The Real Estate Investor's Answer Book

The Real Estate Investor's Answer Book

Moneymaking Solutions to All Your Real Estate Questions

Revised and Expanded Edition

Jack Cummings

McGraw-Hill

New York   Chicago   San Francisco   Lisbon   London   Madrid
Mexico City   Milan   New Delhi   San Juan   Seoul
Singapore   Sydney   Toronto

The *McGraw·Hill* Companies

1 2 3 4 5 6 7 8 9 0   EUS/EUS   0 9 8 7 6

ISBN 0-07-146712-2

This publication is designed to provide accurate and authoritative information in regard to the subject matter covered. It is sold with the understanding that neither the author nor the publisher is engaged in rendering legal, accounting, or other professional service. If legal advice or other expert assistance is required, the services of a competent professional person should be sought.

> —*From a Declaration of Principles jointly adopted*
> *by a Committee of the American Bar*
> *Association and a Committee of Publishers*

McGraw-Hill books are available at special quantity discounts to use as premiums and sales promotions, or for use in corporate training programs. For more information, please write to the Director of Special Sales, Professional Publishing, McGraw-Hill, Two Penn Plaza, New York, NY 10121-2298. Or contact your local bookstore.

Library of Congress Cataloging-in-Publication Data
Cummings, Jack
The real estate investors answer book : moneymaking solutions to all your real estate questions / Jack Cummings.—Rev. and expanded ed.
p. cm.
Includes index.
ISBN 0-07-146712-2 (alk. paper)
1. Real estate investment.   I. Title.
HD1382.5.C854 2006
332.63'24—dc22   2005037583

This book is printed on recycled, acid-free paper containing a minimum of 50% recycled de-inked fiber.

Contents

4. How to Deal with Your Real Estate Broker   45

5. Successful Buying and Selling of Homes   53

10. Income Property for the Twenty-first Century: Buying and Selling Residential Rental Properties   155

11. Buying and Selling Income-Producing Properties   173

12. Managing Your Real Estate to Maximize Profits and Minimize Problems   186

Preface

Everyone who has an interest in real estate should read this book. Buyers, sellers, property managers, mortgage brokers, lawyers, first-time property owners, senior citizens, real estate salespeople, builders, developers, people who rent and want to own, people who own and should rent. Everyone.

This book is designed as a quick and easy way to find the answers and solutions to the 227 most important situations you may face in your quest to maximize your real estate investments. The approach I have taken is to offer you what I think is the very best method you can follow to deal with these situations so that you can make the most of your own real estate investments. In this way, you can take short-cuts to solve or avoid problems and to help you get started in real estate investing, or to improve your present investment strategies.

These questions were selected from thousands of such questions that have been asked of me over the past 30 years. During that time span, I have been committed to the real estate industry in many different ways. These include being a real estate agent, an investor, an investment counselor, a teacher, a lecturer, an author, a talk-show guest and host on both radio and TV shows, a speaker at conventions, and a real estate authority in legal proceedings. In addition to being an instructor of real estate investment techniques, I am also an avid reader of real estate books and frequently take courses and attend seminars covering tax problems and solutions, international investment potentials, and so on.

I believe that priorities and opportunities in real estate investing are constantly changing, and that to succeed in real estate it is important to be as current with the trends as possible. The solutions you will find in this book are backed by years of experience, lots of learning it the hard way, and solid study and research and practice on what works best for which situation. Getting from point A to point Z can take a long time when you learn it out in the field. Take advantage of this experience and use this book to get to the nitty-gritty quickly and easily.

With this kind of background and in preparation for writing this book, I have made it my personal goal to bring you solid information that can give you the kind of answers that will enable you to make a decision, effect a change, or stick by your guns because you now have the data and background knowledge to lean on. You can profit from the experience of others in this way and thus avoid having to make the mistake in the first place.

In reading this book you will discover that the material is easy to digest and without that stuffy textbook kind of writing that is usually the style for question-and-answer books. This book, like all my previous books, is meant to be read and enjoyed. The learning experience will be pleasant.

This is much more than an accumulation of the most important situations you may face in your real estate investment adventure. It is a detailed book of problems and their solutions and is fashioned to illustrate the most prudent approach to each of these circumstances. The goal is to give you a fast reference for solving problems that may be similar to the kind you are experiencing or that you believe may shortly confront you. The idea is to provide solutions and explanations that are clear, concise, and easy to understand. These solutions have the depth to explain and teach about the subject to which the solution was directed. The advantage for you is that you won't have to go any further than right here. The solutions are offered in such a way that you will be able to use the information for your own personal benefit. The situations contained in this book touch on virtually every aspect of real estate, so it is likely that everything you ever wanted to know will be covered.

Take a look at question number 42, for instance, which asks "What are the hidden gems I should look for in a property when trying to get the most value for my money?" The solution gives you the answer and then explains why each of the hidden gems can pay off with profits when the time is right. The right questions combined with easy-to-understand answers and solid backup allow you to build your own knowledge and confidence in how to handle problems and make decisions.

You will find the question or answer that will help you most in one of two different quick and easy ways. The first is to scan the 21 chapters. In the first chapter, for example, you will find questions dealing with the fundamentals of real estate investing. This method may be all you need to get right to the section that fits your immediate need.

However, for a more detailed response to your problem or need, use the key word and subject index, which shows all the different answers that deal with a specific key word or topic. *Foreclosures,* for example, are discussed in the answers to many different questions. By using the key word and subject index, you will find following each key word or subject (*foreclosures, senior citizens, mortgages,* etc.) all the items in which the answers touch on or deal with that specific key word or subject.

This book has many useful checklists and helpful hints on how to head off problems before they hit you. It is designed to be used on a daily basis as you need help or when you just want to brush up on the techniques of buying and selling property. Everything about the book is designed to enable you to quickly find the questions that are most important to you.

Jack Cummings

1

Investment Strategies for a Profitable Real Estate Portfolio

1. What Makes Ownership of Real Estate a Good Investment?

The essence of sound real estate investing is to grasp the benefits which real estate can provide. There are many such benefits, depending on your specific needs, abilities, and goals; however, there are eight primary benefits from which all others will flow.

> **Solution:** Understand the basic key factors that form the foundation for all real estate benefits.

The following eight key factors are commonly accepted as the major reasons real estate continues to be a good investment. For most investors, these factors will be the most critical issues in investing in real estate.

Eight Key Factors of Real Estate Ownership

- Is a necessity
- Is a hedge against inflation
- Produces income
- Appreciates in value
- Provides stability
- Is a fundamental of wealth
- Is easily financed
- Comes with many perks

To understand how each factor can affect your decisions on real estate investments, review the following brief discussion of each of the eight key factors.

Factor No. 1: Is a Necessity. Unless you are homeless, you own or rent real estate or live with someone who does. Housing, clothing, and food are three of the major necessities of life, and all three can be provided from real estate.

Factor No. 2: Is a Hedge against Inflation. Inflation is the result of an increase in the cost of living and can suddenly eat away at savings. When the cost to rent an apartment continually increases every year, those on a fixed or limited income will find their standard of living slipping behind, or the effort to keep up will be harder each year. Because real estate is one of life's basic elements, it adjusts naturally to the usual supply and demand economics that governs most of the marketplace.

A good example of this is an apartment building constructed 25 years ago, when an unfurnished one-bedroom apartment may have cost only $90 per month rent on an annual lease. That same apartment today (25 years later) may rent for more than $500 per month. If you were the owner of that apartment over the same period of time, your ownership costs would not have increased proportionally. Best of all, if you rented the apartment to someone else, you would have experienced a steadily increasing rental income to cover increased cost-of-living expenses.

Factor No. 3: Produces Income. The obvious cash benefit is an offset to inflation, as mentioned earlier. Owning income property is the opportunity to put other people's money (OPM) to work for you. The term *OPM* is a cliché in the real estate industry, but it is a real factor in the ownership of property.

Being a landlord is a position of both status and wealth in most parts of the world. Building wealth in real estate can be as simple as acquiring property with a lot of debt and letting other people use their money to pay off your debt. Once the property is free and clear of any debt, all the income that had been going to mortgage payments now goes into your pocket.

Factor No. 4: Appreciates in Value.   As a result of the first three factors, real estate has a tendency to increase in value. While this fact is not guaranteed, you will discover that by selecting wisely at the time of acquisition, planning prudently, and keeping a watchful eye on the trends in the marketplace, it is not unusual to see real estate values appreciate greatly over a period of a dozen or so years. Even modest increases in value can produce great gains and substantial wealth. For example, because housing is in great need, well-located apartment complexes that are properly maintained should increase in value as the rents charged for those apartments also increase. Twenty years ago, $200,000 could have purchased a very nice 15-unit apartment building. In a conservative investment plan, the investor might have invested $40,000 in a down payment, with the balance being a first mortgage of $160,000 payable over a 20-year term. The obligation to meet the mortgage payment would be covered by OPM (from those who rent the apartments).

If this was your investment and it did nothing for you except provide an apartment to live in and income from the other 14 apartments to pay the mortgage, in 20 years the first mortgage would be paid off. A very conservative approach would show the current value of these 15 units to be $600,000 or more. After all, this is only double the original investment over 20 years. While a 5 percent per year increase may not sound like a good investment, you must remember that the cash investment was really only $40,000, and that in addition to the increased value, you lived free in one of the 15 apartments. The value of the investment has increased 10 times, still not counting living rent-free and more than likely putting some cash in your pocket each year.

Factor No. 5: Provides Stability.   Real estate does not have an instant market, as do other items such as gold coins, stock in IBM, and so on. A buyer must be found who has a use for a particular property or who can see the benefits it will produce. Because this is not an instantaneous market, the values tend to adjust slowly on the downside. However, because real estate involves location and is not a commodity, the need for a specific location or area can cause values to go up much faster.

Factor No. 6: Is a Fundamental of Wealth.   Real estate and the items that are produced on or under it are the basis for most the wealth in the world. Wars are fought over it, divorce lawyers argue about it, and when you own it free and clear there is certain soundness to your sleep at night.

Factor No. 7: Is Easily Financed.   This is a factor that Americans take for granted. However, the fact is that for much of the world financing is a hit-or-miss proposition that can be very expensive. The ability to repay a loan over a long term of 20 or more years at a modest interest rate, spreading the payment out over an amortization table to keep the payment affordable, does not exist in many countries. This means that for much of the world a $100,000 loan might require paying out $10,000 a year in principal plus interest on the outstanding balance of, say, 10 percent. The first-year payment would come to $20,000. While this payment would drop a bit each year, it still is heavy during the early years, when the borrower may need as much help as possible. An annual payment total with a 6 percent 30-year term in the United States would amount to a total annual payment of $7,265.00 for the year. Quite a difference, isn't it?

In the United States, many people are able to borrow all or nearly all of the purchase price, a godsend for a seller who is able to unload his or her property quickly, because in this country the buyer can easily finance the deal.

Factor No. 8: Comes with Many Perks. Investment properties can provide you with more than the investment return you get on the cash you put down. Many families live off the perks that come with owning investment property. Restaurants feed the entire family; hotels and apartment buildings and other such properties can house the entire family, as well as allow the owners to spread the cost of operation to other family members who are hired to do the work.

2. What Is the Best Approach to Real Estate Investing?

Most real estate investors do not have a concept of how to approach real estate when they consider making an investment. After all, everyone knows that you make an offer, it is accepted, and you close. What else is there?

> Solution: The savvy real estate investor knows that many steps need to be accomplished even before deciding to make an offer. The best approach is to build your own comfort zone in order to narrow down the investments that will work best to take you closer to your goals. This is called a *comfort zone* form of investing.

The comfort zone method of investing in real estate is a proven approach to learning all you can about a specific geographic area or type of property. By having a strong focus on a narrow market area, you can quickly become an expert in the property in that area.

For example, Abel decides he will learn everything he can about the area of town where he lives. He knows that potential investment opportunities must exist there. Yet, because he does not know the marketplace, the values of property, rent potentials, and so on, he is unable to recognize opportunities when they are right before his nose. To change this situation to one in which Abel will begin to see the opportunities, he must learn a new procedure. Abel uses the following checklist as the basic formula to start forming an effective comfort zone for real estate investing.

> ## 10 Basic Steps to Establish a Comfort Zone
>
> - Outline the area.
> - Determine the number of properties.
> - List important officials.
> - Learn the zone.
> - Become an insider.
> - Document your data.
> - Recognize opportunities.
> - Inspect properties.
> - Make offers.
> - Learn to do due diligence.

Outline on a Map the Exact Geographic Area That Will Become Your Comfort Zone. It is important that you do not bite off more than you can chew. Start with a reasonable area and build from that.

Make Sure There Is a Minimum of 600 Residential Properties or 200 Commercial Properties in the Area. Be sure to define the area as one that is within one city boundary and, ideally, within one subdivision if at all possible. This concentrates your research to one city and one set of city ordinances. You can expand this area later after you have fully mastered the first. The reason for trying to stay within one city area is to minimize the amount of data you would have to master. Each city generally has its own building codes and ordinances.

Make a List of Important Governmental Officials and City Meetings. The VIPs will include the city mayor, county commissioners, head of the building and zoning department, head of the planning department, and important people recommended by these people, as other VIPs who would be helpful or important to real estate investors. Start to attend city and county council meetings and local planning and zoning hearings. The city manager's office will assist you in finding out where and when these are held.

Get to Know the Comfort Zone Like the Back of Your Hand. You should know everything that goes on in your community that can cause someone to choose or to reject a property or an area of town, and you should determine how much buyers will pay for a property, what the actual market has done in the past, and where it is headed now. Some of these items include bus routes, school boundaries, locations of churches and hospitals, shopping areas, centers of employment, local zoning ordinances, and building rules and regulations.

Become an Insider. This occurs without extra effort because you are getting to know the important people in the community who affect real estate values and who can be influential in helping you make a change in the value of your own property. The key is to make sure that the VIPs of the community you meet know you in return. This is totally within your power because you control your own follow-up.

Build a Property Value Awareness File. Every time a property is offered for sale or rent, research it. Get in the habit of checking the county records on sales and foreclosures of property for the actual sales price. Find out what people have paid by looking at the county deed records at the tax assessor's office. The office staff will provide ample help to show any prospective investor how to use the deed records.

Continually Look for Undervalued Property That Presents an Opportunity for Future Profit. These kinds of properties will begin to stand out as you become acquainted with your comfort zone. The property may simply need tender loving care or a change of use to make it more valuable.

Inspect Properties That Are for Lease and for Sale. Real estate is both hands-on and eyes-on kind of investment. You may never know anything about a stock you buy (other than the broker's recommendation), but real estate must be seen, touched, and understood completely or you may make a mistake—a big mistake. Therefore, look as much and as often as you can. Get to know what people are asking for rent or to sell, and check what they got when it was later rented or sold.

Make Soft Offers on Many Properties. A soft offer is one that you feel sure the seller will not accept, and which, if accepted, would be a windfall for you. The main reason for doing this is to get to know how the process works. Offer, counter, and then counter-counteroffer is a common routine. This process will help you get a handle on what the offer forms look like, what they mean (read every tiny word), and how the process works. Be sure to instruct your broker never to fax a document without sending it in "fine" (or even superfine) resolution. Too many people do not know that their fax machine has a higher, more readable resolution than the standard default setting, which, after a contract has been faxed twice, makes it nearly unreadable.

Learn the Process of Due Diligence. This is the process of double-checking everything you first thought to be correct. Many people wait until they have double-checked and double-checked yet again before they even make an offer. This is generally a big mistake. Why? Because you lose out on getting the property. Savvy investors know that the key is to tie up the property, make the inspections, and then, if things are not as they thought they would be, enter into negotiations to lock up new terms. In the meantime, they have closed the door for other investors to snatch the property out from under their noses.

3. What Is the Most Dynamic Technique to Increase Value and Ensure Profit in Real Estate Investing?

We are moving into the nitty gritty of real estate right off the bat. A number of effective methods and techniques can help you increase your value and ensure profits, but one stands out. This book touches on all of the techniques, of course, but let's make sure that you understand the star performer right from the get-go.

> **Solution:** Grasp the best and most effective technique for this age to ensure your future in real estate. This method is called *economic conversion.*

Economic conversion is an event whereby the property owner makes a change in the real estate that allows the net rent earned from that property to be increased. When this is properly accomplished, the economic return on the invested capital increases.

It is important that the investor study all options available when contemplating a change of any kind. For example, it may be easy to increase rents by making improvements to a property, but the cost of those improvements may actually reduce the yield on the overall invested capital. Be careful not to make a change for change's sake when the real answer to success lies elsewhere, perhaps in improved management or increased rents.

For example, Frances purchased a large three-story home that has a detached three-car garage in the rear of an oversized corner lot, with a large workshop and apartment over the garage. The home has over 1400 square feet on each of the three floors, and the garage has nearly 1200 square feet on each of its two floors.

The property cost Frances $120,000, which she felt was below the market value, considering the location. This was due to the fact the home was in need of repair—a factor that Frances did not mind, as she had different plans for the home. She was able to negotiate with the seller for a down payment of $20,000, and the seller agreed to hold a first mortgage for the balance of $100,000. Frances has a mortgage payment that includes the real estate taxes and insurance on the property of $1500 per month.

Frances selected this home because, after checking at city hall, she discovered that the zoning laws permit several different uses for the property in addition to its use as a single-family home. These uses included professional offices, such as medical offices, insurance company offices, real estate offices, lawyers offices, and so on; multifamily housing that would allow a maximum of five separate apartments; and a mix of professional offices and apartments.

Frances's first thought was to make the needed changes in the buildings to create the maximum of five apartments. Her plan was to make each floor of the main house into a spacious two-bedroom apartment and to convert the garage and its upstairs workshop and apartment into two additional two-bedroom apartments. She studied the rental market for the area before she bought the home and ascertained that she should be able to collect a minimum of $600 per month per apartment once the work was completed.

An architect worked up a preliminary sketch for her to take to a building contractor so she could get a price for the needed conversion. Soon Frances realized that she would need to add four completely new bathrooms and remodel two existing ones to make sure that each of the apartments had at least one bathroom; in addition, she would need to completely relocate or install all the needed kitchens. The "easy" conversion was becoming an expensive nightmare.

The builder suggested that Frances turn the home into professional offices and do some minor repair work on the second-floor garage apartment. The needed remodeling turned out to be nothing more than removal of old carpets, which hid the soon-to-be refinished hardwood floors, and general painting inside and out. The rent that would come from the offices on a triple net lease (i.e., tenant pays all the costs to maintain the property, including real estate taxes) was more than she could collect from all five apartments, and there was still potential income from the garage apartment. Frances calculated that with the rent from the offices, plus a minimum of only $400 from the fixed-up garage apartment, she would end up with over $25,000 at the end of the year after all mortgage payments and expenses had been paid. This was not a bad return on her cash investment of $20,000.

Frances now had the opportunity to make the changes in the building and to find a tenant. Instead, however, she went around to local law firms and medical groups armed with several maps and aerial photographs that showed off her property and pointed out the ideal location for a prestigious office. After a week of contacting likely tenants, she found a law firm that grabbed the opportunity Frances was offering. The lawyers realized that if they made the improvements, they could have a much lower rent, and that over a period of five years they could save considerably over what they were currently paying and, moreover, have a landmark office facility.

Frances was maximizing her use of OPM by giving the lawyers something important in return. The final economic conversion of this property into a lawyers' office did not cost Frances more than a few weeks of scouting potential tenants.

Economic conversions follow many different paths. An old-style motel might be converted into small shops; a drive-in theater might be given added income potential as a flea market by day; a vacant lot might become a parking lot or a "U-Pick-It" strawberry patch.

Sometimes the economic conversion is very subtle, such as when a strip of 18 small shops is converted to 18 antique boutiques. The shops still exist, but because of a change in concept and the development of a theme, the rents can be increased—and tenants may willingly pay for the opportunity to be at that location.

Every real estate investor who wishes to build wealth should look to economic conversion as a logical process to follow. This means that every prospective investment should be considered only if additional income can be created from the property so that the total yield on the investment is increased.

Very small changes in income can make very large changes in value. This occurs because most real estate investors buy an income-producing property based on the yield or return they will get on their investment. For an investor who wants a 10 percent return on his or her invested capital, that means that for every additional

$100 of net income per month there would be $1200 of net income for the year, an increase in value of $12,000 (10 percent of an additional $12,000 in sales price).

If, as in this example, a buyer wanted a 10 percent return on his or her cash invested, a property that has $25,000 of income left over at the end of the year after all payments and expenses have been made would be worth $250,000. As Frances's conversion was destined to have that kind of year-end return, she could see a potential sale of a property that cost her only $20,000 out of pocket and that would return $150,000 (after her payback of the $100,000 mortgage to the original owner).

4. How Can I Put the Idea of Economic Conversion to Work?

It is one thing to approach a property with the idea of economic conversion. But where do you start?

> **Solution:** The best kind of economic conversion for any real estate investor to attempt would be one that was selected after following these four steps.

Four Steps to Successful Economic Conversions

- Do your homework.
- Stay within your comfort zone.
- Know the lender's preferences.
- Learn how to avoid or overcome pitfalls.

Do Your Homework.   Do detailed homework of the existing real estate market and understand all options available. Any economic conversion should not be attempted until a detailed study has been completed of all the alternatives that are allowed under the current zoning or that could reasonably be accomplished through a change of zoning or variance of city ordinances. Once the investor sees what can be accomplished, the next step is to determine what is most likely to succeed. Only by knowing the market area can this be determined with safety.

Stay within Your Comfort Zone.   Work within your own comfort level. Given several viable options, each of which shows promise for economic gain, the best economic conversion would be a change that suited the investor's ability and capability. This extends well beyond the level of competence in property management or business acumen. The total comfort level should include the financial responsibility that will come with the project as well as property management.

Know the Lender's Preferences.   It is good to know which types of real estate the lenders prefer. Even if you have all the cash necessary to accomplish the project, you should find out where the smart loan money is going. This can be a good indicator of which kinds of business operations or real estate properties are going to maintain their value the most. Today, lenders are very conservative, and following their example will produce an equally conservative investment portfolio.

Learn How to Avoid or Overcome Pitfalls.   Be aware of all the potential pitfalls when going to contract on the property. Far too many investors divulge their plans too early. Your great idea might just be picked up by someone else if you are not careful, so make sure you have a firm contract to purchase the property before you talk to a local building official, a banker, or even a friend.

Every investor should realize that time can be both a friend and an enemy when making any economic conversion. The smart investor asks for ample time in the purchase contract to accomplish everything needed.

5.   What Does It Take to Become a Successful Real Estate Investor?

I'd have to admit that having a couple million dollars could be a help in this area, but, without a sound plan to follow, that nest egg could be a thing of the past pretty quickly.

> **Solution:**   There are four elements that all successful investors have and effectively use to fit their own style and talent.

Four Elements That Make You a Successful Real Estate Investor

- Determination
- Positive attitude
- Strong goal orientation
- Self-confidence

Determination.   The most critical of the four elements that a real estate investor should possess is determination. However, having all the determination in the world may not be enough to ensure success without three other elements. The combination of these elements can provide the foundation for a success in any chosen path. Determination is the will to keep going against all adversity. This factor is essential to all those success stories of people starting with nothing and ending up wealthy beyond their dreams.

Positive Attitude.   A positive attitude is harder to obtain and often even harder to maintain. The world is full of adversity, and it is easy to believe that failure is the opposite of success. This is not true: the lack of desire for success is the opposite of success. Failure is simply readjustment time. Try again, or try a different approach, but try. This is where both determination and positive attitude work together.

Strong Goal Orientation.   Add a strong goal orientation, and the plan to succeed has focus and direction. Proper goal development must be learned, however, as it is not acquired overnight. The key to the whole effort is seeing an intermediate goal as a stepping-stone to a longer-range goal and then working bit by bit to attain that step before proceeding.

Self-Confidence.   If you build a ladder to success by doing tasks that have the greatest possible chance of success, your overall goal is eventually obtained and self-confidence is maintained at a high level. An example of this process is becoming an insider in real estate investing. One step is to get to know as many VIPs as possible.

You have absolute control over this process because the VIPs are highly visible, and you can ask one to recommend you to another. By simply having the right attitude about meeting them and then making sure you follow up properly so that they get to know you, your ultimate goal of becoming an insider is ensured. The right attitude, by the way, is not to try to speed up the process. If your first positive event is just to have met a VIP, and the second positive event is to follow up, then you are functioning in a solid, positive mode.

Building one simple success on top of another is the secret to accomplishing anything. To write a book, write one page, then another, while keeping the overall goal in mind. The process of simple successes piled on top of others builds something all the money in the world cannot buy: self-confidence. Once you achieve self-confidence and mix in the other three elements, the world and success are yours.

6.   What Should My First Acquisition Be?

Most people make this decision out of immediate need by buying their first home. This "backed-into" deal may actually be the very best item to purchase, but exactly where it is, what it consists of, and how it moves you closer to your goals may have been overlooked.

> **Solution:** The first acquisition should be a property that helps you move closer to your goal.

This is not sidestepping the issue, as the answer must come from you as you establish your own plans for the future. You should accept the fact that the direction you need to take is to follow your goals. Why? Because goals dictate what you should buy.

Because most people do not set proper goals, it is critical for you to understand that without proper goals your efforts toward any dream can become a series of frustrations and disappointments. To acquire a property simply for the sake of owning something may be a boost to your ego for the moment, but will do little or nothing to move you closer to your goal. The wrong property can and most likely will move you further away from your goals.

If you are currently renting your living quarters, one of the first aspects of real estate ownership should be to consider buying your own place to live. While this concept may not be ideal for everyone, if you are settled in an area and expect to remain there for five years or longer, then in the absence of any other goal at all, this should be your first consideration. But what should you buy—a home, an apartment, an apartment building? Each has its advantages and disadvantages, and your own ability to deal with the complexities of these properties will help you make a meaningful choice.

Clearly, a very handy person, someone who is able to fix up both the inside and outside of a property, may consider a small apartment building that needs a bit more than some tender loving care. Satisfying two intermediate goals at the same time, a place to live and added income to cover debt service, is a sound way to go. On the other hand, a great interior decorator may want to take a condominium apartment and redecorate it, which would be more in line with that investor's abilities. Investors must ultimately develop the comfort zone of expertise that will work best for them.

2

Real Estate Values: Keys to Why and When They Change

7. What Makes Property Increase in Value?

Most of what affects real estate's value is predictable. The most elusive part of the equation is the time factor. However, it is possible to narrow the gap in the quest to pick the right property at the right time.

> **Solution:** Every circumstance that can cause real estate to increase in value can be attributed to one or more of the following critical factors. Each will be discussed in detail.

Eight Reasons Property Values Increase

- Inflation
- Improved infrastructure
- Government control and regulation changes
- Neighborhood sizzle
- Economic conversion
- Increased bottom line
- Capital improvements
- Supply and demand

Inflation.   Inflation is the increase in the cost of any item or service due to the increased cost to reproduce the item or provide the services. In real estate, these increased costs occur because of many different circumstances: for example, bureaucratically imposed costs to obtain building permits, to meet environmental standards, and to construct roads and newer facilities. As new buildings cost more, old buildings become more valuable. Because real estate is tied to a specific location, older, already improved properties may not be directly comparable other than the cost of replacement. This occurs because the value of a highly sought after location often increases beyond the effect of inflation alone.

Improved Infrastructure.   Infrastructure is the total of all elements that make up a community. This includes the roads, the public and private facilities, shopping centers, theaters, banking systems, sewer and water facilities, schools, airports, ports, jails, hospitals, and so on. Improving or expanding the infrastructure of a community can have a major impact on the value of properties. Generally, there is both a positive and a negative impact, and some properties may go up in value while others go down.

This dual potential of improvement to infrastructure requires all real estate investors to be very watchful of proposed community changes or improvements. A long-range benefit may cause a sudden drop in value due to temporary construction or road detours. A property owner or tenant who is operating on a tight budget may find that even a slight decline in revenue can mean economic disaster. This type of situation can present a great opportunity to an investor who can endure the temporary drop in value.

Government Control and Regulation Changes.   Building codes, zoning rules and restrictions, and other factors that are within the scope of governmental control can create windfalls for property owners (or tidal waves). On the positive side of this it is important for property owners to be vigilant about what is going on within all elements of government that can cause any change in what can be built or what their property can be used for. While the general trend in government control is to reduce things like density and negative (in their opinion) uses, there are times when development-oriented policies prevail.

This kind of trend is great for real estate investors who see it coming and can capitalize on buying property ahead of the boom. Trust me on this, if you watch what is going on in the local political arena, you will be one of the first in line to get your foot on in the door. Why? Because few people actually pay attention to what is going on in local political arena (zoning board, planning and zoning departments, and city and county council meetings), those who do are at an advantage.

Neighborhood Sizzle.   You know which neighborhoods have it where you live, don't you? If you don't know, then find out. While it might be too late to cash in on the present hot neighborhoods, you should do some homework to find out what made them so hot. This sizzle factor did not occur overnight, so what made it happen? Likely, it was some kind of redevelopment, or an open residential neighborhood got together and formed an association that made their area a gated community, or some other event took place to add value, and that will be replicated in another neighborhood. Likely the one right next door. Look for patterns like this and jump ahead of the rest of the would-be investors. Cash in on that newly forming sizzle.

Economic Conversion. Economic conversion, discussed in question number 3, is any change of use of an existing property. Not all change produces a positive effect, however, and the overall effect of an economic change should be carefully weighed.

Economic conversion is one of the best ways for an investor to control the ultimate increase of value. The more you know about the local real estate market conditions and trends, the greater your prospect of making a successful economic conversion. A very simple example of an economic conversion would be to take a vacant lot and convert it into a used car sales lot. The lot is converted from a non-income-producing property to one with a positive cash flow. If the income from the car lot warrants a greater price than you recently paid for the lot, then the value has increased due to your conversion of the property.

Increased Bottom Line. When you increase the annual cash flow of an income property, you will most likely increase the value of that property as well. Many factors may cause this increase, such as your improved management, decreased expenses, increased rents, and so on. Because the value of an income property can be a multiple of the net operating income (NOI), which is total rent collected less total operating expenses excluding depreciation and debt service, small increases in the bottom line can mean much greater increases in value. For example, a property valued at 12 times the net operating income (NOI) of $80,000 per year would have a value of $960,000. Increasing the NOI to $88,000 (only an $8,000 increase) will boost the value to $1,056,000, for a total increase of $96,000. This is how fortunes are made.

Capital Improvements. Just as improved infrastructure in a community may have a positive effect on value, so can improvements made directly to the property. However, for income property, these capital improvements should have a direct effect on increased rents for this added cost to increase the value. As an investor, the key is to distinguish between costs needed to restore a property to the value you have paid for it and improvements that increase value. Almost every property on the market will need an infusion of capital just to maintain it or, because of deferred maintenance, to bring it up to standard. You should not expect that improvements will increase the value of your property unless you have taken into account these costs and have already discounted the property value at the time of acquisition.

Supply and Demand. The supply of and the demand for any item will have an effect on its value. Because of the fixed nature of real estate, supply is tied to specific areas of the country or town. Generally, the resulting supply and demand will be closely tied to the community infrastructure and its rules and regulations. Local zoning may limit certain kinds of businesses to specific areas, and the inability to increase the area size limits the supply dramatically. When the cost in an established area climbs too high for new businesses to locate there or for the needs of existing businesses, new communities may compete with the old location, causing a rise in value in these new areas.

Supply and demand curves for real estate are very local in nature. With the exception of the availability of financing, which is a function of banks and less geographically connected, the market trends in one city may not have any consequences on what happens in your town, which may be only a hundred miles away.

8. What Makes Property Decrease in Value?

The same event that causes some properties to increase in value can have a negative effect on other properties in the area. The change in value, either up or down, may be temporary, so the immediate shift can easily mislead an investor who does too little homework on the situation.

> **Solution:** Review the following nine factors that cause real
> estate values to decline.

Each of these factors can be a double-edged sword, meaning that it can push values both up and down. Pay close attention to how this occurs and how one factor can cause others to enter the picture.

Nine Reasons Property Values Decrease

- Inflation
- Decline of neighborhoods
- Adverse effects of infrastructure change
- Negative governmental control and regulatory changes
- Decreases in the bottom line
- Lack of capital improvements
- Economic obsolescence
- Supply and demand
- Urgency to sell

Inflation. Just when it looked like inflation was going to make your investment turn into a gold mine, the same factors that are making a fortune for people across town are turning your costs of operation into a nightmare. When you are stuck with static rent coming in due to long-term leases with no provision to increase them to allow for inflation, your costs to keep the property can go out of sight. Protect yourself by having short leases or a built-in clause to tie the lease to a cost-of-living index adjustment every year (or even a shorter period).

Decline of Neighborhoods.   When a neighborhood begins to decline, for whatever reason, the values of property within that area will fall. It is important to realize that the decline occurs first, and then values fall. Over a long period of time, the area may undergo a fall in value such that new investors see the advantage of making new investments in the area. However, the time from the start of the decline to the rebirth of the area can be very long.

Neighborhoods decline for many different reasons, one of the most obvious and predictable being the lack of building upkeep and maintenance. When this happens, tenants move out, rents are reduced in an attempt to provide some income flow from the property, and the next step is a downward spiral of less maintenance, lower rents, and ultimately, slums. Tenants move out for many reasons, but usually because of an event in or near the area that makes it a less desirable location for a business. This might begin as a temporary situation, such as a long-term road project or some other improvement to the overall infrastructure of the community, but this area becomes cut off and isolated and businesses move out. With lower rents in place, a less affluent economic element moves into vacant business and residential properties.

Novice real estate investors are well warned to stay away from urban renewal projects. These projects are best left to the community itself and to large corporations that can afford to spend and lose a lot of money before a profit is made.

Adverse Effects of Infrastructure Change.   There's a downside to the benefit a new hospital or an expanded airport can bring. All major infrastructure change is likely to cause some properties to go up in value and others to decline. New roadways, especially superhighways, may require new rights-of-way that have the end result of cutting nice neighborhoods into two less desirable areas. Increased traffic, noise, and pollution are some of the negative side effects of almost any infrastructure change.

Negative Governmental Control and Regulatory Changes.   Every bureaucracy has a tendency to expand and become more complex. In real estate terms, this complexity usually increases the cost to build and/or maintain real estate. Building permits and other city requirements may become so expensive that it is not economically feasible to build or to continue to operate a specific type of business or rental property. For small construction jobs, it is not uncommon for the cost of meeting all the rules and regulations and obtaining all the required approvals and permits to be more expensive than the actual construction itself. When this occurs, the value of predevelopment property can decline, while already improved investments increase in value.

It is common for communities to establish building moratoriums or impose expensive impact fees for new construction. These events occur partially because of the natural willingness of the existing residents of a community to pass on costs of the needed infrastructure improvements to the newcomers. The end result is that the new buyer must pay more simply to cover the costs the developers must pay to hold onto the property during the moratorium or to meet the requirements.

Decreases in the Bottom Line.   This is the point where your NOI and, worse, your spendable cash, begin to drop. The causes are many. Poor management is one of the biggest reasons this occurs. Why? Because a good property manager recognizes what must be done to keep the revenue ahead of spending. Also, a good manager will recognize when things must change or when it is time to bail out of that investment.

Lack of Capital Improvements.   This ties in closely with decreases in the bottom line just mentioned. Real estate will deteriorate if money is not spent to keep it up. That means other factors in this list will soon occur and value will surely drop.

Economic Obsolescence.   A large part of any modern building will become economically obsolete over a period of time. Eventually the day comes when major new capital must be invested to support desired income levels. The best economic option may be to demolish the building and start over.

Many property owners do not properly maintain their buildings. They manage to get by because of other positive factors, such as great location, heavy demand in the area, and so on. However, the point of no return will eventually occur, and without added investment, the property will eventually decline in value. Even a well-maintained property that serves an economically obsolescent industry is faced with a property readjustment of value.

For example, an old motel with small rooms, poor location for that use, and no modern facilities for the guests is faced with hard choices. Some of those choices may be to go back to square one, which is to look at the land as the primary source of value. Many obsolescent properties are sitting on land that is worth far more for a different use. Open your eyes to that potential.

Supply and Demand.   Overbuilt situations occur as a natural part of the real estate cycles when builders overestimate the number of units or the amount of square feet needed to meet the present demand. The result is too much supply for too little demand. When this happens the market goes into a tailspin, because most builders and developers operate on other people's money (OPM); when the sales or rental predictions fail to materialize they get in trouble financially and scramble to meet debt service. The sudden results can be a sharp decline in rental rates in brand-new properties as these developers attempt to get all the cash they can. In the end, the lower rents reflect lower values, and if the builders can just barely meet their expenses and debt service, a further decrease in rents hastens foreclosure sale, and bargain prices set in for new investors.

Urgency to Sell.   If you want the value of your property to start to decrease immediately, put up a sign in the yard that says "Owner Must Sell—Moving Out of Town." Wolves, (i.e., aggressive buyers) seem to smell blood suddenly and home in on the potential bargain.

All property owners should review their long-range goals on a frequent basis to see whether their investments are working properly for them. This kind of planning allows the investor to avoid potential situations that may ultimately require dealing with a pack of wolves.

9. How Do I Predict Which Property Will Increase in Value, and Why Is Timing So Important?

Everyone who invests in real estate wishes they had a crystal ball to see into the future. If you think there is no such item, then read on. To set this stage, you likely know people who seem to always be at the right place at the right time. Those lucky dogs, you might think. Well, it is possible that they have found the secret to this crystal ball thing.

> **Solution:** Accept the fact that real estate follows trends, imitates what happens elsewhere, and is best and most dramatically affected by changes in infrastructure and governmental controls and regulations.

With this in mind, the best way to predict the future is to study the past. In real estate terms this is much easier than looking into a crystal ball to predict whom you will fall in love with tonight. Nearly everything that can happen in your area has already happened in some other location. Even though the final value of any property is best determined by the price a person will pay for it, the reasoning that goes into the buyer's decision-making process is predictable.

People buy because of location, use, cost, emotional appeal, pride of ownership, and to make a statement. All of these are human motivations. All are predictable. In fact, selecting a property that is likely to go up in value is pretty easy. The problem is knowing when that will happen.

Good timing is the maker of fortunes in the real estate market. For example, if you attend a city council meeting where a new highway is proposed that will open up areas outside of town, you could presume correctly that this new road will have the potential of increasing the values of the new area to be accessed. If the property is currently farmland and priced accordingly, and if it is in an area that will allow, or could allow (e.g., with proper rezoning), a mixture of commercial and residential uses, then the ultimate profits to be made by buying this property could be tremendous.

However, enter timing: from the day a city council talks about a new road to the day this road opens for traffic can span many years. Worse yet, the actual pathway of the road may vary slightly or be dramatically altered. The value of the land you rush out to buy will indeed go up . . . but when? Will it increase while you still own it, or long after your mortgage was foreclosed and you lost everything?

Short-term speculation is much safer than long-term anticipation, and one of the quickest payoffs is to find a property suffering from a temporary adverse effect of infrastructure enhancement and then wait out the short term.

What is an example of this kind of investment? A bridge is being widened to make way for the anticipated expanding of traffic over the next 10 years. Businesses on or near the approach to the bridge may suffer tremendously during the two years of construction . . . so much so that tenants move out, owners need to sell, and prices of real estate that are destined to jump in value actually decline . . . making the profits that much greater later on, all as a result of timing.

10. How Can I Determine What My Neighbors Paid for Their Property?

The sale of real estate in most parts of the world is strictly regulated and documented. The chain of title (ownership) for any specific property is likely to be maintained in one or more governmental bureaus or departments not far from the property itself.

> **Solution:** Of all the private things in life, ownership and details surrounding real estate is not one of them. Once you have mastered the access to public records you will be able to discover mountains of information about all the property you may want to acquire.

Public records can be accessed by way of computers as well as personal visits to the departments and offices that maintain that data. Real estate is a matter of public record in the locale where it is owned and traded. Counties in every state of the United States as well as similar offices of records in most countries of the world contain information about the ownership, chain of title, tax assessment, past sales, and the approximate (if not exact) amounts of those sales.

Virtually every area has a local tax assessor's office. In the United States this task is left to the local county tax assessor's office. A visit to the local tax assessor's office would be the first place to look for the details on any property.

If the tax assessor's office does not have the needed information, then the property records office of the clerk of the circuit court may. In this county department, information on property transfers are maintained and deeds are recorded.

Every public department and records office is open for you to review almost any public document of record. The people who work in these offices are trained to be helpful and to assist you in getting the most from the data that they can provide.

11. What Can I Do to Cause My Property to Go Up in Value?

A key to answering this question can be seen by a review of question number 7, which deals with the things that make property go up in value. Of those items, a property owner can take six basic steps that have the potential to have a nearly instant positive impact.

> **Solution:** Review the following six steps, which any property owner can take which will have a nearly instant impact on the value of a property.

Review the solutions to questions 7 and 8 before moving to this side of the total picture.

Six Steps You Can Take to Increase the Value of Your Property

- Change the zoning.
- Make an economic conversion.
- Obtain a variance.
- Paint and fix up.
- Relandscape.
- Increase the bottom line.

Change the Zoning.   Because value to a prospective buyer is based on two main factors, location and use allowed, a change in zoning can dramatically affect the value. A farmer sells his strawberry patch to Sylvia. She then goes to the local governing authorities and, after properly filing a petition to rezone, obtains authority to build a shopping center and a hotel on this land. Through the change of zoning Sylvia has created a new use; land that will support a shopping center and a hotel is more valuable than land for a strawberry patch.

Make an Economic Conversion.   This concept may also include a change in zoning, but in general refers to a change in use that is already permitted. Discussed in question 3, this technique is one of the best methods to increase values in real estate. It is also safe and relatively risk-free when properly handled, as you can enter into a contract to acquire a property based on obtaining all the required permits and approvals to make the desired change.

Obtain a Variance.   Sometimes the only thing necessary to increase the value of a property is to get someone to bend the rules just a little. When a property owner is faced with a building regulation or city ordinance that will not allow something to be done, sometimes the city or other governing body will grant a variance to permit the desired construction or other use, despite rules to the contrary.

For example, a new backlighted sign that is built closer to the road than the rules allow might attract the right tenant who will lease the property for more money than the present tenant. This higher rent conveys greater value.

Paint and Fix Up.   Giving a fresh coat of paint and fixing everything that is clearly broken are good steps to increasing property value. Some properties have several years of poor maintenance but are structurally sound and in good locations. All that need be done is cosmetic work.

There are some key factors here. Do not scrimp on important and highly visible items such as front doors and doorknobs. Remember that quality paint does not cost that much more than the cheap stuff, and the bulk of the painting cost is the labor. Often, the better paint can save money, because it may cover better than cheap paint, which might require more coats to give a decent finish.

Relandscape. Existing landscaping is often either too much or not enough. Sometimes all that is needed is to move some plantings or to sell off excess plants that are too big for the property (thereby getting top dollar from builders who want mature plants). Putting in a more modern look allows you to show off the newly painted property. When relandscaping is tied into some of the other elements here, the end result can be a fresh-looking property that will attract buyers, providing a future sale is important to you. If your goal is to increase the bottom line for your own benefit, these steps can put additional revenue in your pocket from a higher-paying tenant.

Increase the Bottom Line. The value of all income-producing real estate is a reflection of the income potential of that real estate. Therefore, the best way to benefit from an increased value is to increase the bottom line of the property. To accomplish this, an investor must do one or more of the following:

1. *Increase rent.* More money in the owner's pocket at the end of the year increases the value of the property that generated that money. The increase or decrease in value can occur with relatively small movements in the bottom line. For example, if buyers will buy a property that produces a 9 percent return on their investment, an increase of the bottom line by as little as $900 dollars can increase the value by $9,000 dollars.

Smart real estate investors look for properties where the existing leases are below the market and may easily and inexpensively be increased. This situation happens all the time and is due to a wide range of events, often occurring at the same time. Absentee management is the top cause of this situation. Other causes are poor management, personal problems, a bad mix of tenants that make it impossible to collect market rent, a run-down property that needs tender loving care, a high vacancy factor, decline in business, roads under construction in the area, and so on. When these events are present, both time and money may be needed to turn the property around. These factors need to be carefully considered before buying the property. While it might be possible to increase rent, if expenses more than outpace the increased rent, then the net effect of having more money in your pocket at the end of the year reverses itself.

2. *Reduce expenses.* Expenses should be considered as a percentage of the gross revenue collected. Assume that the present rent of an office building is $200,000 and the total operational expenses are $80,000. In this situation, the expenses are 40 percent of the income. It may be that the building is renting below market value and that the income really needs to be brought up to $260,000. By implementing a well-thought-out plan to make some improvements in the building, you may attract higher-paying tenants. If the new expenses can be held to a modest

increase—for example, a total of $95,000 instead of the old amount of $80,000—the overall income picture goes up. The adage that sometimes you need to spend money to make money is true.

Old income	$200,000	New income	$260,000
Old expenses	80,000	New expenses	95,000
Old bottom line	$120,000	New bottom line	$165,000

3. *Soften debt service.*   When the bottom line is reduced by mortgage payments, your money in the pocket can take a real beating. However, free and clear ownership of investment real estate is generally not the case. The value of mortgaged real estate is the total of the owner's equity and the amount of debt on the property. When you purchase this property, negotiating the price you will pay is totally oriented to the equity position. For example, a property that has a mortgage of $1,155,000 (70 percent of the overall value) has $495,000 of equity. Offering the seller $495,000 for that equity leaves the debt untouched in the negotiation process. However, if the mortgage payments could be reduced or softened, the net result can be a greatly increased value that occurs the moment you close the deal.

Assume that the $1,155,000 mortgage had been in place for seven or more years at 8 percent interest and has 18 years to go. This mortgage has an annual payment total of $121,272. It may be possible to reduce the annual cost of this mortgage by refinancing at a better rate and/or a longer term. As an example, the annual payment would drop to $96,911, if the loan were restructured to 30 years at 7.5 percent interest. This is a savings of $24,361, all of which goes directly to the bottom line.

12. How Can I Tell That the Value of My Income-Producing Property Is Approaching Its Peak?

The critical word in this question is *approaching*. The actual moment when your property has reached its top dollar is an unknown. It is doubtful that a prospective buyer would say, "I'll pay you one million dollars . . . uh-oh, on second thought, I'll pay only half a million dollars." On the other hand, some clues can tell you that without some major changes in the current marketplace, the value of your property is reaching its peak.

> **Solution:** Pay attention to the basic elements that cause property to go up in value, then apply the social and human conditions and circumstances that make them occur (review questions 7 and 8).

Every investor should keep track of the local market to take advantage of a potential sale, if it fits his or her investment plan, before the market turns downward and property values decline. Five key signals indicate a property's value is approaching its peak. They are usually quite visible if you look for them.

Five Key Signals That Suggest Value is Peaking Out

- Continuing strong real estate market
- Getting top income with little room for improvement
- Sudden small increase in vacancies of similar properties
- Some tightening of the new mortgage market
- Approaching economic obsolescence of major items

Continuing Strong Real Estate Market.   You can check a number of local indicators. I stress *local* indicators because national statistics on real estate are often tied to housing starts, which is an average from the whole nation or wide areas of the country and can be misleading. Your area may have zero housing starts while the national statistic is on an upturn, and obviously the opposite can just as easily occur. The best local indicator can be obtained from your local board of Realtors. They keep track of the sales of their members; strong sales and a high volume of property moved is a good sign. By keeping in touch with the board you can track the local statistics on a monthly basis.

For example, a steady three-month drop in sales during a time of the year that normally shows brisk business can be a definite sign that the market is going soft and may be headed for a decline. The local building departments keep track of the housing starts in your area and can provide you with statistics. Because a decrease in building permits often precedes the actual market decline, this may just be a confirmation of what you already expected. The market may be softer than you thought.

Getting Top Income with Little Room for Improvement.   If a rental property is at the top of its rental potential, if a hotel is already doing better than any other hotel in the area, or if a restaurant has reached its maximum without expanding, then only inflation can increase the gross revenue without added capital investment. Investment property buyers look at such situations and realize that there is no likely direction to go but down. The top value for the moment has been reached. Without some other event occurring, such as an expansion of the facility or a restructuring of debt expense that would contribute to an even greater bottom line after refinancing, the maximum value has been reached.

Sudden Small Increase in Vacancies of Similar Properties.   There are local and seasonal reasons this might occur that would have no effect on the value of the properties in the area. However, if you take that into consideration and still see an abnormal number of vacancies, it may be a sign that the rental market is softening. A softening rental market can have a wide-ranging effect on other real estate values, depending on the actual cause. If you see this happening, then look at the other elements of this section to see whether there is a compounding effect.

Some Tightening of the New Mortgage Market.   The mortgage market has a greater impact on investment property than it does on single-family residential properties. This does not mean there is no impact on single-family homes, as easy money at low interest rates can make ownership of modest housing comparable to paying rent in a similarly valued apartment. However, because investment property is so closely tied to the cash flow of the income and expense statement, a higher mortgage payment will reduce the yield to the investor. Prospective buyers compensate for this by reducing the amount they are willing to pay for the property.

Approaching Economic Obsolescence of Major Items.   Even though your income is up and promises to go up a bit more, your property is facing major expenses due to economic obsolescence.

Building items such as roofs, elevators, air-conditioning and heating systems, boilers, carpets, furniture, electrical wiring, and plumbing all have a useful life. In addition, there comes a point when maintenance of the item exceeds the replacement cost.

13.   What Advance Signals Indicate Property Values in My Neighborhood Are Headed Down?

Rather than discovering too late that no one is willing to pay you the same price you paid for your property, watch for the signals showing that your neighborhood is already in a decline. If you and your neighbors act quickly, it may be possible to reverse the trend.

> **Solution:** If you missed the handwriting on the wall that your value had peaked, then look for one or more of the following six advance signals that suggest property values have leveled off and can be expected to drop.

Six Advance Signals Indicating Property Values Are Headed Down

- Increased crime
- Increased vacancy factors
- Abundance of "For Sale" signs
- Drop in the level of property maintenance in the area
- Detrimental infrastructure changes
- Sudden major job loss in the community

Increased Crime.   If you close your eyes to what is going on, you will be oblivious to increased crime in your comfort zone. Newspapers are quick to point out where crime is taking place, and a visit to the local police department will provide you with eye-opening details.

Increased Vacancy Factors.   If you have not yet seen any vacancies, but begin to notice "For Rent" signs in places where they never were before, then this is a very good indicator that the economic climate is shifting. Checking with the owners of those properties may also produce another grim fact: rents asked are dropping as well.

Abundance of "For Sale" Signs.   This may be a seasonal trend, so check with the local board of Realtors before you jump to conclusions. The board of Realtors can tell you about rentals, too, and whether there are other downward trends. The "For Sale" indicator can mean that people are financially strapped and looking for a change of lifestyle, which is a sure sign of decline.

Drop in the Level of Property Maintenance in the Area.   When a good market shifts downward, the drop in the level of property maintenance in an area can be the last signal to appear. This is not, however, an indicator that the down market is on the upswing.

In a previously well-maintained area, it may take a while for the declining market to begin to affect the pocketbook of these property owners. When the cash flow pattern begins to slip and there is a question of either making the mortgage payment or painting the building, the building does not get painted. A continued decline in the level of property maintenance has a domino effect of causing tenants to move out, thus requiring even lower rents to be offered to attract any tenants at all. The whole demographics of an area can slowly change from one economic strata to a lower one, and values will be reflected through their steady decline.

Detrimental Infrastructure Changes.   I have touched on the importance of infrastructure changes in a community. Some are positive and increase values of surrounding property, while others or the same ones for other property owners have the opposite effect—for example, the bridge over the canal that connects the stylish neighborhood with an industrial part of town, or the new exit off the freeway that increases traffic through your residential part of town. Both of those events can increase or decrease certain property values. The key here is to be on top of what is being planned so that you can act long before the event has even been started. Do not wait until it is finished.

Sudden Major Job Loss in the Community.   The key word here is *sudden*. While any job loss can have a negative effect, the worst ones are those that come out of the blue. It is impossible to anticipate some of these, but others may occur in an industry that has been festering for years. International competition has a way of plowing old unprofitable industries into the ground. Because this is a real situation, it is important to be cautious about investing in an area that has major employment centers consisting of such businesses.

3

Renting or Owning: Which Is Best for You?

14. When Is It Better to Rent than Own?

Even if you can easily afford to own, there are times when it may be much better for you to rent.

> **Solution:** Carry out an honest study of what your total costs would be in either situation and compare those costs with your goals.

For example, if the local real estate market is such that a property can be leased on a long-term annual basis for between 4 and 6 percent of the real value of that property, then the economics points to the lease as a possible benefit over ownership.

Are there markets like this? Yes. In moderate- to higher-priced residential properties it is not unusual for rents to be unrepresentative of the value of the property. I recently leased an apartment in New York City and paid $950 a month ($11,400 for the year) for an apartment that had been sold to a Japanese investor for over $250,000. His combined taxes and building maintenance exceeded the rent I was paying. In another situation, a friend of mine has a home that was appraised for $950,000, and the most he could get from an annual rent was $3,500 per month. This amounts to $42,000 for the year and is less than 5 percent of the value of the home.

If you were to buy that $950,000 home with $200,000 cash down and get a very accommodating loan from the bank, your annual payment of interest only on the debt could exceed $70,000 per year, not including any principal reduction. Moreover, you would owe annual taxes ($12,000 for the year), insurance ($2,200 for the year), and general upkeep ($3,500 for the year). If you wanted to live in this house, would you choose to rent or to own?

Your age and lifestyle influence greatly the determination to own or rent. If you know that you will be firmly established in one geographic part of the world for a long time, then ownership can have obvious advantages—provided that you can afford the economic commitment. One way to make sure you can afford the cost is to acquire property that also produces income to offset some or all of your costs.

If you are retired, have a lot of free time on your hands, or have nothing to tie you to any single location in the world, then ownership can become a real burden. This is another ideal situation where becoming a tenant can be the right choice.

You cannot afford to buy, so you think you have to rent? Stop for a moment. If this is the reason you became a tenant, then change your attitude about buying property and learn how to own real estate. Unless you are solidly on welfare and cannot see any way out of this situation, chances are there is real estate that you can buy.

15. What Are the Most Important Contract Factors I Should Be Aware of When Renting?

Every contract will likely have terms and conditions that you may not fully understand. Because legal jargon can be difficult to understand unless you are familiar with the terms used, it is easy to get into trouble because you thought you understood what was being discussed. Nothing in this book is intended to give you so much confidence about contracts that you will not need a lawyer to hold your hand. However, this book is filled with guides and tips on things that you should look for, and this section is an example. You will discover, if you use lawyers often enough, that they sometimes assume you already understand the business terms of the deal and will spend their time (and your money) looking at potential legal problems presented by the contract.

Business terms include things like *price, date of closing, amount of deposit,* and so on, but they also include the elements I discuss here as they relate to rental agreements, which are in fact legal and binding obligations between the parties.

> **Solution:** Review the 14 important rental agreement factors that are part of the business terms of a rental agreement.

The following is a list of the important elements of any residential lease. In a commercial lease many of these are equally important.

The 14 Most Important Rental Contract Factors

- Cost of living
- Common area maintenance
- Default
- Hidden costs
- Improvements made to the property
- Penalty for late rent payments
- Property inspections
- Property insurance
- Repairs—who does them and who pays for them
- Rights and options to renew
- Security deposit
- Signs
- Tax stop
- Utility costs

Cost of Living.   When a lease will tie the landlord into a commitment greater than a one-year term, a cost-of-living increase provision causes lease payments to adjust upward to reflect an increase in the cost of living. This type of increase may simply be called a cost of living adjustment (COLA). A phrase in the contract similar to the following may be used:

> . . . and therefore, at the beginning of each new year of this lease, the rent will be adjusted according to any increase in the All Items cost-of-living index as is published by the United States Department of Labor, or in the event that index is no longer published, by the commonly accepted replacement for that index. The adjustment will be made by taking the increase in the All Items index over the previous 12 months and increasing the last adjusted base rent of this lease by that same percentage; the new amount will then be the new base rent for the next 12 months.

Common Area Maintenance.   Often referred to by its acronym, CAM is a separate charge to the base rent. The base rent of any lease is usually a net amount that does not include other charges. Your lease may or may not have any other charges. However, if it does, those costs could include the following: sales tax (when charged on residential leases—check with the state sales tax office in your county or area to see whether that is legal); electricity, water, and other utility charges; late-payment charges; damage assessments; pest control; security alarms and protection; door attendant cost; and cable TV, management, public and common area maintenance, general advertising (as with a mall or shopping center); and so on.

One way to limit the increases is to limit the amount your lease can be increased over a year's term. It would be a good idea to contact the Department of Labor (Bureau of Labor Statistics) located in Washington, D.C., or call the federal offices in your state and ask for the nearest facility that provides labor statistics and, most specifically, the cost-of-living index. The Department of Labor can put you on a mailing list to receive the most recent indexes every month. This free service also includes (if you ask for it) a booklet on how to interpret the list.

The staff members in these offices are used to getting phone calls from real estate owners and tenants and are usually very helpful in giving you data over the phone.

While you are getting ready to negotiate a lease, you may discover that the All Items index may have averaged a 4 percent per year increase over the past three years. It should be an obvious benefit to you if in the negotiation of a lease you can tie your first few years of increases to one-half the actual increase in the All Items index.

Default.   Review carefully anything in the lease that would cause you to be in default. Not everything may be specifically spelled out. For example, the lease may state that any violation of city, state, federal, or building rules or regulations will cause your lease to be in default. The key phrase here is *building rules or regulations.* If you are leasing an apartment in a condominium building, you will be expected to abide by all the rules of that building. Make sure you know what those rules are before you sign the lease. They may include rules you do not want to or cannot abide by.

Events that occur once you are already in default may become a function of law, and the landlord-tenant laws may vary from state to state. This is one of the very good reasons to have a lawyer look over any legally binding document.

Hidden Costs.   Some of the hidden costs have already been mentioned, such as increases to rent above the base rent due to cost-of-living adjustments. Other hidden costs can be repairs and replacement of items in the apartment. Most leases dictate that you keep the property in good repair and in the same condition as when it was delivered to you for occupancy. However, did you check out everything? Had you done so, you might have found that all the appliances were over 15 years old and not working well. You should not be obliged to pay for the replacement of a 15-year-old refrigerator a week after you move in, but your lease may give the landlord the right to demand that you do.

There are property inspection companies that will inspect the property before you move in, and although these companies are generally used by a buyer, there is no reason you cannot have them do a minicheck of any items that might become an expense to you. Before you go to the expense of having this inspection, make sure you have a fully executed lease with the provision that it can be canceled (before you move in) if you do not like the inspection report for any reason and that the landlord will fix any items not in good working order, or will allow you to do so and then deduct the cost from your next rent payment.

Improvements Made to the Property.   If you plan to make any improvements to the property you should have a clear understanding in the lease that you are permitted to do so and that you are not required to return the property to its previous condition at the end of the lease.

If you plan to add something that may be considered "fixed" to the property, such as a heater for the swimming pool, an electronic air-filtering system built into an existing air system, or any other expensive apparatus, be sure that you have the option to remove those items. Expect that you will have to return the property to its condition before the installation. You may want to take those expensive items with you and would be prohibited otherwise.

Penalty for Late Rent Payments.   Most leases have a penalty for late payment of rent. Be sure you understand how this penalty is applied. I have seen leases that allow the landlord to subtract the late charge automatically from the security deposit. You may not be aware that this is happening until the end of the lease when you ask for your security deposit back. It is a good idea to have a provision that requires the landlord to give you advance notice before making any debits to any deposits you have given to him or her.

Property Inspections.   Landlords want the right to inspect their own property from time to time, for several reasons. First, they want to make sure that the property is being used according to the terms of the lease and is kept in good repair. Second, they may want to show the apartment to prospective tenants as your lease draws to its close.

Make sure that the landlord must give you reasonable notice before making the inspection (be specific about how many days—usually two working days), and feel free to restrict the weekends and evening hours.

Property Insurance.   Property insurance is a two-way street. First, as a tenant you want to be sure that the landlord has sufficient insurance on the property to cover any damages in the event of fire or windstorm or other natural causes. Also, does the owner of the building have liability insurance to cover you for any negligence on his or her part? Second, tenant insurance is a must, because even if the owner of the building has more than adequate coverage, your personal property will not be covered if you are robbed or suffer a casualty not covered by the owner's insurance.

Repairs–Who Does Them and Who Pays for Them.   Tenants should know exactly what their responsibility is with respect to the repair of an item in the property that is being leased. However, it is one thing to have a provision designating that obligation to the landlord, and another to get the work done and paid for. For this reason I suggest that the following clause, or something similar, be included in your lease:

> . . . and, in addition, should any of the electrical or mechanical items listed below, all of which are owned by the landlord, malfunction or fail to operate properly, it will be the obligation of the landlord to promptly cause the item to be returned to its good operating order, and if not repairable to be replaced with another item of similar nature that does operate properly. Should a period of time exceed 48 hours—from the first notice to the landlord of malfunction or improper function of any listed item—without a service call by a qualified repair person to repair or replace the item, then the tenant may hire a locally licensed repair person to do the needed repair or replacement. The cost for work ordered by the tenant may be charged to the landlord or paid for by the tenant, and if paid for by the tenant

would become a credit in full applied to the next rent and charges due, until such time that payment by the tenant has been completely offset.

Rights and Options to Renew. Tenants should ask for a right to renew their lease, even if at the time the lease is negotiated there is no thought of extending it beyond the initial period of time. There are several reasons for asking for this right. The most important is that without having some clear understanding about a renewal, the landlord could refuse to renew the lease even though your circumstances may have changed such that to move at the end of the lease would be very costly or inconvenient. Another good reason is that by locking up the terms for future rent, at least to a formula (e.g., adjusted to one-half the increases of the cost-of-living index), you can better budget your expenses. That area of town, for example, may suddenly be in vogue and rents skyrocket.

Security Deposit. The first step in dealing with a security deposit is to understand what the state law says about these deposits. Many areas of the country have laws that require the landlord to keep security deposits in interest-bearing accounts; other laws may not be so specific. Even if the state law does not require the landlord to maintain the deposit in an interest account, you can make that a provision to the lease.

It is not uncommon for the landlord to have the right to deduct penalties or assessments for damage from the security deposit. Make sure that no such deduction is made without notice being given to you before the deduction so that you can contest the deduction if you feel it is unreasonable or unwarranted. Otherwise, you may find that your total security deposit has eroded over a long-term lease.

Signs. Some leases have a provision that allows the landlord to place a "For Rent" sign in the window or on the property as your lease draws near its termination. Such a sign may draw unwanted and uninvited visitors to your door at all hours of the day. If any signs are allowed they should be placed so as not to indicate which apartment is for rent and to direct attention to some other place.

Tax Stop. Real estate tax adjustments may be shown as a tax stop, which creates an obligation to the tenant for whatever amount the future real estate tax exceeds a set amount. This is usually the amount of a prior tax, but can be any sum the landlord puts in the lease. This idea can extend to other items that may not be specifically included in any CAM charge.

Utility Costs. When the lease provides that you pay all the utility costs, it is likely that not all those costs are being divided equally among all the tenants in the building. You need to find out if there are separate metering systems for each apartment for each of the utilities. It is not unusual for an apartment building to have one water meter, and if other services, such as garbage collection, are calculated by the amount of water used, then you should see who the other tenants are before you agree to a pro rata division of the water bill. If one of the rentals is a restaurant or a laundromat, you will definitely end up paying for part of their water and garbage collection service.

16. What Should I Check When Looking at Property I May Lease?

In every situation where you intend to become a tenant, it is easy to overlook some important elements of the property you are looking at. To aid you in this task I have provided you with a prelease checklist. As with all the checklists in this book, the items are listed in alphabetical order to the first word(s) of the list rather than in any order of importance.

Solution: Use the following prelease checklist of 17 items that you need to consider before signing a lease.

Prelease Checklist–17 Important Things to Consider

- Authority to make a lease
- Building rules and regulations
- City code violations
- Common area maintenance (CAM)
- Condition of all furniture and fixtures included
- Condition of the exterior of the building
- Environmental problem potential
- Garbage collection
- General security of the building
- Insurance issues
- Neighbors and neighborhood
- Other special requirements
- Parking space(s)
- Pest control
- Safety devices provided
- Sources of noise
- Sources of smells

Authority to Make a Lease.   Are you dealing with the party who is the landlord, or is it his or her agent? You need to make sure that the lease is legally binding, or it may not be enforceable in court.

Building Rules and Regulations.   Is there one set of rules that everyone is subject to, or are some tenants under the old building rules and regulations? If this is the case, you might want to insist that you be subject to those same terms if they are less onerous than the new list of rules and regulations presented to you.

City Code Violations.   Most cities or counties have a department dedicated to ensuring that the city or county codes are not being violated. It is relatively easy, in most cases, to call or stop by this office or department to check on a property you are about to lease. These offices are located within one of the municipal facilities, but the people who staff the department are often out on the road checking for violations. Because of this, prior to going to the office in person, call to check their hours; better yet, make an appointment.

Be sure to give the following information prior to your arrival so someone can check the property information file ahead of time. You want to know if there were any code violations that have not been corrected or that have been corrected but now occur in the part of the property you plan to rent. For example, say the owner was cited for having electrical work done in an apartment or commercial space that is other than the one you want to rent. The inspector may not have checked the entire building and may have cited the owner for only that single incident. You discover that violation, and also see that it had been corrected.

You can ask the city to now inspect the part of the property you plan to rent to check for any additional violations. If there are, you can ensure that the owner corrects them prior to the start of your lease. Keep in mind that finding no violations does not ensure that there are not any. Investors who are anticipating purchasing or leasing a property can have, in cities where this kind of service is available, a prepurchase or prelease inspection.

In nonresidential leases, most cities will make an inspection at the time the tenant applies for an occupational license. This kind of inspection will vary in intensity and can be a quick look-see by a zoning department person to make sure that the zoning allows what you plan to do there. Other times, the inspection is far more detailed and can get into everything from parking to violations of federal laws governing rights of the physically challenged. Any violation, no matter how small, can keep the city from issuing an occupational license, which means, if you have already started your lease, you may be on the hook for rent even though you cannot open for business.

If your lease has a provision that it is your obligation to abide by all local, state, and federal laws (at your cost), you can be shelling out a bundle long before you open for business. Other possible violations that may not be evident from the code enforcement people could be related to fire codes, health department codes, deed restriction limitations, lease rules and regulations, and any state or federal laws that limit use or provide civil rights protection.

Common Area Maintenance (CAM).   While this term and its use is common to most commercial leases, it is also becoming a part of many residential leases. CAM can be everything that pertains to the management, maintenance, and cost to do business of a property. In both commercial and residential leases this term can take into effect additional elements, too, such as a reserve for replacement, common advertising, all insurance, and all real estate and personal property taxes. CAM expenses are essentially operating costs that the lessor is passing through to the tenant rather than including it as part of the rent. It is very important that both the lessee and the lessor pay close attention to this factor if and when it is used in a lease. The totality of what is included in CAM and how it is calculated should be spelled out.

The lease should spell out what qualifies as rent and what qualifies as pass-through expenses. When there is a state or local sales tax levied on rents, as is often the case in certain kinds of leases (generally limited to commercial leases), the tax may be applicable to just that part of the lease that is allocated to rent. The portion that goes to pay for the real estate tax, utilities, management, and so on may escape the sales tax. Following several phone conversations to the sales tax collection authorities of several states, I can tell you that there can be different interpretations on how the sales tax is calculated.

For example, it might simply be based on the rent and CAM amount shown in the lease. One thing is sure, though, when the rent is one combined amount (for which the landlord has taken into account costs that might otherwise apply to a separate CAM), the sales tax will generally be applied to the total paid. The lessor or its management company generally collects the sales tax for the state or local authority and then pays it to them, so there is no motivation on the lessor's part to reduce the amount of tax paid by the tenant. Make sure you are current on this issue and that you do whatever is prudent to avoid having to pay tax on pass through amounts when possible.

Condition of All Furniture and Fixtures Included.   There are several items in this list that deal with the condition of certain elements of the property prior to the start of your lease. In some lease situations, it is important to have photo documentation of the conditions existing at the start of the lease. Why so? Because future disputes may arise due to damaged or lost items or the misuse of the premises that could be attributed to you (for any reason, including the act of a vandal, burglar, or guest). It is a good idea to have photographic evidence of the pertinent aspects of the property. The best way to do this is to take photos and have them processed with the actual date showing on the negative, slide, or CD.

At the time the lease is signed it would be good to have the photos initialed and dated by lessor and lessee. The very fact that you are going through such detail in documenting the current condition of the property is likely to cause the lessor to pay a lot more attention to some of the language in the lease, so don't be surprised if some new language appears that tightens up who is responsible for what. That's okay, and it works to your advantage in the long run.

In regard to furniture and fixtures, it is important that every item be photographed and that some identifying mark be put on the property. This can be a code number or model number that is scratched into a normally invisible location to identify the item and the date your lease starts. In the case where something is left behind by the previous tenant, with the general comment, "If you want this you can use it," you should question this to clarify exactly what is meant. Often the item is from a prior tenant, who may come back and demand the item. Other times, it may be something that the lessor will otherwise throw out or cart away at an expense he or she would rather not have. It is best to say, "I don't know if I can use this, but if you plan on giving it away anyhow, I will see if I can use it. Is it mine, then?"

Condition of the Exterior of the Building.   Triple net leases or leases of the entire premises often have provisions whereby the tenant is responsible for upkeep of the whole building. This may mean the roof, all appliances including air-conditioning, and so on. It is reasonable to request previous maintenance records of the building prior to agreeing to such blanket responsibility. It is possible that the previous tenants bailed out of their lease because they discovered that the entire roof was in need of being replaced and that their lease required them to do so out of their own pocket. Instead, they kept their mouths shut, dealt with leaks for two years, and then didn't renew their lease. Suddenly, you come along and sign a lease, unaware of the leaking roof. The lessor may or may not be aware of the leaks. Never sign any lease that requires you to maintain a property until you know the condition up front. Most buyers would have a commercial or residential inspection conducted prior to purchasing a property. If you are to be responsible for repairs and maintenance, you can do this, too. Even if you are not to be responsible for the repairs and maintenance you may want to have these inspections. Why? What if your occupancy and use requires the continued function of certain elements to the point where even a few days of malfunction could have a negative impact on your business. What if the elevators stopped working or the refrigeration to your 100,000 cubic feet of cold storage failed? Would you suffer negative consequences?

Environmental Problems Potential.   Environmental issues are becoming more and more critical, and new laws come out from time to time that may have an impact on you as a tenant. If you hire an inspection team to inspect the property be sure that you understand exactly what they will inspect and what they will warrant. Most of these companies do not warrant things like code violations of any kind, but environmental problems are not technically code violations. Make sure that every item in this list is either covered in such an inspection or, if *not*, that you seek other inspection sources (even yourself or your lawyer) if you feel you need that protection.

Garbage Collection.   How, when, and where are the first three questions that should be spelled out clearly in the lease or building rules and regulations. A good lease will also provide instructions for extraordinary amounts of garbage and trash that occur during the move-in/move-out and periodically during the year when deliveries of supplies or equipment may arrive. Included in the garbage section should be details on what happens when the tenant has parked an inoperable vehicle on the premises for longer than a certain period of time. Most leases would allow the landlord to have it removed, after a notice to the tenant, at the tenant's cost. When a local ordinance dictates that garbage be separated into recyclable containers, the building rules should reflect that. Violation penalties for a tenant's failure to abide by these kinds of rules are for the benefit of the tenants who do abide by them.

General Security of the Building.   There can be some security issues that are covered in code violations. For example, is there a swimming pool or other water hazard (a place where someone can drown) on the property? Does it need to be fenced off from wandering children? Are the rails on stairs or balconies up to the current code? Do doors meet fire codes and physically handicapped requirements? Is there storm protection for windows and doors? These are just some issues that may have an effect on your insurance.

Insurance Issues.   Security, as mentioned, can create important insurance issues. Most leases require the lessee to maintain certain levels of liability and possibly other insurance that also name the lessor as co-insured. In some instances, the lease may specifically pass on the responsibility for certain kinds of damage (say, for broken windows) to the tenant's renter's insurance. You need to understand what your obligations are, and what insurance you can reasonably get.

Neighbors and Neighborhood.   Choosing a commercial space on a late Sunday afternoon or a residential apartment or home on a late Monday morning may not give you a true picture of the neighbors, or for that matter the entire neighborhood. It is a good idea to pick times and days for such inspections that will demonstrate the amount and kind of traffic that is generated in the area. Who is in the building, whether residential or commercial?

Other Special Requirements.   Your need to adequately use the premises can dictate special requirements that are critical to you. No checklist can effectively take every such possible element or location into account.

Parking Space(s).   Any tenant needs to know the parking situation. Many older buildings, both residential and commercial, do not meet the current parking codes. This can greatly affect your use of the premises being leased. Be sure you understand the building rules that govern parking. For example, where can your guests or employees park? Are there limitations on parking? In commercial space, is there signage that limits parking to, say, 30 minutes, to ensure a turnover of space? Is there parking that is specifically designated and identified for you? Make sure you understand the parking situation. Be sure to check the building rules, too, as they may include items that relate to parking.

Pest Control.   *When* and *how* are the two most important aspects of this element in a lease. Will the company have access to the property when no one is there? What problems and issues can that create? A lease simply stating that the lessor provides pest control does not answer those questions, and more data should be included in the lease.

Safety Devices Provided.   Most rental property, both commercial and residential, is subject to local ordinances that relate to safety devices such as fire extinguishers, smoke detectors, alarm systems, and so on. Be sure that, if required, they are not only there but are in good repair and meet the existing codes. Fire alarms are subject to testing from time to time, and you can ask to see the latest inspection report.

Sources of Noise.   As with neighbors who can become a major source of noise, you should be aware of other possible sources: airports, railroad tracks, highway systems, schools and their playgrounds, auto body shops, junkyards, factories, lumberyards, and other places where the beep-beep-beeping of trucks backing up can drive you crazy. They can all be quiet during the hour or so you are at the property, but can become great sources of noise and vibration. If your use and enjoyment of the premises is dependent on peace and quiet, you need to check these things out.

Sources of Smells. The direction of the wind and the time of the day can all lessen a stench that surrounds the location the rest of the time. The great thing about smells is that the person who has been in the neighborhood for a while may not even notice the manure factory that is right behind that row of trees next to the property you want to lease. However, the five or six months it will take you to become used to that or other smells is something you want to avoid. The point here is never to ask the neighbor if there are bad odors in the area. Drive around and check it out yourself.

17. How Can I Negotiate the Most Favorable Lease Possible?

Get ready to meet the landlord or his or her agent. This is an event you need to plan for, because in any contract negotiation nothing is ever etched into stone. Leases are prepared by the lessor or its management company and almost always are one-sided agreements. The legal aspects of the lease should be reviewed with your lawyer, who should always be the one to give the final approval for you to move forward (more on that later).

However, the actual negotiation of the lease is often best done by you if you think you can handle the negotiation elements that are provided in this section.

> **Solution:** Use the checklist of 14 negotiating factors for all leases that follows.

Checklist of 14 Negotiating Factors for All Leases

- Ask for cleanup time.
- Be ready to negotiate.
- Demonstrate your financial ability.
- Get move-in time.
- Get approvals on leasehold improvements you need.
- Give the landlord your must-have list.
- Have excellent references.
- Lock up renewal terms up front.
- Make a *good* impression.
- Negotiate in person.
- Negotiate soft terms—one at a time.
- Never give in until you are ready.
- Question cotenants.
- Your lawyer or other third party gives the final okay.

Of all these items, several will likely stand out for you, depending on your situation. For most would-be tenants, the key things you should *not* do follow.

What Not to Do When Negotiating a Lease

1. *Do not negotiate in person if you cannot give a good impression.*   If you become easily flustered in any kind of negotiation activity, then have your real estate agent or lawyer be the one to have the face-to-face meetings with the lease agent or the lessor.

2. *Never be so firm in your demands that you burn a bridge.*   Know what items you can and cannot live with. A good negotiating tactic is to shoot for a win-win result. This means that the lessor and the lessee should both end up believing that they won something in the negotiations. It is okay to be willing to walk away if you and the lessor cannot come to an agreement. What you want to avoid is having the negotiations end badly. The real estate world, when viewed on a very local scale, is small. You may run across this lessor or that management company in the future, so play it cool. Share your disappointment at failing to come to terms if that happens. Let the other team know that you really hoped to work it out, but your finances just are standing in the way. Tell them you are going to have to look for something more in line with your terms. That final move by you might allow you to reopen the door at a later date. They may even call you the next day to make a final, slightly improved offer.

3. *Never make an offer until you have exhausted your negotiations on what the lessor wants.*   By this I mean that you start out by asking what rent they want. They will tell you, leaving off the element of CAM or other costs to the tenant. Ask them, "Are there any other costs?" and they spring things like CAM, security deposits, advance rent, and so on. This is when the negotiations begin. You must continue to ask questions and obtain information until you know the full picture *before* you begin to negotiate any of the items.

4. *Never begin negotiations on the big items.*   This means that you will generally begin with the CAM items first.

5. *Never negotiate on cost until you have negotiated the "free" items.*   This means that you start with those elements that do not cost the lessor anything out of his or her pocket. Naturally, if you get three free months, it may ultimately cost the lessor the loss of that revenue, but on the other hand, there is no assurance that the property will rent in the meantime. Some lessors offer free time up front anyway.

6. *Do not negotiate at all until you have done your homework.*   This includes knowing what the competition offers to you, as a tenant, in the way of perks. It is also a good idea to have a friend or your real estate agent call the lessor or the management company and ask frankly what they offer to get a good tenant.

7. *Do not use all your negotiating power until you get to the really big item that is most important to you.*   You should save something that you can do or give to close the transaction. Remember, your final yes is still predicated on your lawyer's approval of the lease. This means that you will save this one final push to wrap up the lease until you come back from seeing your lawyer. That event would go like

this: "My lawyer has some reservations about a couple of items; however, I am ready to move forward on this lease anyway and sign it right now if we can deal with one final issue." You take a couple of big breaths and lower the boom. "I want you to reduce the rent by 20 percent for the first 12 months [don't call attention to the free time you have already negotiated and that the lessor has okayed], and to demonstrate my sincere interest in this property I will pay you six months' rent up front as my security deposit."

There is a lot to be said for a bird in the hand, and if it comes paying six months' rent up front, that bird is more like a golden eagle.

18. What Can I Do If the Landlord Will Not Fix What Is Broken?

If you think all landlords are good repair people who are just sitting at home waiting for you to call them to tell them that something has broken, think again.

> **Solution:** It is wise to address the likelihood that something will eventually break or need repair. In essence, be sure the lease agreement is clear on these issues.

The simplest approach would be to have a provision in the lease that will allow you to fix anything that is broken at your own expense and then deduct it from your future rent. While this is indeed simple and will solve the problem, most landlords will balk at this blank check to make repairs. If the lessor won't agree to this simple approach, suggest that this provision should not come into effect until after a reasonable time has been given for the owner to remedy the problem and that it is only a safety step for you. I would, however, make sure that things like loss of electricity and water be put on a fast-track repair cycle of, say, 24 hours or less.

If you do not have such a provision already in a lease, and you are faced with a broken refrigerator, and the landlord cannot be reached or will not respond, then you may have no choice but to fix the broken refrigerator yourself and hope for the best.

However, before you have that problem, write the owner or his or her agent and ask for the policy on such matters—be sure it is given to you in writing.

19. Where Can I Find the Most Important Laws That Protect Me as a Tenant?

Many laws protect the tenant. They fall into city, county, state, and federal jurisdictions and cover a long list of possible factors that may contradict (and override) provisions that the lessor has included in your lease.

> **Solution:** Be sure you have a basic understanding of your rights as either lessee or lessor. Review this section to explore the suggested sources for free information.

Every level of government has its fingers in landlord-tenant relationships. Because of this, a great diversity of rules and regulations result. The best place to start is either at the top or at the bottom, which is to say, start with federal laws and work down to the city jurisdiction, or vice versa. For the sake of expediency, do not start in the middle and work in both directions.

The city and county rules may be very simple, dealing with things such as minimum dates when heat is to be supplied (e.g., in New York City) and dates that bulk garbage is picked up. State laws may mirror other state laws, but do not count on that. Federal laws deal with issues such as discrimination and the right to equal treatment for all people, especially those who are physically challenged and senior citizens.

The best source of information, and the one most likely to be up-to-date, would be your own real estate lawyer, who is used to dealing with tenant-landlord issues. However, not every good real estate lawyer deals with these issues, so dig into the Internet and you will find a wealth of information. Some of it will be free, too. All you have to do is to search in several different ways. For example, search the following categories, plugging in specific information that applies to your area. For the sake of this example I will use Miami, Dade, Florida, and Federal in my search requests. You would use your own city, county, state, and federal district with your requests.

Seven Ideal Internet Search Areas for Data on Tenant's Rights

- Miami-Dade tenant laws
- Miami-Dade tenant-landlord rights
- Dade County tenant-landlord laws and rights
- Florida tenant-landlord laws and rights
- Federal tenant laws
- Federal tenant and landlord laws and rights
- HUD tenant and landlord laws and rights

---

20. What Can I Do to Reduce the Cash Cost of My Lease?

During the negotiation of a lease, the prospective tenant has a certain advantage, which cannot be denied: the landlord has a vacancy that needs to be filled, but the prospective tenant has multiple places that he or she can rent. The tenant's task, once everything has been negotiated and the lease is just about ready to be signed by both parties, is to attempt to reduce the initial (and possible continuing) cash cost of the rent.

> **Solution:** The strategy is to get the business terms out of the way, then be creative in coming up with ways to reduce your cash portion of the rent while at the same time not diminishing the benefits of the lease to the lessor.

The key with this strategy is to understand that the tenant has already gone over every item the lease contains. This means that every strategy in this book, plus whatever the tenant comes up with on his or her own, has been thrust into the negotiations. All that remains is to sign the lease. But wait . . . there is this last minute attempt to replace cash, or at least some of it, with another benefit.

One of the easiest benefits to negotiate comes from the barter or exchange of goods. Barter is a simple approach whereby you offer the landlord something other than cash for all or part of your rent. This form of exchange can be anything from cleaning supplies or other products that come from your own business to the use of a time-share you own in Orlando, Florida, so the lessor can take his or her family on a holiday (or an annual holiday for each year of your lease). If you do not own anything you can barter, become creative.

Make a deal with a travel agency to sign you up as an outside agent, then barter a $12,000 deluxe cruise to Europe for a full year's rent. Of course, you will have to pay for the cruise, but you may get back a big commission, as some cruise lines pay hefty fees to agents in the slow time of the year—often over 30 percent. If your cut of the commission is 70 percent, this would equate to nearly three free months for an $800-per-month rental (30 percent commission equals $3,600; your cut is $2,520).

Sweat equity is similar to barter, but instead of a product or item, you actually perform a service or do work for the landlord: sweep the halls, pick up trash, cut the lawn, do bookkeeping, collect rent, paint walls, fix the plumbing—whatever.

The success of these two techniques may depend on your attitude and presentation to the landlord. For example, indicate that you might be having a rough time over the next few months, and then suggest an alternative to reduce your monthly outlay; at the same time, show that you are conscientious and do not want to fall behind.

21. How Can a Senior Citizen Negotiate a Super Lease?

All prospective tenants should make every effort to get the best lease they can. Some landlords are very successful at intimidating their tenants by making them feel as though they are doing them a favor by allowing them to occupy their property. In some instances this might be true, but those rare situations might occur in cities like New York or San Francisco.

> **Solution:** Prospective tenants should take a long look at what benefits they can bring to the landlord and use those benefits as negotiation chips to get the best lease possible.

Take a look at some of the benefits that a senior citizen can bring to the negotiation table.

Nine Great Benefits Senior Citizens Offer a Landlord

- Great references
- Stable tenancy
- Pride of ownership
- Quiet neighbor
- Around a lot
- Steady, on-time rent
- No children
- No wild parties
- Knows prospective tenants with similar advantages

Use these benefits, if you can back them up, and landlords will be glad to have you in their buildings.

22. How Can I Get Free Rent When Negotiating a Lease?

The answer is a simple: "ask and ye may receive." In reality, it is important to know what to ask for and how to ask it.

> **Solution:** Asking for free rent takes proper timing and knowledge of the rental marketplace. Review the strategies that may end up with free rent.

To begin this solution let's look at some key words you should use and some you should avoid. Let's start with the positive key words.

Seven Positive Phrases That May Produce Free Rent

- Long-term lease
- Cleanup period
- Move-in expenses
- Fresh paint expense
- Recarpet expenses
- Rental commission
- Renewal bonus

Two Negative Phrases That Will
***Not* Give You Free Rent**

- Free rent
- Free anything

How It Works

The key here is to understand how savvy landlords think. They all want good tenants who pay their rent on time, do not abuse the property or other tenants, are ideal neighbors, and do not balk at the building rules and regulations. Okay, this has just described you, right?

Now, most landlords know that they may have to be soft on certain things in the negotiations, but if the tenant does not ask for those things, then landlords will not bring them up. This usually amounts to "free rent" for a period of time. But we are not going to call it free rent, because landlords hate to give anything away for free.

In exchange for your willingness to sign a long-term lease and to be all those nice things mentioned two paragraphs ago, you want something in return. Here is what you shoot for: cleanup period, which is time you need to clean up the space before moving in (but allowing you to move in during that time); some extra time to offset your move-in expenses (some landlords actually may offer to pay for your move-in expenses); time or money to paint the inside of the space (the landlord supplies the paint, of course). At this point, you will want to include a similar request for fresh paint and new carpet when you renew your lease two years from now. Don't ask for time at this point, but if the landlord does not offer it, say you will paint and recarpet in exchange for a rebate of a month's (or two months') rent. You can also ask for a rebate in cash (or in rent) as your rental commission (which the landlord doesn't have to pay to a real estate broker). Just as the army will give a bonus to a soldier who reenlists, don't you qualify for a rental renewal bonus? Sure you do.

4

How to Deal with Your Real Estate Broker

23. Do I Need a Real Estate Broker or Salesperson?

If you are buying or selling property, you do not need a real estate broker or salesperson. However, members of the real estate profession can save you a lot of time and help you sidestep problems. The professional Realtor has a tremendous amount of data at his or her fingertips. While it is possible for you to obtain similar data via the Internet or by subscribing to real estate data services, the time and effort it takes to navigate those programs is not worth your while unless you do it often enough to become an expert in those tasks. In the end, either as buyer or seller, you most likely will benefit from their services.

As a professional Realtor for more than 30 years I can vouch from experience that it is very difficult to sell your own property yourself. After some bad experiences representing myself, I now use another broker or an agent to represent me as the seller. As a buyer, I work extensively through agents who bring me properties. Because I am candid with them and let them know exactly what I want, where I am headed, and what my goals are, they know they can spend the time to help me find what I want.

24. What Is the Difference between a Realtor and a Licensed Broker, and Is That Important to Me?

The National Association of Realtors is an organization made up of licensed real estate brokers and associates from many different states. This association has its own code of ethics and functions through the hundreds of boards of Realtors located around the United States. These boards of Realtors are local branches of the national association, and each has a membership from a specific geographic area.

All the members of any board function as a marketing unit, and several boards combined (say, south Florida or southeast Texas) make up a nucleus of members who cooperate with each other in their marketing efforts. To assist those efforts, the board of Realtors operates a multiple listing service (MLS) in which the members can list the properties they represent. This MLS varies depending on the size of the board, and can be a book or series of books, issued monthly or more frequently, that contains information on thousands of properties offered for rent, exchange, and sale. Most interestingly, only Realtors are supposed to have access to this listing service. These are some of the advantages offered to a prospective buyer or seller who uses the services of a Realtor.

A licensed broker or associate who is not a member of the National Association of Realtors cannot use the term Realtor. A nonmember may be qualified to serve your needs, depending on what those needs are. The fact that this person does not have the networking available to Realtors may not be a disadvantage to you.

Many real estate brokers and salespeople choose not to join the National Association of Realtors (and become Realtors), not because they would fail to qualify, but because they see no benefit. Often, such real estate firms and agents are far more selective about the number of properties they market, and they can devote more time and attention to their clients' needs. In deciding whether to use a Realtor or an independent agent, interview several brokers and go with the one who best relates to your needs and in whom you have the most confidence.

25. How Can I Maximize My Benefits from Real Estate Agents?

Both buyers and sellers use real estate agents to assist with their purchase, sale, or rental of real estate. It is important to understand the relationship between you and the agent, from a legal standpoint as well as where their responsibilities and loyalties are focused.

Solution: Review the following seven elements that you should discuss prior to entering into any agency agreement or relationship.

Seven Prelisting Elements to Discuss with Your Broker

- What are the benefits to the agents?
- Do they understand your goals?
- Can you help them be creative?
- What are their energy zones?
- Consider using them as buyers' brokers.
- Would you make them part of your team?
- Can you get a cut of the commission?

Show Agents How They Will Benefit.   Agents are in the real estate business to make money, not to be tour guides. Be sincere about your dealings; express that you are a buyer or seller and that you want to use their services; state that in return you expect them to do everything they can to help you attain your goals; the result can be very rewarding for all.

Be Sure the Agents Understand Your Goals.   They have to be working in the right direction, and this will depend on the signals you have given them. If you are a buyer, the agent will ask questions that will help in finding the right kind of property. If you are vague about what you want, which might indicate that you have undefined goals, then the effort the agent spends can be frustrating, because nothing will seem to fit what you think you want. Formulate your goals; then clearly express them to those you choose to help you.

Help the Agents Become Creative.   If you are going to delve into real estate, then you should do all you can to learn some of the creative techniques for buying and selling. You should not rely on your agent or anyone else to take you by the hand. You should take the lead; this may mean you have to express the willingness to use creative ideas and techniques to reach your goals. Most agents are not assertive in making creative deals because they are not trained to do so.

Discover the Agents' Energy Zones.   Everyone responds to praise and appreciation, so do *not* wait until the property you want has been found and the deal closed to praise your agents. The life of real estate agents can be filled with frustration and disappointment. It is, generally, a life dependent on commissions, and when deals fall apart there is no income, despite much work and effort. Pat your agents on the back from time to time if they are working hard on your behalf. They will respond with a positive attitude toward you and their task to help you.

Consider a Buyer's Broker Relationship.   In this kind of agency relationship, the agent works directly for you when you are a buyer. This means that his or her responsibility and total loyalty is on your side of the negotiations. Some buyers fail to recognize that the commission is really paid by them anyway (after all, it comes out of the proceeds the buyer brings to the table), so why not be properly represented? Remember, when you deal with the seller's agent, that agent is bound to get the best deal possible for the seller, not you, the buyer.

Make Your Agent a Part of Your Team.   You should have a team of people who assist you in all your legal, accounting, business, and other important aspects of your life, even if you are an expert in that same task. The idea of working for a team is appealing, and it can build loyalty from agents, who are insiders to the real estate industry. Insiders like to deal with other insiders, so having them on your team is a benefit.

Cut Yourself in for Some of the Commission.   Check to see if this is legal in your state by checking with the state department that establishes agency rules and regulations. As a principal in the transaction, as either buyer or seller, you may be allowed to get a piece of the commission in the transaction. As a buyer, this could help you meet the down payment percentage the lender insists on; as a seller, it allows you to pocket more of the proceeds of the sale.

26. What Are the Most Important Factors I Need to Know before I Sign a Listing Agreement?

There are a number of critical factors you should review whenever you place your property in the hands of an agent through an exclusive listing agreement. Remember, this document is legally binding to both you and the agent for a period of time.

Solution: Review the following prelisting checklist.

The Seven Most Important Prelisting Agreement Factors

- What is the real estate firm going to do for me?
- Does the agent understand my goals?
- Is the agent willing to work hard for me?
- Does the agent have enough time to devote to my property?
- What is the commission I am expected to pay?
- How will the listing firm split the commission with a co-broker?
- What is the term of the listing?

What Is the Real Estate Firm Going to Do for Me? The firm should do whatever it promises to do: advertise, keep the property open, network the property, make a color brochure, put a sign in the front yard, or whatever. Make sure you have these commitments in writing and get a timetable of when you can expect these events to happen. If the items are important to you (they should be), insist on the right to withdraw the listing if the agents fail to keep their promises and timetable. Let them suggest the timetable: most agents will be overly eager to impress you and are apt to cut short the actual time they will need. Review that schedule and add on a reasonable period to take account for the lead time it takes to put any good marketing program into effect.

Does the Agent Understand My Goals? The agent who works toward the wrong goal may well end up there, at no benefit to you. Explain to your agent exactly what you are trying to accomplish. For example, if you want to build your real estate portfolio to the point where you eventually own 100 apartment units and you now own none, be sure the agent knows you want to start slowly, with 20 units or so, and not to jump right to that end goal. If you have a change in your plans and goals, be sure you let the agent know so he or she can shift the property search accordingly.

Is the Agent Willing to Work Hard for Me?   You cannot just take the agent's word on this—you have to look at his or her past record for job performance. Ask for references and check them out. Following through is the key to success as a real estate salesperson, and that takes persistence and the ability to overcome frustration. Do you have an agent who can handle that? If not, find another one who will meet those roadblocks head on and win.

Does the Agent Have Enough Time to Devote to My Property?   Some agents use their charm to get listings, but end up with too many and are hard put to sell them all. They may become successful, however, because if they keep the listing long enough, some other agent may sell the property and the listing agent will get a commission. You really want an agent who is an aggressive seller, not the charmer who can list too many properties to work with. Some real estate firms have figured this out and work their agents as a team. If you find a team that combines charm with aggressive marketing, you may have found a team that will take you to great wealth.

What Is the Commission I Am Expected to Pay?   Due to the illegality of price fixing, there is no standard commission. Each brokerage firm is allowed to establish its own guidelines, and many are flexible within those individual guidelines. Remember, when you pay a commission you are paying only for results. It is not unusual for real estate commissions in the United States to be as high as 10 percent for vacant property. Residential properties may vary between 4 and 7 percent. The listing agreement should be very specific about the price you are offering and the percent of the selling price you will have to pay as a fee. Be sure the listing agreement specifies exactly who gets the fee. Do not get into a situation where you start talking directly to other brokers who do not know you already have a listing agent, because you might end up being obligated to pay two commissions.

How Will the Listing Firm Split the Commission with a Co-Broker?   If you are using a Realtor who will list your property in the MLS, there is a good chance that an agent from another firm will actually sell your property. The selling agent will be paid a percent of the fee you are paying. It is customary for the two firms to split the total commission in half, but this is not always the case. Some listing firms simply show the total percentage, not how it's to be divided between the offices. In my opinion, if the division is not a 50-50 split between the two offices, the advantage should go to the selling office. You want the best effort in selling your listed property, so insist that the listing firm not get more than the selling firm and that your property be exposed to as many prospective buyers as possible. This means that the listing office should not sit on the listing and try to sell it without letting the listing be shown by or become available to other Realtors.

What Is the Term of the Listing?   How many months do you tie your property up with this real estate firm? The listing should be very specific about this and should show the actual date the listing expires. If the property does not sell by the expiration date, the agent will ask for an extension. If you are satisfied with the efforts and wish to continue the listing, be sure the extension is valid only with your approval. Avoid any listing contract that allows for automatic extension for a specific term if you fail to withdraw the listing by a predetermined date. Most state laws prohibit automatic listing renewals in the absence of an owner's withdrawal.

27. How Does the Real Estate Law Affect My Relationship with My Broker or Agent?

State laws may vary in regard to both the broker-buyer-seller relationship and the broker's obligations. In general, business relationships you can have with a real estate agent take one of five forms.

> **Solution:** Find out exactly what rules and laws the real estate brokerage industry must abide by in your state or whichever state you are doing business in. You may find out that the laws vary between those states.

You must be informed about which of the following forms of agency you are dealing with. Some state laws are stricter than others about the method of notifying the parties, and as a practical matter both buyers and sellers should ask the question and get the answer in writing. Then find out how your state law governs the agent's fiduciary responsibility to you and the other parties to the transaction. Call the nearest board of Realtors in your area and ask how to get in touch with your state bureau governing licensed real estate brokers and associates.

Five Forms of Real Estate Agency

Subagents Become Coagents.   This occurs when licensees acting for other real estate firms serve as coagents (as through the board of Realtors multiple listing service). Even though your listing agreement is with company A, a salesperson working for company B may become a subagent of yours by attempting to sell your property.

Single Agents.   Single agents are licensees who act as either a seller's agent or a buyer's agent but never represent both parties in the same transaction. These agents may adopt the policy not to become subagents when working with other brokers.

Seller's Agents.   A seller's agent is a licensee who is employed by and represents only the seller in a transaction. In this situation, the agent owes total loyalty to the seller. However, state laws may require the seller's agent to make certain disclosures to buyers of known property defects and similar issues. This is a form of a single agency.

Buyer's Agents.   A buyer's agent (or buyer's broker) is a licensee who is employed by and represents only the buyer in a transaction. This is another type of single agency. This form of agency occurs when the buyer delegates to a licensee the right to act on his or her behalf in a real estate transaction, regardless of whether the commission is paid by the buyer directly or by the seller through a commission split.

Dual Agents. Dual agents are licensees who attempt to represent both the buyer and the seller in the same real estate transaction. This is the usual type of agency and, with careful notice to all parties, is legal. This form of agency places a great deal of pressure on the broker to maintain a proper fiduciary relationship with both parties of the transaction. Because of the potential conflict of an agent accidentally and unintentionally violating the fiduciary relationship with you or the other party, it is a good idea to insist that your agent act as a single agent and represent you as either a buyer's agent or seller's agent, depending on whether you are a buyer or seller at any given time.

28. Should I Use a Different Agent for Buying and for Selling?

Review question 27 regarding the five different forms of agency.

> **Solution:** My recommendation is that as a seller you always insist that your agent represent you as a single agent, a seller's agent, and if you are a buyer that the agent become your buyer's agent. Your agent must then notify all other agents or property owners with whom you deal of this situation.

The same broker can represent you in each situation provided he or she maintains the status of single agency each time.

29. What Is the Usual Commission, and Who Pays It?

There is no "usual" commission because of anti-price-fixing rules and regulations; however, within any community there will be a common range of commissions charged. From a practical point of view, the commission will range from 4 to 10 percent. International transactions may be higher.

> **Solution:** As with every other item in a contract between the parties, the commission is open for negotiation. However, once the broker has it in writing from the party who will pay that broker, the broker has the right to expect to be paid accordingly.

When a seller lists a property with an agent, the seller usually pays the fee in the event of a sale or other disposition (exchange, lease, lease option, etc.). However, the seller may elect to list net of commission, indicating that the seller expects to get a certain price and the agent can add on whatever commission he or she wants. While the idea of a net commission sounds attractive to a seller, agents are reluctant to agree to this kind of commission because they have no control over what the seller will actually take, nor can they control what a buyer offers. Agents who are savvy in real estate brokerage will not work on a net listing.

5

Successful Buying and Selling of Homes

30. How Can Buyers Improve Their Success When Negotiating an Offer?

The art of negotiating is not a talent that we are born with. It comes from watching, listening, and following a simple, learnable example.

> **Solution:** Discover the buyer's 11 steps to improve sales contract negotiation skills.

The following steps will enable you to approach the entire spectrum of acquiring real estate with self-confidence, knowing that you are well prepared for the negotiating process. Success in a one-on-one negotiation depends on this inner confidence, not only for your own sake but to impress the other parties. Everyone likes to do business with a successful person; at the end of the deal, everyone can go away from the closing feeling good about that person. This process builds good reputations. Make this one of your goals.

> ## The Buyer's 11 Steps to Successful Contract Negotiations
>
> - Be positive about everything you do.
> - Know your goals.
> - Find properties that move you closer to your goals.
> - Set financial and personal ceilings—then expand them.
> - Do your homework.
> - Discover the seller's motivation.
> - Learn how to handle timing.
> - Get started on the right foot.
> - Understand the fundamentals of motivation.
> - Establish a deadline on the deal.
> - Be patient.

Be Positive about Everything You Do.   If you have a negative attitude about anything, then your whole outlook on everything you do will be slanted. You cannot be a positive person if you allow negative thoughts or negative people to become part of your life. Positive people attract other positive people. The more positive you are, the more difficult it is to say no to you.

Know Your Goals.   You should have your goals written and posted where you can see them every day. I know this sounds oversimplified, but this is for your benefit alone—them, no one else need see them. By keeping your goals in clear sight they will also be clearly in focus when it is time to negotiate that contract to buy or sell. By knowing where you are going, you will be less likely to overpay when you buy or to hold onto a diminishing benefit when you sell.

Find Properties That Move You Closer to Your Goals.   This is easier said than done, but if you follow a plan and get to know your investment area and local market conditions, you will begin to see the opportunities that were there all the time but that you did not recognize before. Everything you do that is directed toward your goals should fit a pattern and should be attempted in a logical order. The key to success is to avoid being sidetracked from your main purpose. Determination is, after all, only one of the necessary attributes to success; a clearly focused goal, self-confidence, and persistence round out your chances for success in everything you attempt.

Set Financial and Personal Ceilings–Then Expand Them.   You have only so much money and economic strength, and your personal abilities will carry you only so far—that is, for the time being. As your confidence increases you will be able to raise your investment sights. Your success in raising your goals will be your honesty with yourself. Engage in periodic self-reviews of things you should be doing to increase your abilities. For example, if you are struggling with accounting or have a hard time understanding the income and expense statements sellers show you, then sign up for a night course in bookkeeping. Most communities have adult education programs that cover just about every aspect of real estate. Take advantage of these inexpensive and mind-broadening programs; they will pay off.

Do Your Homework. Doing homework in real estate is called *due diligence.* It is critical if you want to avoid risky mistakes. No one said that making a fortune in real estate was going to be easy. There is a lot of information that you need to gather and then learn. The local marketplace is dynamic, and the person who learned everything two years ago and did not keep up-to-date is dealing with yesterday's news. Get into the habit of carrying a notebook around with you at all times, and when you see a "For Rent" or "For Sale" sign, write down the phone number, the address, and what type of property it is. Then call and get the details. Even if you are not interested in the property, ask if you can see it. This allows you to learn more about property in the area, and also to meet either an agent or the owner. Either one can be a good source of information if you take the time to ask for it.

One very important aspect about due diligence is the greener-grass syndrome. You have experienced it many times before: the sensation that the grass looks greener over there, on the other side of the fence. Often, even the smartest real estate investors forget that more than location changes as you go from one part of a town, a state, or a county to another. A buyer used to the high prices of homes in New York City or San Francisco, for example, can come across a comparable home in Georgia or a thousand other places for one-third the price. Without due diligence, that investor has no valid perspective on the real value of "away from home" property. Do your homework.

Discover the Seller's Motivation. All sellers have a reason for selling their property. Knowing what has prompted a seller to want to dispose of the property you would like to own can be very helpful in how you structure your offer. You will discover that sometimes the reason is based on a wrong premise. For example, a person moving out of town who must now find another place to live elsewhere may not know that he or she could exchange the property, offer a long-term lease with an option to buy, and so on. Discovering the reason for the sale is to find out what "benefit" the seller is seeking. Sometimes you acquire property by helping the sellers achieve their goals (i.e., by helping them gain the benefit they want).

Learn How to Handle Timing. All salespeople know that timing can ruin a deal if not properly handled. "Strike while the iron is hot" is certainly true when negotiating a sale. Both the buyer and seller can become colder than a block of ice if the deal does not progress. It can be very easy for either party to become fatalistic about the transaction if the other party seems to be throwing unwarranted delays into the transaction. It is a good idea to use an agent for that purpose, however, as this removes anxiety about the transaction. However, make sure your real estate agents understand that you expect them to keep on top of the deal until it has been accepted by all parties.

Get Started on the Right Foot.   Good communications skills are very important when dealing with other people. In real estate negotiations these skills are best used to make sure that you give the right signals to the other party and do not disrupt a transaction that was moving in the right direction. In the very beginning of any transaction it is a good idea to express your thoughts about the property and make sure the other party understands what you are thinking. For example, "Mrs. Seller, I think your home is absolutely perfect for me, and I hope that we can get together on price and terms because I know my wife and children will just love this neighborhood." Later on, as you close the gap on the price and terms, you can continue to let the seller know that you and she are on the same side of the fence. After all, you both want the seller to sell you the home.

Understand the Fundamentals of Motivation.   There are many reasons people are motivated to do what they do. Your task as a buyer is not to attempt to motivate them to do what you want but to allow their own motivations to lead them to a decision that is mutually agreeable. Motivation plays a strong role, because many people cannot make a decision. A decision as critical as accepting an offer on their home or other property can often be put off so many times that the buyers give up and move on.

The importance, then, of dealing with motivation is to help the seller come to that mutually agreeable decision. A good salesperson can be worth his or her weight in gold in this part of the negotiation process, but if you are dealing directly with the sellers yourself, continually look for the benefit they are seeking—the real reason they want to sell. Eventually, you may find that the real reason is a pending divorce, a health scare, or financial problems. Work within the scope of the seller's goals whenever possible by opening options to them that they may not have realized.

Establish a Deadline on the Deal.   It is a great feeling to negotiate a deal and finally come to a successful conclusion. However, if you let yourself get bogged down in endless meetings and countless back-and-forth offers and counteroffers, then you have not given the right signal to the seller or perhaps to yourself. Every deal should have a deadline for the current negotiations. I say current because even if you are not successful this time, you can, as long as the property is still for sale, come back again. But you should not let the seller know this . . . and in fact, if you break off a deal this afternoon, by tomorrow you may have found something you like even better, which may take you out of the picture altogether as a buyer.

So set a deadline. Put it in the contract: "If this offer is not accepted by noon of the seventh day following the date executed by the buyer, then this agreement shall be considered null and void and each party hereinafter released from further obligation to each other." In counteroffer situations, this provision can be modified or removed. However, the initial posture is to make sure everyone knows that you are a ready, willing, and able buyer and that if you cannot acquire this property you will go elsewhere—and soon.

Be Patient. Patience is the virtue that makes deals fly. However, the ability to sit back and let the transaction move forward on its own is often difficult. It is easy for a buyer or seller to become impatient with the lack of progress or the inability to get a decision from the other party. Yet patience should not be employed without persistence. To sit back and do nothing is a good way to frustrate the other parties in the transaction. When any transaction seems to stagnate, it is time for a good salesperson to step in and help things get back on track. Principals should never appear anxious in the heat of negotiation. That should be the task of the salesperson. "Mr. Seller," the real estate agent can say, "I hate to see this deal go down the tube simply because you are unsure how to counter the buyer's offer. Let's go over the details of her offer again. I think you will realize that all of your objectives in selling this property can be reached."

31. What Should All Sellers Know When Negotiating a Contract?

To win any game, you must know the rules and techniques and, most of all, your opponent. In the heat of negotiations, each party to the transaction may assume that the adversary in the deal is the other party—buyers against sellers or vice versa. In reality this could not be further from the truth.

> **Solution:** Discover the real enemy that can stand between the buyer and the seller, and how to deal with it.

After all, the buyer wants to buy the property. The seller wants the buyer to buy the property. Is that an adversarial relationship? Actually, the two parties sometimes forget that they both really want the same result. The problem, then, is not negotiating an agreement on the end result but simply knowing how to get there. For the buyer, the end result (I want to buy, and I know the seller wants to sell) was decided the moment he or she told the salesperson to write up the offer.

When the seller approaches a transaction with this nonadversarial frame of reference, the whole negotiating process will be less traumatic and far more successful for both parties. After all, they both want the same thing. The following checklist will help the seller keep the end result firmly in focus while the negotiations are moving toward that destination.

> **The Seller's 11-Item Contract Negotiation Checklist**
>
> - Never be insulted by an offer.
> - Review your goals.
> - Know what benefits are given up.
> - Can you use the benefits gained?
> - Avoid saying no.
> - Help the buyer to become an owner mentally.
> - Keep all options open.
> - Be creative.
> - Never insult the buyer or the buyer's agent.
> - Let the agent absorb the heat.
> - Look for win-win situations.

Take a look at each of these factors. If you have been a seller before, did you go over any of these prior to entering into negotiations?

Never Be Insulted by an Offer.　As a Realtor for nearly 30 years I have had hundreds of sellers toss the buyer's offer back into my lap and tell me they were insulted by the offer. Their insult may have been prompted by the low price offered, the terms, or a dozen other things that rubbed them the wrong way.

It does little good for me to suggest that if they are insulted by an offer, how do they feel about all the people who did not even like the property enough to make an offer?

The point is, there are ready, willing, and able buyers who want to win points in the deal. If they do not win points, they will not buy. It is simple as that. However, before jumping to conclusions that it is you that must lose points, think back to a time when you may have walked out of a store even though you'd found exactly what you wanted to buy. For some reason, however, you felt slighted and you left, perhaps to drive all the way across town and buy the same thing for more money, just to prove something, win points, or not to lose face. This idea about losing face may sound silly, but it is not.

Why do buyers have to win points? There are dozens of reasons. Here are some of them: to impress someone (e.g., girlfriend, neighbor, the agent) and prove that they are capable of getting a good deal; to play the game they think they are supposed to be playing; to try to get a steal; and because they are novices at real estate and are being led by others.

The initial offer from one of these people may indeed appear too far off your target. However, if you throw the offer back or counteroffer with a price and terms exactly matching the listing terms, then you have removed the potential of any points being won, and the game may be over for you.

Review Your Goals.   You should review your goals every day, so thinking about them before starting to negotiate with a buyer should not be an exception. It is a good idea to pay very close attention to the reason you decided to sell the property in the first place. This will help you clearly focus on where you want to go after the sale.

Know What Benefits Are Given Up.   The property you own may have some very positive benefits to you, despite the fact that you want to dispose of it. As you go over your goals, look at the positive factors of the real estate you own. You would not be the first seller who has decided to keep your property after discovering the benefits cannot be replaced at the price a buyer is willing to pay.

Can You Use the Benefits Gained?   Circumstances of a sale may seem to solve your problems or move you closer to your goals. But do they? Take a hard look at the bottom line, the end results after you make the sale, pay your taxes (if any), and then move on with your life and investment planning. This would be particularly important if you were to take another property in exchange to facilitate the transaction. Can you use the other property, or does it now become a bigger problem?

Avoid Saying No.   You should never commit yourself, no matter how much the buyer or the agent may press for a commitment, until you understand the total offer being made. Once you have a clear understanding of the total offer, you should not say no even if the offer is not acceptable as presented. Instead, you should adapt the offer to terms and conditions that are acceptable to you and make the counteroffer. There are many ways to change the agreement, allowing the buyer to win some points that have little or no effect on your end results. The better approach is to say "Yes, Mr. Buyer, I think we can get together on this deal, and I do appreciate your interest in this property. I think your family will love this neighborhood and that your children, as have my children, will enjoy this home. I have made a few modifications in the offer and have accepted it."

Help the Buyer to Mentally Become an Owner.   The quicker the buyer begins to see him- or herself as the owner of your property, the smoother the negotiations will go and the quicker you will have a firm and binding contract. Sellers can aid this process by giving the buyer positive signals that all is going well in the negotiation process. Let the wife come over to measure for new carpets and drapes, ask or have the agent ask bonding questions such as, "Will you move in right after the closing?" or "The seller said he will have the rooms repainted right after he moves out, would you like to select the colors?" This kind of question can be a closing question for a salesperson, because it allows the buyer to say yes (to buying the property) by agreeing to a small item.

Keep All Options Open.   No one knows everything, so do not enter negotiations with a closed mind or with such a narrow focus that you will not explore something new and innovative. A buyer or an agent may have an idea of how you can attain your goal, and the buyer his or her goal, at a price or terms that you may not have agreed to earlier.

Be Creative.   There are many books written about creative real estate. You might enjoy learning some of the different techniques that can make a deal work for you. There are perfectly legal tax angles that can save you thousands of dollars or give you a fast deal if you will just open up and be creative.

Never Insult the Buyer or the Buyer's Agent.   Having been both a buyer and (in another situation) a buyer's agent, I know how I have felt when a frustrated seller explodes and unloads that frustration on me. Although I understand the situation and have been able to take my own advice (see the next factor), I know many agents who have been reduced to tears and have not been able to face their prospective buyer as a result of being insulted by an irate seller. Naturally, by insulting either the buyer or his or her agent, you run the risk of burning a bridge that was about to take you to your desired goals.

Let the Agent Absorb the Heat.   In the usual situation, the real estate agent is working for you, so you should let that agent absorb the heat of any anger or frustration thrown off by either side without passing that onto the other party. There is no reason for the agent to tell you what uncomplimentary name the buyer or seller called you when your counteroffer was presented. Agents can be anxious to make a deal because of the commission they will earn, and they can be determined to get the deal signed even if it means going back and forth a dozen times until midnight or later rather than to let the deal rest over the weekend and the buyer "go cold." Far too many deals collapse because each side attempts to be so cavalier that someone else beats them to the draw, or fate enters the picture and minds change.

Look for Win-Win Situations.   When you keep your eye on the goals and benefits you want to gain and on those you are happy to eliminate (because they no longer help you), then you will find more win-win situations are possible. To some degree negotiations are give-and-receive processes. Only in the hottest of real estate markets will sellers be able to sit back and wait for their exact price and terms. But remember that waiting is time, and time is money. You may win more by accepting a slight modification in your price or terms than by holding out.

32.   What Does It Mean When a Buyer Says "I'll Pay Your Price If You Accept My Terms"?

This strategy is well known to savvy real estate agents and insider investors. To some degree, it means, "There are other ways to skin the cat."

> **Solution:** Learn the quid pro quo between price and terms, and don't let the seller's price turn you off if there is a way to make the terms work.

Assume a seller sets a price for a vacant lot, say, at $100,000, payable as $54,000 cash and a mortgage of $46,000. Along comes a buyer who says "I will pay your price of $100,000 if you will accept these terms":

BUYER: I will assume your mortgage of $46,000.

SELLER: Agreed.

BUYER: I will pay you $5,400 per year for 10 years—that totals $54,000. Okay?

This offer totals what the seller wanted, almost. The only difference between what the seller wants and what the buyer offers is time. Time, then, becomes one of the fundamental negotiating elements in real estate. If I can pay you what you want, but not exactly when you want it, then perhaps we can negotiate not on money but on time. This works most of the time, but it is not the only factor to consider.

The amount of money the seller will have to reinvest after the transaction can also be used by the creative buyer for negotiations. Consider this same seller who, 15 years ago, paid only $10,000 for this vacant lot, now worth $100,000. This means that the individual has a gain in this transaction of $90,000. Oh, but wait. There is a mortgage outstanding of $46,000 on the lot, which is $36,000 more than what was paid for the lot. So far, the seller has had the use of this extra capital ($36,000) without having to pay any income tax on that amount. However, when the lot is sold, everything above the book value (called *basis* in real estate) will be treated as a capital gain—including the $36,000 that the seller has most likely already spent.

If, because of other income and expenses in the year of the sale, the seller's overall tax rate is only 15 percent, the amount of tax to pay on the gain would be 15 percent of $90,000, or $13,500. If he gets $54,000 cash at closing he would pay the tax from that amount and end up with $40,000 in his pocket (not taking into account any closing costs or real estate commissions).

What was the seller going to do with the money, anyway? The lot is being sold because the seller sees no benefits from it. In fact, it is a liability because there is a mortgage on it, and annual real estate tax causes a cash drain. What are the seller's goals? Or is the seller like so many others, who have no real goals in sight and are just trying to unload a problem?

A creative buyer may present an alternative: "Let me give you my six-unit apartment building in exchange for your lot." The details on the apartment building are as follows: price, $180,000; existing first mortgage, $120,000. If the seller holds the second mortgage of $6,000, the equity in the apartments is $54,000, an even swap for the lot equity.

Does this new benefit help the seller of the lot? It may not, but it does present an alternative that may not even have been considered. This kind of exchange would likely qualify as a tax-free exchange under IRS Code 1031, so there would be no loss of reinvestment power. If the apartments are capable of paying off the total debt of $126,000, then that will be a future benefit, and if there is income now, then this is much better than the seller having to make payments on the previous $54,000 mortgage.

Successful deal making in real estate depends on both the buyer and seller not getting bogged down in a price battle. Each party can look for other ways to skin the cat.

33. How Should I React When a Prospective Buyer Finds Fault with My Property?

Many sellers avoid being around when their property is shown to prospective buyers. However, when buyer and seller do end up together during a property showing, sparks can easily fly. An aggressive (or just anxious) buyer or seller can confront his or her opposite party and engage in what might be simple banter between them. Suddenly, the buyer puts a nasty look on his face, and even without words passing between them (at that point) the seller is insulted. What should you do if you are that seller?

> **Solution:** Take heart. Negative looks and/or comments may really be a buyer's signal that he or she is warming up to the property. Read on.

What do you do? How about rejoice and be happy? Most real estate agents know that the moment a prospective buyer starts to find fault with a property, it is a buying sign. Of course, if the buyer makes the statement, "This place is like a pig's pen" and the reference is valid, then this may not be a buying sign.

The signals from the buyer can come in the form of body language as well as spoken language. Each can be very subtle and at the same time can be taken as an insult by the sellers if they are watching or listening.

For example, the prospect says, "I can't stand the color of that carpet." The seller, in his or her mind, adds "What idiot picked it out?" and is insulted. In reality, the prospective buyer is thinking, "This is the first thing I will change when I buy."

Most agents learn how to deal with buyers' negative comments and nasty looks. A good agent would ask this buyer, "What color will you install?" Dealing with negative statements is all part of finesse in bringing the closing to a point where the deal is signed and accepted by both buyer and seller. It is important to remember that just because some negative comments or looks may be closing signals, the opposite, a positive look or comment can also be a distinct closing signal. When the seller says, "This paint color has got to go," that is most definitely a closing signal, and so is, "I love this color; our leather love seats will go nicely here."

34. What Are the Most Important Buying Signals I Should Watch For?

As mentioned in solution 33, every person who inspects your property will give off some signals that can give you a clue regarding how they feel about the property. However, some of these signals can be misunderstood by novice agents or by sellers who may be present. The following positive signals are solid buying signs.

> **Solution:** Become familiar with the following important buying signals.

The Nine Most Important Buying Signals

- Spouse there this time
- Nitpicks
- Starts to talk about redecoration
- Asks about structural items
- Asks about hidden factors
- Wants to know the seller's motivation
- Introduces time to the negotiation
- Comes back several times
- Brings up the issue of price

There is no particular order in which these signals may be displayed, if at all. Some buyers are very warm and open, others as cold as ice; each may be a real buyer for your property or may hate the place. Anytime you start to see one or more of these nine signals, both you and your agent should start to close in on this buyer . . . and not let him or her get away.

Spouse There This Time. This is an important signal that some people (brokers and salespeople) often overlook.

Nitpicks. When buyers start to pick apart a property, this can be a sign that they are attempting to appear disinterested. One or two nitpicking statements may not give a clear signal, but four or more do.

Starts to Talk about Redecoration. "Can my decorator come over?" is a strong buying signal, as are comments about where they would place their furniture, what color to paint the walls, and the like.

Asks about Structural Items. Unless there is some interest in the property, there is no reason to get into technical details. Any such questions are strong buying signs.

Asks about Hidden Factors. Hidden factors can be anything from "What is behind this wall?" to "Have there ever been any termites?" It could be that the buyers are looking for a hidden gem that will help convince them to buy. "Are there hardwood floors under this carpet?" may be a signal meaning "Please let there be so I can say yes right now and close tomorrow."

Wants to Know Seller's Motivation. These questions indicate that buyers are thinking how to structure an offer. You have to look beyond the casual "Why are they selling?" because that question might simply be raised to pass the time during the visit. Once the buyer starts to ask for more information about the seller's motivation, some solid interest is being manifested.

Introduces Time to the Negotiation. This can be a very strong buying signal. "How soon could you move out?" is about the strongest question dealing with time.

Comes Back Several Times. This sign is hard to assess because it is both a buying signal as well as an unsold signal. Buyers who have not made up their minds may revisit properties several times and then not even make an offer.

Brings Up the Issue of Price. When this comes either early or at the end of the sequence of visits, that is a very good sign. It often means that the would-be buyer has exhausted every personal conflict that might preclude buying.

To lose a sale at the juncture where the buyer has given one or more of these signals is usually the fault of the sales agent by not picking up on these factors. Of course, you have to understand that the agent (if not your agent) has his or her own agenda and may be trying to sell another property where the commission is greater. This does happen, which is why it is a good idea to have your own agent in the middle of the negotiations. It is clear that these people are having a hard time making up their mind and thus may not make a decision without some help. A good agent should make an effort to resell your property rather than push for a decision.

35. How Do I Get Rid of Mildew Smells?

When God made man and woman, one of the true masterpieces of this work was the sense of smell. If it were not for the fact that virtually any human is able to adapt to any smell, there would be many places in the world void of human presence. That is the good news. The bad news is that the home or building you own and now want to sell may have a smell about it that is so bad that a prospective buyer (and tenants, too) are turned off the moment they get a whiff of the odor. You cannot trust your own nose in these situations, and you need to listen to the advice of your fresh-to-the-property sales agent. It's not that you like the smell, but that you don't even notice it.

> **Solution:** Get rid of the source of the smell, remove the
> lingering odor, and stop the cause.

1. *Get rid of the source of the smell.* If it is old carpeting or other easily removable material that has embedded mildew or other smells, then get rid of its source. When the mildew has found a home behind a wall, perhaps in insulation between the wall studs, there may be no simple solution. If this is the case, you need to contact a professional cleaning firm that has equipment to fumigate the mildew and kill it within the walls.

2. *Remove the lingering odor.* What if you have removed everything that might be causing the odor and yet the smell remains? Perhaps there is mildew inside the walls or under the wallpaper, or perhaps the odor has soaked in and will linger for a very long time. First make sure that it is only odor you are dealing with. Removing wallpaper is important because behind it might be more mildew. The same can be said for mirrors and wood paneling. Once you are sure that the coast is clear of mildew or other molds itself, and only the smell remains, then wash the walls with a mild solution of trisodium phosphate (TSP) and chlorine, say half a cup of each in a gallon of water. Let the area dry, then paint, wallpaper, or panel.

3. *Stop the cause.* Mildew and toxic mold are both plantlike life forms that grow almost anywhere in an environment with some humidity, warmth, lack of circulating air, and little or no sunlight. For example, a good place for mildew to get started is leather shoes and jackets in a dark, warm, moist closet. Another possibility is when rain soaks the interiors of walls due to an undetected leak; there may be no visible water stains, but you notice the smell of mildew and other unpleasant odors. The best way to handle this is to repair any leaks, air out rooms frequently, and use circulating fans to keep the air moving in a room that is closed up for any period of time. However, make sure you kill the old mildew by washing down the area with a chemical made just for that job or with the mixture of TSP and chlorine mentioned previously. Any hardware store will have several fine products from which you can chose.

36. What Are the Key Moneymaking Aspects about Landscaping?

Landscaping can be one of the best improvements you can make to any property. Because of this it is important to landscape your property with an eye to how long you plan to keep the property. If you are a builder and plan to sell the property quickly, then invest in mature plants to best show off the property. On the other hand, if you are like most homeowners, you may plan to keep your home longer than 10 years, perhaps for a lifetime.

Solution: **Plan (with professional help) your landscaping for a seven-year maturity period.**

The key time factor is seven years. Even a modest landscaping program should be planned with a seven-year maturity in mind. This does not mean that you have to wait seven years for results; you will see continual improvement beginning in only a few months.

If you want the best possible results from landscaping, have a professional lay out your plan. Explain your seven-year plan and provide the parameters of your economic budget. This will enable the landscaper to design an overall master plan, either for implementation now or to be staged over a period of time. The most critical concern should be the slowest-growing plants. Get them in the ground as soon as you can, and buy plants that will reach an attractive size within the time allowed.

Work on the front yard and the living areas of the backyard first, mainly because you want to enjoy the home yourself and not just be a slave to your master plan. Fill in the rest of the landscaping as you go.

Ask the landscaper to include plants that provide edible produce . . . but only if these plants fit the overall plan. Citrus, mangos, avocados, bananas, and other such plants complement property in tropical areas, whereas pecan, walnut, apple, plum, peach, almond, and other trees can be used in cooler areas to produce a beautiful and functional yard that may attract the buyer you will be seeking years from now.

37.   Should I Sell My Property Furnished or Unfurnished?

If the property is presently furnished, then you may face the time when you should consider offering it as furnished or unfurnished.

> Solution: **If the question of keeping the furniture need not be considered, offer the home for sale unfurnished.**

When you list your property for sale unfurnished, do not state in the listing that the furniture is also available. Such statements automatically encourage a buyer (who likes the furniture and wants to buy it) to ask you to throw it in. In other words, the buyer makes an offer that includes the furniture. You can always discuss the furniture in the negotiations, but it is best to require the buyers to ask for it. Why? Because if they ask for it, this is another buying signal: "Would you include the baby grand piano?" Your answer should be, "Are there any other conditions to your offer to buy my home?" Keep in mind that your agent may be the one who makes that remark, not you.

When the furniture is not really an issue, meaning that neither you nor the buyer is interested in it, then you can offer it to a family member, give it to charity, or barter it for something you can use.

38.   How Can I Get Rid of Dog and Other Animal Smells?

The human nose has a wonderful fail-safe ability that eventually accepts odd or distasteful smells as normal. People who have lived near paper mills for a few years do not even notice the smell, which you might find very unpleasant. The same goes for any smell, including old damp dogs, kitty litter boxes, and even your household llama. However, your agent knows the smell is there, and so will any prospective buyer.

> Solution: **The first step is to accept the fact that there is a dog or other animal smell in the property. Review the solution for problem 35, and add to this solution the following three steps.**

1. *Wash, and wash some more.*   Like the mildew problem, you first must get rid of what is holding the smell. That means cleaning the dog bed well, changing the kitty litter daily, and bathing the dog and the llama more often. Then wash the area most frequented by the animal with fresh-smelling soaps, and use odor-killing sprays.

2. *Keep odor-holding elements clean and deodorized.*   In cases where puppies and other animals have wet the carpets a number of times, the carpets may have to be replaced. A rug shampooing cannot totally solve the problem, but if the carpets are in good shape, contact a carpet cleaning firm that will give you references (which you should check) and ask for advice.

3. *Have the animals checked for a medical condition.*   The dog, cat, snake, or whatever may be ill and may be producing odors that your nose has long ago forgotten exist.

39. What Should Sellers Do When Showing Their Home to a Prospective Buyer?

Many real estate agents cringe at the thought that the owners will be around when prospects show up to view the property for sale. Generally, I tend to agree with the idea that it is best for the agent alone to deal with people who come through the property. But there are many times when this is not possible, and it might be better to let the prospective buyer see inside an occupied home (or other property for sale) than to miss out on a potential sale.

> **Solution:** Follow the 10 sales-producing steps to owner-hosted open houses.

10 Sales-Producing Steps to Take When the Buyer Is Going to Inspect the Home

- Remove pets from the site.
- Spring-clean the whole house.
- Make closets and storage areas as neat as possible.
- Show off the garage as best you can.
- Neatly cut and trim the yard.
- Clean and polish the front door.
- Clean bathrooms and hang fresh towels.
- Make sure the kitchen is spotless—clean, empty sink and uncluttered refrigerator.
- Turn on all lights, as a bright home is a happy home.
- Remember, pleasant-memory smells drown out old smells.

Take into consideration seasonal items—snow cleared off the drive and walkways, air-conditioning adjusted properly in the middle of the summer, and so on.

40. What Are "Memory Smells," and How Can They Entice a Prospective Buyer?

This is a multifaceted problem that has no simple approach. However there is a solution.

> **Solution:** Review this section on memory smells and apply its suggestions.

Memory smells can be both good and bad. Everyone has some of both, and the idea is to introduce one of the good smells into a property when prospective buyers are coming to inspect the property—for example, when brokers hold open houses or when you have been notified that a prospective buyer is on the way.

Each of the following smells can be created in relatively short time, if you plan for it. There are many variations on these, and many others are not mentioned at all. The idea is not to produce the smell that you find pleasing, but rather a smell that is safe and generally accepted as having a pleasant-memory smell for most people.

The All-Time Top 14 "Good Memory" Smells

- Fresh flowers
- A clean, nonchemical smell
- Bread baking in the oven
- Cookies baking in the oven
- Pies baking in the oven
- Turkey baking in the oven
- Freshly brewed coffee
- Heated hot chocolate
- Candy as it is cooking
- Freshly popped corn
- New leather
- Fresh paint (the kind that smells good)
- Bubble gum
- A hardwood fire

To top off the delightful smell, if it is food such as candy or cookies, having a sample for prospective buyers to taste can be a real winner. It works for supermarkets—why not for your home?

41. What Steps Should I Follow When I Am Ready to Buy a Home?

Most successful people work hard at obtaining their goals. The key word is *goals*. The unfortunate fact for many people is that they have no real goals in focus. Many people function on a day-to-day basis with dreams and not with well-formulated goals. They do not know exactly where they are going, do not have a timetable to get there, and do not do all the right things to ensure they are equipped for and capable of getting where they want to be. In essence, it is hard work to set and obtain goals directed toward one final result.

With no clearly defined goal there is no purposeful plan, and actions tend to be random and often without any real satisfaction, because there is no way to judge what progress has been made, if any.

> **Solution:** The process of buying a home is not an everyday event. Your approach to this task should be taken very seriously, and the more deliberate your approach, the greater your success in making the right decision. The following 13 steps will help you organize this important event.

---

13 Steps to Follow When Buying a Home

- Write down your needs.
- Discuss the plan with all family partners.
- Review your financial capability.
- See if there are preliminary matters to deal with.
- Select the area where you want to live.
- Check the lifestyle values in the area.
- Firm up your plans and start looking.
- Select one or two agents to work with.
- Inspect a minimum of a dozen properties before making any offers.
- Check the prices of recent sales in the area.
- Get prequalified for a loan.
- Look for value-enhancing attributes.
- Be ready to act.

It is possible that your specific needs may add several steps to this list, so do not limit your advance work to just these 13 items.

Write Down Your Needs.   Study them for a few days; you are bound to make some changes. Goals take time to develop and need to be adjusted to the current situation from time to time. Your needs differ from your wishes, however, so start first with the basics and work from there. If you can afford to go beyond your present needs, then you should definitely have those extra comforts. After all, you worked hard to get them.

Discuss the Plan with All Family Partners.   This is an important decision, and everyone who will either live in the home or help you pay for it should be involved in the plan.

Review Your Financial Capability.   Are you ready to make this financial commitment? You may discover that you have to go back and make changes to the list of needs in the first step. One approach might be to look for a home that includes income potential, such as a duplex with two units or a small apartment building, to add to your financial stability.

See If There Are Preliminary Matters to Deal with.   Do you have a home you might have to sell first, or can you exchange it for the property you want to buy? Do you need to get settled in your new job? Plan ahead and anticipate the time it will take.

Select the Area Where You Want to Live.   Think ahead. Think about schools for the kids, hospitals for health problems, closeness to work, and so on. Check out several areas of the town you plan to live in. You may discover new areas that you like better than your first choice.

Check the Lifestyle Values in the Area.   A neighborhood you drove through on the way to work might seem like a paradise. But drive through on a Saturday morning and you may find many children playing, numerous sporty cars parked on the streets (indicating the likely presence of teenagers), street parties of friendly neighbors, police cars driving around because of a crime problem, unwanted people loitering at street corners, and so on. It does not take long to find out what a neighborhood is like if you do some legwork. Ask around; check with the police and fire departments. Are there any problems you should know about? Ask the neighbors: "Hi, I'm considering buying a home on the next block and, well, would you mind telling me, will I like living here?" This question might just give you the answers to help you decide for yourself.

Firm Up Your Plans and Start Looking.   There is no better time than the present, so once you know what you want to do, go do it! Looking for property to fit your needs should be both a fun time and a learning experience. As with every-thing you do, however, map it out, and keep records of what you see.

Select One or Two Agents to Work with. Real estate agents know most of the other agents who work a specific area of town, so it will be counterproduc-tive for you to work with more than one or two agents. Even though the agent technically works for the seller in most cases, you will find that each agent has many different sellers. Also, if the agent is a member of a local multiple listing system, he or she will have access to the vast majority, if not all, of the listings in the area.

Inspect a Minimum of a Dozen Properties. Do not worry if you miss an opportunity while you are learning about the area. It is much better for you to be aware of what is going on in the local market, and this requires you to do home-work. One of the most important steps in this process is to see as many for-sale properties as possible so that you can begin to get a feel for two important aspects of this search: to find out what you can get for your money and to adjust your needs to what you can afford.

Check the Prices of Recent Sales. Most areas of the country have easily understandable property records that indicate what the current owner paid for the property and how much other properties have sold for in the recent past. This information allows you to see a pattern of values in a specific geographic area. Keep in mind that prices for property sold in other areas and neighborhoods may have little relationship to prices where you are looking, so check whether the areas are very similar in the aspects that are important to you.

Get Prequalified for a Loan. Most banks and mortgage brokers will take you through the process of prequalifying for a loan. This will enable you to know exactly how much you can afford, unless you have some extra cash hidden some-where. If you are looking for income-producing properties, this prequalification may not be highly accurate, but it can give you a good idea of how much borrow-ing power you have. Keep in mind that if you are going to use seller-held financ-ing, then you may find a far more motivated lender, as you are solving the seller's problem—buying his or her property.

Look for Value-Enhancing Attributes. These are elements of a neighborhood or the property itself that you may not specifically need but that may add value to the property when it comes time for you to sell (if ever)—things like proximity to churches, schools, and shopping, added privacy because of extra landscaping, or the absence of high-rise buildings looking down on the home. Some personal items might appeal to larger families or to prospective owners with no children. These items should be noted, as they may be a deciding factor when it comes time to pick between two or more properties.

Be Ready to Act.   Once your plan is made and you have a good feel for the market and what you can do, do not let any opportunity get away.

42. What Are the Hidden Gems I Should Look for in a Property When Trying to Get the Most Value for My Money?

Even in homes that are only a few years old, some of the valuable aspects of the property may be covered over and eventually forgotten. In older properties it is not unusual for the existing owner to be unaware of some of the hidden gems that exist. These gems will vary by area of the country, and many others are not specifically mentioned, such as a wine cellar or root cellar that was boarded up long ago and forgotten.

> **Solution:** Know in advance of your property inspections what kind of hidden gems you might find. Keep in mind that there may be some that are very unique to your area of the country, so discuss the potential gems that are sometimes found in your area.

Look for the following top 14 hidden gems.

The Top 14 Hidden Gems You Might Find

- Solid brass fixtures
- Hardwood floors
- Slate, terrazzo, or tile floors
- Hardwood tongue-and-groove paneling
- Copper plumbing
- Copper roofing
- Higher-than-normal ceilings
- Large attic spaces
- Crawl spaces under the building
- Large and dry basements
- Tons of storage space
- Fruit trees in the garden
- A working fireplace
- Ability to expand the building without going up

Solid Brass Fixtures.   Years of paint may have covered up these beautiful fixtures, and they may now be not only very valuable but irreplaceable. Scrape some of the paint away with a knife where it will not be noticed—after asking permission, of course.

Hardwood Floors.   Peek under the wall-to-wall carpet. If you spot hardwood, do not assume that it is everywhere or that it is in good condition where it is covered with carpet or other flooring. It is possible that the carpet is there to cover up the places where the bad hardwood has been removed and replaced with plywood. If the hardwood is viable, you may find it worth refinishing. Always make a thorough inspection of any hidden gem to be sure it is not partially fake. If restoration is needed, be sure to get the advice of an expert before you assume you got a bargain.

Slate, Terrazzo, or Tile Floors.   If you do not see hardwood floors, you might find slate, tile, or (who knows?) even marble floors. Most of these types of floors can be refinished, and if they suit your preferences, you may have found a real gem at last.

Hardwood Tongue-and-Groove Paneling.   If the wall appears to be wood but has been painted or papered over, it may be worth checking to see whether you have genuine hardwood tongue-and-groove paneling. This can be very expensive to install (unlike the much less expensive, thin, plywood-backed paneling), and while it is costly to remove layers of paint, it might be worthwhile.

Copper Plumbing.   When you have the property inspected, this can be a very pleasant find. When a seller knows the plumbing is copper, make sure the buyer is told of this valuable asset.

Copper Roofing.   If you find copper sheeting over the whole roof, you have made an important discovery, as this can be the best kind of roof you will ever have. Copper scuppers and drains are a plus, even if the roof is of more conventional material.

Higher-than-Normal Ceilings.   This is a great perk when you find it. Many homes that were built 70 years or more ago had high ceilings, but did not have large rooms unless it was a palace. High ceilings are great.

Large Attic Spaces.   Extra storage space in the attic can be a windfall. And if the space can be finished into extra living space, then it's a real find.

Crawl Spaces under the Building.   Some homes and commercial buildings have crawl spaces either under the building or between walls for access to the plumbing and electrical installations. This may be very important to the buyer of a motel or hotel and is good news to any home buyer of property that is 10 years old or older.

Large and Dry Basements.   Like the attic space, a basement can be a real asset if it is a dry one. A wet basement can be a source of mold and smells and an endless headache. But if dry (or if it can be made that way), and especially if it can be finished into extra living or recreational space, then it is truly a gem.

Tons of Storage Space.   Any kind of space will do, but having a lot of closets and other kinds of storage is a real find.

Fruit Trees in the Garden.   Actually, any trees that do not overpower the property can be a hidden gem. They can also be a nightmare if you have to remove them. Look for fruit trees first because they bring presents at least once a year.

A Working Fireplace.   This is a great find as long as it is not the only method of heat for the property.

Ability to Expand the Building without Going Up.   This may not have any appeal to you now, but it can be important to you later on if you want to add an extra room, or just to pass that attribute to the new owner. To expand without going up is the least costly way to add living space, but it will be necessary to have the room to add space without crossing beyond the building setback lines. This will require you to check out what the local code requires and to double-check the survey of the property to ascertain where those lines are in relation to the existing building and where the property lines lie.

43.   What Are the Most Common Time Bombs I Should Look for before I Buy a Building?

Do not assume that the following list includes all the potential time bombs that you might encounter, because it does not. Each area of the country has some special problems that are likely to be more critical than any of the following, and you need to know what those special problems are. They can include, for example, the potential for sinkholes, which are caused by underground cavities that have eroded over hundreds of years before finally collapsing. Such sinkholes have been known to swallow up whole houses. Earthquake zones, tornado areas, falling rocks, avalanches, and rising rivers all pose threats to life, limb, and property.

> **Solution:** Review the following list of "time bombs" which may be waiting to ambush you. Remember, every item may have a dollar amount to correct the problem or defuse the bomb. The total sum may be the negotiation factor you should apply if you want to continue with the acquisition.

---

12 Property Time Bombs You Should Be Aware of before You Buy Real Estate

- Termites
- Broken plumbing
- Roof leaks
- Property line encroachments
- Environmental hazards
- Code violations
- Pending special assessments
- Title problems
- Structural problems
- Moisture damage
- Subsoil problems
- Pending negative development in the area

Termites.   There are several kinds of termites; all are preventable, and their damage can be kept to a minimum when encountered early. However, termites may come and go and leave behind substantial damage. It is important in most areas of the world to check for termites and their damage. The question "Are there any termites?" may not disclose their damage. Have a professional check all property to ensure that neither termites nor their damage exists. If either are found, then it should be up to the seller either to make the necessary repairs and have the property treated, or to adjust the price accordingly.

Broken Plumbing.   Only your plumber can tell whether the plumbing is in need of repair. One sign of a potential plumbing problem is a large water bill. Water charges for amounts over and above presumed use can signal a broken water pipe underground. Even a steady flow of water from a pipe several feet underground may never be noticed aboveground. If the pipe is underneath a building, the damage may be undetected until the building falls into the hole that was eaten away by the flow of water. Plumbing repairs can be very expensive.

Roof Leaks.   If you buy in the dry season, it might be several months before you find a leak. You can, however, look for ceiling or wall stains, which indicate that there was a roof leak at one time. Of course, these stains can be painted over and hidden, or the roof could have been fixed. It is a good idea to make sure a complete roof inspection is a part of your prepurchase checklist.

Property Line Encroachments.   Not all property line encroachments are visible, and not all property lines are obvious. Underground septic tanks or drain fields may extend from one property to another, from the neighbor's property or from your own. In either case, problems can arise. A recent survey can help prevent most of the property line encroachments, but not all, because not all underground installations may show up in public records. One key is to make sure the survey marks all the corners of a property. Make a physical inspection of these corners. Are they what you thought them to be? Draw lines between the corners—use a heavy cord or colored surveyor ribbon where buildings or landscape allows. Ask each neighbor if he or she knows of any underground installations from either property that cross under or near these boundaries. Check the local building codes to be sure that all buildings on the property do not encroach setback lines.

Environmental Hazards.   There are several important environmental problems that you may want to check. The most important is radon gas inside a home or apartment. This gas occurs in a natural state as the result of the decay of uranium, radium, and thorium. This gas is found in minute particles in the air, dissolved in some springwater, and within certain minerals that contain uranium, radium, or thorium. Because this gas is colorless and odorless and is a heavy gas, when it seeps into a home or apartment the concentration can quickly build up. This gas is highly radioactive and can be very dangerous. Test kits are available at most well-equipped hardware stores, and all property inspection companies are capable of testing for this gas.

Outside the home, hidden underground time bombs are toxic chemicals, oil products dumped into the ground, and other unpleasant items that simply await your shovel. A check into the usage and recent geologic histories is helpful and may show that the site was once a landfill area, that an oil refinery once occupied the site 50 years ago, or that there is a deep-burning coal fire two miles under that very spot.

Code Violations.   Past, present, and future code violations should be checked. A visit to the local building and/or zoning departments that have jurisdiction over the property would be the place to start. If any violations have been recorded against the property you should check to make sure that the problem has been corrected. Are there any present violations? You can ask for an inspection; this may occur automatically if the property being purchased is commercial in nature and you are attempting to apply for a business license. Future violations do not require a crystal ball. Often, laws are passed that give property owners lead time to prepare for the code change. No violation may exist now, but a change in law may require you to do something soon, something that might be very expensive, such as provide interior fire sprinklers in every enclosed space, fire alarm devices, and new enclosed fire exits. These future violations might be the very reason the property is offered for sale at such a great price.

Pending Special Assessments.   As with code changes, it is possible that pending special assessments are planned but have not yet been implemented. This is more likely to occur with a condominium or cooperative apartment than a single-family home, so check with the building association. Is a plan being discussed or has one already passed that will impose a special assessment on the property you are considering purchasing? If so, find out how much, and take that into consideration when you make an offer.

Title Problems.   In the United States, many properties have a clear chain of title that is evidenced by an abstract of title. This is an actual history of recorded documents showing the chain of title as far back as legal action requires. In Florida, for example, an abstract of title starts with the original land grant from Spain. If an abstract of title is not available, the history of title can be checked through a title search. This requires a manual review of recorded documents to confirm that the present owner has good title and can pass it on to you.

Problems that occur with title are often nothing more than an improperly executed deed or mortgage satisfaction, or a lien that had been discharged but not properly documented. Death of a partner or spouse of a past owner can also pose complications and require the seller to take legal steps (not always expensive, but sometimes taking years to clear up) to produce good marketable and insurable title.

Structural Problems.   Every building should be checked for both obvious structural problems and latent ones. The obvious problems show up in the form of cracks in the walls and/or floors, whereas latent ones are often noted by looking at adjoining buildings. If an older building next door has cracks around the foundation level, it might suggest that the ground is soft or has shifted and that similar cracks may soon occur in the adjoining building you are considering for purchasing. It is possible, of course, that the structural problem has already been spotted by the current or previous owner and has been corrected or dealt with.

Moisture Damage.   Finding moisture damage can be indicative of mold and other problems. Moisture damage can be hard to find unless there is evidence of a wet ceiling, peeling paint on a wall or baseboard, or the odor of mildew. There are technical ways to test inside the walls for high moisture content and mold, so if your inspection team suggests it you may want to go that extra route prior to buying the property.

Subsoil Problems.   The condition of the soil around a building can be very important. If it consists of muck or clay there can be shifting of the soil or sinking of a building built on it without a proper foundation designed for those conditions. This can be a major problem or a relatively minor one. It is best to find out which if someone on your team believes that there is such a problem. This is often easy to spot because the building records of adjoining properties may show that a different and more substantial foundation has been used compared to the one under the building you are looking at.

Pending Negative Development in the Area.   I have mentioned that there are few secrets about future plans in real estate. They often take years to come about—

and years longer to show up next door to your recently purchased property. However, those future development plans (a new highway or jail or . . .) can be the very reason the prior owner was willing to sell at that bargain price. Be sure to check with the local planning and zoning department and the local department of transportation to find out whether such plans exist. Your real estate agent should also know what is going on, but it is best to do some of this homework yourself.

44. What Should I Do When I Am Ready to Sell My Home?

I will assume the decision to sell is a goal-enhancement decision. Some sellers, however, are faced with the immediate need to sell based on economic or job-related reasons. Urgency to sell is an important issue that will speed up this process when time becomes the most critical element.

Solution: All prospective sellers should follow these five important steps in their decision making before they list their property for sale.

Five Important Steps to Follow before You Put Your Home on the Market

- Review your present benefits.
- Balance those benefits against future needs.
- Examine all other options.
- Weigh those options against your goals.
- Establish your timetable and price accordingly.

Review Your Present Benefits.   Take a hard look at what you are about to give up. Are you ready to do that, or do you plan to add to those benefits with your next property? Do you need those added benefits? This reminds me of the seller who calls the listing agent and comments that "After reading the advertisement you placed in the newspaper about my home, I didn't realize how wonderful my property really was . . . so take it off the market, please!"

Balance Those Benefits against Future Needs.   Once you have taken a good look at what you are about to give up and have examined what your finances will be after the sale, are you able to meet your goals for future needs? If so, then proceed; but if not, and if you are not forced to sell, then you may want to take a harder look to see if your goals may need adjustment or just your plans.

Examine All Other Options.   Many people wait until they are overcome by problems and have few options to follow. Even if you did wait until some options are no longer available to you, there still remains more than one avenue to follow. Most sellers think that the only way out of debt is to unload what they have by selling it at any price, which may be the proper course. However, under the right circumstance, a gift to a charity can solve the problem and offset future income at the same time through a deductible contribution. Alternatively, perhaps a real estate exchange to put your equity into another kind of property would be better.

Weigh Those Options against Your Goals.   This emphasizes a point that has been stressed throughout this book. Goals are the focal point of everything positive. If your goals are correctly set, that is, written down, set in intermediate, easy-to-reach steps that are attainable by you, clearly in focus, and reviewed on a regular basis, your decision process will be easier and the options open to you more abundant.

Establish Your Timetable and Price Accordingly.   Time is both the friend and the enemy of real estate investors. If you use time properly, you will have the lead time necessary to accomplish the maximum benefit in the sale or disposition of a property. If you do not manage time well, you will become overly anxious, or worse, a desperate seller.

The key is to know what your timetable is and to work according to those needs. For example, if you know that by the end of 12 months you will be moving to another state, put your property on the market now. You can agree to rent it back for up to a year to aid prospective buyers to purchase now, even if they do not need the home right away. Start looking for a property in your new location and be an aggressive buyer in that area via an exchange of your old property. Be active . . . let time work for you.

45.   What Inexpensive Things Can I Do to Fix Up My Home to Improve My Chances of Getting Top Dollar?

Naturally, you will have to do whatever is necessary in the following list within your budget. If money is not a problem, then go through the home and do everything you have been putting off that you know should be done.

Ask your listing agent to make a detailed list of anything he or she thinks would help to sell the house if it were fixed, changed, cleaned, moved, or thrown away. You might be surprised. If your agent is very candid with you, you may soon have a very big garage sale. By the way, it is best to get rid of all this unwanted, unnecessary stuff right away, because it will make your home look less cluttered.

> **Solution:** The following list contains what I believe are the most important things you can do to maximize the value of your property.

Some of the items on this list can be done over a period of years. They will be the items that you might want to put on your to-do list the day you decide to purchase the property.

---

16 Inexpensive Things to Do to Maximize Your Property Value

- Get professional help to redesign the landscaping.
- Plant fruit trees.
- Have flowering plants.
- Upgrade kitchen appliances.
- Modernize electrical switches.
- Paint or replace the front door.
- Make sure every door functions properly.
- Trim lawn and landscaping neatly.
- Fix all obvious broken items.
- Paint walls.
- Clean—clean—clean.
- Remove all clutter.
- Put new brass street numbers on the house.
- Have a clean and neat refrigerator.
- Install closet expanders.
- Get rid of bad or offensive house smells.

---

46. How Do I Set a Price for My Home?

Successfully selling your property means getting the highest price possible from the present market. The last thing you want to do is to ask your neighbors what price you should put on your home. If they're glad you are going, they will give you a rock-bottom (quick-sell) price, and if they are sad to see you go, the price will be out of sight.

> **Solution:** Ask at least two prospective real estate agents to give you a market analysis.

Some agents may have different names for this report, but the report will be a compilation of all the recently listed and recently sold properties in your area. A well-prepared report will stress properties similar to yours and show the actual listed price, the actual sales price (if already sold), and the length of time the property has been on the market (which should also include unsuccessful previous listings).

Based on this report, the agents will suggest a price range for your property and will recommend that you list your property at the middle to upper end of that range.

This kind of report is usually accurate on the high side, that is, homes often sell at the price below which they are listed, so no matter what price you put on your property, buyers tend to offer less; therefore, sellers generally build in a buffer for negotiations.

With all this in mind, you should go with the best property report or analysis, trust in the agents with whom you have developed a rapport, and let them help you arrive at a fair market price.

47. What Can I Do to Speed Up the Sale of My Home?

The saying goes like this: Time is money. This means that getting the maximum price for your home, or any property for that matter, may take longer if you are out to get the top dollar. There are, however, some exceptions to this, so take a good look at the following solution.

> **Solution:** Review the goals and your timetable to selling your property and then apply the following checklist of six elements to this process.

The Six Elements to Speed Up the Timetable of a Sale

- Keep your goals in sight.
- Work at the counteroffer process.
- Keep the house open.
- Be realistic about your price.
- Be creative.
- Keep an open mind.

Keep Your Goals Clearly in Sight. This will help you stay on track with your investment plan.

Work at the Offer-Counteroffer Process. You should be proactive in this process. Make offers to exchange if that takes you closer to your goal. Do not say no to any offer without making a counteroffer. Never be insulted because someone wants to solve your problem, just work at the price.

Keep the House Open. Do it yourself if the salesperson cannot. Do not let a busy or lazy salesperson stand in the way of a quick sale.

Be Realistic about Your Price. Review any offer with your agent. If you are way off, then there may need to be an adjustment. Never let price stand in the way of trying to work out the deal. Perhaps you can get better terms in exchange for the lower price, and thus increase your value.

Be Creative.   Would a lease option work for the buyer and be good for you, too? Look for options to do a deal. If time is important, you may have to find a compromise between the timetable and your goals.

Keep an Open Mind.   No one has made an offer? Well, perhaps selling is not what you should be doing anyway. Review the basic reason you decided to sell in the first place and look at other options. Stay put; lease; exchange; enhance, then sell . . . look at all options.

48.   How Do I Select the Best Agent to Sell My Home?

In many communities, the only profession more prolific than real estate is the legal profession. Finding the right agent can be a problem unless you have read the following solution.

> **Solution:** Do your due diligence in locating an agent with whom you feel comfortable and who understands your goals. The following steps will help.

Five due diligence steps to find the right real estate agent

- Drive around your neighborhood and nearby areas (two miles in all directions should do) to see which real estate firm has the most listings.
- Make a list of all the firms in the area advertising property for sale. Put checkmarks by the firms that represent properties similar to or more valuable than yours (rather than less expensive).
- Call the firms with checkmarks and talk to the agents about the houses they are representing. Do not tell them you live in the area and want to sell. First you want to find out how they deal with a prospective buyer. If any irritate you, cross them off your list.
- When you find an agent you like, make an appointment and meet in person. You should meet with a minimum of three agents before you decide which one is for you.
- Insist that the agents go over all the details of the listing agreement and put in writing all that they are going to do for you.

49.   What Is the Best Technique for Selling Real Estate in a Slow Market?

A slow market doesn't always mean a buyer's market. What can happen is that even in a hot market where properties seem to be selling lickity-split, your property may still sit there without anyone making an offer. Why? This is just the nature of the market. It might be your price, the location, or even the color of the house.

> **Solution:** The very best technique to sell any real estate is to become an aggressive buyer for some other property for which you are going to offer your property in exchange.

To do this effectively you must have a strong focus on your own investment goals and then seek only property that will move you closer to those goals than will the property you are trying to sell.

For example, your home or other property has been on the market for nearly a year. It is admittedly the most expensive home in the neighborhood, with many features that are not common for the demographics living in the area. Nonetheless, the value exceeds the price you have placed on the property. The buyers, however, have not measured up to the home's worth.

Worst of all, you have not even had an offer that you could take pleasure in turning down. Then you remember my advice about being proactive with your property. You take a hard look at your goals and find some room in your plans that may allow you to take on a very passive long-term investment as a part of the sales proceeds of your expensive home. Mind you, this is only one of many options you might be able to include in your ultimate goals and plans. Others might allow you to own a large sailboat or a villa in Bosnia (a large number of those might be available).

You decide that a large tract of land almost anywhere in the path of growth might work out nicely. You do, however, narrow the area to something east of the Mississippi River and south of Virginia.

You let your real estate agent get this information out to the wide market you have chosen. Any savvy agent knows how to do this, and often the response is very fast. The agent puts out this information:

> Free-and-clear mansion in Fort Lauderdale's most established area of town available for exchange. Owner will consider a large tract of land in the path of progress, prefer SE USA, but will look at anything that makes sense. Value of this beautiful six-bedroom home with deep-water dock, tennis court, and 10-acre polo field is $3.8 million. Will take up to $1 million in exchange property and willing to hold a long-term first mortgage at 6 percent interest for 20 years.

Stand back and watch what comes in.

50. Should I Consider a Real Estate Exchange, and If So, for What?

Many people shy away from a real estate exchange, and one of the usual reasons for this is because they do not understand how exchanges work and the benefits that can come from them.

Solution: Become familiar with the benefits of the 1031 exchange as well as all exchanges.

A real estate exchange is a very good way to increase your end-result benefits. The answer to question 32 illustrated one example of how an exchange could introduce a benefit that the seller had not thought of before. Saving on taxes that would be due in a sale can be strong motivation, but that should not be the principal reason you would take a property in exchange. The key to exchanges is to think and act as though you are a cash buyer. It is possible that in the right transaction the seller of the property you end up with can also get cash out of the transaction as well as other benefits.

For example, say you have a home in Chicago you have been unable to sell. It has been on the market at $175,000 for some time and is free and clear of all debt. You cannot afford to buy a home in Tampa, where you want to go, until you sell your Chicago property. Therefore you are stuck in limbo. Or are you?

You take a trip to Tampa and start looking for what you would like to own. Because you are going to retire, you want to get a place to live and also own income property. You find several small apartment buildings you would like to own, and you start making offers. One such building is a 10-unit property that has a nice owner's apartment. The fair asking price is $400,000. The seller has a first mortgage of $100,000 on the property. You offer your Chicago home plus $125,000 cash. The deal looks like this:

The apartment complex:	$400,000
Less the existing debt:	100,000
Seller's equity:	$300,000
Your Chicago home:	$175,000
Plus your cash:	125,000
Your equity:	$300,000

You get the $125,000 in cash by casting a new first mortgage on the apartment building of $300,000 (a reasonable 75 percent loan-to-value ratio). After you pay off the first mortgage of $100,000 and give the seller $125,000, you are left with $75,000 less some closing and loan costs.

The sellers of the apartment building may or may not want your Chicago home, but because they have solved a major problem, they may be in a much better position to absorb the Chicago property by making it easy for a buyer to acquire it. They do not have the same problem you had . . . after all, they got rid of their Tampa property and received cash on top of that. They might be satisfied to hold a low-interest or *soft* mortgage (easy terms) or to trade the Chicago home for a blue-water sailboat and head for Tahiti.

In the preceding example, we did not even look at the benefits that might have come from a 1031 exchange. Keep in mind, however, that the tax-free benefits of such an exchange are available to you only if the properties you are exchanging and obtaining in the exchange qualify as "investment properties." I will get into that later on in the book, and there are some really solid tax reasons for doing a transaction that will allow you to avoid capital gains tax that would otherwise be due on a cash-out sale.

51. How Is the Tax on a Sale of My Home Treated If I Buy Another Home?

The IRS is kind of like a candy box with the name "Pandora's Treats" embossed on it in gold lettering. You never can be sure if there is something grand or gross waiting inside for you. So it is with the capital gains tax when you sell that home you have lived in for 30 years (or, for that matter, only a few years).

> **Solution:** Expect anything the IRS gives you to be subject to change, but for the moment there is a great IRS rule that opens up a major loophole to save when you buy (and sell) your personal residence.

This rule is called the "residential capital gain exclusion," and to help explain it, let me first give you an example.

Marlow and his wife have owned their home in Tampa, Florida, for 12 years and have decided to retire to the mountains of North Carolina to enjoy cooler summers and a change of seasons. Their cost basis in their home is $185,000. This is what they paid for the home plus some capital additions they added during the 12 years they lived there.

Because values in Tampa have climbed through the roof during these past 12 years, it was not a surprise when they received an offer for $650,000 net of all closing costs and commission for the home, which they were glad to take. Better yet, their real estate agent explained to them they would not have to pay any capital gains tax on the profit (i.e., everything over their cost basis). This meant that the full amount of the sale, $650,000, would remain in their pocket. Thanks to the IRS exclusion rule, they would pay no tax at all on the $465,000 profit as a result of the sale ($650,000 − $185,000 = $465,000).

The program works like this. The IRS has a set of rules, which, if you qualify for them, allow the seller of a home to exclude up to $250,000 of the gain from any tax liability. As Marlow and his wife owned the home in both their names as joint tenants, the exclusion of up to $250,000 could be applied by each of them. Therefore, the full $465,000 was covered and no tax was due.

Had the sale been $785,000 their profit would have been $600,000 and they would have exceeded the exclusion maximum of $500,000 by $100,000. In that instance, they would have to report a taxable gain of $100,000 and apply the appropriate tax to that amount.

IRS Rules

What about the IRS rules? Well, they are not difficult to understand, so take a look.

How to Double Up and Get the Maximum $500,000 Exclusion. To accomplish this, all of the following four questions must be answered *yes*.

1. Are you married, and do you and your spouse file a joint return for the year of the sale?

2. Do either you or your spouse meet the ownership test?

3. Do both you *and* your spouse meet the use test?

4. During the two-year period ending on the date of the sale, have either you or your spouse excluded a gain from the sale of another home?

Okay, let's assume that you have answered yes to each of those questions. This means that you can, if you qualify for the tests mentioned in questions 2 and 3, qualify to double up on the exclusion. Let's look at the nitty-gritty of these tests.

The Ownership Test.   You must have owned the home for at least two years during the five-year period ending on the exact date of the sale and transfer of the home. Miss that date by one day and you fail. If you are close, delay the closing until you meet the test. If the buyers push you, then either don't sell or enter into a lease with option to buy or some other creative technique that will give you the added time to meet the ownership test.

The Use Test.   Also, during the five-year period ending on the day of the sale and transfer of the home, you must have lived in the home, as your main home (legal residence), for at least two years. This two years is counted as a total of 24 months, or 730 days. These do not have to be continuous periods of time as long as your occupation time during those five years totals 730 days. If you rented the home during the winter or summer season each year for short periods of time and still occupied the home a total of 730 days, the rules (as they are written at this time) allow you to qualify.

There is some leeway in these rules, too, so even if you do not qualify in the way the rules have been shown here, don't give up hope until you finish reading this section.

Rules That Can Be Bent.   The five-year period can have suspensions of time. These breaks in time, which might extend the total time to more than five years, can be applied if the break in time occurs because of military service, foreign service, qualified official extended duty, disability, previous homes being destroyed or condemned, homes transferred from a spouse by death or divorce, and other circumstances that might meet with IRS approval and that you can prove occurred without your voluntary action.

The ownership-use test has some circumstances that can mitigate the strict application of its rule. For example anytime you must sell because of the following factors, check with your accountant (before the sale whenever possible) to see whether the rule will apply for your situation: a change in place of employment that forces the sale; a health problem of you or a relative you care for; to provide finances for the diagnosis, cure, mitigation, or treatment of a health problem; unforeseen circumstances such as death, unemployment, or change in employment that reduces your ability to pay for the home; divorce or legal separation;

multiple births from the same pregnancy; terrorist attacks; inability to financially keep the home; or a change in the property that makes it unsuitable as a home.

You can see that as complex as this rule is, it is not hard to comprehend. The complications begin to enter the picture when you do not meet all the tests right off the bat. As I have indicated, do not assume that you are left out of the box. See your accountant or tax lawyer to get the full and current interpretations of the rule.

As an added bonus, you can reinvest the tax-free money (not just the profit but the amount you originally invested, too) into another home, and at the end of the next five years you can do this again.

One word of caution: The IRS is fickle and changes rules all the time. This exclusion may have changed between the time I write this and you read it. You can go online, search IRS rules, and then use the key words *residential gain exclusion* to get to more current rules.

52. How Can I Avoid the Pitfalls of a Title Closing?

Closing is the term used for the event that occurs when the buyer and seller actually transfer funds and the deed. At this time, mortgage notes and mortgages and all other necessary and important documents are signed and executed. Most of the time these events take place without any problems, but not always.

> **Solution:** Go over the following preclosing checklist and make sure that your broker, lawyer, and closing agent agree on all the items it contains. Any problems will need to be cleared up, and it is possible that a new set of purchase terms may be required or you will walk from the deal.

The Buyer's 13-Item Preclosing Checklist

- Have a qualified inspection company inspect the property.
- Make sure you know what they will and will not inspect or warrant.
- Get a clean bill of health from the code enforcement departments.
- Preview the property.
- Verify the survey.
- Verify the legal description.
- Check for good title.
- Ask questions about hidden time bombs.
- Review and verify inventory.
- Question all repaired damage.
- Have a closing agent go over the procedures with you.
- Read and understand all documents you are to sign.
- Understand your legal rights and options should problems occur.

This checklist is not something you should attempt to do solely on your own. Obtaining professional advice in any legal transaction, especially one as important as the sale or purchase of real estate, can be the least expensive part of the whole transaction. It is much better to avoid a problem than to fight your way out of it in court. To help you properly deal with this checklist, each item is briefly discussed.

Have a Qualified Inspection Company Inspect the Property.   This is something you do after you have an accepted contract to purchase. The purchase agreement is generally subject to your approval of this and other inspections. If things arise from the inspection that you cannot live with, then you either walk from the deal or you renegotiate the deal.

Make Sure You Know What They Will and Will Not Inspect or Warrant. This is an area where you can get into deep trouble. Not every problem may be found by the inspection team because they do not look for everything. You need to understand exactly what they will inspect. Ask them what they do not inspect. They may be vague about this, because that list might be rather long, and they may simply say, "Here is our list of things we check . . ." Ask your real estate agent, lawyer, and closing agent what other things you need to know about. Here is a partial list of items potentially excluded due to local circumstances: code violations, fire department requirements (those coming up but not yet in force), zoning changes in effect that make this property okay for now but would disallow rebuilding if it burns down (e.g., it could only be something other than what it is), subsoil conditions, encroachments onto or from neighbors, confirmation that it is really the right property (oh, you would be surprised to find that no one checked the address against the survey), utility easements, deed restrictions, and title problems.

Get a Clean Bill of Health from the Code Enforcement Departments. Many cities have a city building and code enforcement check that you can pay to check out these kinds of problems. It is generally worth the expense for most properties—and an absolute necessity for multifamily or commercial properties. This can show, for example, that there is a running fine from the city that may now be in the thousands of dollars because of outstanding code violations, or worse. Check it out and get the seller to verify that there are no problems other than those you find, and let that warranty survive the closing so you have someone to go back against when you have to pay $100,000 to tear down the detached garage that was never permitted.

Preview the Property.   Prior to the closing, and as close as possible to the actual time and date of the closing, you should have a detailed walk-through of the property. The sellers should be aware that you are going to do this well in advance so that there will be no last-minute delay or difficulty getting into the property. The reason for this is to ensure that the property is exactly what you expect it to be. Are the furniture and equipment you contracted for still there? Has any of it been replaced with cheaper items? Are all the trees and other plants still there (don't laugh)?

As you go through the property it is a good idea to have a copy of the property inspection report, which you had arranged for some time prior to the closing. If there were items to be repaired or replaced, check to be sure the work was done as ordered.

Verify the Survey.   Do the property and the recent survey match up? To find out, as you take your reinspection tour make sure that you locate the survey markers. Be sure to take a long measuring tape so you can double-check distances. I did this once on a parcel I had purchased and discovered the surveyor was 80 feet short! The surveyor was cutting corners and had transcribed the measurement from an old, incorrect survey.

It is a good idea to order survey markers (iron rods are best) with the approximate location marked on them by the surveyor who did the survey, as well as on the actual survey document, in the event the markers are accidentally moved or hidden by landscaping. Check the measurements. Are they the same as the legal description and survey indicate? Does the survey show any encroachments? If so, this must be dealt with before you close on the property.

Verify the Legal Description.   If the legal description is given in metes and bounds, the actual property border dimensions will be given. Do they match the survey and your actual measurements? Does the legal description match the actual property dimensions, as shown on a city subdivision plat? Errors do happen, and you would not be the first person to buy a property next door to the property you thought you were buying.

Check for Good Title.   This is a job for your lawyer, title insurance company, or escrow closing agent. That agent can review the history of title transactions and can tell you if there is a possible problem with the title. Most of the time, these matters are rather simple to clear up and signify nothing more serious than an unsigned deed or a death not properly recorded. However, other problems can arise that are very serious and expensive to clear up . . . some that may not be able to be cleared up at all. Do not close unless you know the title is good.

Ask Questions about Hidden Time Bombs.   Be sure you discuss with your agent, lawyer, accountant, and insurance agent any possible hidden time bomb that might occur after the closing. You may overlook something that might initially seem insignificant but that later can require you to pay more taxes than you need to, to have a potential legal action filed against you, or to jeopardize your rights to file legal action against someone who wronged you.

Review and Verify Inventory.   Checking inventory can be a tedious job, but it is important and should be done. It is not unusual for an inventory list that is made when the property is first put on the market to differ greatly from a final inventory taken or checked on the day of the closing. Often, the differences are accidental or the items have been misplaced in different rooms, but sometimes the items have been removed from the property.

Question All Repaired Damage.   If you do not question it, who will? Some closing agents will suggest that you close, even though the damage has not been repaired, by putting a sum of money equal to the estimate for repairs in an escrow account. I do not recommend this procedure unless you have other plans for the area that would need the repairs. For example, if there is damage to the concrete decking around a pool and your plans are to remove the concrete anyway and put pavers over most of the backyard, why do any repairs at all? Take the money.

Have a Closing Agent Go over the Procedures with You.   Find out what is going to happen the day of the closing before that day arrives. It is not necessary for you and the seller to be at the closing at the same time; in fact, sometimes it is advisable that you not meet that day. Why? Lots of strange emotions are going on when a home is sold, and even the smallest problem seems to blow up into something much bigger. Good friends can become lifelong enemies.

The actual procedures of the closing are simple, and the buyer can arrive before the seller and complete all the documentation needed, deliver the check or other items necessary, and leave. The seller then comes along and signs the deed, the documents are recorded, and the closing is finalized. Some closings take place entirely by mail.

Read and Understand All Documents You Are to Sign.   Some of the best closing agents will actually read the document to you and explain every item without your having to ask questions. I like this kind of closing agent because he or she wants to make sure that no person is intimidated by anything that goes on at the closing.

If your closing agent does not do that, request it. If there is anything you do not understand about any part of the documentation, then ask. In fact, ask a lot of questions until you are comfortable that you understand not only the document you are about to sign, but also the potential problems that can occur as a result of the document and what your obligations and liabilities are after you have executed that document.

Understand Your Legal Rights and Options Should Problems Occur. What can you do if there is termite damage? Can you claim damages from someone in that case? What do you do if you find out that the agent lied to you about something important, something that you relied on in deciding to buy? What about the mortgage you signed, only to find out later that the lawyer did not uncover a previous mortgage when he or she checked the title, one that the agent and the owner did not tell you about? Who do you sue?

You should go over these and other pertinent questions with the closing agents, and make sure you are comfortable with the answers they give you.

6

The Keys to Buying and Selling Condominiums and Cooperative Apartments

53. What Are the Most Important Differences between Condominiums and Cooperative Forms of Ownership?

Any kind of property can be owned and held in various forms of ownership. This is true of residential apartments, office buildings, commercial space, and even single-family homes. The form of ownership may not be readily apparent from the property you see.

> **Solution:** Learn the differences between condominium and cooperative forms of ownership. The following snapshot will set you straight on this course.

Condominium properties take many different forms of construction, ranging from what appear to be normal single-family homes to more conventional high-rise apartment buildings to professional office space and other commercial and industrial buildings. The method of condominium ownership is not new and resembles a form of subdivision of ownership that has been popular in Europe for hundreds of years. In essence, the building or property is divided into segments, generally apartments or office space, or even lots, and each owner holds a deed to that specific space. Along with ownership come the obligations of ownership in regard to a portion of public space (halls, stairs, entrance area, meeting rooms, recreational space, parking area, green space, and so on). In general, lenders prefer to lend money on a condo apartment rather than on an individual's interest in a cooperative unit.

Cooperative properties make up a building that is owned by a corporation whereby shares in the corporation give the shareholders rights to certain space in the building. This usually relates to apartments but can also relate to commercial space. One share or a block of shares, depending on how the corporation is set up, gives the holder the right to occupy a specific apartment. Upkeep costs are divided by all owners based on a percentage of the space (square footage) that they own. This form of ownership can be found in various parts of the country and is very common in New York City. There are no specific advantages to ownership through a cooperative, and in light of the advantages that exist through the condominium form of ownership, few new cooperatives are being developed.

One distinct disadvantage to cooperative ownership is, for the moment at least, most financing of these properties is done by a master mortgage that covers the entire structure or property. Individual owners underwrite the entire loan and assume obligation for a share of that mortgage. When buying an interest in this kind of property, you are required to assume that obligation. This form of loan structure can present distinct problems, and prospective buyers are cautioned to ascertain the full details of this underlying debt. It is possible that there could be separate loans secured by the individual's interest as well as this master loan.

This does not mean, however, that under the right situation and circumstances the cooperative form of ownership could not be the desired choice, so do not simply assume that a condominium is always best.

54. What Critical Factors Should I Know When Buying a Condo or a Co-op or Any Other Form of Multiple-Entity Ownership?

What other forms of multiple entities are there? I list here several other common forms, all of which may present critical issues that you should research in detail.

Seven Common Forms of Multiple Ownership of Real Estate

- Condominium
- Cooperative
- Joint venture
- Tenants in common
- Interest in a corporation
- Limited partnership
- Syndications

When you buy a home or business or any real estate that is owned in any of these forms (a joint venture can take any of the other forms, and a corporation or limited partnership may own interests in any of the other forms), several aspects need to be carefully checked.

> **Solution:** Review the following list—these are the nine most important items to become familiar with. Remember, there may be other elements unique to any of these forms that will require special review by your legal representative.

The Nine Most Critical Factors When Buying Multiple-Ownership Properties

- Ownership rules and regulations
- Original founder's rights
- Annual assessments and charges
- Debt and mortgage obligations
- Ownership balance sheet
- Existing owners
- Management
- Individual rights
- Method of sale

Each of these items must pass your test or you might be headed for trouble. Review each carefully.

Ownership Rules and Regulations. The building owner's association or other form of ownership setup has very distinct rules and regulations that may differ from any other property you have looked at. State law may regulate the extent of those rules and regulations, but usually there is ample flexibility within the law for rules to be imposed that may not be to your liking or that may be too lax or too strict to suit your needs. These rules may govern simple things such as furniture being moved in and out of the property and hours when trash and garbage may be thrown out. For residential or commercial properties where the owners may occupy their own apartment or commercial space, stricter aspects, such as rental limitations and the requirement of master approval of future tenants, may be difficult to accept.

Original Founder's Rights. The original developer or founder of the property may have some unique rights that none of the other owners have. These might include future buyback provisions or rights of refusal in the event of a future sale. These rules can be imposed on everyone and may be absolute to the extent that they cannot be changed by democratic rule of the majority of the owners. These rights may include management of the property, which can be a future problem that may be difficult to deal with.

Annual Assessments and Charges.   The cost to keep up a big building, with 24-hour security, swimming pools, meeting rooms, workout rooms, saunas, steam rooms, and all the other facilities that may come with an upscale lifestyle may not be as expensive as you think. By the time the cost to maintain all those facilities is added up and divided among the owners, the annual fee may not be any more than you would pay for a gardener and pool cleaner to come to a private home. However, sometimes special charges that cost small fortunes are incurred to take care of the replacement of major items such as elevators, central heating or air-conditioning, or building painting and roof work. Such costs are not usually levied without advance notice, and more often than not, such assessments follow a year or more of political infighting within the association of owners. Make sure that such an impact is not about to be slapped on the property you just bought. You have a right to ask questions of the building management, but the best way to get this information is to contact the owner and his or her agent, ask the following questions, and get the answers in writing:

Are there any possible building repairs or improvements that are being discussed by management or the building association board of directors?

Have any assessments been planned but not levied?

Does the building have a reserve for replacements, and how much is it?

Debt and Mortgage Obligations.   If the property is a condominium, then mortgage information can be checked in the same way as for a home. All mortgages of record would be recorded in the public records under the legal description of that property, and any liens against the owner would be recorded against the owner by name. Potential problems of unrecorded mortgages can be circumvented through a careful title search by your lawyer or title insurance company. A land lease or recreational lease (where allowed by state law) would also be recorded in the public records and should be checked. All such documents should be read to find out the fine-print terms. Leases and mortgage interest can escalate, balloon payments can come due tomorrow, and options to buy can come and go without your knowing about them.

Cooperative mortgages usually come in two stages. First, there may be an overall mortgage that covers the entire building. When this is the case, each of the apartment owners would be obliged to pay a share of that mortgage. A default on their share may ultimately cause them to lose the shares they own in the cooperative, and with them their rights to the apartment. However, everyone understands that a mortgage must be paid or they will suffer the consequences. It may be difficult to get information on the amount of the total mortgage owed and what your share of that mortgage would be once you own the apartment. You should insist on knowing how much the mortgage is and not just assume that because the monthly maintenance charge includes the mortgage that the $700 dollars a month charged now will continue that way forever. You may find that six months after you close, the underlying mortgage balloons ("Oh, you didn't read the mortgage document? It's in the public records"), and that your share of the payoff is $50,000. Remember, when you buy a property that has outstanding debt, the total debt must be added to the cash and other equity you pay to find out exactly what price you really paid. Co-op owners in New York City have frequently told me what they are paying to buy their apartment without even knowing what their underlying debt is . . . "Oh, it's just in the monthly maintenance payment."

Ownership Balance Sheet.   Every well-managed building should have a reserve for replacements. If you are looking at two apartments in two different buildings and cannot make up your mind between the two, look at the balance sheet of the building ownership. Do they owe six months of contract wages? Is the building replacement and repair account at zero? If one building has been accruing funds more than 10 years for a major building replacement, and the other has nothing in the bank and a major replacement just around the corner, then choose the building with the reserve for such replacements.

Existing Owners.   In the case where you will occupy a space in the property, it is important to check with the neighbors and co-owners about the present situation. After all, the people who live around you can make your life either pleasant or troublesome. When selecting a home or business location, I recommend prospective buyers walk around the area at several different times of the day and night. Saturday at midmorning can present a different picture than noon on a workday.

A condominium or cooperative presents a different problem, but the need to check the neighbors is even more important. These people will not only be living and working in your neighborhood, they will have something to say about how you must act when you are there.

If the building has recreational facilities, such as meeting rooms and swimming pools, then visit the building several times during the hours when these facilities will most likely be in use. This may be the only time you will see your potential neighbors. Feel free to talk to them and ask them about the building and the management. Ask what they dislike most. You might uncover something very important.

Management.   You will want to know how management is chosen and how decisions are made that affect your ownership rights and occupancy of the property. In most non-owner-occupied properties, the management has obtained some preapproved management rights and does not need to deal with every decision by a democratic vote of the owners. Where you are an occupant of the property, it is critical to know how far those preapproved rights can and do extend. The method of replacement of management is always important, and sometimes management is farmed out to other entities. A condo hotel, for example, may be managed by Hilton, or by some other such company with a direct connection to the use of its name. If you get rid of the flag management (hotels with national or international name recognition are called *flag hotels*), you and the property would lose the use of that name. In these instances, the management expects to exercise a wide range of management decision making without ownership input.

Individual Rights.   Get your individual rights very clear in your mind. Can you sell your interest to anyone you want? Do you have to first offer it back to the existing entity or the former developer or someone else? Can the existing ownership stop you from selling to anyone? Can you lease out your commercial space or apartment to anyone? Do they have to be approved, and if so, by who and how? I could go on here, but by now you get the picture. Whenever there is multiple ownership, you will have a very long list of rules and regulations that define the extent of your specific rights. Get to know them well prior to buying.

Method of Sale.   I touched on the sale in the preceding individual rights section. But how a sale is made is important because it might not be just your interest at stake. Can less than 100 percent of the ownership decide to sell the property and thereby commit everyone to that transaction? In many multiple-ownership enterprises, this is the case. You need to know how this can happen, which state laws may conflict with the rules and regulations of the entity. State law rules.

55.   How Is the Association Maintenance Charged against the Unit I May Buy, and What Potential Problems Do I Need to Look For?

Association charges for maintenance may be charged monthly, quarterly, or semi-annually. Rarely are the usual charges collected on an annual basis, but special charges can be.

> **Solution:** Look at the ownership bylaws to see how the present collections are outlined, but also check on how changes in the bylaws can occur.

The hidden time bomb comes in the form of special assessments that are about to be levied, or worse, that are already past due but not yet paid by the seller. Lax management may not have gotten around to placing a lien on the apartment, so it may remain undiscovered when your lawyer or title insurance company checks the title they may not find a lien. However, this assessment can be charged against you anyway, after you have closed on the unit.

Remember, the copy of the bylaws or rules and regulations given to you by the owner of the interest you are about to purchase may be out-of-date. Such rules and regulations are frequently modified, changed, or stricken from the everyday use. Sloppy management, often the case in small residential or commercial multiple-ownership entities, may not get around to making up new manuals and may simply notify owners of the changes.

It is a good idea to ask the management for a list of current owners who are delinquent in their maintenance or assessment payments. Ask these questions: What is the total outstanding delinquency? What is management doing about collection of delinquent payments? What kind of political infighting is going on between the owners? Is there discussion going on now about problems that may lead to future assessments?

56. What Factors about the Apartment Do I Need to Consider before Buying?

The overwhelming answer is another question: Do you really want to live there?

> **Solution:** In addition to rereading the solutions to previous problems in this section, look at the following suggestions.

Many people move from a home or some other kind of private residence into a condominium or cooperative. These same people may have, at some time in their past, lived in a rental apartment and may relate to that experience. However, living in a condominium or cooperative that you own is not the same as living in an apartment that you rent, for the following reasons. When you rent, there is always a "temporary" feeling about living there. You learn to live with the neighbors because they, too, are temporary and if you want, you can move. When you own your apartment, the temporary nature of living in a rental apartment disappears.

If you are used to coming and going as you please, working in your own yard, skinny-dipping in your own pool, then your life is in for a change. Are you sure you want to live there? If so, then be sure you check out the following.

Does the apartment need to be remodeled? Check out just how far you can go prior to needing a special ownership meeting and majority (or more) approval.

Read the minutes of a dozen or so past association meetings. This will give you a solid idea of what the politics are and whether you are up to dealing with them.

57. How Should I Prepare for the Interview by the Owner's Association to Improve My Chances of Being Approved?

When you buy into a condominium or cooperative, it is usual for you to meet before a review board prior to your contract becoming valid. This is just one of those difficulties that makes association ownership different and annoying. On the other hand, the idea of not letting just anyone live in your building has its advantages, too.

> **Solution:** Think of the interview as an opportunity to see how the building regulates who they allow into the building. You will either like what they ask you or hate it. Review this section for more tips.

The review committee could come under much scrutiny from potential legal actions should they violate someone's rights. The problem is that some committees spend most of the time looking for ways to reject you legally. Forestall such action by not giving them any legal reason to reject you.

You should prepare yourself by knowing the state laws that govern such home associations. Ask your real estate agent to get you a copy. Also, get a copy of the building rules and regulations if you have not done so already, and be familiar with the rules you are expected to abide by once you live there. This will give you a clue about what kind of questions the review board will ask. After all, they want you to like the same things they like.

Use political pull if you have it, or get your agent to pull some strings within the review board. These associations have their demagogues, and bureaucracy can be a critical part of living and surviving in a condo or co-op. It is often better to flow with the tide than to fight it. And dress conservatively, no matter what you normally like to wear.

58. What Are the Most Important Strategies to Use When Selling My Condo or Co-op?

Selling any property is simply a question of letting the property meet the expectations of the prospective buyer and satisfy the buyer's needs. Some properties will do that all by themselves . . . all the agent has to do is introduce the buyer: "Buyer, meet your new property." However, this is a rare event, so take a look at the following proven sales strategies that work.

> **Solution:** There are eight sales strategies that seem to work well for most condominiums and condo apartments. Review them below.

Eight Proven Sales Strategies for Condominium and Co-op Apartments

- Stress the security.
- Highlight all the benefits.
- Name-drop important neighbors.
- Show off party rooms during a party.
- Discover the buyer's motivation—then use it.
- Introduce the buyer to compatible neighbors.
- Be creative.
- Have all important facts in writing.

Stress the Security.   Many people buy an apartment because they no longer feel secure where they presently live. The idea of 24-hour security, banks of television monitors that telecast views from a dozen hidden cameras, armed and uniformed guards roaming around the building to protect life, limb, and property can be very appealing. Therefore this factor should be stressed. No matter how lax the security is in your building, it may appear to be a sanctuary to the buyer. Enforce this by showing the buyer all the special security features, such as hidden cameras and one-way doors that allow people out but not back in unless they have the right passwords, and stressing the number of guards on duty at any time.

Highlight All the Benefits.   It is not unusual for people who live in a condo or co-op to be unaware of some of the benefits of their own building. You will need to know them all and build on them. For example, mail is usually a closely awaited event in many large apartment buildings, so much so that when mail arrives it becomes a social hour. I have seen buildings that hoist a flag in a courtyard that is visible to all apartments the moment mail has been put into the boxes in the mail room. Turn this normal event into a special benefit. Mail is collected for you and kept safe, even if you are out of town for a week, a month, or longer.

Health facilities, exercise rooms, tennis courts, and swimming pools are all bonus features, but there is probably more to offer. For example, the facility could offer yoga classes where the teacher comes to the building instead of tenants having to run across town, private tennis lessons just outside the back door, or scuba lessons in its own Olympic-size pool. Any of these benefits might be the one thing that motivates the buyer.

Name-Drop Important Neighbors.   "Oh, Mr. and Mrs. George Bush live across the hall. And, did you know, the head of cardiac surgery for the Cleveland Clinic lives two floors down?" Note the subtle nature of not mentioning who lives higher up. Use that approach when possible. You should not just drop names of famous people, but names of the kind of people you think the buyer would relate to. This might require a quick judgment call on your part, unless you have a clue from the agent. Or perhaps the agent, who already knows the client, drops the name.

In general, it is best to play up the benefits of the building through the names you drop. "Oh, Jimmy Connors lives here, and it is not uncommon to see him out on the tennis courts . . . or in the sauna afterward."

Show Off Party Rooms during a Party.   As a Realtor, I have taken prospective buyers through some of the most elegant condominium buildings and visited absolutely beautiful party rooms that left everyone disappointed, because the rooms were not designed to just be beautiful, they were designed to be enjoyed during a party. It takes a party to see them put to their intended use.

Brokers can arrange a special cocktail party and invite likely prospects or invite other brokers to bring their prospects to this very private showing of your property. If that is not possible or timely, and you know there is a party planned, then try to schedule a showing of your apartment when you can also take the prospective buyer through the party room in the midst of a social gathering of neighbors (if the neighbors are friendly).

Discover the Buyer's Hot Button–Then Push It.   When buyers look at the apartment and all the other amenities that go with it, watch their eyes, listen to their questions, and pay attention to their body language. All that they do will lead you to their motivation. Questions about the depth of the pool, for example, might be a sign of interest in scuba lessons or a fear of drowning (themselves or a child), so be careful not to react the wrong way. Be safe and stress the security at the pool; then find out why the question was asked.

Too many agents rush through the building part of a property, showing and stressing the apartment itself. This is wrong. People do not buy an apartment; they buy a lifestyle. Somewhere the motivation can be uncovered, and it may manifest itself as approval of the apartment. For example, saying "What a beautiful view" may mean they are really thinking that the view is beautiful because they can sleep safely and securely, even with their windows open at night since they are 20 floors up.

Introduce the Buyer to Compatible Neighbors.   This is a very good closing technique and is generally saved for the second visit, unless you are lucky and run into someone whom you know to be compatible with everyone while you are walking around the building.

On that second visit, invite a friend in the building to come over for coffee at the same time the prospective buyer is coming. Tell the buyer you thought he or she might like to meet one of the neighbors to ask about the building from the standpoint of someone who is living in the building.

Be Creative.   Already you have seen some very creative techniques, most of which have rarely been used by agents. However, there are many other areas in which you can be creative in finalizing a deal. You can create a successful negotiation by being open-minded and letting the prospective buyer mentally transform into a buyer. This happens if you give strong but not desperate selling signals.

Take the posture that you and the buyer both want the same thing: that the prospect buy your apartment. Once a potential buyer is sold on that prospect, the only business that will remain between you is defining the terms of that sale. The more the buyer thinks of him- or herself as owner, the smaller that gap will become. You can drive buyers away by not responding to their need to own that apartment.

Have All Important Facts in Writing.   If your property is listed for sale, the agent will have a copy of the listing to give to the prospective buyers. This is okay, but it may be just like every other listing the buyer has seen. You want to give them not only the facts but to do so in such a way that they will remember the elements that count. Reinforce everything that has been mentioned earlier by giving the technical details on all the benefits of the building. If you have cable, stress the top-of-the-line wiring system and that the building also has satellite antennas with more than 200 extra channels (if it does, of course).

Also, mention the security system, which is not an ordinary security system but one with state-of-the-art equipment. Remind buyers that the tennis courts are of special construction. Remember what Elmer Letterman stressed: to sell the steak you sell the sizzle.

Have a photograph of the apartment, and if you really want to make sure prospects never forget the building, take a Polaroid snapshot of them as they try out the grand piano in the party room.

7

Insider Secrets for Buying, Selling, and Owning Vacation Properties

59. Do I Get Any Tax Write-Offs with Vacation Property?

The love affair with vacation homes and apartments continues stronger than ever. The give then takeaway of the IRS has played with second-home vacation property for some time, so it is not unusual that many people are confused about write-offs or deductions from earned income such property owners can take advantage of.

> **Solution:** As with any IRS rule you have to double-check the current position of the IRS. However, at present there are some perks that owners of such property can take. Take a look at the rest of this section.

As I'm writing this book, the IRS still allows certain expenses of a second home to be deductible from income. The rules that govern these deductions fall into different categories, depending on the amount of time you use the property and how much time you rent it out (if you rent it out at all).

Use and/or Rental

If you rent the home for more than 14 days a year and also use the home for more than 14 days, or 10 percent of the number of days rented, whichever is greater, this property is considered to be a personal residence. The IRS allows you to deduct interest on up to $1 million of combined debt on two personal residences. If you own more than two, use the two with the most interest to deduct. Property taxes are generally deductible, no matter how many homes you own. *Use time* is considered to be the total time used by you, your family members, and people who rent from you at less than the market rental rate.

Expenses that are incurred (other than interest and tax) need to be separated into two categories: *personal use* and *rental expenses*. First of all, in calculating these expenses, the rental expenses are taken for taxes and interest for the percent of a year in which the property was rented. One month of rental would be one-twelfth of the total tax and interest, six months' rental would be half of the interest and tax, and so on. If you rent for a greater period during the year than you use the property (vacant time is considered as personal use time), or if you use the property less than the greater of 14 days or 10 percent of the rental days, then the property is no longer considered to be a personal residence and things get a bit more complicated. If this is the case, be sure to check with your accountant to brush up on the current rules.

If you rent a lot, and that time is greater than the 14 days or 10 percent that you use it, then the property is considered to be a rental property, and the taxes and interest will be prorated between the time you actually use it and the time it is rented out. Expenses that apply to the rental side of that equation will be allocated over the rental portion of the year. In this way, if the property is rented for 200 days and you use it for 18 days, then the personal portion of the interest and taxes is 18 divided by 200.

The divisions between personal and rental use are for IRS procedures only, but they do have an impact on what you can deduct in the year of the expenses if you have more expenses than income. This can trigger the "passive income" rules that I would rather not get into here, which simply means that if the income comes from a passive activity (e.g., if the home is rented and managed by an outside company the income is considered passive), then the maximum deduction you can take would be the amount that brought your income to zero for the year. However, the IRS does allow you to carry any excess loss forward to be used in future years. If this situation matches your circumstances, speak with your accountant about it.

60. What Are the Nine Major Pitfalls of Owning Vacation Property?

Every vacation homeowner has or will experience one or more of the eight pitfalls of owning vacation property.

> **Solution:** If after reading this section you are still bound to own a vacation home, then prepare yourself because one or more of the following pitfalls will surely find you. You can run, but you cannot hide from them.

> ## The Nine Major Pitfalls of Owning Vacation Property
>
> - Location
> - Keeping up with the maintenance
> - Absentee management of rental use
> - Long-distance problem solving
> - Undetected crime
> - Financing
> - Extra record keeping for tax purposes
> - Being out of your comfort zone when buying or selling
> - Potential estate problems

Your ability to deal with and in some situations avoid the pitfalls altogether will be enhanced if you review each item in detail.

Location.   The location of the vacation home is the very reason you wanted to own it and is apt to be the very reason you will want to sell it. To some degree this will depend on your attitude about the property and that location. If the area is a part of the country where your family has been going to for years, and you have lots of vacation time and friends who either live in the area or visit the same time you do, then you are likely to continue going to that location for a long time.

However, many people fall in love with the warm winter sunset from the wraparound balcony and buy the property without realizing they might become bored looking at that sunset night after night when there is nothing else to do.

People buy whole-ownership vacation property thinking that if they owned it they would go there more often. The same rationalization is often given by the owner of a boat, which may end up tied to a slip at a marina, growing sea grass on its bottom.

If you can afford whatever you want to do, then none of this may matter to you, but if you are looking for a good buy and an investment you can use and eventually profit from, then use this tip: Find a nice property in the area you think you want to own and rent it for 12 months. This will cost much less than buying property and will give you all the time you need to slip away to that vacation hideaway and enjoy your life as you envisioned you would. Also, it will give you time to try out other seasons of the year to see how well you like them.

If all goes well, then take part of that 12 months and look for a real bargain that will serve your needs and meet your goals for years to come.

Keeping up with the Maintenance.   When you live in a home on a long-term basis, you may take for granted the little things that you do to keep the place in good working order and as clean as you like it to be. Add a second home to this scenario and problems start to multiply.

First, during the time you are not there, dust settles everywhere; while you can cover almost everything with sheets, the floors, walls, tops of counters, edges of frames and doorjambs, and in general everything not protected by dust covers can accumulate a thick layer of dust, which, for some reason, seems to harden. Or rather, it all seems to harden except the dust that has settled on the sheets you have used to cover the furniture. You arrive late in the evening because your flight from Chicago was delayed 12 hours and all you can think about is a warm fire in the fireplace and a good night's sleep. You start to pull the dust covers off the sofa, chairs, and lamps—and suddenly clouds of dust blossom everywhere. Welcome home!

Oh, this is just the start, too. A winter water pipe has broken due to an ice blockage, and the house floods as soon as it thaws (the heat from that roaring fire in its hearth). While you sleep, neighbors (who arrived for a weekend visit to their vacation home down the hill from yours) realize that a waterfall coming from under your front door has completely flooded their home too.

One tip that will help you survive such problems is to buy a second home that is no farther than three to five hours of driving time from where you live. Then you can run over there a couple times a month just to do some cleaning and general maintenance. If that is not possible, then make sure a reliable maintenance service is available in the area to watch over your property and solve any problem that comes up. If the cost for such maintenance is too expensive, then perhaps you really should not buy the second home.

Absentee Management of Rental Use.   Distance may make the heart grow fonder, but when it comes to having a vacation home that you hope to rent out when you are not using it, distance can create some very special problems.

The most critical is that a potential tenant may destroy your property. This does not happen with every tenant, but sooner or later, unless you are very careful, it will happen.

Absentee management of rentals is very difficult, so you will then be forced to use a local rental office. If you get the right one and lay out some very strict rules to abide by, then you may have no problems. But remember, when prospective tenants are on vacation they are less likely to treat your property with tender loving care.

Long-Distance Problem Solving.   This is a two-way street. When you own a vacation home you feel obligated or compelled to spend time there that you might otherwise have spent. This means that because you are at your vacation home you may have additional problems where you normally live. Distance is the reason for the potential problems, not at which end of the road you are located at any given moment.

Distance problems can be kept to a minimum, of course, by trying to be logical and practical about your purchase. That hideaway on the top of the mountain or on a rocky shoreline on Costa Brava in Spain might have taken your breath away, and the breathless emotion may have caused you to sign the contract where reason might have made you stop and think: "Hey, what am I doing?"

If you cannot live without being in the area and having a second home there, then start looking at each of the pitfalls listed here and find the solutions to them, or find a property that does not have such a high probability of potential problems.

Undetected Crime.   There is a criminal element that loves vacation time for two reasons. When you are on vacation you are not at home, and when you are at home your vacation place is empty. These criminals have the best of all worlds. Because they constantly travel in the off-season, they can get two shots at you for the price of one.

Becoming a victim of burglary is not the end of the world. It can happen when you are sleeping or going out to a movie. The problem, however, is that you might not know about the criminal act until you arrive, say, at midnight after driving for 44 hours in heavy snow, on icy roads, to find that every stick of furniture as well as the central heating unit has been removed. This can be an economic blow as well as a major inconvenience.

Security becomes a major factor that you should consider when buying a second home. Alarms may not be sufficient, however, so strong door locks and storm and burglarproof shutters or decorative bars may be necessary. The best solution is to buy property in a secure community, such as on the twentieth floor of a condominium with 24-hour door attendants and roving armed guards with attack dogs. In absence of such extremes, do what a friend of mine did. He installed a state-of-the-art alarm system and a video system with several cameras. It had a battery backup system and transmitted a signal to a Web page set up just for him. He could, whenever he wanted to, go online (on the Internet), access that Web page, and see for himself what was going on at his place in the mountains. The video system did not run 24/7, only when motion, sound, or both triggered it, so he could quickly scan several hours that might represent several months of coverage. Check with your local alarm people to see whether they can handle it, or ask for names of someone who can.

Financing.   One of the most difficult residential investments to finance is the second home. Because of this you may be required to put more cash down than you are comfortable doing or, alternatively, to look around for someone desperate to sell (i.e., going through all of these eight pitfalls), who is willing to hold soft paper with easy payback terms and take a low down payment.

When you buy, you should provide for the possibility that you too may want to sell this property sooner than you think. The way to do this is to make sure that any mortgage you assume or take out when you buy will be assumable by a prospective buyer when you sell. Otherwise, you might find that you have to reduce or, worse, pay off the amount owing on your existing mortgage just to entice a buyer.

Extra Record Keeping for Tax Purposes.   Any property you own adds to your own administrative process. Not only will you need to keep copious records to get the maximum benefits from the IRS, you will have to keep track of those monthly expenses that must be tended to: mortgage payments, association fees, management costs, light, water, and phone bills, annual taxes, and so on.

A tip that will make record keeping easier is as follows. First, have a record book where you can keep notes on every obligation, expense, payment of income, and so on that pertains to that property. If you have several other properties, either keep separate record books or have a journal with dividers to separate each property. Second, on the first page of the journal make a list of every recurring expense for that property. Be sure to record the usual payment due dates, amount owed, account numbers, and the names of persons to whom payments go, along with their addresses and phone numbers. Write this in pencil, because this information is apt to change over time. Third, have a large master calendar for the year with a full page for each month and squares for each day that are big enough for you to make notes of those and other obligations. In addition to being a reminder of what you need to do at a quick glance, such planning enables you to free up brain cells for more productive things than worrying about deadlines.

Being out of Your Comfort Zone When Buying or Selling.   This can be the worst pitfall of all—making an investment in something you know nothing about. For example, I have seen people come to Florida who are accustomed to prices in New York City pay far more than they should for a second home, simply because their point of reference regarding value was based on what they knew of New York City, not the actual market in Florida.

It can happen to anyone, and I have been tempted by what I thought were bargains in foreign countries or in other cities in the United States when looking at prices that were one-half or one-quarter of what the same kind of property would bring in my own backyard, within my comfort zone.

Any prospective buyer can do the necessary homework to create a comfort zone in any location in the world. However, this takes time and effort, which most people do not want to spend when they are on a holiday.

Potential Estate Problems.   Whenever you own property that is not in the state where your legal residence is, you may have potential estate problems on the death of any of the owners of the property. If you are from New York, for example, and you own a vacation home in Arizona, on your death, Arizona may want to tax your entire estate. The same goes for other combinations of states. One way around this is not to hold the title for vacation property in your own name, but in the name of a limited liability corporation or some other entity. Seek sound legal advice about this issue.

Don't Forget the Bonus on the Residential Exclusion of a Gain Trick.
Look back at question 51 and review the factors that occur when you have owned a property for five years and lived in it for two years. You may jockey back and forth between new homes, and every two years or so you can qualify to forego

paying capital gains tax. In this instance, you would need to have the property in your own name(s).

61. What Is the Most Important Thing to Know before I Buy a Vacation Property?

I would hope you would already know the answer to that question.

> **Solution:** When you start looking for a vacation home, there is one question that you should write in big, bold print on a 5 × 7 inch card. Every time you see a place you might consider, pull out this card and read it very slowly out loud: "Do I really want to live here?"

Play the devil's advocate with yourself and push for a detailed explanation to any positive reply you might give to that question. Think about the pitfalls mentioned in question 60, and try to dissuade yourself from buying. If you survive this test and buy, well, at least you have done so with your eyes open.

62. What Are the Most Important Factors When Renting Out My Vacation Property?

There can be factors I have not included, depending on the property and how much rent you plan to charge. But this section gives you a heads-up start on making sure your venture into the vacation rental market is a favorable one.

> **Solution:** Check and recheck the status of your property in relation to the 10 important factors listed here.

The following factors can make the difference between a well-operated rental program and constant worry. As any property manager will attest to, the real key to a well-maintained rental property of any kind is the kind of tenants you cater to. When it comes to vacation properties, this can be very important because of the attitude that often prevails when people are on holiday. I call it the "take the hotel towel, ashtray, and television home with you" syndrome. Do not let that problem become yours.

The 10 Most Important Factors When You Rent out Your Vacation Home

- Have management that is local to the property.
- Have a plan for the security of the property.
- Have more than adequate insurance to cover losses and lawsuits.
- Know the tenants.
- Have strict rules about occupancy and enforce them.
- Get a sufficient damage deposit.
- Check inventory before and after.
- Check utilities before and after.
- Check for damage before and after.
- Plan the major cleaning to occur before one of your visits.

Have Management That Is Local to the Property. Never think adequate management can function at a long distance—not your own good management skills or those of others who are nearer, but still far away. Most important, don't count on friends or family members to do the work for you unless they are in the management business and you pay them according to their abilities.

Have a Plan for the Security of the Property. This means that every potential security situation has been discussed with the ultimate management team. Storms, fire, theft, floods, vandals, bad tenants who trash things, and so on all can affect the security of the property and your assets there. The management team should have a written plan for these potential events, and you should know what it is and expect it to be carried out in a timely manor.

Have More than Adequate Insurance to Cover Losses and Lawsuits. Go over this situation with your insurance agent and perhaps your lawyer as well. Know what exposure you may have when you rent out a property that is a thousand miles or so from where you live. What if the management team forgets to do something that causes the building to burn down with the tenants still asleep in their beds? What if you never rent out the place, but you let a friend stay over one weekend while you are on a cruise and something happens. Insurance is not cheap, but the peace of mind it can provide makes it worthwhile.

Know the Tenants. I do not mean you should just know their names, but make sure you have copies of picture identification, home addresses, home and office phone numbers, names of references, type of car (if it is owned and not rented), auto license, and so on. The more data you get and the earlier you get it, the better equipped you are to do some homework and check to make sure you know who these people really are. One simple but comprehensive rental application plus different identification cards placed face down on a copy machine can give you everything you need.

I know some property owners who let anyone rent their property as long as the tenant pays a rather expensive security deposit. Keep in mind that it will be impossible for you to charge anyone sufficiently to make up for the possible damage they can do. Even a grandiose deposit for damages cannot compensate you for everything that can happen. For example, when the renters leave for some foreign country that has no extradition agreement with the United States and have left your mountain cabin empty of furniture, the central heat turned to 110 degrees with all the windows open, all the water spigots on full blast, and no one will be there for two months, you will understand what I mean.

Have Strict Rules about Occupancy and Enforce Them. A list of your rental rules and regulations should be given to the prospective tenants prior to their arrival, with the understanding that if they do not like them or feel that the rules are restrictive, then they need to either discuss the problem with you or make other arrangements. It might be possible to bend one or two rules slightly for the perfect tenant, but by maintaining strict rules you may actually attract other people who respect what you are doing.

What goes into the rules and regulations? The first and most important is the actual rental contract. That agreement should be properly designed to protect you to the maximum. Do not use one of those standard rental forms you can buy in an office supply store. Those forms are too evenly balanced between the tenant and the landlord to serve your needs to obtain the maximum benefit. Get a good one from your lawyer or from the rental management company you may use. Be sure you understand everything in that contract, because even if you do not sign it yourself, your management company may bind you to any agreement it executes in your behalf.

Once you fully comprehend the rental contract, you can start to list any rules that are imposed by others on you, such as association regulations or condominium rules. After that, the best rules you can impose will regulate the following: total occupancy; pets; smoking; cooling and heating temperatures; use of phone; check-in and checkout times; security deposit conditions; your rights to inspect with reasonable but short notice, or at predetermined times and dates; use of facilities; off-limit rooms or closets (if any, keep them locked if possible); and whatever you feel is important to you.

However, it may be difficult to enforce your rules. After all, you might be 5,000 miles away and totally dependent on local management. Regardless of how you operate your lease program or how well you know the people who are renting your property, make sure you have someone who can do the check-in and checkout procedures. It is an unfortunate fact that some of the worst offenders of your rules and regulations may be your friends, because they will assume that those rules are not for them but for people you do not know.

Get a Sufficient Damage Deposit. *Sufficient* is a relative word in this situation. As has already been mentioned, it will be impossible for you to get a deposit that will cover any possible loss. There is a limit to the amount you can effectively charge someone and keep them as a tenant. One way to soften the security charge impact and increase your security is to get some money up front in addition to rent, then have the tenants sign a credit card slip, which you properly validate and hold against any damage. Rental car companies do this, and many rental management companies have the facilities and arrangements with major credit card companies to accommodate this service. A very good rental contract is essential to cover all the obligations the tenant has agreed to in the event of damage to your property or loss of items previously checked off during check-in as being part of the inventory.

Check Inventory Before and After. Everything that is available for tenants to put their hands on, from the teaspoons to the television set, should be listed on the inventory checklist. You will expect these items to be left in like condition when the tenants check out.

This is usually the most lax of all management obligations, and you should stress this as critical. You can even pass the obligation for replacement of stolen or missing items to the management company if it does not follow the proper procedures for check-in and checkout. Things will disappear anyway, but at least you will have some way of tracking down blame, and you will have an opportunity to deduct the cost from the damage deposit or take legal action if need be.

As a part of the check-in procedure, it is important that tenants sign a statement that they have checked the inventory list against the actual inventory in the property and verified that everything listed is there and working or, conversely, have noted what is missing or not working. From that moment on, tenants can and should be held responsible for missing or broken items.

Check Utilities Before and After. Did someone leave water running or the heat on? This might seem to be overly simple, but a full checklist of all the things that someone should check both before tenants arrive and after they leave is essential. After all, airline pilots who take off and land hundreds of times a month still go through a checklist every time they pilot an aircraft.

Ask all the logical questions, "Did they leave a pot of water boiling?" or "Is there propane gas in the tank outside?" In addition, make sure that unauthorized phone calls have not been made. This might be difficult if you haven't restricted use of the phone until you get the phone bill several months later. If you do not want to ban phone use completely, and you cannot limit it through equipment controls, then be sure that your rental contract allows you to charge tenants for any phone calls made during the period of their occupancy. Phone bills usually show the exact time and date of any long-distance phone call, so having tenants record the exact time they check in and out will give you an opportunity to collect for such charges.

If you rent your vacation home on a regular basis, you may want to invest in a phone system that can be coded not to allow phone calls that begin with 1 or 0. If your apartment or villa is part of a complex, there may be a way to have all the outgoing phone calls channeled through a central operator.

Check for Damage Before and After.   This is another very important check that should be a regular procedure. Many property managers may overlook the check-in procedure, feeling that if the property was okay when the last tenant checked out, then why bother checking for damage when the next tenant checks in? The reason is because the cleaning team, a repair person, or someone sent to check something else might have caused damage.

Plan the Major Cleaning to Occur Prior to One of Your Visits.   The reason for this is to give you a nice fresh vacation home to stay in. Why show up to find that the only cleaning has been the in-between service provided by the management? Every vacation property needs at least one major spring cleaning, where repairs are made, carpets replaced if needed, and so on. Let that be just before you arrive.

63.   What Is a Time-Share Vacation Resort and How Does It Work?

The development of time-share vacation properties is one of the fastest-growing kinds of real estate properties. A time-share, interval ownership, or vacation time (three names for the same thing) usually consists of a resort-style property that is made up of apartments, villas, hotel rooms, or a combination of all three. They vary in many ways, however, and it is important to have a good understanding of those differences, how maintenance fees are calculated, and how you can make the most out of the worldwide exchange programs that the salesperson touted as the real bonus.

> **Solution:**   Become a time-share insider and maximize your time-share benefits by following the tips and avoiding the traps outlined in this section.

What You Buy

The form of ownership can vary from outright ownership 100 percent of the time (with or without limitations on the owner's personal use) to ownership of a specific week of the year, called the *interval,* or of a nonspecific week of the year, called *floating time.* Some developers sell points rather than a specific unit. This would create difficulty in doing an exchange for another resort that has specific intervals, except that the developers have made arrangements with the exchange programs to actually bank a week for you in return for a deduction in your total points held on reserve. Some of these programs give you a deed to that interval week much like any other real estate transaction. If the developers are selling you leasehold time, it is really your ownership of time for a limited period, at the end of which the lease expires and the developer gets the property back. Is this what you have? Well, don't say no too quickly. You might have received a "deed," but somewhere in tiny print it might say, "This is a deed representing title in the Master Lease held by XYZ Corporation, which expires without possibility for renewal on the twenty-first anniversary of the date on this deed," or something similar.

Foreign time-share resorts, that is, those outside the United States, may function entirely unlike any entity you recognize. Mexico has some unique ownership rules, and the key is to know exactly what you are buying and how you can sell it if you want to.

Vacation Exchange Networks

Most of the vacation time resorts are members of one of the two exchange associations that have made time-share ownership a truly interesting phenomenon. The largest organization is Resorts Condominiums International (RCI), and the other major company is Interval International (II). Each of these organizations provides time-share developers with the opportunity to participate within its system. Each has high standards to which the developer or the resort management must adhere. If the resort does not maintain those standards, then it is dropped from membership, or at least the association attempts to have improvements made in the facility. Each of these two associations ranks its time-share resorts with some kind of designation, like "Gold Crown," or "Resort of International Distinction," or some such. I have seen these resorts up front and have a hard time telling much difference between them. Be sure to check the major pitfalls in time-shares in this section for more on this subject.

These exchange associations have created major potential benefits for the property owners and other members. When a resort is a member of RCI or II, its time-share owners, who are also members of the association, can deposit their time into a space-bank operated by the association. This allows any other member of that organization to swap into the unit. This format of vacation ownership allows the owner of one vacation time condominium to go to any of the thousands of locations around the world, paying only the modest administration fee.

When you purchase a one-week period in a resort, for example in Orlando, Florida, that time period may be a set week each year that may begin on any given day of the week. However, as most check-in days are Saturday, the ownership may be recorded as week 27 of unit 216 of Orlando International Resort. Week 27 would begin on the twenty-seventh Saturday of that specific year.

The Orlando International Resort is a member of RCI as well as being a Fairfield Resort. Fairfield is a time-share development company that develops and manages many resorts. These resorts also have their own internal form of exchanges, which at this writing are less expensive for owners than going through RCI or II for a unit outside the system. In any event, Fairfield is not alone in setting up internal systems for its own resorts, which may in turn also be members of either (or both) RCI or II.

If you own multiple weeks (in either one resort or several), you need only one membership in the master associations (such as RCI, II, or Fairfield as examples). As a member, you would be able to deposit your vacation time in RCI or II or the internal space-bank. This can be virtually any kind of unit or points you own. This would allow you to draw against your banked time by making an exchange into available resorts around the world. The exchange facilitator, such as RCI or II, will charge you a fee to process that exchange, which together with the membership fees and rental charges is how these companies make money.

Each of these associations and most developers offer different kinds of programs from time to time in an attempt to meet the needs of their clientele, and they do the most they can to see that banked weeks are used. Even saying this, there are many weeks banked but never withdrawn from that bank by another member. This may have nothing to do with the quality of the resort, although poor resorts will have a history of high vacancy, and members owning those weeks will have their banked time given a low rank in the exchange process.

The time-share industry has taken much criticism for many years due to the investigation of dishonest developers. Most states have very strict marketing laws that govern the sale of time-share resort properties, and in general the concept is a good one.

There are many pitfalls, however, that a prospective buyer should be wary of. The following are the most important.

The Top Six Time-Share Pitfalls

- Buyer's inability to say no
- Confusing rules
- Poor management
- Exchange problems
- Fees too costly
- Resale problems

Buyer's Inability to Say No.   There is a saying in the time-share business that no one ever wakes up in the morning and says, "Today I am going to buy a time-share apartment." Sales are made in the millions of dollars each week across the country to people who are glamorized and emotionalized into buying, but virtually none of them thought they were going to buy anything that day.

The salesperson does not have to be smooth or overly slick, as many are not and yet they still produce large sales. What works is the technique, the sales pitch, the beauty of the product, and the idea of a lifestyle of traveling around the world and staying in deluxe apartments for the cost of a small hotel room. Time-share vacation units are a very good example where "sizzle" is the key. If you are a salesperson or want to learn a lot about selling, visit a time-share resort and pretend to be a prospective buyer (but be careful, you might end up being a real one).

Confusing Rules.   As time goes by it is not uncommon for the management or the exchange association that provides the perk of worldwide exchange privileges to the owners to make changes in the rules of operation. Both Interval International (II) and Resorts Condominiums International (RCI), have modified, changed, and completely confused their staff and members from time to time. As a multi-time-share owner, my wife and I travel a lot, using both our own time-shares and those we exchange into. It is not at all uncommon for me to discover that the people I deal with over the phone to make the exchanges are not as up-to-date on the new rules as I am. If you are confused, stick with the issue until someone explains it properly. Make sure you keep a log of the date of your phone conversation and the name of the person(s) you talk with.

Poor Management.   Exchange organizations such as II and RCI are supposed to police their resort members to make sure that the properties are kept up to snuff. In this they are similar to franchise hotel operators such as Holiday Inn and others who want to maintain and even improve the quality of the experience that guests have at those locations. However, things can get tired, be in need of fresh paint and a new carpet that does not smell of old wet fur, and so on. There are many bright new time-share properties that look great as long as the developers are still selling units, but look at them a few years after the "Sold out" sign is hung on the door. It is important for members like you and me, who have purchased time in these resorts, to complain not only to the management team on the property, but to the exchange network (II or RCI).

If your resort is part of its own internal network system, which is a separate exchange program with resorts that associations have either developed or lined up to cooperate with them (e.g., Fairfield Resorts), then the complaints should be directed to the head office of that internal network as well as to the master II or RCI affiliation.

Exchange Problems.   Every year, thousands of weeks have been banked by their owners in the exchange pool only to go unused. Yet many owners are not able to find a resort when they enter the exchange program at the time and/or place they would like to have their holiday. This problem is growing, even though the number of time-shares is expanding. The key, but not solution, is to bank early and not rely on the online Internet program to sort things out for you. Nothing beats using that voice at the other end of the phone (which might be in India, Ireland, or wherever) to help you work out the exchange of your dreams.

Fees Too Costly.   Paying too much for a week is a frequent argument of owners who start to add up the total cost at the end of the year. It is possible to pay as much as $30,000 for a week, although that would be rare, and to have an annual charge (for your one week) of $500 or more by the time you take into consideration your RCI or II membership. This might sound like a lot of money, but that cost must be balanced against the benefits. As for overpaying when you buy, this will happen with any real estate if you do not shop around. There are bargains in the time-share market if you look for them.

Resale Problems. Problems in resale do occur with many resorts. This happens for several reasons, and if you are careful you can limit your risk of experiencing this pitfall. First, take a look at the size of the project. If it is a large complex, which would be any resort with 100 units or more, then the developer can retain control of the market for that facility for a long time. There will be little opportunity for resale at anywhere near your purchase price until the developer is out of the project. However, if you want to sell and are creative, you might get a good price even while the developer is still around by offering your available week to other owners who own the week just prior to or just after your week. This is called *double loading,* and a happy owner may want to increase his or her vacation time at that resort by another week.

I have sold some of my time-share weeks at very good prices in this manner. National newspapers such as *USA Today* and the *Wall Street* journal often display advertisements from marketing companies that resell vacation time-resort weeks or that represent lender foreclosure sales for them. Often, these are prime resources for buying an inexpensive week that will allow you access to the entire space-bank system.

Seven Critical Factors of Time-Share Ownership Use

1. *Is it RCI approved?* While Interval International is not a bad second choice, it is still in my opinion a second choice. If you are bargain hunting, stick with RCI properties.

2. *Stick with "red time."* Red time is the code for prime season at resorts. When you plan to use the space-bank system, you will find that in a normal long-lead-time reservation exchange (one you plan for three or more months in advance) you can exchange to a *less* active season of the year, but not the reverse. Stay with red time.

3. *Watch out for high maintenance charges.* It is not uncommon for a vacation time resort to have an annual charge for maintenance and taxes of more than $400 per week. Your key is to find a resort that meets all the requirements of these tips and will not cost more than $300 per year including taxes, maintenance, and your annual RCI dues.

4. *Pick units that sleep a minimum of four or more in privacy.* The key word here is *privacy,* which means that people (usually meaning two to a room) can sleep in such a way that no one has to pass through their sleeping area to exit the building or use a bathroom or go to the kitchen or living room. The number of people the facility will sleep is also part of the space-bank exchange criteria. Both the color code and the number of people the unit will sleep affect the long-range reservations, so this aspect can be very important. With a long-range swap you can exchange for a smaller unit, but rarely can you exchange for a larger unit. A unit that sleeps four is often a one-bedroom apartment with a living room that converts to a sleeping room for two people. A unit that sleeps four *in privacy* has two distinct sleeping areas and may actually accommodate a total of six. Because you are

going for the bargain, price the units that sleep the most people in privacy. If there is little difference in price, go for the larger unit.

5. *Do not pay the price the seller asks.*   Negotiate, negotiate, negotiate. You will find a seller willing to meet a reasonable offer sooner or later.

6. *Whenever possible buy directly from the owner.*   Look in local newspapers. Keep in mind that if you want to own a unit in Orlando, then look in an Orlando newspaper. If the owner still owes money on the purchase mortgage, then you might make a deal just to take over the debt. If you do, make sure that you get a letter from the lender stating the exact amount owed, which might include all past interest, maintenance charges, and taxes. This may be a small deal, but there is no reason you should be lax about checking the title.

7. *When you buy, make sure the future time has not been traded in the space-bank and already slotted to someone else.*   Because the owner could have banked his or her advance time, and as that time might already be taken in exchange by another RCI member, your ownership of the week would not give you that time back. By knowing the owner's name, RCI account number, and the legal description of the vacation time unit, you can call RCI and find out the status of the future time.

Resorts Condominiums International (RCI) can be reached by phone at 317-876-8899. Interval International (II) can be reached by phone at 305-666-1861.

64.   What Are the Advantages and Disadvantages of Time-Shares?

When discussing the advantages and disadvantages of time-share vacation resorts, it is important that you compare apples to apples. When you own your vacation home, you may use it for only a very limited time each year. However, you pay for that facility 100 percent of the time and generally have a substantial sum of money tied up in the real estate. You can rent it out, of course, but that presents many problems, and when you do want to use it, you have to go to that location whether you like it or not.

Solution: Buy because you like the location, but also value the exchange rank.

Time-shares have taken much of the sting out of vacation ownership. Now you need only own the time you want, and in fact, if you use some of the special programs such as space-banking and bonus weeks, you are not limited to a specific time or location. The world can indeed be yours.

I would not be the person to tell you not to buy a time-share vacation resort apartment, because I own a dozen of them myself. However, I will tell you not to buy one without shopping around, and then buy to fit your needs rather than your emotions.

For example, I own five weeks at the Orlando International Resort. It is a nice facility, but in the 15 years or more of my ownership, I have used my weeks at the resort a total of only four times. Is that a bad deal for me? Not at all. I space-bank most of them, and because Orlando is one of the most requested areas in time-share locations, my banked weeks are taken by another member almost as soon as they are listed in the database. This in turn gives me a computer-calculated advantage over people who own time-share weeks in remote parts of the world or in nice areas during tornado season. If someone who owns a week in July in Tierra del Fuego (wintertime in South America) makes a request the same day I do for a resort in San Francisco, I will get it and the other owner will not because my resort and the time I banked are in much higher demand. My Orlando (Disney World area) time-shares are ranked rather high. But they are by no means ranked as high as the same category (say, red time sleeping six in privacy) in London, Paris, or San Francisco. Of course, the purchase of those locations would likely cost double or more what my weeks cost me.

My weeks have cost me anywhere from $4,000 to $8,000 per week. By using the space-bank exchange, I have traveled around the world and have stayed in resorts whose purchase price may have been as much as $30,000 per week. The key, then, is to own a week that will allow you to maximize the space-bank system rather than pay top dollar for a location you will rarely visit.

As you travel in these remote parts of the world, it is a good idea to check out the time-share resorts that are in or near those locations. They are easy to find; look them up in the exchange association you belong to or one that exists in the area. Generally, you can find these on the Internet by going to the home page of either RCI or Interval International.

The reason you want to check these resorts out should be clear. All the photos in the world can not expose you to the mildew smell of a damp building. You will find nice and not-so-nice places, but you are looking for the great time-share resorts. As my wife and I have found out while staying in an area only to later exchange into it time and time again, some small resorts sold out years ago operate in great locations. You can no longer buy them but can use them through the space-bank exchange.

65. What Can I Do to Increase the Value of My Vacation Property?

As with all real estate, you can do things to improve its value, no matter what it is.

> **Solution:** The key word *vacation* is your clue to improvements that will best suit vacation property. Stress those first.

Think about what makes a memorable stay. I have provided a list of things you have some control over that you can work at to enhance the value of your vacation property. Some of the items take into consideration elements that create value to the rental of the vacation home or apartment, and even if you do not want to rent, pay attention to them. The next owner of your property may want or need to gen-

> ### 11 Things You Can Provide to Increase the Value of Vacation Properties
>
> - Romantic setting
> - Lots of fun things to do
> - Comfortable setting
> - Nice furniture
> - Beautiful grounds
> - Great amenities
> - Privacy
> - Good security
> - Great management
> - Maintenance-free property
> - Good follow-up

erate some extra revenue from the property so he or she can pay that big price you are asking.

Romantic Setting.   A combination of the other elements in this list can help with this, too. People like to return to romantic settings, so do what you can to create that memory.

Lots of Fun Things to Do.   Add things to the property that make it fun to be in, and have a "fun to do" book that lists all the things that make the area special. If the property is part of a condo association, then serving on the board will give you some voice in what goes on and what improvements are made.

Comfortable Setting.   One of the most comfortable settings I can remember was my last visit to a Ritz-Carlton hotel. Okay, not fair, but read on. It was great, but the place I really want to return to is a log cabin at Jenny Lake Resort near Jackson Hole, Wyoming. Comfort is relative to what is going on at the place, so enhance the style of comfort that people are looking for at your particular location.

Nice Furniture.   Expensive furniture is not essential, but it should be nice, clean, fresh smelling, comfortable, and in good taste. To keep your furniture and interiors with that nice fresh smell, insist on the following rules: no pets and no smoking (install smoke detectors that are very sensitive and that blast sound at the first hint of a cigarette or cigar). If you have a wood-burning fireplace, install a natural gas log and ban any kind of wood burning in or out of the unit. A wood fire can end up sending smoke into every room (and the carpets and furniture, too).

Beautiful Grounds.   Some of the most beautiful grounds are the small patios and backyards in Charleston, South Carolina, so grounds need not be spacious.

However, if there is the space to work with, then let your landscaper help you plan for the future. Trees and other plants can turn anyplace into a beautiful setting, given time and TLC.

Great Amenities.   Provide a fireplace in the mountains, a back porch overlooking the marsh behind your building, a gazebo on the hill next to your apartment with an unbelievable view, or whatever your property lends itself to.

Privacy.   Privacy is a valuable item, and its absence is greatly noticed. Privacy is more than being out of sight of prying eyes; it is being not heard, too. There are ways to attack both problems if they exist. Landscaping will help remove prying eyes and ears, and it will protect you and your guests or future owners from hearing or seeing the neighbors, too.

Good Security.   Security means entrances and exists are well lighted at night, doors have strong and easy-to-use locks, and windows can be securely locked, too. A sufficiently large safe that is securely bolted to the floor or wall can provide additional security for everything from camera equipment to cash. An alarm system is not expensive, and video equipment can even offer the opportunity to check your vacation paradise via the Internet when you are thousands of miles away. It takes only a click of your mouse.

Great Management.   Even if you don't rent out your vacation property, it is a good idea to have a management company check on its condition from time to time. The same companies that manage rental properties generally offer this kind of service. They will clean the property just before you arrive so you don't have to deal with a dusty arrival, and they can stock your refrigerator with what you might need until you have time to visit the market yourself. Well-cared-for vacation property can enhance its resale value.

Maintenance-Free Property.   Okay, there is no such animal. But you can reduce the maintenance and improve the value at the same time. How? One good way is to get rid of carpeting wherever possible. This may mean an initial cost to replace it with flooring such as wood, tile, or terrazzo, but in the long run you'll be free of dealing with old, damp, or soiled carpet. Carpet captures smells (kippered herring, cigarette and cigar smoke, smoke from a closed flue in the fireplace, dog smells, etc.), which are instantly noticeable to would-be tenants or buyers.

Good Follow-Up.   Good management knows how to do this. When the place is rented they follow up with the tenants they would like to see come back again. You can do the same, even if you have outside management. I once received such a follow-up from the owner of a condo unit we rented one summer in North Carolina. The unit was well managed by the condo resort complex, but the owners took the time to send what looked like a personally handwritten letter thanking my wife and me for taking such good care of their unit during our visit. It included a 200-minute calling card for use anywhere in the United States. A nice touch, and we continue to seek reservations at that same unit. But guess what? It has always been booked. I guess I need to look further ahead.

66.   How Can I Syndicate My Own Vacation Property?

So, you found that beautiful villa by the sea, or the one with the magnificent mountain view, but you can't quite make the economics work. Why not get a few friends together and form your own syndication? In essence, form your own private time-share. What do you need to do to make it work?

> **Solution:** **Establish your own limited partnership or limited liability corporation and sell interests to the kind of people you like to associate with.**

The best way to start this process is to discuss the possibility with a few friends who get along with each other. Ask what features they would like to see in the "ideal vacation villa" and remind them that flamboyant features cost money. Once you think you have a good idea of the kind of place that would work for everyone, then develop that into several choices. Sure, this may require you to take a couple of weekend trips, and you will need real estate agent help wherever you go. As you are scouting for the ideal property, be working on your business plan. I will discuss that in a moment. However, try to find several places that are close to your ideal. Go ahead and make offers on the properties, but be sure to give yourself some solid due diligence time to put your act together. Now that you have locked up the places to show your friends (with offers that are binding to the sellers, not to you), finish your business plan and get everyone together and show them what you have. You are in control now, because the offers are in your name.

The Business Plan

The business plan has to be very well thought out and presented. You want your prospective coinvestors to see that you are serious and have thought out the whole idea in advance.

The business plan is simple enough. Collect the following data and plan the method of use up front. The more detail you have in this plan, the less discussion you will have later on. Be firm and strict on certain rules, such as no pets and no smoking. If you are a smoker and want to allow it at your vacation home, then so be it, but that may affect the resale value, as nonsmokers are unlikely to rent or buy when that becomes apparent.

Putting the Plan Together.   Here is a very brief example of how the major elements of a business plan can be treated. Assume that there will be 12 equal divisions of ownership.

The most important factors are ownership and use. Ownership will be by limited liability corporation that will be divided into 12 interests or shares. Each shareholder will be liable for one-twelfth of the cost to operate and maintain the subject property and will be assessed this amount on a monthly installment basis. The cost will be the total of the following items: debt service, management fees, rental commissions, utilities, cleaning services, estimated cost for breakage and replacement, insurance, real estate and personal property taxes, a reserve for major repairs and replacements, and other such costs. Any net rental revenue earned during the year will be divided between the shareholders equally and not held in lieu of the shareholders meeting the obligation to their one-twelfth share of the cost.

What about Shareholders Who Do Not Pull Their Own Weight? Carefully plan what will happen in the event a shareholder fails to meet the obligation of any monthly share of that cost. The founder (or his or her replacement) of the limited liability corporation can call the delinquent shareholder in default. If the delinquent shareholder does not remedy the default, together with a late charge equal to the amount of delinquency, within 15 days of receipt of notice, the founder will offer the delinquent share for sale to the remaining shareholders. On such an offering, the remaining shareholders will first be asked to bid on the share at an absolute auction, where the highest bid, no matter how high but at least sufficient to cover the amount of delinquency plus penalty and to include auction costs, is deemed the buyer. If no bid is offered, then the share will be offered at an open auction where any party can bid for the offered share. The proceeds of the auction will first go to the amount of the delinquency.

This default method just outlined is rather severe, but I can assure you that the tougher you make it, the better the initial owners will like it. Each will assume that he or she would never be the one to default.

Continued Upkeep. An essential part of the business plan is the continued upkeep of the property. This means that a sufficient reserve for replacements must be built during the ownership of the property. An initial sum should be placed in a bank account and a contribution added each month.

Third-Party Management. General management of the property should be in the hands of a third party and not one of the owners. This might be best if it were a local rental management company (even if the unit is never rented out). Each user will, however, be treated as though he or she is a renter and has the same responsibility to the property as a tenant. If you break it, in essence, you pay for it.

Management will be responsible to determine when something needs to be fixed or replaced and will notify the owners of this decision. If the owners do not object or if they have set a level of expenditure for which notice to them is not required, that should take care of most of the replacement problems. Essential items that need to be periodically replaced should be built into the fund by predetermining when such things need to be done (e.g., replacing carpets every four years unless management says they are still in good shape, that sort of thing).

Who Uses What When? This is generally the biggest problem, but once a formula is established it should work out for everyone. If the property has more than one distinct season, perhaps a great ski season and a great "cool off in the summer" season, then those who don't ski will work nicely with those who do. A revolving period of time can be established whereby each owner gets both in-season and off-season time, which can shift somewhat every year. Say, for example, 12 owners each have two weeks in season and two weeks off season, this time shifts forward in the every calendar year to even out the periods of time. Once a five-year period has been established, a new fifth year of time division would be made each year. In this way, the keeper of the calendar (or Web page), can continually inform the owners of who has what time. The individuals themselves can swap time between each other. Say you wanted four weeks in a row; okay, you swap time with another member to work it out. For really important times of the year such as holidays or special personal occasions, effort would be made to allocate them fairly over a period of years so that everyone would benefit equally.

Possible "Rent-Only Time."   When the holiday property includes some truly valuable vacation time, that time might be set aside as "rental time only." It is possible that over a two-month period of prime ski time, or during fall foliage, or whatever, rental revenue could provide the bulk of the operating expenses. This can work out nicely if the number of owners is reduced to say four to six, and there is ample time for both owner use and rental.

What If an Investor Wants to Sell His or Her Interest?   The potential need for someone to sell his or her share of the property should be anticipated, and here's one good rule: Any owner wishing to sell his or her portion must first offer it to the remaining owners. If they agree, then they accept an equal division of the share. For example, if the share was offered to a remaining five owners at the price of $50,000 for the one-sixth share, then each of the five remaining owners would pay $10,000 and would divide that share between them. If not all the owners chose to purchase a portion, then any of the five could buy the entire share at the offered price or make a counteroffer. If the seller does not accept the counteroffer, then the sale fails.

Get 100 Percent Agreement on Every Detail *Up Front.*   Be sure that your business plan is agreed to by all members before letting them join the group. Remember, you are the founder and you have the contract to acquire the property. You are giving your friends and acquaintances the opportunity to join you. The business plan is *your* plan, so resist any changes, because that opens the door for even more changes.

You Must Like the Place First.   You are doing this for your benefit, so look out for your own interests first. Once you have found a property that you believe will also suit everyone, make sure to offer the opportunity to more people than you need. If you want two-twelfths of the ownership for yourself, and you plan to offer the remaining ten-twelfths ownership, you will want to have more than 10 people on your list in case one or more decline your proposal.

Present Your Package and Push for a Quick Decision.   Have photos, video, and as much information about the property and the area as possible. Have a purchase agreement worked out between you and the seller of the property. Show the actual use of the proceeds from the transaction to the new owners who are going to be your partners (so to speak) in this venture.

Assume the property costs you $275,000 (including all sales and closing costs), and you want to add $25,000 in new improvements to the home or apartment, and you have a reserve of $10,000 for management costs, plus legal fees of $2,500, and you want to get a founder's fee of $30,000, then your total start-up costs in this venture are as follows:

Purchase cost	$275,000
New improvements	25,000
Reserve	10,000
Legal fees	2,500
Founder's fee	30,000
Total	$342,500

Against this total cost, you have arranged financing of $200,000, so the required per-share cost is now as follows:

$342,500
−200,000
$142,500 divided between 12 interests (making the initial cost of each interest $11,875)

The debt service and other annual costs to operate and maintain the property could easily run $26,000 per year. This would mean that each one-twelfth owner would be obligated to pay an annual fee of $2,167, which breaks down to $180 per month. Any rental revenue would be divided among the owners.

This kind of syndication would give each owner a full 30 days a year vacation time and good equity in a property that will be well cared for, with the likelihood of some revenue to offset the cost.

67.   How Can I Get the Most for My Money When I Sell My Vacation Property?

In addition to rereading this entire chapter, especially the answers to question 60, there comes a time when many vacation home owners are ready to sell.

Solution: Review the seven great tips that help you maximize the sale of your vacation home.

Seven Tips to Help You Sell Your Vacation Home

1. *Be ready to sell just prior to or during the prime season.*   Many sellers overlook the fact that the prime holiday time for that area is when emotions are highest, and at those times it is easier to sell the benefits of your property to prospective buyers.

2. *Make sure the agents sell the sizzle.*   Selling a vacation property is easier when all the sizzle is emphasized. One of the problems that occurs is that the local real estate agent is apt to be a year-round resident of the community and may take for granted many of the qualities that bring the vacationer to the area. As owner of the property, be sure your agent has not forgotten what made you fall in love with the property.

3. *Leave a fun-time photo album open for buyers to see.*   This is a simple but very effective tool—photos of you and your family having the time of your life in the home and enjoying the area.

4. *Clean, clean, clean.*   Because dust can accumulate quickly when a property is not occupied, make sure that the place is kept spotless even when you are not around. As long as there is a chance a prospective buyer will want to inspect the property, have someone keep up with regular cleaning. You do not want to leave the furniture covered with sheets.

5. *"Good memory" smells entice buyers.*   Be sure the agent brews coffee or puts some apple popovers in the oven just before the prospective buyer arrives.

6. *Have absentee management lined up.*   Even though you did not need management, keep in mind that prospective buyers might. Make sure your agent has several management firms (in addition to his or her own, if appropriate) take a look at the property, give an opinion of what the accommodations would rent for, and offer an estimate of management fees.

7. *Be creative in helping a buyer finance your property.*   If you are following a sound plan, the sale of this property should be moving you closer to your goal. Have you reviewed all your options to get you to your goal? Could you lease with an option? Would you be in a position to hold a first or second mortgage for a long period of time? Would you consider an exchange for all or part of your equity? A positive answer to any of these questions will start you on the way to being creative in financing the sale.

8

Questions That Every Senior Citizen Needs Answered

68. Why Should a Senior Citizen Look at Real Estate Ownership Differently than a Younger Person?

When I was younger and just getting started in real estate, I discovered that *time* is the equalizer to every real estate truth, myth, and lie. Give any real estate situation enough time and it will cycle right through all truths, myths, and lies.

Now that I am approaching the world and life as a senior citizen, I have discovered a new dimension to time. Give any real estate owner enough time, and he or she will move beyond the realm where that real estate satisfied earlier goals. Because I believe that real estate ownership should be goal-oriented (i.e., acquired and kept only to attain or advance the investor's desired goal), a person's approach to real estate should be reviewed and reassessed as time passes.

> **Solution:** If you are a senior citizen, your primary concerns should focus on the following items and how they apply to your estate.

There are only a few items that seniors will focus on with a different point of view than that of a younger person, but they require a synergy between all members of the family.

Six important Items All Seniors Need to Include in Retirement Planning

- Financial independence
- Taxes
- Inheritance
- Lifetime goals
- Management abilities
- Health care needs

It is recommended that all investors anticipate the date when they will be honored to be senior real estate owners; they should seek advice early about the right form of ownership to fit their needs and goals. As goals should be constantly reviewed and adjusted, it is logical that as a person matures, lifetime goals will eventually level off, or at least take a different direction from the time when growth of assets and wealth may have been more important.

In the youthful years of real estate investment, elements such as risk and sweat equity apply at completely different levels of importance than they do for the senior real estate investor, whose thoughts dwell more on good health and the maintenance and enjoyment of assets attained than on expansion of wealth and holdings. Naturally, some senior citizens go to their grave with a purchase contract for another shopping center clenched in their hands, and for these people this chapter may not apply.

69. How Much Can Retired Senior Citizens Afford to Pay for Their Housing?

Many senior citizens arrive at that point in their life as though they have just been ushered into a surprise party.

> **Solution:** Do not suddenly become a senior citizen; plan for it well in advance.

A good rule of thumb that works for most is that your housing cost should not exceed 25 percent of your total spendable income available. Several factors could cause a different percentage to apply, however. Here are some.

Extraordinary expenses may create an extra burden on the available income. Often, it is possible to insure against this kind of expense, and people approaching retirement should have supplemental insurance when they can afford it.

Retirement home living can consume a greater share of available income because it usually includes other costs that would not be associated with living in your own home. A full-care facility can, of course, require the majority of a person's income.

Debt service on existing property can continue to drain income until the property is paid off. One good plan is to schedule your mortgages to be paid off prior to your retirement. Having a free and clear home can be a good nest egg and hedge against future extraordinary expenses. There is a mortgage program that allows seniors to borrow against their equity and receive a monthly payment over a period of time. This reverse mortgage allows the total loan to build up to a fixed or adjusted (upward as values rise) amount and in reality to be paid off from the sale of the property after the death of the owner.

Personally, I do not recommend this kind of loan as a planning tool because loan policy can change overnight, and that kind of loan may not always be around. However, if you need to use it, and it exists, shop around, because very likely different lenders offer a wide range of terms.

70. What Are Some of the Options of Ownership That Senior Citizens Should Be Aware of for Their Housing Needs?

This is a problem whose solution must be tailored to fit the individual's unique situation.

> **Solution:** Every senior citizen needs to discuss their specific circumstances with a qualified estate attorney. Planning for the future where estate considerations need to be reviewed can mean considerable savings for heirs and a better lifestyle while you are still alive.

The first option to consider when it comes to real estate housing would be to not own any at all. This concept has been discussed in the answer to question number 13, and a review of all of Chapter 3 may be a good idea if there is a chance that your option may lean toward renting rather than owning. The other primary options of ownership are as follows:

Gift the title to others (heirs) and retain a life estate.

Gift the title to your spouse.

Form a family trust.

Put the title in the name of a corporation (with or without a leaseback).

Hold the title jointly with your spouse.

Hold the title in your own name only.

Exchange the title for a life residency in a retirement living facility.

Consider other options.

Before you choose one of these options, make sure you have discussed your plans with your spouse as well as with both your lawyer and your accountant. Each decision can have a different consequence, depending on your present or future estate and the goals you want to accomplish. Because this matter is absolutely unique to your own situation, providing answers for every scenario would require a separate book that would be larger than this one.

71. How Can Senior Citizens Reduce
Their Annual Housing Cost?

The first step to any plan is to review the current situation and the options available. This means examining the total picture before contemplating any decision.

> **Solution:** You need to review five major areas of
> consideration with your spouse (or companion), lawyer,
> and accountant.

The Five Major Items to Review to
Reduce Housing Costs for Seniors

- Fixed income that will not change
- Income subject to change
- Fixed expenses
- Expenses subject to change
- Benefits available

The first four are self-explanatory. Income and expenses are the critical factor, because if your expenses exceed your income, you are already in trouble. If that were the case, you need to increase income, reduce expenses, or a combination of both to attain a positive end result.

Previously overlooked benefits may offer an avenue toward other options, and these need to be studied on a case-by-case basis as applied to your unique situation.

For example, if you have an unused capital gains exclusion as allowed by the IRS ($250,000 for an individual and $500,000 with your spouse), then at your retirement you may want to take advantage of moving your equity into a smaller and less expensive property and generate tax-free cash that can produce some added income.

This provision was discussed in detail in the solution to question 51. Now would be a good time to review that situation.

Other benefits that may be available include a Veterans Affairs (VA) loan entitlement that you may have forgotten you had coming to you or that you never knew you had. You might sell your present property and buy another with such a low-interest VA loan.

Homestead exemption provisions, when they apply to your state, may reduce the annual taxes on property substantially owned by you, and those savings can make a difference in the standard of your lifestyle. This benefit is lost by many people either because they do not know about the laws or they have not properly filed to take advantage of them. This factor may change your thoughts about giving actual ownership of a property to another person, because to qualify for a homestead exemption you must be the owner and have occupancy as of the first of the taxable year.

72. What Is the Single Most Important Estate Factor a Senior Citizen Should Take into Consideration?

In seeking council from lawyers and accountants for my own estate, I have heard about everything from planning for future tax consequences to making sure that my heirs have the fewest possible problems. My lawyers argue that my will needs to be letter-perfect, my insurance just the right amount, and every *i* dotted and *t* crossed. My accountant insists that dealing with the IRS should be considered in every possible detail and that state laws are critical as well. Both my lawyer and accountant want to know my state of residence in case a state where I own a time-share suddenly decides that my multi-billion-dollar estate (or whatever it will be in the future) belongs to North Carolina instead of Florida, where I live. All of this is important, but the most important item has not yet been discussed.

> **Solution:** The single most important estate factor senior citizens should take into consideration is whether their estate will take care of their own and their spouse's expenses in their retirement years. Once that question has been answered properly and planned for, then the other important needs can be dealt with.

What are those other needs? They are many, such as a continuing income stream for family members dependent on the estate, as would be the case of children or relatives who are handicapped or cannot otherwise provide for themselves. All those things the lawyers, accountants, and insurance agents harp on are also important, but they come next in line.

73. What Is the Best Way for a Senior to Transfer Ownership of Real Estate to Reduce or Eliminate Estate Taxes?

In general, it is always safe to assume that anything having to do with taxes may change between the time a book on the subject is written and the time you read it. With this in mind, consider the following solution to this problem.

> **Solution:** Read this section and then discuss this potential problem with your lawyer and accountant. If your estate is already set up to maximize the existing tax and estate laws, you are likely sitting pretty. Even so, it is a good idea to review whatever plan you have from time to time, as laws change and you need to make sure your estate plan is properly matched to current rules and regulations.

The four good ways in which property (both personal and real) can be transferred to reduce or eliminate future estate tax are as follows:

> **Four Ways to Transfer Property to Reduce Estate Inheritance Tax**
>
> - Transfers by gift
> - Transfers by exchange
> - Forming a family trust
> - Transferring the asset into a corporation

Keep in mind that both federal and state laws may vary, so if you live in one state and your gift or exchange property is in another, make sure you know the specific laws and how they may affect your intended plan. A long-range plan is helpful in establishing a pattern that will be easy to follow and that will enable your advisors to better assist you in maximizing your future benefits. The idea is to balance your long-term goals with your present circumstances.

Transfers by Gift.   The IRS allows you an annual year-end tax exclusion for gifting up to $10,000 per person. This means that a husband and wife can make a combined gift of $20,000 to any individual without incurring any federal gift tax. This gift does not have to be cash; it can be an ownership interest worth that sum.

Estate planning requires accurate, up-to-date information on the tax laws, and it is important to know that estate taxes are one of the areas that frequently come under attack. In 1992 the Democratic-controlled Congress floated a bill to reduce the gift and estate tax exemption from $600,000 to $200,000; although it did not pass, this kind of legislation could reappear in the future as Congress searches for more tax revenue.

If you make a gift of a property you need to live in, then make sure that you retain a life estate or long-term lease to secure your goal.

Transfers by Exchange.   In any qualified Section 1031 exchange (often called the "tax-free exchange") you can shelter a capital gain and avoid paying taxes on the profit. This kind of transaction requires considerable care, however, because its application in real estate deals with investment property and not your personal residence. The rules are complicated and are the principal subject of a recent book I wrote for John Wiley & Sons in 2005: *The Tax-Free Exchange Loophole*.

The IRS Section 1031 allows an investor to buy a property, then exchange at a later date for another qualified property, and exchange yet again at a later date for another property, and so on. If carefully planned, each subsequent transaction will shelter the gain within the estate of the owner. On death of that person, the property would (if properly set up) end up in the hands of the heirs with the stepped-up base, which would be the value of the property at the time of death. Depending on the size of the estate, it is possible that there would be no tax on either the estate or on any capital gains.

Forming a Family Trust. Sometimes a good place to park an asset is in a corporation or family trust. I will get to the corporations in a moment, but first let's look at the family trust.

A family trust is established carefully by a lawyer experienced in these matters. It may allow for the continued control of the assets placed into that trust and can, in some situations, allow the value of the assets, and their growth in value, to remain untaxed at the death of the original owner. Many different things can occur in a trust, and the use of insurance funds, charitable gifts, and so on may have the unique ability to accomplish certain goals that would not otherwise be possible. Seek your lawyer's advice in any such matter.

Transferring the Asset into a Corporation or Other Legal Entity. This could also include limited liability corporations and limited partnerships, to name two additional entities. Again, the choice of which vehicle to use will depend on the amount of the assets, the kind of assets, and the end goal you want to accomplish. The moral of this section is that there are many different ways you can go, so focus on exactly what you want to accomplish and let the experts guide you toward the accomplishment of those goals.

Keep in mind that tax laws change, and there may be other methods to save taxes and retain the maximum benefits from your estate. Be sure to discuss these matters with experts in these different areas.

74. How Can Senior Citizens Use the Installment Sale to Their Best Benefit?

When anyone is faced with the sale of property that produces a substantial gain, it is always wise to seek the help of an accountant familiar with the different loopholes that the IRS Code provides for such situations. One such code is the installment sales treatment on the sale of a property.

> **Solution:** Discover how to use the installment sale to soften the blow on the sale of a property that does not qualify for the capital gains exclusion.

The installment sale is a provision that allows the seller to postpone tax on a capital gain and can help a senior balance the need for income and the ability to legally avoid paying a capital gains tax by either spreading the gain over a long period of time or by moving it to a future date. The rules to qualify for an installment sale have been greatly simplified over past years, and now all that is required is that the seller receive a portion of the proceeds of the sale in one or more tax years other than the year of the sale. Let's see how the installment sale works and can be used to benefit a senior citizen.

Albert owns a vacant tract of land that he purchased more than 20 years earlier. It was rented to a farmer for much of that time as a "U-Pick-It" farm, which served the purpose of providing some revenue and keeping the property in an agriculture classification to hold down real estate taxes. Although Albert paid only $30,000 for the property, its present value is at least $1.3 million, which is the amount a developer wants to pay for it. As the developer wants the land primarily as an entrance to a major office park he plans to build on the adjoining 500 acres, ownership is key for the developer.

But Albert wants to maximize income from the site to build up his estate and to postpone the capital gains tax (which might eliminate it altogether) or at least spread it over a longer period. He has considered using the IRS Section 1031 (tax-free exchange) to move his equity to another property, but is fearful that he will not find a property that suits his estate.

To solve his problem, he sells the property for $200,000 cash down and agrees to hold a first mortgage at 8 percent interest for 10 years. The mortgage has a provision that says there is no principal payment to be made on the mortgage of $1.1 million unless Albert demands one, and then he must do so within 180 days of the anticipated payment, and the payment of principal during any given year cannot exceed $200,000. Other than those principal payments, the new owner of the land cannot prepay the mortgage in advance of the tenth-year due date.

In this way Albert will have an initial capital gains tax to pay on that portion of the $200,000 that represents a gain. During the period of time he holds the mortgage, he will pay earned income tax on the interest portion he receives, and only if he demands a principal payment will he have a capital gains tax to pay on the gain portion of that principal payment.

If he keeps the mortgage at the $1.1 million principal due, he will collect $88,000 in interest each year. He will pay income tax on that amount based on his current tax bracket.

The installment sale can also be used to hold back the receipt of large amounts of taxable gains in a year when there are already large amounts of earned income. If you were already in a high income tax bracket by the middle of the year, a sudden receipt of cash from a sale (even a sale that occurred several years ago) could bump you up into a higher bracket. This could have the effect of discounting the funds you actually receive. If the sale were a new one, then rather than avoid the opportunity to make the sale you simply take little or no principal of the sale in the time period in which you may jump to a higher bracket. If the sale occurred some time ago and you are holding a mortgage that is interest-only (i.e., no capital gains funds are being paid to you, only interest, which is of course taxable), then the sudden payoff of that loan in advance of your planned payout could have a negative impact. There may be no way for you to stop the payoff of the loan unless you include a provision in the mortgage document that would not allow a prepayment, or if allowed that it would come with a penalty (to cover the negative effect of the added tax).

75. How Can Seniors Save Money When They Own or Rent Real Estate?

Some senior citizens miss out on some simple approaches to saving money by paying taxes at a rate higher than they need to. The same can be said for overlooking savings on other small items, like the tiny leak in the toilet that adds up to lots of money each year.

> **Solution:** Take a look at the following eight tips that can add up to big savings and added spendable cash flow at the end of the year.

Eight Money-Saving Tips for Seniors

- Apply for maximum homestead exemptions.
- Change to free checking.
- Pay off high constant-payment mortgages.
- Check for special Seniors-only insurance rates.
- Get tax advice on active, portfolio, and passive incomes.
- Shift to income property in a down market.
- Rent out part of the property.
- Form a management company to manage your own property.

Apply for Maximum Homestead Exemptions.   When your state has a homestead exemption law, this allows you to reduce the tax assessment by an amount to determine the final taxable value. Most states with a homestead exemption allow different amounts to be deducted from the value based on tenure of residency, with extra exemptions for widows and widowers, as well as for certain disabilities.

Change to Free Checking.   Many banks provide seniors with free checking accounts. If you have more than one account—for example, one for each rental property you own—and your bank will give you only one free account, then open an account at another bank or sit down with the president of the bank and get approval for additional free accounts. Other services the bank offers may also be free, such as money orders, cashier's checks, traveler's checks, and so on. If you are a good client, ask for a free safe-deposit box, too—even if you do not use one at present. If you get it, you will find use for it.

Pay Off High Constant-Payment Mortgages.   Many people overlook the actual cash drain a mortgage causes and look to the contract rate for the interest they pay. For example, take a 30-year mortgage that is in its final 3-year term. At the time you took out that mortgage the interest rate may have been 7 percent. If the original principal balance was $100,000, and your mortgage payment was based on a full amortization of principal by way of 360 equal monthly payments of principal and interest, the mortgage history would look like this:

Original mortgage loan:	$100,000.00
Interest rate:	7 percent
Monthly payment of principal and interest:	$665.30
Constant annual rate year 1:	7.984 percent
Owed at the end of year 17:	$21,546.80
Constant rate for year 18:	37 percent

Because the monthly payments for this mortgage will remain the same, $665.30 per month for the entire 30 years, the usual method of principal reduction for most mortgages is weighted to heavy interest payments in the early years, and the principal is paid off slowly. As you can see, with only three years left, there is still $21,546.80 outstanding.

The debt payment on the $21,546.80 is $7,983.60 per year. If you had $21,546.80 in savings earning at 3 percent interest (only $646.40) and you paid off the mortgage, you would add $7,337.20 in cash flow to your annual income ($7,983.60 less the 3 percent income you were getting of $646.40 equals $7,337.20).

Check for Special Seniors-Only Insurance Rates.   Some insurance companies have rates that are good for senior citizens. The only way you can find out about them is to ask your insurance agent or to become a member of one of the national associations that cater to senior members of the community.

Get Tax Advice on Active, Portfolio, and Passive Incomes.   The IRS has different rules and regulations that govern what and how much you can deduct from these different categories of income. By proper planning, you may discover you can shift income into a better category to suit your individual tax needs or obligations. Seek professional advice on all tax matters.

Shift to Income Property in a Down Market.   Use a down real estate market to shift to income property. If you want to sell your residence, for example, but the market is down, then try converting it to an income-producing property. Either rent it out as it is, convert it to something else, such as a professional office complex, or add more units. Later on, when the market improves, you can sell it, or, if you have established another residence in the meantime and do not need or do not qualify for or have already used the $125,000 capital gains exemption, ask your accountant if you could qualify for a tax-free exchange under the provision of the IRS Section 1031 exchange.

Rent Out Part of the Property.   Often senior citizens find that they are living alone in a home that was once suitable for the family they raised. Rather than selling the large home, it might be wise to consider renting out part of the home to generate additional revenue while at the same time keeping the older tax basis. This may result in a lower real estate tax than if they sold and purchased a smaller place to live.

This does not have to mean the loss of privacy, unless you welcome the company of a tenant living in the home with you. Modifications may be possible (if the zoning laws allow it) whereby a garage is converted to an apartment or the home is subdivided. My grandmother lived in my neighborhood in her later years, and she had a nice home with a separate garage. Over the years she converted the garage into two apartments and added a room to the house, doing some subdividing at the same time, and she ended up with a nice two-bedroom apartment for herself and three apartments to rent out. Later, when she decided to move to Fort Pierce, Florida, to be near her son, the property sold at top dollar because of both its living and income potential.

Form a Management Company to Manage Your Own Property.   Having your own corporation can provide you with many advantages. When you legitimately use that company to manage your own properties, you can legally use the management fee to cover expenses for which you may not get personal deductions. In addition, your private company may qualify as an S corporation, giving additional benefits to some. It would be a good idea to discuss all of your holdings and income sources with a good tax lawyer to ascertain what kind of corporation you should form, how you should channel income into that company, and how to take expenses to maximize your year-end cash flow. One added bonus that may appeal to some taxpayers is that corporations are less likely, I've been told by several certified public accountants (CPAs), to be audited.

76.   What Are the Five Best Insider Tips That Would Help a Senior Citizen in Ownership of Property?

1. *Know your goals and plan for them well in advance.*   Everything discussed in this book underscores the importance of goals. The sooner you have them and the quicker you establish a sound plan to attain them, the better off you will be. Remember, better late than never, so if you have no discernable goals and no active plan, start now. A husband and wife team should be able to recite their mutual goals and understand the plan.

2. *Document everything that deals with ownership, investments, real estate, insurance, and the purchase and sale of any of them.*   This can be a vast task for anyone, but with a little organization it is not as difficult or time-consuming as you might think. Each element should have its own file or box or folder in which the details are maintained. Deeds, bills of sale, insurance papers, and so on should be kept in a safe or safety-deposit box. Be sure you have an inventory of what is in that deposit box or you can go nuts looking for something you thought you put in your second drawer under your socks three years ago. Things that require frequent attention, such as mortgage payments (owed by you or to you), insurance premiums, certificates of deposit that need to be rolled over, and so on should have one calendar log that maps out two years of such payments or deposits. At the end of one year, you should advance the schedule by adding a second year to the existing year.

3. *Maximize your own lifetime benefits.*   Far too many people work all their lives building, adding, and investing for the future, but never seem to find the time to sit back and enjoy what they have. Do not let life pass you by without smelling the roses.

4. *Establish measures to maximize your surviving spouse's benefits.*   This should be the primary purpose of estate planning, as I have mentioned elsewhere in this chapter. Once that has been taken care of, then other members of the family can be considered, as needed. Beyond that, everything else is subject to your own wishes.

5. *Have a will drawn by a tax lawyer versed in estate planning.*   Not just any lawyer can advise you properly. Many very complex matters go into proper estate planning, and not everything deals with federal tax alone. Each state may have a different application of tax laws that can eat away at your final estate. A final disposition of your assets should be planned well in advance. In many situations your lawyer will want you to set up a trust fund that will administer your estate, and in some circumstances the surviving spouse can be the administrator of that estate. This kind of structure can postpone or save thousands of dollars in taxes on the death of the first spouse. It is essential to review your will, as well as any trusts you may have established to implement changes driven by new tax laws.

9

Master Wealth Builder: Buying and Selling Land

77. Why Has Raw Land Been the Millionaire Maker of the Past, and What Is Its Future?

Many millions of dollars of wealth have been made through the purchase of vacant land. Some of America's wealthiest families have made their fortunes from the thousands of cheap acres they purchased or obtained through land grants. Others have profited by buying farmland that skyrocketed in value as towns grew. While the original purpose of the land might have been to raise cattle or sheep, drill for oil, or grow cotton, the land itself became valuable in the long run.

The natural growth of cities into rural areas, where land that once sold for $100 per acre in the recent past now goes for $500,000 per acre or more, is not at all uncommon. This kind of growth is well documented and is still possible today.

However, unlike the investment patterns of the past, investing in raw land today can be much more risky. Gone is the throw-a-dart-at-a-map-and-buy-wherever-it-lands (TADAAMABWIL) method of investing. Today more elements of control govern the use of a property and therefore affect the ultimate value of that property.

The fundamentals for the selection of raw land that is destined for growth potential do still apply.

> **Solution:** Review the six key factors that govern the appreciation of raw land.

Six Key Factors That Govern the Appreciation of Raw Land

- Growing population and demand
- Improved infrastructure, making growth easier
- Increased spending power building top-end buyers
- Political and environmental pressures limiting and shaping growth patterns
- Decline in supply of land available for development
- Increasing savvy of property owners and investors

Generally, these six factors work in unison, some providing positive directions to the appreciation of land and others functioning to direct or redirect the pattern of growth to other areas. But when any of the elements are present, property that is in the path of outward growth from any city will experience an increase in value. The key for an investor is to recognize the proper timing of the investment. The usual mistake made by an investor is to acquire the land too soon, so that growth does not come as quickly as the investor anticipated. This factor, plus the inability of the investor to generate the needed income from the property, can overwhelm the investor with costs.

It is very possible that the cost to hold onto a future gold mine will be more expensive than the investor can support, which is substantiated by many unfortunate examples where being at the right place at the wrong time has been a recipe for economic disaster.

78. What Are the Key Steps to Buying Raw Land?

If there is a pill that you can take to make you wealthy, it is found in the following solution.

> **Solution:** Learn the 12 key steps that will give you the crystal-ball answers to where growth is headed and which property is going to appreciate the fastest.

The following 12 steps will aid you in the quest to purchase raw land. All of the information needed to accomplish these 12 steps comes from your local community. You will find that a local real estate broker can be very helpful in providing much, if not all, of the basic data; however, it is highly recommended that you get involved by attending city and county council meetings and other public meetings that deal with your community and the real estate in it. The idea is to become an insider in the market. The best way to do that is to meet with other insiders to learn their secrets to success and soon you'll become one of them.

> ## 12 Key Steps to Buying Raw Land–
> ## Your Aspirin to Wealth
>
> - Plot growth trends.
> - Understand zoning regulations.
> - Recognize use zones.
> - Classify areas demographically.
> - Isolate target areas.
> - Attend planning and zoning meetings and city council sessions.
> - Get to know DOT officials.
> - Obtain utility expansion plans.
> - Review historic examples of similar growth.
> - Maintain contacts with lenders.
> - Learn how to rezone property and why.
> - Prepare your investment team.

Review each of these steps and put them into the context of your own situation. You may have already taken care of some of the steps without really knowing it, and once you see the whole picture you will begin to see how everything fits together.

Plot Growth Trends.   Start with a map of the area and go to the county planning office. Ask one of the senior planners to help you plot out the business, industrial, and residential growth of the community over the past 30 years (more or less). The idea is to see how areas have grown and where the upper-income areas of town have established themselves. These are the primary areas on which to focus your attention.

Understanding Zoning Regulations.   Zoning rules and regulations are the most important of all the local restrictions that control use and therefore value. Visit each of the different zoning offices that govern land in the area you are researching. This may require visiting more than one city, as well as a county office for unincorporated land areas. Get copies of the zoning ordinances and read through them. Make sure you understand each classification of zoning and the differences among the various communities.

While you are at the zoning department ask whether other restrictions may apply that are unique to the specific area of your interest. It is possible that environmental controls may be even more restrictive than zoning rules. If the property fronts a lake, river, or ocean, has marshes, endangered plants, or animals, is part of a tidal system, was once a landfill, was or is used for mining minerals or drilling for oil or gas, or has any other unusual characteristics, then make sure you mark that area with a big red warning banner: Many potential problems may exist.

Recognize Use Zones.   Areas of a community often develop into use zones. Downtown areas, for example, may become mostly office use, with little or no residential activity, even though the zoning may allow it. Suburb areas may be overly heavy in single-family homes with little apartment or commercial use even though the zoning may allow it. These patterns may indicate possible profit centers if you can take advantage of an allowable use in an area where that use is sparse. The key is to understand why an area was developed for the particular use that exists, even though the zoning of the area was flexible and permitted other uses. You may find that, historically, the area went through a change. For example, maybe a city center area became so commercialized that residents moved out to the suburbs; perhaps apartment buildings were slowly torn down and replaced by higher-rent office buildings. Sometimes these areas can and should revert back to mixed use to create live-in city centers.

Classify Areas Demographically.   Code your areas to the demographics of the community. Some residential areas will cater to a higher-income-level property owner than others. When you see growth moving outward from one of these areas, you might assume that the demographics of the new area will be equally high or even higher. However, do not assume this without examination of all other factors. The key to good information is to cross-check the data against several different sources. The tax assessor's office can give you information based on property values, whereas the telephone company will have areas broken up into demographics of phone bill charges. The American Express credit card company segments areas into zip codes as well. By selecting several sources, you end up with a better picture.

Isolate Target Areas.   You need to limit the area of your research as quickly as possible or you will be frustrated by the monumental task of finding the right property to acquire. Try to stick to one set of governmental controls by staying within one city and county rather than several different ones. The key to selection of a target area is to have a general idea of all the possible optional areas first.

Attend Planning and Zoning Meetings and City Council Sessions.   Once you know which city and county you plan to invest in, start going to the planning and council meetings. The insiders attend these meetings, and to become an insider you need to attend them, too. You will learn more about your own community in two visits than you ever thought possible, both good and bad. Be sure to make notes of all the people you want to meet personally. Start with the mayor and work down. The key to attending public meetings is to obtain an agenda, understand the procedures of the meeting, make notes of the VIPs at the meeting, and take steps to meet them.

Get to Know DOT Officials.   The officials in the local departments of transportation (DOT) are very important because these departments have the greatest available data on potential property value changes. These departments are found at three levels: state, county, and city. Each is critical and each will have a long-range master plan that is available to you. While these master plans are subject to (and frequently do) change, they will provide you with a reliable forecasting tool showing areas that will experience improved traffic flow or will become open to new traffic. The key to getting to know any official is to maintain contact with that person to ensure that he or she gets to know you. This is a primary step in becoming an insider—the fact that local VIPs recognize you as someone who is on the inside.

Obtain Utility Expansion Plans.   The local water, sewer, city gas, and electric utilities, cable television and telephone companies, and other such providers each have a master plan and timetable to ensure that they stay ahead of the growth patterns. Because it is difficult to build homes in areas where there is no electricity, the electric company would be the first place to start.

The demand levels for future services expected by each utility in different areas of the county or state is highly useful information for any real estate investor, and absolutely indispensable information for the vacant land speculator. The key to obtaining data from utility companies is to request the information in such a way that it appears to have already been offered.

For example, contact the company to get the name of a top official, say the director or the president. Call that person and ask who would be the best individual to talk to about public relations information and other data that would be helpful for a report you are compiling. Then call the public relations person and tell him or her that the president of the company (or whomever you talked to) asked you to call him or her about the demographic and planning data.

Review Historic Examples of Similar Growth.   Go back to the first step and take a look at the patterns of growth you plotted out. How did the growth occur, and what were the results? If you know a new airport is planned for an area that is nothing but farmland now, then look around and find a community not too far away where a similar event occurred 10 to 20 years ago. Examine how its growth evolved and how it changed land values. Be sure to make adjustments for price levels, and be aware that some of the mistakes that happened before just might happen again. The key to getting useful historical information is to make every effort to find past events that are as similar as possible to the situation you are studying. This is often very hard to do and may be one of the most difficult of the 12 steps to complete satisfactorily.

Maintain Contacts with Lenders.   It is important for you to know which types of situations appeal to lenders for loan approval. Even though you might not be a developer and are looking at a tract of land only as a speculator, you will find that the more you know about the problems a developer goes through, the better you will be at selecting the right property in the first place. Smart developers build what they can finance.

The advantage of dealing with lenders is that they get to know you as an insider who is or may become a future customer. This requires you to introduce yourself as a real estate investor looking at the local market to determine whether it is a good place for you to invest. As a potential client, the mortgage broker or banker will supply you with more information than he or she would otherwise.

Learn How to Rezone Property.   The ultimate and maximum profit you get from a vacant tract of land may come only after you change the zoning to a different use. Because value is a function of use, you should begin to become aware of all the steps necessary to effect a zoning change. To accomplish this, you should first make an inquiry at the zoning office about the necessary paperwork.

The next step will be to attend several rezoning meetings to get firsthand information about how the professionals do their job. It is both interesting and highly informative. You will meet the people in town who specialize in rezoning and will quickly spot those who are more adept at that task than others. The key to rezoning is to know what new zoning is likely to produce—economic conversion of the property to your benefit.

Prepare Your Investment Team.   Your team should include all your partners (your spouse being the most important), a real estate lawyer, a good tax advisor (lawyer or CPA), and one or more real estate agents. All the members should know your goals and be committed to helping you attain them. The key to forming an investment team is to shop around. Find and use people who are compatible with your needs and who understand that you expect them to assist you in the attainment of your goals.

79. When Buying a Vacant Lot, Is It True That Location, Location, Location Is the Single Most Important Factor?

There is a cliché that the single most important aspect of real estate is "location, location, location." The point of the triple play on the word is to stress that real estate is a function of location.

Broadly speaking, this is a fact; that is, location may be the only element of a given site that cannot be changed (although you *can* move a building to another location). In many respects, it is the location that separates real estate from being a universal commodity. The universal nature of, say, stock sold on the stock market is how Wall Street would like to categorize real estate, yet Wall Street continues to fail to grasp that what happens in Chicago may have absolutely nothing to do with a New York property that has a similar size, shape, and location (e.g., the corner of two very busy commercial streets). The value of each of those two corners depends on other considerations, of which the following three property analysis factors play a very strong role in comparing two or more properties.

> **Solution:** First of all, forget this myth that *location, location, location* are the three most important words in real estate investing. The reality is that location is part of the equation,

but only in unity with two other equal partners: *use* and *approval.*

A property has its location, which might be ideal for some uses and not so ideal for others. The ultimate use is critical to maximizing the price for that property. Approval also is essential in today's modern, politically run, planning and zoning departments. The best use at the best location doesn't mean much if the city will not approve a building permit.

80. How Do I Compare the Differences among Various Vacant Tracts?

This is one of the most difficult of all investment decisions. Which of the various opportunities available should you choose? Most investors get sidetracked from their original purpose, however, making the decision even more difficult and complex than it has to be.

Solution: Follow the guides shown in the following checklist for vacant land comparisons.

Six-Item Vacant Land Comparisons Checklist

- Review your goals.
- List the important criteria of those goals.
- Get all the important data on current uses allowed.
- Discuss possible uses that you can add to the site.
- Negotiate to find the seller's bottom line.
- Buy the property that moves you closer to your goals the quickest.

Review Your Goals.   Step back and remember what it was you started out to find, and why. The important thing is to stay focused on what you started out to do. If you want to find or develop a great site for multifamily housing, then stay in tune with everything that will advance that goal. This means knowing the lay of the land, its laws and rules, and how far you can stretch them. The dollar amount of anything you want to buy is not the important issue as long as you know how much added value your efforts can add to the equation. Profit is your motive, and that is where you need to stay headed.

List the Important Criteria of Those Goals.   A tract of land that you can use for raising pigs now, with the prospect of building homes later, will have different criteria than one for a winter hideaway with the possibility of future recreational use. Remember, we are talking about vacant land here, and that means time will be one of the factors that can work for or against you. If there is a long time (several years or longer) in the process of turning a vacant tract into a gold mine, then you need to know the cost to hold that land and to continue the improvement process.

Get All the Important Data on Current Uses Allowed.   Then study that information carefully. Do the present zoning ordinances allow for your desired use, or would you be required to seek a zoning change?

Discuss Possible Uses That You Can Add to the Site.   It might be possible to rezone a subject property. This is done all the time, and many multimillionaires succeeded by learning how to do exactly that. They either develop the property or sell it at great profit to developers who don't want to mess around with the political side of rezoning.

Negotiate to Find the Seller's Bottom Line.   After all, this might be the final and most important criterion of all. By using letters of intent, which are not binding contracts, or offers with contingencies that give you a release from the agreement, you can see just how good a deal you can make with the seller. Sometimes the key factor is time. If you can tie up the site long enough, for example, without being committed to buy it, and can get the present zoning changed, you can ensure a profit without much risk.

Buy the Property That Moves You Closer to Your Goals the Quickest.   Once you have reviewed your findings on several different tracts of land, considering all the preceding factors, it is likely that the obvious winner will stand out like a sore thumb. However, if several options look like winners, it could very well be that they are.

81. Why Is Zoning So Important When Buying Vacant Land?

By now you should understand that *location, use,* and *approval* are the three most important words in investing in vacant land as well as in any developmental property.

> **Solution:** Learn the zoning and other use codes and restrictions that you will have to deal with in your area. Location is what it is, and approval is the process you have to go through to get final go-ahead to implement your plan. Concentrate on *use*.

Zoning is the primary factor that determines the use of any property. As an investor in vacant land, you would want to know the answers to the following five questions.

> ## The Five Important Questions about Use
>
> - What does the present zoning allow?
> - What optional zoning categories are available?
> - Of the optional zoning available, which is likely to be obtained?
> - What is the approval process going to cost in time and money?
> - Can I get the seller to give me the time to obtain my approval?

Review each question to see how to deal with them in the context of buying vacant land for profit.

What Does the Present Zoning Allow?   Vacant land that is outside of town is often zoned into an agricultural type of zoning. This farmland category may vary around the country and may not be limited to growing crops or raising animals. Some farm zoning allows limited residential use, mining, oil exploration, certain limited industrial use, and so on. This broad-spectrum use can cause problems when developers attempt to build residential communities next to land zoned farmland on which a 2,000-acre pig farm or chicken hatchery may be constructed (upwind, too).

The goal for a speculator in vacant land is to buy property that is presently zoned at the lowest possible tax base and located in an area that is poised for the greatest possible growth in high-demographic use. This ideal sometimes happens, but usually there is a trade-off somewhere along the way. Clearly, not all vacant land in the path of growth will experience the same upward growth in value.

What Optional Zoning Categories Are Available?   A study of all zoning categories used by the local community is a good start. One of the critical aspects of this study is to determine which communities to visit. As towns grow into unincorporated or county-governed land, one of the cities may eventually absorb the area and assign its own zoning restrictions, which may supersede those of the county. But which city will absorb the area first? This can and frequently does make a very big difference—so much so, in fact, that developers who are looking at the acquisition of a large tract of land (or the sellers of that tract) may approach different cities to see which community can offer the best development package should the property be taken into its boundary.

Of all the zoning available, look for zoning that seems to fit the pattern of growth and at the same time falls within the high end of demographics. If the tract of land in question is large enough to have a mixed use, then an overall site plan might be required to establish this mixed use through a rezoning process.

Of the Optional Zoning Available, Which Is Likely to Be Obtained?   Local politics can be the toughest obstacle to overcome for an investor in vacant land or for the ultimate developer of that land. Because of this, before the land is purchased, you want to get a good feel for the political attitude in that community about development in general and developers specifically.

You do this by visiting the local planning and building departments (not always at the same place) to discuss the past, present, and future trends of the city and county. You also explain why you are asking questions, as your interest is to be a better-informed real estate investor and property owner in the community. Be specific about the site or location of the property you are considering. You may find that some controversy is involved, and you will learn more about the property and the area than you can imagine.

From the building and planning departments, you would then go up the chain to the city or county teasers—the council and commission members. Make appointments with each of these officials and get their opinions on what is going on in the area and how they view growth. Are there upcoming changes of which you are unaware, such as new roads, bridges, highways, canals, airports, or trash dumps, that can affect the area in a positive and/or negative way?

Ask these officials how they would view a specific zoning request, or which category of zoning they see as being viable for the area.

In asking these questions you should be prepared to get a variety of answers, depending on whom you talk to. The end result of this study should, however, reveal a trend that can aid you in making a decision about buying the land. Keep in mind, however, that political officials do not always retain their jobs, and there may be an election between the day you get their opinions and the day you expect to profit from those decisions.

What Is the Approval Process Going to Cost in Time and Money? You don't want to plow all your potential profit (which you don't even have yet) back into the carrying cost of the property. A prolonged fight with a reluctant building department or city hall can cost you hundreds of thousands of dollars and take a year or more out of your life. I have seen property owners and developers fight city hall for a decade or longer before they (or their estates!) finally win. That's the wrong way to pave your path to heaven.

Can I Get the Seller to Give Me the Time to Obtain My Approval? You are down to the nitty-gritty question. Say you find the best location available for your intended use and you discover that you can expect a mild city hall fight to get the approvals you want, but it will take at least 90 to 180 days to get the approvals that will lock up your use. What do you do if the owner of the property will only sell contingent on a 60-day due-diligence period (i.e., approval time)? This can be a tough call, but one that most builders would have no qualms making if the seller holds firm at 45 days. The decision is simple: Bye-bye.

However, when there appears to be a light at the end of the tunnel, then what do you do? Sixty days slips past pretty quickly, and in the heat of the summer, when people are on vacation, or during the frozen months of January, when city planners head for Florida for a holiday in the sun, it may be best to avoid the burned-out brain cells you will likely end up with and move on to a more motivated seller.

Which brings up another subject: sellers who don't understand that developers will pay big bucks for a property they can put to their intended use. Take away the potential of that use, and it is not the developer who suffers. Why not? Because the developer will simply move to another property or deal with a seller who understands this process.

I wish I had $100 for every would-be seller who says, "Thirty days, take it or leave it; why, hell, I'll develop the site myself and keep all those millions of dollars of profit."

How many do? Very few.

82. What Is a Master Plan, and How Does It Affect the Future Values of Property?

A master plan is the overall plan for the development of a community. This plan is usually a function of several overall plans that may start at the state level and work down through the county planning office to end at the community or city level for final implementation. Often, the least comprehensive of the plans is the one at the state level, as it may govern elements such as water supplies, funds available to repair roads, money to build bridges, and so on.

When environmentally sensitive or public properties (e.g., near oceans, lakes, or rivers) are involved, each underlying level of authority may impose certain restrictions.

The county government establishes a countywide master plan to which each of the cities within that county must totally or substantially conform. This may allow the city to adjust within its boundaries certain areas to create a slightly different balance of commercial areas over residential areas, for example. Generally, however, once the county sets up its master plan, each city has a given period of time to make those adjustments in its own plan.

When the city has a master plan that is approved by the city council members, which generally follows a long and often very heated battle between property owners and political leaders, the property owners within that city soon discover that any change in a use of existing property must conform to the new plan.

If the property in question is currently a motel, it could be that the new master plan has designated the location as low-density residential use only. If that is the case, then conforming to the new plan would require a use other than the motel. Usually, however, the motel would be "grandfathered."

The term *grandfathered* means that a change in the building code or zoning ordinances that occurred *after* the present use was established would be allowed (sometimes only to the present owner, other times to subsequent owners as well), but that any change to the existing structure may require the entire property abide by the new use codes and ordinances in effect. This can and frequently does cause hardships on property owners who have a fire or other damage; when they seek a new building permit (for substantial repairs or rebuilding), they may discover that the new laws will not allow them to rebuild their business.

> **Solution:** Discover that the master plan is really the investor's blueprint for success. It doesn't matter too much what the plan says, as long as the investor understands that it will dictate the pattern of growth for the next decade or longer. As nothing happens quickly in overall community development, these master plans serve the communities to coordinate their own lower-level plans with the state and county plans that oversee their own growth. Study them as if they are the DNA of future real estate in your area.

Of course, keep in mind that master plans are not etched in stone. As if to prove that fact, communities frequently undergo changes in their master plan and every so often devise new ones just to show the outdated thinking of several years earlier.

Knowing the future thinking of those in charge of master plans for your area is very important, but should not be viewed as the final word. A long time can elapse from a thought to a plan to the implementation of that plan; the final product may not even closely resemble the original thought. The closer you are to the mind-set of the local political environment, the more likely that you can use this long-range thinking as your own long-term investment strategy. This is just another of the many reasons I have pointed out in this book thus far that you should become closely entwined with the political thinking of the community. Please note, by "becoming entwined" I do not mean that you should become a political combatant. Observe like a benevolent United Nations observer, but take note, and act quietly.

83.   What Are the Major Pitfalls When Buying Vacant Land, and How Can They Be Overcome?

Pitfalls often come in twos. When one happens, another can soon be on the way.

> **Solution:** Review the following nine major pitfalls of buying vacant land.

Nine Major Pitfalls of Buying Vacant Land

- Change in zoning
- Change in building regulations
- Decline in neighborhood
- Building moratorium
- Changes in community infrastructure
- Concurrency requirements
- Political mind-set shifts
- Dry-area water retention
- Dried-up finance capability

Take a look at these pitfalls. If one has already occurred, it can be a prelude to another.

Change in Zoning. When the local officials change the zoning of your property or of property around yours, this can signal a shift in the demographics and use zones of that area. This factor does not, by itself, mean the value of the property will go down, but it does indicate that there is going to be a change and that the value of some properties may go up and others may go down as a result.

Change in Building Regulations. Any change in what you can build or how you build it also triggers a change in the status quo. Usually, building restrictions become more stringent and costly rather than the reverse, so this added cost may cause values to go down. These regulations may include increased setbacks, reduced density, lower building heights, more comprehensive fire sprinkler systems, and so on.

Decline in Neighborhood. Long-range investing takes into account a steady improvement in the status quo. With a downturn, however, the best-laid plans become worthless. Declines in neighborhoods can come slowly or suddenly. A slow decline can be seen coming, and investors who continue to invest in the area, rather than seeking a way out or reversing the decline, do so with ultimate losses. A sudden decline usually occurs because of a major infrastructure change or improvement.

A new highway may be viewed as an improvement to the overall traffic situation of a community, but for the formerly attractive residential subdivision that is now sliced into two less desirable areas, it can mean a sudden and dramatic drop in property values. Foreclosures can result; banks then dump their real estate owned (REO) properties; the economic demographics of the area plummet.

Building Moratorium. A building regulation that developers fear most is a moratorium on development. Communities often establish a period of time in which no construction permits are granted to enable new rules and regulations to be formulated or to allow infrastructure to catch up with development demands. These moratoriums can effectively halt development for long periods of time, causing builders to shift their attention to less-restrictive areas of the city, county, or state.

Changes in Community Infrastructure. This factor has been stressed several times. Whenever a community does something for the betterment of some of its members, there is apt to be a reduction of benefits for others. Every citizen of a community should be wary of improvement for improvement's sake. Also, at some point after the completion of any infrastructure improvement, the law of diminishing returns sets in. It is rare for any highway to continue to meet the demands put on it (because the demand increases) or for any bridge to solve forever the problem for which it was designed.

Concurrency Requirements. If you give a land planner who is hell-bent on stopping development enough time and a dictionary, he or she will come up with some of the darndest things you have ever heard. In Fort Lauderdale these types have come up with some real doosies. Here's one: "New development must be compatible with the neighborhood." This is one of those strange things that is put into a zoning code to stop a developer when nothing else in the code seems to fit.

In Fort Lauderdale, some areas of town are in desperate need of redevelopment. There are slums and truly old properties that are worth a lot of money simply because the dirt under them (the land) has become valuable. You can build there, but only if it is something worthy of the community, valuable to the tax rolls, and will increase the value of the neighbors' property. Okay, but if you can only build what is compatible with a slum, what can you build?

Then there is the "shadow study" that says you cannot build a building that shadows more than 50 percent of a public area adjoining your building (by property line). Public area may be a park, the beach, playgrounds, or other public land. There are those who argue that the shadow study should be conducted at noon. Think about that for a minute.

Dry-Area Water Retention.   The newest thing going on is called *dry-area retention,* which is an area that you have to provide on sites without storm drainage to hold the first couple of inches of rainwater so it does not run off onto other properties. Okay, but things can go too far. For example, I owned a site that I purchased a long time before such a rule. This commercial land is bordered by a county drainage canal on two sides (150-foot-wide canal system) that is maintained at a higher-than-normal level to keep the ocean from depositing salt onto farmland that is no longer existent; and I cannot use the canals (which I was paying an annual fee to maintain) as a resource to carry off some of my rainwater. "Okay," I demanded, "City Fathers, then buy my property." (They did.)

Political Mind-Set Shifts.   Did you vote? Did you know who you were voting for? Do you know what those people you voted for have voted to do to you? I'll bet that the answer to those questions is no for the vast majority of readers. Almost worse, you said yes to the first but no to all the others.

"Ouch" is what you say when you accidentally hit your finger with a hammer. "Shame on you" is what you say when you vote for people you should have known were not going to act in your best interests.

On the other hand, and in defense of you, political figures may change their minds in midsentence. What are you to do?

Stay on top of what they do. Read the newspapers; go to the meetings (often you can watch them on local public TV, although that is not the same as being there).

Dried-Up Finance Capability.   It is harder to finance vacant land which you are buying as an investment. If you have a sound business plan, however, that you can show the lender how you plan to soften the carry cost for the next few years by turning the site into a parking lot, or a u-pick-it farm or whatever, that can help. The key is to have a sound use for the property down the road. Show the lender that your plan will work, even though it may take you several years to bring the value of the land to the point that it is ready to be developed (or sold, you don't say to the lender, to a high rolling developer).

84.   How Can I Maximize Income from My Vacant Land?

This picks up right on the heels of the previous question. A creative approach to turning vacant land into income-producing property may be nothing more than putting a sign on it that reads "For Rent."

> **Solution:** Look to the city's book of uses, the zoning code. This and some creative thinking on your part will give you some ideas on how to generate income from vacant land.

One of the first steps for creating income from vacant land is to find out what the current zoning allows, and if that is not productive enough, find the zoning you can likely get that will offer income potential.

11 Examples of Uses for Vacant Land That Will Produce Income

- Parking lot for local community members
- Parking for rental car companies and nearby businesses
- Storage lot for trucks, boats, and so on
- "U-Pick-It" strawberry patch or other crops
- Temporary grazing land for local farmers
- Used-car sales lot
- Equipment sales lot
- Landscape sales lot
- Fruit stand
- Flea market
- Paintball recreation area

The list can go on, but you get the idea. As you drive around your area, imagine what businesses might function with little or no property improvements other than showing the product they sell or displaying the services they render.

A longer-term program for a large tract of land would be the planting of growth timber or other landscape material. Do not let the land just sit there without putting in some effort to increase the value by improving it. Often, the effort alone attracts investors who suddenly are interested in a site they had not noticed before.

85. How Do I Entice a Buyer to My Vacant Land?

Every seller can be active in the development of a sound marketing plan.

> **Solution:** Take a look at the following nine strategies that
> work.

Nine Proven Strategies to Entice Buyers to Purchase Your Vacant Land

- Change zoning.
- Landscape for value.
- Target users.
- Show flexibility.
- Offer an exchange.
- Offer easy buyer terms.
- Lease back all or part of the land.
- Offer a "soft" joint venture.
- Line up a build-to-suit tenant.

Change Zoning.   As zoning is the determination of use, and use is the guide to value, you may find that by petitioning the governing bodies to grant you new zoning you will broaden the market for your property.

Landscape for Value.   Landscaping can produce long-range benefits regardless of what plants you put into the ground. The best results come from using landscape material rather than timber, but timber works in the right situation.

Target Users.   Once you know what your zoning is or has been changed to, you can make a list of all the possible users for the site. Do not worry about your idea of the viability of the site for users—let them make up their own minds. The key to selling anything for top dollar is to find that buyer out there who is attracted by what you have to offer.

Show Flexibility.   In a buyer's market, sellers have to be creative and flexible. By learning of some of the different creative-selling techniques, as well as creative-buying methods, you will be in a better position to deal with a buyer who may need to be enticed to buy your property.

Offer an Exchange.   One of the best ways to sell is to become a buyer. By turning the market in your favor (if it is a buyer's market), you may find you can solve your problem of selling your property by using it to acquire another one.

Offer Easy Buyer Terms.   Remember that deal about "I'll pay your price if you accept my terms"? Well, it works in reverse. "I'll take your deal and give you terms you will like."

Lease Back All or Part of the Land.   As the land is vacant, offer to lease it back for a short while. You might already know someone who will help you in this by taking some or all of the land and paying part or most of the rent. Remember, your goal is to unload the land, so if you have to eat some of the carrying costs (which you are anyway if you can't sell the land), then do so.

Offer a "Soft" Joint Venture.   If the buyer is a builder, then find out what he or she wants to build. Perhaps you will do better if you offer the land at a lower price and take part of the profit in the sale of the condos or commercial space that the developer/buyer is planning to build.

Line Up a Build-to-Suit Tenant.   Some people may have approached you in the past and asked whether you would build a facility and rent it (or part of it) to them. Keep those names, and when a buyer comes along who will build such a building, you may have a deal already done and didn't know it.

86.   What Are the Key Steps to Follow When I Sell My Raw Land?

One of the most important factors when it comes time to sell real estate is this: Did you have an exit strategy in mind when you purchased the property? If you did, and if you modified it along the way, you would be in the best position to sell your property. However, even most people who start out with an exit strategy generally fail to keep it up-to-date. Here is what you do.

Solution: Go back to the basics that follow.

Nine Key Steps to Maximize Profit When Selling Raw Land

- Have a plan that fits your goals.
- Gather demographic data.
- Show growth trends.
- Plot areas of similar use.
- Estimate future uses.
- Show how easy it will be for the buyer to acquire your site.
- Develop a marketing brochure.
- Insulate yourself from the buyer.
- Help the prospect mentally become an owner.

Have a Plan That Fits Your Goals.   Everything starts from this point, and by keeping your goals clearly in sight you will be less apt to make a mistake.

Gather Demographic Data.   As part of your marketing plan, this information can help you target the right buyer or deal with that buyer when he or she appears.

Show Growth Trends.   This reinforces the reason for growth of value. Steady growth trends should also indicate room for more growth. The buyer may want to know that there are still value appreciation possibilities in the site.

Plot Areas of Similar Use.   Show that a similar lot down the street has doubled in value over the past few years.

Estimate Future Uses.   This will help you target the right buyer and at the same time show flexibility in use to the investor who has no ready use in mind.

Show How Easy It Will Be for the Buyer to Acquire Your Site.   Offer a purchase package that works for the buyer. You do not have to be the cheapest property on the block to attract a buyer, only the one that works best economically. Use some creative techniques that allow the buyer to use the IRS to the best advantage and to save money while paying you more.

Develop a Marketing Brochure.   Give all the facts and then more. A picture can be worth a thousand words, and advertising pays off. Any up-to-date print shop can take your data, such as an aerial photograph you order from a company found in the Yellow Pages, and produce an inexpensive brochure that looks very professional. Sometimes, all you need to do is give that buyer something to think about at the end of the week when he or she has inspected a dozen properties and must now select the one to buy.

Insulate Yourself from the Buyer.   List the property with a qualified real estate agent. Pick one who handles the kind of property you are offering, and make sure the agent understands your goals and is committed to helping you reach them.

Help the Prospect Mentally Become an Owner.   Give a lot of "sold" signals as he or she is negotiating for your property. Until a buyer is mentally an owner, there is always the risk of losing the deal.

10

Income Property for the Twenty-first Century: Buying and Selling Residential Rental Properties

87. How Can I Successfully Acquire Residential Rental Properties?

Your good friends, that is, your goals, will have a lot to do with how you approach this task. Why? Rental properties have considerable flexibility in their use, in both present and future applications. For example, you may acquire a small rental property as your starter home, with the bonus of having income attached. This is how my wife and I started out, and more than 40 years later we still own that property. Its use has changed as our goals have changed. Its rents have gone from an average of $80 per month to an average of more than $800 per month. The original mortgage of $35,000 has long since been paid off, and the property has become a solid income producer. It is about to enter a new stage in my goals, by way of an interesting switch of events, too.

The neighborhood where the apartment is located was always a good one, and over the years it improved. It is near downtown, a mile from the beaches of Fort Lauderdale, and two blocks from the ever-elegant and popular Las Olas Boulevard, with its neat restaurants and fancy shops. The zoning is such that most of the old homes are actually built on lots that allow multifamily properties to be constructed. So now, properties are being gobbled up and razed to make way for elegant and expensive town houses. Some are selling at more than $1 million. Guess what change in use may soon occur to our little four-unit starter home plus income producer? Right, four elegant townhomes, one of which just might be our new "starter" townhome for our new phase of life.

Once you have your current goals firmly in focus, look at the area where you want to purchase property. Your primary goal is to seek properties that allow you to add value. This might mean tearing down the existing buildings and then enhancing the dirt under them by building something that generates a greater return (taking into consideration the added investment capital that is likely to be needed).

> **Solution:** Review the following checklist and seek properties that offer you the potential of added value from steps you undertake. Take special note that although this checklist is geared toward residential rental properties, it can be applied to virtually any kind of real estate.

---

12 Steps to Adding Value to Any Real Estate

- Know the local market conditions.
- Know the local income and expenses for rental apartments.
- Make detailed inspections.
- Watch out for hidden time bombs.
- Know the current and possible future zoning and uses allowed.
- Review existing leases and tenant records.
- Be ready to negotiate for time and terms.
- Look for management deficiencies.
- Seek seller financing.
- Know where to go for the best financing available.
- Have all solutions ready to go when you close.
- Set target goals with timetables.

Know the Local Market Conditions.   This step is never finished, because the local market is constantly going through changes. If you anticipate being able to find properties for sale that represent an opportunity for you, then the most critical element to master is your own local market conditions.

Each community and each area within that community will have something about it that makes it unique and different from any other part of town. The factors that cause this difference may be very subtle, such as a slightly lower tax millage (the percent of assessed value that represents the basis for real estate tax in any given year), a better water system, or a highly sought after school district.

Even the obvious, an area close to high-paying jobs, will create different economic layers within a small area, and those layers will translate into different rent zones. These rent zones will establish the likely maximum rent that can be charged. This is very important, because if your total experience is within the top demographic zone, and you are used to charging top rents, a deviation could cause you an unpleasant surprise. Rental property several blocks away may look very attractive, and you may decide to acquire it simply because you have applied your thinking and knowledge to that property; however, your conclusions could be very wrong unless you know the market for that rental zone. You need answers to the following questions:

What will lenders offer loans for with favorable terms?

What does the average investor expect to get as a return for his or her invested capital?

What is the trend for the neighborhood?
- Is employment up or down and which way is it headed for the future?
- Is this a buyer's market? Are there special factors that give buyers the edge?
- Which lenders in the community like to make loans on residential rentals?

The key to getting to know your local market conditions is to start observing what is going on. Attend local city council and county government meetings and read the public announcements in the local newspaper—each of these events provide early signals about what may transpire. Get to know several perceptive real estate brokers who have been working in the area for a long time. Ask them what they think may happen. Check with the city and county planning officials and find out what they have planned for the community.

Walk the neighborhoods where you plan to invest. This gives you a slow and easy way to observe everything. Sometimes you spot things that disenchant you about the area, which can be the most important thing that could happen. It is better to know the bad things before you buy. Best of all, walking the streets of the neighborhood can reveal a lot about the owners in the area and give you the opportunity to meet many of them personally. In a few months, you can become an expert on what has been happening and what is about to occur within your community.

Know the Local Income and Expenses for Rental Apartments. The income that you can expect to collect from a rental property can be accurately estimated once you know the local market conditions and the vacancy level you will encounter. The actual rent you can collect will be a function of the rent zone where the property is located. However, it is possible to raise a property from a lower rental category to a higher one when the geographic situation warrants it. For example, if you find a property that can be cosmetically improved and the standards of the units enhanced to match or exceed those in a higher rent zone, you can increase the income level of a property considerably. This factor then becomes one of the important elements you should look for.

While property management is approaching an exact science, many local factors affect the overall cost of the operation of any specific category of property. Make an effort to learn what the local expenses should be for any rental property you may be interested in owning. This is most critical for residential properties because this kind of property is usually more management-intensive, and fewer expenses can be passed on to the tenant. A shopping center owner is used to having add-on charges for common area maintenance (CAM), real estate taxes, sales taxes, advertising, security, and so on. The residential tenant's payment customarily includes everything (except, in most cases, electricity), and if any part of the fixed cost to operate a property increases, the owner has to absorb that cost.

Where can you get local income and expense figures? Try your local tax assessor's office. Often, this department conducts a detailed study on many different aspects of the local market. Assessors are looking for backup information to use when they appraise the real estate within their jurisdiction. This information may contain some or all of the following data, all of which is helpful to real estate investors.

- Income levels by geographic zones
- Property values by geographic zones
- Rent zones
- Numbers of rental units available by geographic areas
- Employment by geographic areas
- Vacancy factors for all rentals by zone
- Vacancy factors by percentage of gross revenue
- Growth trends
- Expenses for rentals by percentage of gross revenue
- Real estate taxes by percentage of gross revenue
- Utility cost by percentage of gross revenue

Make Detailed Inspections of the Property.   It is very important that a property inspection be completed by a team of professionals prior to your being fully bound by the purchase agreement. This is important for two reasons.

1. *You do not want to spend the time, effort, and money for a detailed inspection of the property and the review of that study unless you have the property tied up.*   Too many would-be owners have spent a lot of time, effort, and money only to have another investor snatch the property away from them.

2. *You do not want to be bound to the contract in the event you discover something wrong that exceeds your level of interest in that property.*   Some real estate agents and most real estate standard-form contracts provide for property inspections and

have a provision that requires the seller to "fix or repair" any item found to be in need of it. Often there is a blank space that the buyer or seller can fill in setting the maximum exposure for such risk to "fix or repair," and some contracts designate that if the blank is not filled in there is an automatic limit of 2 or 3 percent. This inspection provision may work for you, but in most situations, it will not be adequate to take care of all the possible problems that can come up. First, 2 or 3 percent off the gross price may be an amount the seller is already anticipating will be returned to you. Why? Because the seller knows something you do not but that you might find out about during the inspections.

It is more prudent to add to this standard inspection provision a paragraph that addresses your need to be absolutely sure that you agree to accept any potential problem that the property inspection may uncover. An example of wording I would use is shown here. Before adding anything to a standard form (or for that matter, before using a standard form), make sure you get good real estate legal advice.

> . . . and in addition to the terms of the inspection provision paragraph of this agreement, it is herein agreed between the parties that if for any reason the Buyer is not fully and completely satisfied with the findings of the property inspection report(s) that have been completed within the deadline for said inspections as provided, then the Buyer retains the right to withdraw from this agreement by giving written notice to the Seller that this agreement is no longer in effect, and in that event the Buyer shall have promptly returned any and all deposits that the Buyer has placed in escrow pending the closing of this transaction.

Practice your inspection procedure by looking at as many properties in the area as you can. Go to open houses held by real estate agents or owners, and call phone numbers on "For rent" or "For sale" signs and ask to be shown the property. You will learn what to look for by asking the agent or owner to point out the benefits of that property for a buyer or tenant.

Watch Out for Hidden Time Bombs.   Many time bombs await the lax real estate investor; do not let any ruin your investment dreams. Fortunately, if you follow simple guidelines, the chance of your being affected by a hidden time bomb is small. The key is to know the most damaging time bombs that might exist and how to avoid them. The following are some of the worst and most expensive problems to fix if they are present when you buy a property.

- Hidden legal action exists due to problems that occurred months before you even looked at the property.
- You have been given bad title and now have legal problems as a result.
- There are existing code violations and the local building department wants you to tear down a building because of them.
- Termites are having a feast on your property and you are faced with having to rebuild a major portion of the building.

- The lot size is much smaller than you thought it was, even though you have been given all the information that would have indicated the exact size long before you made an offer—but you did not know what to look for.

- There is another mortgage on the property that no one told you about, and the lender wants payment in full now.

- Existing contracts bind you to pay for leased equipment, telephone service, advertisements in the Yellow Pages, employment contracts, future advertising commitments, and so on. This can add up to a lot of money.

Fortunately, all these problems can be dealt with before you close on the property, at least to the extent that if one of them occurs you will have some recourse against the seller. This list of time bombs by no means contains all the things that can go wrong.

Know the Current and Possible Future Zoning and the Uses Allowed.
You already know that zoning (i.e., uses allowed) is a critical factor in any real estate. When it comes to old established neighborhoods, it is an absolute must to know this, because often the zoning is not what you see. In the case of my little apartment building, I knew when I bought the vacant lot, even though single-family homes surrounded it, that it was permissible to construct those four units. Nevertheless, what about the hundreds of old single-family homes that made up the neighborhood? All were zoned for multifamily properties. Do not trust what you see, because real estate is frequently contrary to the "what you see is what you get" (WYSIWYG) principal.

Knowing what the zoning is and what uses it allows can reveal the value of property that is otherwise underdeveloped when viewed from the present-day perspective. You might be surprised but many people do not understand or even know what the zoning is for their own home. They assume that it is what they see.

A word of caution about zoning. The local planning and zoning officials and the city and county commissioners can change the zoning and the allowable uses of your property right in front of your eyes, and you may never know what you lost or what was stolen from you. The rule of the land requires that they give you notice, and they do this with hard-to-read legal notices, often typed in all-capital letters, and filled with legalese jargon that even lawyers marvel at the skill it takes to tell you that your rights are about to be snatched away from you. Sometimes they make these changes so subtle that you do not even understand that what they are doing. They will tell you that they are not changing the zoning but are increasing setbacks, or reducing maximum heights, or altering the meaning of *floor-area ratio,* or reinterpreting some other building term. It is still theft, so be observant about what your elected officials and their hired staff can do to you.

Review Existing Leases and Tenant Records.   The ambiance of any rental project is determined by its makeup of tenants. However, to maintain a quality tenant list takes hard work and the willingness to incur expense to run credit reports and to follow up with reference checks. When management gets sloppy, anyone with some cash for a deposit may end up with an apartment. When the wrong kind of tenant moves in, the right kind frequently moves out, hastening the decline of the property. Lax management also generates sloppy rental contracts with provisions that do not meet your criteria: options to renew for several years, the right to paint the interior of the apartment without your approval, allowing pets, or an okay to have five children and three adults in a two-bedroom apartment. All these are conditions that you may not want to live with. When you find leases like this, put a provision in your purchase contract that the seller must "buy out" those leases and deliver those apartments to you free of any tenants you want to exclude. The seller may not want to do this, or the tenants may refuse to move, but at least you have made an attempt to rectify the situation.

Be Ready to Negotiate for Time and Terms.   In real estate, the single most important factor is time. In contract negotiations, the most important element is the term of payment. By combining these two factors, you have the basis to make any transaction work.

For example, you want to buy a 25-unit apartment complex and the sellers are asking $1 million for the property. It is free and clear of debt and the sellers indicate they will hold up to 80 percent of the price in the form of a first mortgage. There is a balance due at a closing of $200,000 if you buy the property at the asking price. You take a hard look at the tenant situation and decide that if you could increase the rents by 15 percent the property will be worth more than the asking price.

You make an offer as follows: You agree to give the sellers $200,000 at closing, and they hold a first mortgage of, $800,000. On the surface this looks like you have offered them the full price of $1 million. However, you structure this offer so that $120,000 of the down payment is two years of prepaid interest on the mortgage. The mortgage is at 7.5 percent per annum ($800,000 multiplied by 7.5 percent equals $60,000 per year). Your real purchase price then is closer to $880,000 ($800,000 mortgage plus $80,000 principal paid at closing). Notice I said *closer to* $880,000 rather than exactly $880,000. This is because you have prepaid $120,000 in interest, and that has a discountable value for the buyer. For the seller, prepaid interest is worth more because of time. If you paid the interest as it actually came due, say in monthly installments of $5,000 per month for two years, that total would still be $120,000. Now the seller gets the full amount of interest at day one, reinvests it, and earns additional money during the following two years.

In the preceding example, you have used both time and terms to structure a deal that pays the seller's price but allows you to use time and terms to your benefit. You could play with this concept and come up with several other possible combinations that may work better to help you achieve your goals and that would be acceptable to the seller.

Look for Management Deficiencies.   One of the most common reasons for a property to be for sale is that the owner is sick and tired of the hassle of dealing with the property. Even when there is outside management at the property, the problems that property owners face can be too much at times. Often, the management gets lax and sloppy because the owner does not seem to care about the property. When you see sloppy management in place, look very hard at the condition of the property itself, as well as the tenant makeup. Sloppy management can be fixed, and generally the result is a more profitable property. However, fixing can take time and money and must be reflected in the price you pay for the property, or you will start out with at least one foot encased in a bucket of cement.

Seek Seller Financing. Often, one of the best ways to soften the blow when acquiring a property is to use the seller's motivation to sell the property by having that seller hold a mortgage or assist in some other way. The earlier example of using part of the down payment as prepaid interest on a mortgage the seller holds is one such way to increase your cash flow over the time you are not making those payments. Also, by using exchanges of other real estate or items or services you have can become a criteria that will help you decide on which property to purchase. Clearly, if it boils down to three different properties, the one with the most motivated seller can sway you toward that property.

Know Where to Go for the Best Financing Available. You will not be able to rely on the seller's good graces in holding a purchase money mortgage. Part of your due diligence, which you should do prior to even looking for real estate, is to establish a working relationship with lenders in the area. It is a good idea to visit with the head loan officer or even the president of several banks and savings and loan institutions in the community. Practice by starting with the ones farthest away and work toward where you will be investing.

Have All Solutions Ready to Go When You Close. You want to list everything that needs to be or should be done that will have a fast impact on the income of a property. If the plan is to make some physical changes to the property, such as landscaping, new signage, or remodeling, you need to anticipate that you will likely need to obtain building permits for some, if not all, of that work. If that is the case, you want to get started with the paperwork side of any such work before you have closed on the property. Building permits can take weeks or months to be approved, so get started early.

Set Target Goals with Timetables. Everything you plan over which you have control should have a timetable attached to it. This helps you track your progress and will help build your confidence in being able to deal with the complexities of owning and managing real estate.

88. What Are the Most Important Risk Enhancers I Should Avoid When Buying Residential Rental Properties?

The last thing you need is to increase your risk when it comes to buying anything.

Solution: The key is to avoid risks by knowing what they mean, and then discount the price of the property accordingly. If you cannot buy the property with these risk factors already discounted, then avoid purchasing the property.

---

11 Special Factors That Increase Your Risk When Buying Residential Properties

- Deferred maintenance
- Nice cosmetics but obsolete equipment
- Hidden lease terms
- Hidden debt terms
- Environmental problems
- Late-paying tenants
- False income and expense statements
- An appeal to your greed
- A scheduled decline in income
- Income already maxed out
- Access limited due to new roadwork already planned

Deferred Maintenance.   Sloppy management or, worse still, absentee management usually allows a property to slip into disrepair. At first, it may be small items that begin to suffer from lack of preventive maintenance, such as air-conditioning equipment, pool pumps, plumbing, unpainted wood, cracked walls, and missing tiles or shingles on the roof. Also, landscaping may start to die because the lawn sprinklers no longer function, doorjambs may start to rot due to leaks, plaster crumbles, and wallpaper falls off the wall.

Some sellers recognize too late that their property has gone downhill, and in an attempt to sell, they paint and patch but do not really fix the problem.

When purchasing a property that has not been maintained for a long time, the word *caution* should flash bright red in your mind. The fact that the property is run down is not a reason to avoid it; indeed, it could be that the very reason the property is for sale is that it is a management nightmare for the owner. If you can turn the property around, you may find one of those gems you have been looking for. However, know what you are getting into. Repairs can be expensive and should never be taken lightly.

Nice Cosmetics but Obsolete Equipment.   Some properties look great and are, except that too much money has been going to maintain obsolescence. Even the best-looking property may have a lot of old equipment that is at or near the failure point. This is another reason why a detailed inspection of a property is essential. The key to avoiding this problem is to check the age of everything that will eventually need to be replaced. Start with the roof (you can count on a maximum of 20 years unless it is copper or lead sheeting) and work down. Everything electrical, mechanical, rust-prone, rot-prone, or subject to wear and tear should be listed, along with the maximum life expectancy for these items in your area of the country. You can find the life expectancy by checking with other property owners, lenders, and savvy real estate agents in your area.

When you find a 25-unit building that has 25 water heaters that are all 20 years old and look to be in good condition, you should anticipate that within a few years you will have to replace all of them. While the life expectancy will vary, the same can be said for kitchen appliances, air-conditioning equipment, asphalt paving, patios, wood decks, and so on. Add the costs that you would have to spend to bring everything up to present-day standards and take that sum into account when you buy the property. If the asking price is already low enough to take obsolescence into consideration, then move forward.

Hidden Lease Terms.   Sometimes a lease is modified by a letter or other communication that may not show up in the file the seller hands to you when you review the leases. Because of this, it is essential prior to closing that you obtain estoppel letters from each of the tenants to verify that the copy of the lease attached to the estoppel letter is full and complete. This letter simply states that the document attached to it (also described in the letter) represents the total of that contract as of the date of the letter.

Hidden Debt Terms.   Just as a lease can be modified, so can a mortgage or other debt. This may be something as simple as an extension of the payment terms to include two or more years' payout, an increase of interest, or the agreement to balloon the payment next year.

The same type of estoppel letter used to verify lease terms will work for mortgages.

Environmental Problems.   We live in an age where Love Canal, old dump sites, junkyards, and other possible pollution sources are rampant. Old farmland might contain underground fuel tanks that have been leaking oil into the ground for the past 40 years. Residential sites can be built on top of landfill that is leaking methane into the buildings. Former phosphate mines have been leveled and office buildings constructed over them only to have dangerous levels of radon gas accumulating in the basement and subsequently circulating through the building by the heating system.

The only way you can be absolutely sure there are no problems is to test the entire property environmentally, which can be very expensive. The alternative is to do spot-checks and obtain indemnification from the seller against problems that may occur later.

When it comes to environmental problems, it is best to avoid a property that has any potential problems.

Late-Paying Tenants.   There is nothing more frustrating than to have a building filled with tenants who are constantly late with their rent. If the seller or his or her management company has let that develop, you will be able to correct the problem, but you may lose some tenants along that path. Of course, you may *want* to remove these tenants from the building, in which case such violations may give you grounds to call their lease in default. If they choose to fight that action you could have more problems ahead of you. Be sure you seek legal help before you start a war with your tenants. Remember, the lease will not show whether tenants paid promptly or late, so insist on seeing a rent collection log. If the management does not have such a log, then ask to see the bank deposits, which should show a time schedule of tenants' payments. If the leases call for late-payment penalties, has the management collected such payments, or are they still outstanding? If there are any outstanding payments as a result of penalties of any kind, be sure that your purchase agreement does not allow the seller to charge you in the closing of the transaction for future collections that you may or may not attempt to collect.

False Income and Expense Statements.   Many property owners are very sloppy about the records they keep, and when it comes time to give a prospective buyer a summary of the income and expenses for their rental property it becomes fairy-tale time.

There are several ways you can get close to finding the actual truth, but it is unlikely that you will ever learn the whole story of income and expenses. The following list will help.

Five Important Sources of Income and Expense Data

- Sales tax reports may give you a way to figure out the actual rents collected. For example, if the owner has made a report to the state sales tax department, and the monthly reported average is $300, based on a sales tax of 6 percent, you can ascertain that the monthly rent on which tax was paid would be $5,000 ($300 divided by 0.06 equals $5,000). This works only when there is a state sales tax applicable to that kind of rental. Remember that sales tax may vary among states and communities within the state.

- Income tax reports to the IRS may show the actual amount of rents collected. Some owners do not want to show you their year-end income tax report because they have combined other income and expenses into one report.

- Bank deposits can be helpful to track the rent collections. To be accurate, however, you would need to see both the bank statements and the deposit log.

- Canceled checks are what the IRS would ask for in an audit, so why not ask to see them, too, but make sure you have the checkbook stubs as well. Often, the stub differs from the actual check. The idea is not just to know how much was paid out, but its purpose.

- Copies of bills and invoices that have been paid can give you a trail to follow that may lead to the truth. You may find a check that corresponds to a stub in the checkbook, say for $5,000, indicating payment for work to repair a roof when in fact the invoice shows payment for a cruise to Hawaii.

An Appeal to Your Greed.   Sometimes a seller will look you in the eye and tell you that the property is really a gold mine because so many of the tenants pay in cash, the laundry room is awash in quarters every week, and the money from your soda machines has to be collected twice daily.

Many owners of rental properties (as well as other types of income property) do not report every dime that is collected or earned. However, when the seller cannot verify what is collected and simply winks at you and pats his or her pocket, then watch out.

An appeal to your greed is the oldest game in town, and if you play it you may end up losing.

A Scheduled Decline in Income.   Sometimes an event is scheduled to occur that will guarantee a drop of income. This drop usually comes from a greater-than-usual-vacancy factor and a result of a decrease of potential renters or renters who shy away from the property.

A plant closing, a long-term strike, or some other labor problem can turn a small community into an economic disaster. A new highway, bridge, or other major construction can make the rental project undesirable for temporarily or even permanently. However, none of those future events may be evident right now. Make sure you know what is going to happen in the community that might affect the property you wish to buy.

Income Already Maxed Out.   Be careful of the gold mine that may be about to run out of gold. Some properties are operating at their maximum potential for the present time and use. If that is the case, your opportunity to add value will depend on how well you can maintain that revenue stream while at the same time reducing some of the expenses you have to operate the property and pay the debt service. If your interest in the property is to change the use, and you have no long-term interest in the source of the current income, you can actually get a short windfall from a maxed-out property by forgoing maintenance (and its attendant costs) for the short time it takes to end the existing leases.

Access Limited Due to New Roadwork Already Planned.   A natural bureaucratic delay occurs between the time the decision is made to do roadwork and the time it actually starts. Get into the habit of checking with the local authorities to see whether traffic to your potential new shopping center (or any other category of real estate) is to be disrupted. Nothing will spoil your plans to increase rents quicker than having access to your property severely hampered for six months or longer. Tenants with short leases may opt to move out, and filling vacancies will be difficult if not impossible until the work is completed.

There might be a bright side to this, however. Will the new and improved traffic have an ultimate benefit? If that is the case, you may need to renegotiate the deal to buffer the downtime while the work is going on. It is likely that the seller knew all about the pending work, too. It could even be the very reason the property is for sale.

89. Which Is Better to Own: Seasonal Rentals or Annual Rentals?

This is an interesting problem for many vacation areas of the country, or for properties that are located near sources of temporary renters. In areas where there is a strong rental market for the long-stay vacationer, furnished apartments can be an attractive way to go. It is not uncommon for mountain, beach, or lakefront areas to have two distinct strong rental seasons plus off-time when the owners can close down and take their own holiday.

> **Solution:** Decide first if the switch from one form of rental to another has the potential to produce greater income. Then review the benefits and expenses that come with that kind of a decision.

The first step in deciding which way will suit your goals is to get a 12-month calendar that shows all the months on one large page. Mark on the calendar, using a red felt pen, the number of days from each month that your property would rent and how much rent you could get if you were able to offer fully furnished units on a short-term basis. The actual term you choose can be a one-week minimum or any other period you might select for the kind of units you have.

To fill in the calendar correctly, you will need to do some homework. One of the best ways to discover this information is to look at properties similar to yours or properties you are contemplating purchasing that rent to temporary or seasonal tenants. Through a review of the year-round occupancy on a week-by-week basis, you will quickly spot the trends for your local area. The more such properties you review, the more accurate the information you will obtain.

While inspecting properties for sale, you can find an enormous amount of information that will be useful to you. The amount of rents that can be charged, the usual expenses a property will incur, and so on, begin to crystallize as you make comparisons. Of all the data you find, one of the most important will be what is called the *average daily rate* (ADR) or, in the event of weekly minimums, the *average weekly rate* (AWR). This is usually compiled on a monthly basis and is found by dividing the actual income collected for any given month by the number of nights (or weeks) of actual occupancy. For example, if a 25-unit property has a seven-day minimum and a gross rental collection of $50,000 for the past four weeks, during which time all units were rented, that would indicate an AWR of $500 per week.

Seasonal rentals will have some of their own management problems and expenses. First of all, the units are always furnished and may also require you to clean them, supply bedding and towels, and have working kitchens that are sufficiently equipped; and they will likely have items such as furniture, carpets, and fixtures that need to be constantly inspected and occasionally replaced or renewed.

Some benefits from this kind of rental are that revenue can be greater than the annual lease, and when it is off-season time you can lock the doors and take a cruise. Or you can offer working holidays to people from distant places to come and stay in your part of the world for a while, during which time they paint your building, fix the roof, replumb your pipes, and so on.

In areas where the revenue potential is strong and points toward seasonal rental, there may be some interesting possibilities that owners of annual apartments have not taken advantage of. A 12-unit apartment building that brings in $800 per month per apartment when rented annually might bring in $3,200 or more per month by renting it on a weekly basis at $800 or more per week. A year with 26 such weeks at 90 percent occupancy would bring in $224,640 in revenue per year ($26 \times \$800 \times 90 \times 12 = \$224,640$). This assumes that there is no revenue for the other 26 weeks of the year, just for this calculation.

What would it cost to operate this kind of a property? A good friend of mine who owns hotels suggested that it would cost half of the revenue to operate with good service and upkeep. That would mean $112,320 would go to the expenses, and the same amount would be net revenue. Rented at 100 percent occupancy as an annual building at $800 per month, the gross revenue before expenses would be $115,200 per month. After expenses, that could drop substantially, even though the expenses would likely be no more than 40 percent of the gross revenue. Therefore, the potential, using these numbers, is as follows:

Work 26 weeks a year and pocket $112,320.

Have little work to do with annual apartments and pocket $69,120 per year ($115,200 less 40 percent expenses).

To check this out in your own area, look at properties that are for sale that are operated as seasonal rentals. See how much money they take in and what they cost to operate. It will be a good education for you, I promise.

90. What Are the Key Steps to Follow When I Want to Sell My Residential Rental Property, and Why?

The path to getting the best value from any rental property is to have a sound business plan that is firm when it needs to be firm and flexible enough to allow you and/or management to adjust to the current changes in conditions.

> **Solution:** Establish your rental rules and regulations and be quick to react when tenants violate them. Follow this list of management techniques.

Eight Steps Designed to Maximize Property Value

- Keep good rent collection records.
- Maintain a property maintenance and replacement log.
- Keep income and expenses separate for each property.
- Establish a programmed upgrade policy.
- Keep expenses within local margins.
- Create strict tenant standards and enforce them.
- Document violations.
- Set the rental price 15 percent above the market.

Keep Good Rent Collection Records.   This works to your own benefit. Have a log or chart with each tenant's name and apartment number at the top. Indicate the monthly rent and the date due each month. When the payment is made, record the date and indicate whether a late charge was also collected, if applicable.

Maintain a Property Maintenance Log.   This is a very helpful log or diary to keep. Some of the important facts about the building should be recorded in this log in addition to maintenance records. For example, recording the brand name and color of paint used in the building will make it easier to touch up needed areas rather than trying to match colors. When repairs or replacements are made, the log should indicate the following information:

- Description of work done
- Date the work was done
- Apartment or building area where the work was done
- Name of repair or service company
- Quality of the work
- Date payment was made
- Check number and amount of payment

Keep Income and Expenses Separate for Each Property.   It is a good idea to keep a separate checking account for each rental property you own. This will allow you to account properly to the IRS and will make a review of the records by you or prospective investors much easier.

Establish a Programmed Upgrade Policy.   There should be some automatic upgrades that you effect when a tenant moves out of an apartment. In addition, certain repairs or preventive maintenance should be put on a timetable so that you keep ahead of the problems rather than constantly react to them.

Keep Expenses within Local Margins.   If your expenses are greater than the local standards, find out why. Utility bills that skyrocket may indicate a problem somewhere. A leak in a water line can increase your water bill to many times what it should be. A faulty electrical meter can give readings that are several times greater than the actual usage. A tenant may have a faucet that leaks but is afraid to tell you about it for fear that you will raise the rent. Track down expenses that are greater than the norm and deal with them.

Create Strict Tenant Standards and Enforce Them.   If you do not allow pets and yet find them in the apartment when you meet a repair person, then you need to act quickly to either make a change in the policy or enforce your rules.

Strong tenant rules generally do not scare away tenants; rather they help establish a certain quality of tenant. Whatever rules you establish should have some muscle behind them to allow for enforcement. Make sure you have an official, published list of tenant rules and regulations that spell out the rules that all the tenants are expected to abide by. This should be a part of the lease and should include a paragraph that says the tenant has read the lease and the rules and regulations. These rules can list things such as where tenants park and that the vehicle(s) registered with the building management are operable, have no flat tires, and are licensed; when and where they empty garbage; hours of quiet; which items they cannot store in their apartment or residence; and many more.

Document Violations.   At the first violation of any kind the tenant should be sent a notice of violation, which can be a form letter explaining that a violation was observed on a certain date. Be absolutely sure that the violation has occurred and that there is at least reasonable evidence that the tenant (and not someone else) actually violated the lease as you are alleging. Include a copy of the rules and regulations, or when the tenant comes in to pay the fine or penalty, ask that person to read the rules and regulations in your presence and sign a notice to that effect. This should be done even if the lease contains those same rules and regulations.

Keep a separate file for violations to the rules and regulations that shows what action you or management took and what the tenant did to comply with those rules and regulations. Put a copy of any correspondence in the tenant's file folder and make note in the violations file of letters or calls made to the tenant.

This record will prove to be important if you have continuing problems with this tenant. When you wish to call the lease in default and seek to evict such a tenant, this history of violations can be important in any court action.

Set the Rental Price 15 Percent above the Market.   When you attempt to sell your rental property you should make an effort to ascertain the market conditions. Have several real estate agents who deal with apartment rentals similar to yours in the same area give you their opinion of what the market price should be. Then increase that price by 15 percent and price the property at that level.

A well-maintained set of records such as I have just outlined will demonstrate that you have a pride of ownership and can enable you to continue to improve both the property and its tenant list. Best of all, prospective buyers will view such a list as a valuable tool for their smooth entry into the ownership of this property.

91. How Do I Set My Rental Prices to Ensure Low Vacancy and Top Rental Income?

Never buy a rental property unless you have a good idea of the highest amount of rent you can charge without sustaining vacancies.

> **Solution:** Balance rent charged with a tenant selection process that is designed to keep the property well maintained, and at the same time attempt to attract a quality tenant.

One of the keys to successful management of a rental property is to keep the vacancy factor at a low level. Some property owners attempt to accomplish this by keeping their rents slightly below the market in the hope and belief that this strategy will ensure them of tenants who stay put. While this can work, there should be no reason to do that if the market supports a higher rent structure. In any event, it is important that a firm and precise management practice accompany the lease and have fair but strong tenant control. Management should always attempt to use tenant selection as a way to improve the property. Effective management deals with both the rent level and tenant control. Begin by finding the right level of rent to charge.

Finding the Right Level of Rent to Charge

As mentioned earlier, it will be impossible for you to ascertain how much rent your property can bring unless you know the market, what the competition has to offer, how much they charge, and how your property compares to what is available on the market.

Compare rental properties in two ways. First, make a *categorical comparison* (e.g., two-bedroom, two-bath garden apartments in your area rent from $900 to $1,500 per month). Second, calculate a *per-square-foot comparison*. For example, say that in your area the average square footage of a two-bedroom, two-bath garden apartment is 1,300 square feet. If the average rental is as stated, the square foot equivalent would be from $0.692 cents to $1.138 per square foot per month (divide the monthly rent by the square footage).

The square-foot comparison enables you to fine-tune your market analysis once you have isolated the properties most directly comparable to your own. Before those detailed comparisons, make the overall categorical comparisons. If your final analysis indicates that apartments similar to yours are on the market for $1,000 per month in an annual lease, then this would set your maximum rent to ask at that level, or certainly no more than 15 percent above that amount. Naturally, if your apartments are larger or have special features, then your asking rent can be adjusted upward. Note the words *asking rent*. It would be reasonable that you could modify rental terms for the ideal tenant who might appear as well as to give you some negotiation leverage. Savvy tenants know that they can ask for lease concessions, and they frequently do and expect them.

The Tenant Selection Process

Many apartment buildings have a "For Rent" sign on the property even when they have no vacancy. When there is on-site management or the owner does not mind getting frequent calls about such a sign, this is a good idea. It enables the property owner to establish a waiting list for upcoming apartments. Naturally, many people on the so-called waiting list may not be around or still looking for an apartment when a vacancy comes up, but it does give the owners a backlog of possible tenants to call when they know an apartment is soon to be vacant.

Having a waiting list also gives the owner of the units the chance to take an application from prospective tenants in advance of the actual date an apartment is vacated. Unfortunately, many property owners do not put up a vacant sign until the previous tenant has already left and the apartment has been made ready (new paint, carpets cleaned, etc.). This method of looking for new tenants potentially increases the vacancy factor.

It is a good idea to charge the tenant a fee for the application to cover the cost of a credit check, and some management companies recommend that the fee be applied to the last month's rent if the tenant is accepted.

This application fee can be used to cover the cost to order a credit check of the tenant. You will find a list of companies that do these credit checks in the Yellow Pages of your local phone book under "Credit Checks."

The review of information given by a prospective tenant is very important. The makeup of tenants in any building can determine the future of that property. Because the person who lives in a building contributes to the ambiance and social nature of the facility, property owners should strive to be as selective as possible within the laws that govern tenant-landlord relationships.

The U.S. Civil Rights Act of 1968 (42 USC 3601-17) establishes that a landlord cannot discriminate against a person on the basis of race, religion, sex, or national origin. Many states have gone beyond the parameters of this act, and it is essential that you be aware of all the rights you have within your state as either a landlord or a tenant. Contact your local tax assessor's office as the first source for such information, and if not available there, call the closest board of Realtors to see whether they have a booklet that covers those rights. If that proves unsuccessful, call your state senator's office and ask the administrative assistant to help you find the information you are looking for.

11

Buying and Selling Income-Producing Properties

92. How Can I Determine the Best Kind of Income-Producing Real Estate to Invest In?

The selection of any type of investment you want to make should follow a detailed study of all the advantages and disadvantages of each kind of property.

> **Solution:** You should carefully review your own goals in an attempt to discover which kind of property is suitable for you in line with reaching those goals. The ultimate answer to "What do you purchase?" will depend on your own assessment of the following questions.

Ask Yourself Four Questions

- What are your own attributes and talents that will aid you in achieving success in a specific investment property?
- Will acquisition of any specific property help move you closer to your goals quicker and more safely than some other type of investment?
- Do you have the capital available to make the investment safely?
- Do you have the time to meet the obligations of the investment?

A careful analysis of these four items is essential. If you have not already done so, you should make a written list of all the talents you have that will aid you in achieving success through real estate ownership. Some of those talents may not be limited to any specific kind of real estate; for example, you might be a great carpenter, painter, or landscaper. The idea of being a good handy person, able to fix anything and build anything, may direct you to properties that are more in need of being fixed up. If you are a whiz at bookkeeping, then record keeping will not bother you. Management is often the area that is lacking, and usually only because of a lack of experience in dealing with tenants.

Your goals are the key to your ultimate success, so you need to keep them firmly in mind. I know investors who stick to one kind of property until they master it. It does not matter what kind of property it is, just as long as owning it fits your goal.

Having sufficient capital to handle the investment is important. The single most critical reason that people fail in a business or with an investment is because they are undercapitalized. This factor should not frighten you away from a challenge, as many investors have made it on nothing more than sweat equity. Sufficient capital does not mean you must have a bundle of cash in the bank, only that you should have enough so that you can weather a storm of vacancies.

For many first-time investors, the hardest part of a selection of any specific kind of property to buy is the inability to ascertain how much time will be needed to make the investment work. Time can work for or against you. Time should always be set aside, and, like a demanding child, it will require more time than you may have thought necessary.

93. How Do I Analyze an Income and Expense Statement?

When buying or selling an income property one of the key pieces of information for the buyer is the income and expense statement the seller presents as an accounting of the economic benefits of the property. Another name for similar information would be a *profit and loss statement.*

The essence of these statements or reports is to show the total income less the total operating expenses and in so doing provide a detailed accounting of debt service and depreciation. Take a look at the following example.

Example of an Income and Expense Statement

Income	
Gross income collected	$125,000.00
Expenses	
Advertising	750.00
Contract services	6,800.00
Insurance	2,550.00
Miscellaneous expenses	850.00
Professional fees	1,550.00
Repairs	6,500.00
Supplies	1,775.00
Taxes (real estate)	14,000.00
Utilities	4,900.00
Total expenses	$ 39,675.00
Net operating income	$ 85,325.00

This statement shows the total income collected without any accounting for total possible income less vacancy (as might be shown in a pro forma or estimated income and expense statement). The expenses shown are typical of bills paid and include real estate taxes.

Before looking at a more complex income and expense statement, you should be aware of what is missing, as well as what is apt to change once you become the owner of this property.

Two Important Items Often Missing in Income and Expense Statements

1. *The owner's time* is usually the most critical missing element. You will notice that there is no expense labeled *management.* Small businesses, small rental properties, and so on that are managed by the owner usually do not have a management expense included, or if it is included, it is for a resident manager and not for the actual time and work done by the owner. If your ownership plan includes outside management rather than your own efforts, then the expense of management becomes a real out-of-pocket cost that must be taken into consideration when you analyze the property or compare different properties. At best, you should take into consideration the time you must spend as manager of your own property and be compensated for that time and effort over and above the investment return. In essence, pay yourself a salary to keep your property honest.

2. *Adequate repairs and maintenance* would be the next item that is usually understated or missing altogether. Several years of poor maintenance can be glossed over with a coat of paint just before the property goes on the market, yet potential problems can surface in a short time when the paint flakes off the wall, termites swarm, or a heavy rain shows leaks at their best. However, by looking at several past years' income and expense statements, it is easy to get a picture of what has been done to keep the building in good repair. If you see either small amounts spent on repairs or big lump sums spent on repairs, you should question these amounts and ask for copies of bills. It is possible that what appears to be a major repair was really a cruise to Hawaii.

Four Items That Are Bound to Change Once You Own the Property

1. *Real estate taxes* are likely to go up the year following your purchase. The reason for this is the local tax assessor's office will see a record of the sale, compute the purchase price (or pull it from recorded documents), and assess the property, taking into consideration new information of the market values of your property along with similar sales in the area. If there has been a big positive change in the price of the property or other properties in the community, then the real estate tax can jump up quite a bit. The amount of possible increase will vary a great deal among communities, so it would be a good idea to sit down with an official at the

county tax assessor's office and discuss this situation in general before you enter into a contract to buy any property. A 50 percent increase in real estate tax can eliminate the profit you were counting on.

2. *Property insurance* is surely going to go up once the insurer sees what you have paid for the property. You might get by for a year or two if the insurance agent isn't paying attention to the local real estate market, but sooner rather than later your insurance will have to be tied to a true replacement value, not to the old value paid by the seller when he or she purchased the property.

3. *Debt service* may increase simply because you increase the total debt on the property when you acquire it. It is critical for every investor to make an estimated income and expense analysis showing all the possible expenses that would be likely after the sale.

4. *Depreciation* is an allowable deduction from income for tax purposes and is a very important calculation. The amount of depreciation that the existing owner shows as his or her own deduction will not (in most situations) be the amount of your deduction. This is because your tax basis, or book value of the property, should be much greater than the present owner's, unless you acquire the ownership corporation or exchange another property with a lower basis for the new one. In any event, depreciation is variable, so you should seek the advice of your own accountant, who knows your personal tax situation, so that a depreciation schedule will be established to obtain the maximum benefits allowed under the IRS rules.

An Example of an Income and Expense Statement with Depreciation

Income by departments	
Rooms	$ 500,000.00
Food	85,000.00
Beverage	300,000.00
Telephone	45,000.00
Miscellaneous	70,550.00
Total revenue collected	$1,000,550.00
Expenses by departments	
Rooms	245,200.00
Food	80,150.00
Beverage	195,000.00
Telephone	30,000.00
Miscellaneous	60,255.00
Total expenses paid	610,605.00
Cash flow before debt service	$ 389,945.00
Financial and other expenses	
Interest	250,000.00
Depreciation	200,000.00
Total financial and other expenses	$ 450,000.00
Net profit <loss> from operation	<60,055.00> loss

In the preceding profit and loss statement, the final result shows a loss; this is partially due to the introduction of depreciation into the picture. Depreciation is a "paper deduction" that accounts for the reduced life (and therefore reduced value) of the assets owned. Many investors consider this deduction the real value to many real estate investments because it allows the investor to shelter income from income tax. In investment days prior to the IRS revisions of 1986, this shelter meant much more than in 1993, as the investor converted this income, which would have been taxed as earned income, to a capital gains tax when the property was eventually sold.

Depreciation is an expense that needs to be taken into consideration at least partially as an eventual expense. Every item that is depreciated will someday need to be repaired or replaced to some degree. Over a period of time, the cost to repair and then eventually replace an item can far exceed the original cost. Investors need to pay very close attention to these items when reviewing any income property.

Departmentalized income and expenses show up in the profit and loss statement as total numbers, but there would be a separate accounting for the income and expenses in detail. If you are given only the summary page that shows totals, and not the makeup of those totals, you do not have sufficient data to establish a clear picture of the property.

94. What Are My Benefits When I Own an Income-Producing Property?

Most people tend to associate property ownership with wealth. If you have one, then you must have the other. While that is not always the case, ownership of real estate does offer benefits that owning other assets, such as stocks and bonds, for example, do not.

> **Solution:** Ownership of income-producing real estate has several distinct advantages and benefits for its owners. Eight of the most important follow.

Eight Major Benefits to Owning Income-Producing Real Estate

- Tax shelter
- Added income
- Long-term appreciation
- Benefits and allowable business expenses
- Personal housing
- Your own boss
- Employment for family members
- Opportunity to maximize OPM and double-dip

Tax Shelter.   Using depreciation as a tax shelter has already been described. For many investors, this is the prime reason to own income-producing real estate.

Added Income.   It is always nice to be able to add supplemental income. This is a clear and obvious benefit and a primary reason for owning income property. For some investors this income may be the rent from one or more units in a small apartment building where they also live; the rental income pays the expenses to maintain the property and pay off the mortgage. This is an example of using other people's money (OPM) to build wealth.

Long-Term Appreciation.   Consider that your investment is not only going to come with a basketful of benefits, it is going to go up in value as well. Long-term appreciation has been a major source of wealth for many of the wealthiest of people in the world. Well-located and well-maintained real estate can greatly appreciate in value over even a short period of time.

Benefits and Allowable Business Expenses.   When you are managing your own real estate, you will discover you can legally deduct many expenses that you might not be able to deduct if you were working for someone else. For example, if you own a property and use your car for some of the activities related to that property, have your accountant show you how to pay the car expenses from the rent you collect. Your personal insurance, travel, and other expenses often become legal business expenses when you follow your accountant's advice.

Personal Housing.   Solve your basic need for housing by providing an apartment or home for yourself as well as income.

Your Own Boss.   You can become your own boss if the property becomes your major or sole source of income. Financial independence is, after all, one of the elements of life that most people dream of obtaining. Real estate can be a good way to reach that goal.

Employment for Family Members.   Keeping the income in the family is a benefit of every family business. This can work nicely for real estate that is also a business. Employment for family members can be created and is often the main reason some investors acquire labor-intensive real estate. Farms, hotels, restaurants, and so on are often owned and operated by whole families, each member working toward their own economic goals.

Opportunity to Maximize OPM and Double-Dip.   When you borrow money to buy an income property, you are using other people's money. When you pay back that loan with money your tenants pay, you are double-dipping. Only with income-producing property can you build wealth quickly and safely this way.

95. Why Does Ownership of the Same Property Affect Different Buyers Differently?

Consider that a property is much like a boat; it might look the same to everyone who sees it, but each person may choose a different destination or derive a different recreational sport from it.

> **Solution:** The benefits and perks that come from real estate will depend on how you buy it, what you do with it, and what you want to get out of it. Discover how to adjust your purchase terms and debt payback to fit your goals. Apply your abilities where you can, and be ready to sell when the time is right.

A vacant lot can become anything that is allowable under the existing or altered zoning. A building can be converted into something else or removed so that cars can be parked on the empty lot created. Even the same use of a property can produce different end results, depending on the method of operation and the goals of the owner.

The multiple use and varied results that any property can give is one of the most important aspects that cause one buyer to be willing to pay more for a property than another. Investors who anticipate that one day they will want to sell their property should learn as much as they can about the different benefits their property can provide to different owners.

96. What Are the Steps to Successful Acquisition of Income-Producing Properties?

Every income property owner experiences firsthand the problems that come with property. Smart owners learn from these problems and discover how to avoid problems with future properties by following steps designed to help them find properties that fit their goals. The best steps follow.

Seven Key Steps to Successful Acquisition of Income-Producing Property

- Know your goals and abilities.
- Know the local real estate market well.
- Choose the right kind of property to buy.
- Do not bite off more than you can chew.
- Negotiate terms that will help you sell.
- Avoid short-term payback financing.
- Avoid pitfalls.

Know Your Goals and Abilities.   By the time you finish this book you will have repeatedly read of the importance of maintaining your goals just a step above your abilities. You do this because you should continually strive to improve your abilities. This creates a constant positive thrust, and as you enhance your abilities, you can move your goals up another notch or two.

The key to personal improvement is to increase your knowledge of the subjects that are needed so that your self-confidence is reinforced. The local adult education division of the junior college in your area may have a wide selection of beneficial courses, from bookkeeping to vocational classes in electrical installations to plumbing. Property management courses will prove to be highly effective and worth the time.

Know the Local Real Estate Market Well.   Everything you do in your community can have direct input to your knowledge of the local real estate market. One good way to keep on top of local events is to vary the way you drive to work each day so that you see what is going on, spot new "For Sale" signs, or locate the site mentioned at a planning and zoning hearing the night before. Several times each month, plan on spending a few minutes at an open house or talking to an owner of a building that is for rent or for sale.

Investors can become experts in their local communities. It is easy; all it takes is proper guidance to the steps you need to take, and the time to do it.

Choose the Right Kind of Property to Buy.   Take a look at question 92. Your success in real estate is tied to many things, and it is possible to overcome a bad investment. However, with care and the proper implementation of the comfort zone method of investing you will gravitate toward the right kind of investment. My own personal experience in real estate investing has been oriented toward vacant land. Other investors I know do nothing but buy restaurants that have gone out of business and convert them into theme restaurants that work. Still other investors look for single-family homes in areas where the zoning will permit more than one residential unit. They then use their carpentry skills to add, change, and convert the building to several apartments.

Your first investment may be targeted to attain the most basic of goals: your own housing, or a place for your business, or income to supplement your salary. Why not combine these into one acquisition?

Do Not Bite Off More than You Can Chew.   This relates to all facets of the situation: *money*, *ability*, and *time*. It is okay to push one or even two of the trio, but to tax all three to the limit may be stretching yourself a bit thin. Once you know how the game is played and have the rules down pat, then you can take a few risks, but in the beginning, do more homework and take less risks.

Negotiate Terms That Will Help You Sell.   When you make an offer to buy a property, and as you negotiate the counteroffers, keep firmly in mind that the terms you negotiate now may be critical to your selling the property later on. Because of this you should learn as much as you can about different forms of mortgages, techniques such as land leases, options to buy, real estate exchanges, release provisions to mortgages, subordination to other financing, and so on. Check the index of this book to learn where these items are discussed in more detail.

Here's an example: You are trying to buy a 10-unit apartment house. The seller is asking $400,000 for the property and has a first mortgage of $150,000. He has indicated he would hold some financing if he can get at least $80,000 cash down. You offer the full price of $400,000 and agree to give the seller $80,000 cash, providing he will hold a first mortgage of $170,000 on another property you own. Because the mortgage he is asked to hold is a first mortgage, you should negotiate for a lower interest rate than the seller might demand for a second mortgage. Where are you going to get the $80,000 cash? You make the offer subject to your obtaining a new first mortgage on the property you are trying to acquire at terms to your liking, and tie up the property for a period of 45 days in order to shop around with some of the local lenders.

Because all you really need to borrow is the payoff of the first mortgage, the cash to the seller, and the closing costs of the loan and the real estate purchase, your total loan need not exceed $250,000.

Payoff of the existing loan	$150,000
Cash to the seller	80,000
Closing cost estimate	20,000
Minimum loan request	$250,000

If you close on this basis, you will have acquired this property without spending any of your own money. The seller would get the $80,000 in cash he wanted and the balance of his equity of $170,000 in a first mortgage on another property. Your position in this apartment house is established, so you have $150,000 of solid equity. If you want to sell this property in a few years, after you have built up the value to $500,000 you would have many different options open to you: exchange your $250,000 of new equity for a larger property, sell and hold back a high-interest-rate mortgage, or do a combination of the two.

One interesting result of the preceding example is that the property on which you have moved the seller's $170,000 equity to a mortgage now has excellent financing on it should you want to sell it to an investor.

Avoid Short-Term Payback Financing. The preceding example would not be very attractive if the seller insisted on a three-year term on the $170,000 mortgage you gave to him. It surprises me how many smart investors end up buying property with short-term mortgages on them. Such short-term mortgages with big balloon payments can give you many sleepless nights and sometimes a bad day on the courthouse steps as your property is auctioned off. Do not let that happen to you.

Avoid Pitfalls. The best way to learn about pitfalls is to learn from the mistakes made by others. Contrary to what many people will tell you, the best way to learn is not to make the mistake yourself. However, if you do make a mistake, the key to learning anything is to acknowledge that you made a mistake, review the steps that led you to the resulting problem, and see whether you can pinpoint the moment when you could have avoided the mistake by choosing a different path or by making a different decision. Fortunately, when it comes to real estate, few mistakes are made that have not already been made by others, and virtually no pitfall can trap you that has not already trapped someone else. This book gives you many different lists and examples of such pitfalls, and as you deal in property and become an insider you will hear and witness other such problems and pitfalls.

The next question gives you a good insight into some of the most critical pitfalls that await unsuspecting buyers of income-producing property.

97.   What Are the Most Dangerous Pitfalls to Avoid When Buying Income-Producing Property?

It is easy to say "Avoid pitfalls" when in reality the difficulty is to know what you are to avoid.

> **Solution:** For most successful investors, getting out of trouble has evolved into the art of staying out of trouble. This requires experience, but fortunately it does not have to be your own experience that formulates the learning process.

The Seven Most Dangerous Pitfalls When Buying Income Property

- Having out-of-focus goals
- Exceeding your management abilities
- Being undercapitalized for the investment demands
- Having excessive and onerous debt
- Operation cost exceeding your estimate
- Income falling short of your estimate
- Having improper timing for your investment

Having Out-of-Focus Goals.   Good clear goals are the key to any kind of success. When you do not have those goals firmly in sight, or you stray from the intended plan by letting another goal slip in front of your primary goal, then you are headed for trouble. Of all the pitfalls that await you, the most damaging is to start off without your goal firmly in focus. There are many distractions that cause people to stray from the chosen path, and while an occasional diversion may not put your desired goal out of reach, the trip can be longer and rougher than expected.

One way to help keep your goals firmly in focus is to have goals that are attainable, measurable, and staged as intermediate stepping-stones that constantly move you forward. One other aspect is very important: the goals should be written down and 100 percent approved by any other family member who is a party to the attainment of the goal. By having the goals in writing, there is no misunderstanding about what you set out to attain. You should set goals that you can reach, even though you might have to stretch from time to time to get there. Unreasonable goals that sound good, such as becoming a millionaire by the end of the year, may not be realistic for you.

Nothing can damage your self-confidence more than to strive constantly to attain something that is impossible. Start small; take short steps; and plan goals that can be attained simply by your own actions (e.g., "I will meet three city officials this week"). Taking small steps is easy to do and, if connected to a plan, will have a positive result. Small goals are also measurable; using the previous example, you know when you have met all three officials; if it was easy, plan on four next week. However, remember where all the steps are leading, and view the final result as the long-range goal that is firmly in your sight.

Exceeding Your Management Abilities.   Some people find it absolutely impossible to delegate any task to another. These people pride themselves in never asking anyone to do anything they would not do themselves, and because they think they do it better than anyone, they do it themselves. These people generally are poor managers and will have difficulties in owning property that requires management of people.

The technical aspects of management of real estate can be learned by most people. Record keeping, dealing with prospective tenants, setting up leases, and dealing with lawyers, accountants, and other professional advisors are relatively easy to learn once you have taken the time to acknowledge that you do not have a skill. Either set about to learn it or hire someone else to do it for you.

Know your own limitations and do not exceed your abilities—but do take steps to increase your skills so that you can expand with confidence and with a good chance for success.

Being Undercapitalized for the Investment Demands.   This is not a question of inexperience. Some of the most experienced people in the hotel business, for example, get a few friends together and buy a hotel to run on their own only to have miscalculated the need for deep pockets. When the money runs out, it might be possible to borrow more, but that may just feed the fire, and the added expense of the increased debt may hasten the foreclosure sale.

Undercapitalization means there are no funds reserved to cover normal expenses if income drops for an unexplained or unanticipated reason or to pay off expenses that were not expected, despite how well the income flow is maintained. Acquiring a property with the hope that income will go up and expenses can be held at the status quo or even reduced is very risky. Some people manage to succeed and are able to make a lot of money from a very meager start. However, far more people lose their savings and their dream by not having sufficient capital to cover expenses.

Having Excessive and Onerous Debt.   Overleverage, that is, a greater cost to pay the debt than the property produces in income, is not by itself a wrong business decision if other benefits offset the negative cash flow and if you have the capital to carry the debt. When you buy a vacant lot, for example, or another property that has little income, and you plan to add more buildings or construct something new that will have a solidly positive income stream, the initial debt can be higher than any income produced. Excessive and onerous debt is another situation. This is when the debt is structured with *doom* written all over it. Short-term debt, for example, looks good because the payments for five years are interest-only, or even less than interest-only, with the principal that is owed growing. This kind of payment schedule maximizes cash flow, allowing you to meet the debt payments from the cash available, and works only when something definite is going to occur that will allow you to bail out of that debt.

When you structure debt on a property you buy, you should attempt to obtain mortgage terms that give you room to build the income and increase the value of the property in ample time to meet the demands of a possible refinancing of the property. Real estate cycles up and down, and when people get really hurt it is because they were thinking "up" while the market went down. To refinance in a down period may be impossible, and unless the lender wants to weather the storm with you, you can lose the property to the bank or the previous owner who is sitting on a second mortgage that just came due.

Operation Cost Exceeding Your Estimate.   The more properties you look at before you buy, the greater your opportunity to learn about the income and expense for that kind of property. However, to learn, you have to do homework, and this means that you should dig into the books and records of the properties you look at, not just take a 10-minute tour through the property with the real estate agent.

A seller should be willing to let a prospective buyer look at the income and expense records of the property. Even if you have no real interest in a specific property, if you ultimately expect to own a similar property, then spend the time to learn what is going on in the market.

See if your local tax assessor's office publishes a standard of income and expenses for the type of real estate you are interested in. If it does not, sit down with one of the appraisers and ask a lot of questions about standard expenses for the area.

The key to expenses is to know what they should be and then to take the expenses that the seller represents to you as "100 percent real" and see what might be understated or missing altogether. Make your own pro forma estimate, and be very sure that the criteria you use are not below the standards for the area.

Income Falling Short of Your Estimate.   Unless something happens to cause a high level of vacancy, the income picture is the easiest to estimate if you stuck to the market rents for an area. A buyer gets into trouble when a property is being upgraded from the top rent for the zone to a higher rent that the area may not immediately support. Old habits are hard to break, and if other buildings in the same area are asking 30 percent or greater less per square foot, your nicer property may stay vacant a bit longer than you would like it to.

Other events can cause a dramatic downward shift in your rental income. For example, a new roadway in front of your property could be a great long-range benefit, perhaps, but for the next two years your property may become a vacant building while the roadway is under construction and no one can get to your property. Bridges, overpasses, tunnels, and other improvements in local infrastructure can bring similar results.

Having Improper Timing for Your Investment.   Timing is very important. You get the seller at the right moment and she says yes; you are pleased because you read about the new hospital that is going to be built across the street and you plan to expand . . . but it turns out that a homeowner's association around the corner interferes with the hospital plans through 10 years of legal hassle. Many different things can happen that will bring a sudden change in plans. Some of these changes may be to your immediate benefit, others quite the opposite. However, most of these events do not happen overnight, and when they do, a prudent investor should have anticipated that possibility. When in doubt wait. If you do not want to wait, then go to contract for the property you want to buy with an option that gives you the time you need to learn whether the timing is truly right.

12

Managing Your Real Estate to Maximize Profits and Minimize Problems

98. What Are the Secrets to Successful Property Management?

Management of any rental or investment property falls into three categories of importance: Focusing your goals, attention to the property, and the quality of your tenants.

> **Solution:** Remember these three categories of importance. What I call the "open-eye" system of management requires you to carefully maintain all three elements of the property.

The idea is to know your goals and to periodically update them to any changes in your investment life. Everyone will have to take stock of what they have and where they want to go. You may start out debt-heavy as you start your investment portfolio, only to discover 20 years later that your investments are free and clear and have become cash cows. Have you now arrived at your investment destination? Or have you not made the necessary adjustments to keep up with your evolving goals?

Look at the following 13 secrets to successful property management.

13 Secrets to Successful Property Management

1. *Manage to meet your ownership goals.* By this, I mean it is important that you have a plan for the real estate itself. If you are going to tear it down in a few years, you will manage it differently than if you want to hang onto it and continually improve it so that it produces more income. If your investment is a temporary flip because you know the value is going to jump through the roof (you discovered something grand is about to happen to the area), then you may do nothing but wait.

2. *Have an adjustable exit strategy.* Whether you knew in advance about a significant impending change, you should have an exit strategy that is designed to take care of emergencies should they occur, as well as to provide you with steady improvement of the property and the tenants. Always remain true to your goals.

3. *Always look to upgrade your tenant demographics.* A good tenant is critical in any long-haul situation. However, a good tenant can also be one who will gladly agree to rent your property (which you are going to flip or tear down shortly) on a short-term lease, or a lease you can cancel on a short notice.

4. *Have clear unmistakable rules.* Make sure they are not only enforceable, but also strictly enforced.

5. *Do a detailed tenant check.* This means checking credit, employment, references, banking history, whereabouts of family members, and so on.

6. *Be responsive to tenants' needs.* Whenever the property is inspected, the tenant should sign a statement verifying existing problems and then later acknowledging that those problems have been corrected.

7. *Keep detailed records.* Document payment records, repairs, improvements, outside work done, payment of expenses, and so on.

8. *Publicize goals for continual property improvement.* Let your tenants know what you plan for the building only if you are then going to follow through. When the planned improvements are finished, let them know you have attained your goal.

9. *Know your market and seek to increase your rental category.* By a slow but continual upgrade of the property, you can increase your rental base.

10. *Practice problem prevention management.* Act before a small problem becomes a big one. As you learn to anticipate problems, you will stop them from occurring.

11. *Make periodic property inspections.* Record the date of the inspection and exactly what is discovered, both good and bad.

12. *Make needed damage repairs immediately.* When you set a pattern of immediate response, you can also expect the tenants to respond to you in an equally timely fashion.

13. *Promptly impose penalties to tenants when allowed by the lease.* A rental complex is a closed system, and when one tenant breaks the rules, it will not be long before others will attempt to try the same.

99. What Can I Do If My Tenants Are Constantly Late Making Rent Payments?

Dealing with tenants who constantly make late payments can be a problem, and the larger the rental complex, the greater the problem can become, unless you are aggressive in dealing with this situation.

> **Solution:** Maintain contact with your tenants, and review the answer to question 98. For the specific problem of late payments, be sure to follow these five steps to effectively deal with late payments.

Five Steps to Effectively Deal With Late Rent Payments

1. Document the payment records so that you have a detailed record of that tenant's payment schedule. This will give you proof of a tenant's rental record and allow you to act quickly if the delay in payment starts to grow.

2. Make a detailed property inspection to ensure that there are no other problems building. Following the inspection, ask the tenant to sign the inspection report that it is correct. If you discover there are no problems in the apartment, that everything is working properly, and that there is no evident damage, then so indicate. If there is damage, then address it immediately according to the remedy under the terms of the lease.

3. Give notice of pending default to give the tenant every benefit of the doubt about the situation. Let your tenants know that your computer will send out past-due notices automatically if their rent is not received during the grace period. Tell them you treat everyone the same and they should not think they are being singled out.

4. Renegotiate to convert the lease to a month-by-month basis if the tenant has a long-term lease and you want to see whether that tenant can become a better-paying and more responsive tenant.

5. When nothing else works, start legal proceedings according to the laws of your state to evict the tenant. You can stop the procedure anytime the tenant convinces you that he or she is worth keeping.

100. What Can I Do If I Get Stuck with a Bad Check?

Virtually every business experiences an occasional bad check tendered for payment of goods, services, or rent. This is not always intentional, but it can be chronic.

Generally, the chronic situations come with sob stories that can melt even the hardest heart. You know how it goes. "The check is in the mail" is just the first line you will hear. "My bank has made a mistake" may sometimes be true. "My deadbeat ex-husband is five months late on child support" may come as a surprise, because you didn't know there was a child living in the apartment. End-less lies and excuses issue forth. I have even bent my own "crack the whip" rules on occasion.

> **Solution:** **Bone up on the tips that follow.**

- *Get to know your state laws governing bad checks.*   Each state can have a different set of rules about how bad checks are treated.

- *Do not accept postdated checks.*   If you take a check with a date later than the current date, then you have no recourse to collect on the bad check. This rule may vary among states, so check the laws in your state. It is better to tell the tenant you will hold the check for a few days and let them trust you rather than the reverse.

- *When a check comes back marked nonsufficient funds (NSF), you can legally collect a redeposit fee plus a service charge to handle the check a second time.*   If your lease has a late-charge penalty, you may collect that, too, by following your legal rights. One step would be to send notice to tenants that they are in default and that you are applying their security against the bad check. They must either make up the security deposit immediately or they will have violated their lease and be in default.

- *If that does not produce results, check with the court that has jurisdiction over small claims in your area.*   Get the forms and data necessary to use the legal system to collect what is due you.

- *One word of warning: When you follow legal proceedings you should be aware that the tenant may have more rights than you suspected.*   It is possible for you to be 100 percent in the right and the tenant to be several months behind in rent, and you may still have a long drawn-out battle to evict. If the tenant has any reason to make a counterclaim against you, the process can go on for quite a while.

- *Be prompt and legal.*   The key is to make sure that you, as landlord, have documented your position correctly and have not tried to sidestep the law in any way. The very moment that you feel the tenant is going to be difficult you should get the advice of a good real estate lawyer.

- *Commercial leases and residential leases will give tenants different rights.*   Know what those rights are (in your state and local jurisdiction), and make sure you do not violate any of a tenant's rights.

101.   How Can I Reduce or Eliminate Tenant Complaints?

Most complainers have more than one agenda—generally three important ones. The most important is to be recognized; the second is to voice their frustrations or dislikes in the form of a complaint; and the third is to obtain some satisfaction or remedy.

> **Solution:** You never want to completely eliminate tenant complaints. You want them to focus on situations that need your or your management's attention. Circumstances that need to be corrected should be dealt with promptly.

When you can generate the right kind of complaints, you can continue to move the property in the right direction for continued improvement. Continued improvement can generate increases in rental income. Your tenants are your on-site watchdogs and should be encouraged to bring any complaint to your attention.

You will reduce or nearly eliminate tenant complaints by removing the reason for such complaints. When you have a chronic complainer, you need to take steps to distinguish what is genuine and what is not; then have a meeting with the tenant in your office or someplace other than the rented premises and explain that you have made every effort to keep the tenant happy, and if the tenant is unhappy he or she is free to vacate the property.

I have had virtually every possible kind of chronic complainer. Some can drive you nuts if you let them, and others are always pinpointing the same subject or object of the complaint. Some tenants will exaggerate the item about which they are complaining. Nonetheless, the most important question you and management should ask yourselves is this: Is this tenant helping the overall management of the property? In essence, is this tenant worth keeping? If the answer is no, then let the tenant know that the frivolous complaints must stop or else the tenant will not have his or her lease renewed.

102. How Can I Avoid a Tenant's Midnight Move?

A midnight move occurs when a tenant, for whatever reason, wants to break his or her lease and simply disappears one night. Such tenants are most likely behind in their rent, so they wait until midnight some dark evening, rent a truck, and take whatever is valuable. These valuables may include *your* refrigerator, range, and air-conditioning equipment, and your tenants depart for unknown vistas. They leave behind old sofas, moldy mattresses, and soiled clothes; if the refrigerator is not worth taking, that, too, may be filled with rotting food, because the electricity was shut off by the power company.

> **Solution:** Remember the value of a good tenant. Know that the only way to keep good tenants is to do your homework both before and during their occupancy of the property.

The only sure way to avoid this is to ensure that it will not be worth the effort for the tenant to make such a move. Most midnight moves are tenant responses to getting behind on their rent to the extent that they feel it is better to bail out of the place and start over somewhere else.

This tactic may be a blessing for you if they will make the move and leave the premises in good shape. However, this is often not the case.

Midnight movers have been known to strike out against the property and trash the place. A good friend of mine leased his beautiful restaurant to another operator when he became ill and was unable to continue the operation himself. The tenant could operate the restaurant for up to five years and exercise an option to purchase anytime during that period.

However, it turned out that the success of the restaurant was due to my friend's good management, and the new operator turned the business into a nearly instant failure. Instead of simply asking to be relieved of the lease, or even simply exercising a midnight move, these renters fell behind a couple of months and then trashed the place. They poured concrete down the toilets and drains, broke all the china, punched holes in walls, and poured milk on all of the soft material (carpets, chairs, covers, etc.). In a matter of one weekend, with the ac set on heat, those items were ready for the trash heap.

Periodic inspection of the property and its business operations (if a commercial lease) can often provide clues that a tenant might be headed for economic problems. This, in turn, leads to late rent, then a couple of months of late rent.

Strict rules on late rent allow you to act quickly, before tenants fall behind to the extent that they owe you more than the security deposit. As soon as that happens and they owe you more than you are holding in security, there may be nothing you can do to stop a midnight move, so concentrate on getting tenants out before they damage the property.

Nine Telltale Signs That Tenants Are about to Disappear

- Their parked auto(s) are inoperable.

- Rent is getting harder to collect.

- Inspections show sloppy housekeeping.

- A check with the power company reveals they are late with utility bills.

- All windows are suddenly covered with drapes, blinds, or paper so no one can look inside.

- Phone calls to them are not returned.

- Your keys no longer work their locks.

- Power has been shut off.

- Mail begins to back up. (If you have not acted by this time, the midnight move has already happened.)

---

103. How Do I Evict a Tenant with the Lowest Cost and the Fewest Problems?

The steps to evict a tenant who does not want to leave can be very costly and time-consuming. Often, the biggest cost, however, is not the legal charges but the lost rent and the cost of repairs needed to return the property to rentable condition. Review the answer to question 101.

> **Solution:** The key then to keeping the cost down is to make sure that you act quickly when the situation begins to develop. The mistake that most landlords make is to wait until the tenant has gotten way behind in the rent rather than initiate a legal proceeding to get the tenant either to comply with the lease or to get out. Follow these three steps.

Three Steps to Save Money When You Must Evict a Tenant

1. *Act immediately when a tenant's rent is late.* This means to start your procedure that may lead to court action. See the answer to question number 99.

2. *Know your rights.* Have your lawyer keep you informed about the current rules and any changes to your local and state laws and tenant eviction procedures.

3. *Send proper legal notices to the tenant the first moment you can.* This does not mean you need to follow through with the eviction, but why wait? You can tell the tenant through a phone call to expect a legal notice, but that you would like to work the matter out as quickly and as painlessly as possible. But protect your legal rights and start the time clock running. It can take a long time to evict a tenant who does not want to move and who has a lawyer friend who may file or threaten a countersuit out of spite.

104. When Can I Use a Small-Claims Court to Collect Past-Due Rent?

Unless tenants have fallen way behind in their rent or you are dealing with a commercial lease and the sum of rent for a single month exceeds the amount you can sue for in a small-claims court, you can use this action in an attempt to collect what is owed to you.

> **Solution:** Stop by your local clerk of the circuit court's office. Ask for information on how to file a claim to recover unpaid rent through the local small-claims court.

Small-claims court is designed for people with relatively simple claims to settle. If you file such a claim, you can see a lawyer both before and after the court hearings (a very good idea), but the lawyer cannot attend the court hearings with you. However, if you are the one being sued, your lawyer can appear in an attempt to have the suit moved out of small-claims court and put into a jurisdiction where the lawyer can attend to the trial.

Each state may have different rules for their small-claims courts, and each judge may have his or her own preferences ideas about procedures. You can go online and search for some free help on this subject that is beyond the scope of this book. Search phrases such as "small-claims court for [your state]," "[your state] small-claims court," "how to file an action in small-claims court," and so on. You will find help.

The amounts for which you can sue vary, but generally are up to $5,000. We are talking about rent and rent deposits here, so late rent can be bundled into one suit if it does not pass the limited amount; or divide it into monthly increments and file a new suit for each one.

There are fees for this, but it is possible that you can move the problem to a quick solution through the small-claims court. Keep in mind that some states, like Florida, will require tenants to post a bond or put up the amount of rent in question if they plan to defend their rights or if they think they have grounds for a countersuit. This requirement often brings the people to the table to seek a compromise or to immediately pay up.

105.   What Kind of Lease Should I Use?

You must remember that a lease is a formal agreement that binds the parties to its terms. The *lessor* is the owner of the property being leased, and the *lessee* is the person who is leasing the property. The lessee will have payments to make and a time period in which to make them, the term of the lease. Options to renew and other forms of extensions can make the lessee's obligations grow into a considerable sum of money. As the lessor is giving up the property to the lessee, the lessor's rights to access are somewhat limited. The potential for damage to the property can be considerable, and that is one of the areas of risk for the lessor.

> **Solution:** Every lease you offer to a prospective lessee
> should protect your rights as property owner without
> violating the legal rights of the lessee. As these rights may
> vary from state to state, you should avoid using a standard
> contract. Have a lawyer either draft a lease format specific to
> the laws of your state or recommend a standard lease form
> that has been approved for use in your state by the local
> lawyer's bar association, the state board of Realtors, or
> another qualified group.

No matter what, as a property owner you should have a lease that is owner-friendly. This means that you should avoid a standard store-bought lease. The type of lease that you can find in a business supply store is apt to be a middle-of-the-road type of lease. While it may properly address some of the legal aspects that are important for both you and the tenant, it is apt to be slanted toward the tenant and not the property owner.

Do you want to know where you can get a great landlord lease for free? Spend a weekend and visit several large rental apartment projects in your area. Ask for a copy of the lease; you can bet management has spent a lot of money with some top-rated law firms in the area to hammer out a lease that protects the company's rights completely. Read over several of the leases from such projects to make sure you understand everything. If there is something you do not understand, ask the rental agent of that project to explain it to you. In a very short time you will be able to spot the difference between a lease that protects you as a property owner and one that does not.

Take the best lease and let your own attorney look it over. He or she may want to add something that fits your specific situation better or that brings the document up-to-date with current laws and or regulations.

106. What Are the Most Common Problems Encountered in Property Management, and How Can I Solve Them?

I have tried to pinpoint the majority of problems that are common to most leases, either residential or commercial.

> **Solution:** In general, most of these can be dealt with quickly and without any lasting problems by having strict rules, requiring tenants to pay their rent on time, applying swift penalties, dealing with valid complaints, and maintaining the property in good condition. Take a look at each of the following 42 specific problems and how to deal with them.

---

42 Common Management/Tenant Problems and Tips on How to Deal with Them Quickly and Successfully

- Abandoned property
- Application left blank
- Animal smells
- Barking dogs
- Bounced checks
- Broken windows
- Clutter in windows
- Clutter and trash around the area
- Common-area maintenance
- Damaged carpet and damaged furniture
- Derelict cars and other vehicles
- Driveway damage due to oil or gas leaks from vehicles
- Drugs
- Encouraging pests to breed
- Extra people living in the apartment
- Fire or fire hazards

- Fleas
- Hanging things out of windows
- Holes in the walls
- Illegal or improper use of rented space
- Improper number of tenants in the facility
- Improper parking
- Inoperable appliances
- Inoperable and/or unlicensed vehicles
- Letting plants die
- Loud music and other noise
- Missing items
- Nails in the walls
- Nonpayment of rent
- Not keeping yard maintained
- Offensive behavior
- Parking lot damage
- Peeping Toms
- Shoddy tenant improvements
- Storm damage
- Theft and other crimes
- Trash accumulation
- Uncleaned appliances
- Unreported casualty damage of any kind
- Unruly or dangerous pets
- Unruly children
- Use not conforming to lease terms

Abandoned Property.   Often, tenants in residential and commercial properties depart the leased premises and leave behind something they do not value or otherwise want or that they don't have room in the trunk of the car for. If the departure follows the proper rules, that is, the tenants notify you they are leaving at the end of their lease and you inspect the property. If there is damage (e.g., a blood-soaked chopping board where they cleaned chickens for their KFC knockoff restaurant) or even worse problems, put them into the "another deduction from the security deposit" column of your checkout list. Sadly, most leases do not end quite that way. First of all, the tenants don't notify you promptly, or they leave early after being late for the month's rent and notify you that you can take their security deposit in lieu of that month's rent. There you are, the security is used up in rent, the tenants are gone, and the damage plus the cost of a new chopping block far exceed the deposit. What do you do? At this juncture, not much. You can take them to small-claims court, or simply be glad they are gone. You stop this from happening by nailing them when their rent is late. When their lease is up, you watch them like a hawk until they leave.

Application Left Blank.   Okay, so you forgot to have the tenants fill out an application and you took their word on everything without checking out any references. Every lease should have a detailed application for residential leases and a full information sheet for commercial leases. It is wise to get Social Security numbers, copies of driver's licenses, and a list of several banking references as well as personal and/or corporate references, with contact names, phone numbers, and addresses. Then *check on them*. Credit checks are not expensive and can be done online with little more than a Social Security or corporate tax ID number. Have prospective tenants pay the costs for the credit check. Be sure you know how to read the credit report; if you have never seen one, you may not know how to navigate its material. Have someone from the credit reporting company walk you through the first couple.

Animal Smells.   Your lease should clearly spell out every detail governing a pet. Be sure to include conditions on disposal of animal waste and a strict penalty for failure to abide by the rules. Conduct a periodic inspection of the leased premises whenever pets are allowed, and a pet-cleaning deposit should be added to the lease to provide cleanup money in the event the animal has soiled or damaged items in or on the property. Be sure that the cleaning deposit requires the tenant to replenish the cleaning deposit as needed.

Barking Dogs.   Noise control of all kinds should be a part of the lease rules and regulations. Have strict time periods to eliminate loud music, TV, radio, and parties and to cover barking dogs at all hours. Make the violation of this and any other rule or regulation a default in the lease. The best way to deal with this problem is, of course, to forbid dogs on the premises at all. Generally, I do not mind one cat per apartment, but dogs are out. Cats and other pets that do not bark are okay in my book. If the dog is needed for the tenant's assistance, then the law protects that tenant's right to have a dog as long as it truly is of assistance.

Bounced Checks.   Check your state laws about bounced checks. In most situations, it is illegal for a tenant to give you a check from an account that has no funds to cover it. However, from a practical viewpoint this can happen to almost anyone, so you may want to be lenient on the first occasion. Make sure that your lease allows you to charge the tenant for any returned checks. You can add a reasonable service charge to the bank charge, as well as impose a late penalty, but make sure the lease spells out these charges in detail.

Broken Windows. When tenants break something that is part of your property they should be charged for it. If you have a security deposit, then apply the repair against the security deposit, and make sure your lease requires the tenant to replenish the security deposit.

Clutter in Windows. Unsightly window clutter can be a problem for residential and commercial property owners. Rules and regulations can limit this problem by addressing it directly. Commercial tenants should be allowed to display only approved (by the landlord) signs that also meet the local sign ordinances. Residential tenants should be restricted from having any window clutter visible from the exterior of the property during daylight hours.

Clutter and Trash around the Area. Strict rules and regulations should either make it a violation to clutter or provide a common-area maintenance charge to pay for the cleanup.

Common-Area Maintenance Payments. It is a good idea to have a CAM charge regardless of what kind of rental property you have, provided there's more than one tenant. This spreads the cost of trash pickup, driveway vacuuming, window cleaning, and so forth among all the tenants. The CAM provisions in the lease should allow you to pass through increased costs directly to tenants with a minimal notice (say one month).

Damaged Carpet and Damaged Furniture. There is a clear and undeniable difference between normal wear and tear and absolute destruction of a carpet; however, there are many levels of carpet conditions. Some landlords have found that with the right tenant a carpet can last 10 years or more, while other tenants seem to wear out their carpet in 12 months. Keys to any kind of damage control follow.

Three Keys to Damage Control

1. Periodic inspection of the premises
2. Prompt application of a security or damage deposit to repair any damage, requiring the tenant's prompt replenishment of the security or damage deposit
3. Good screening of prospective tenants

Derelict Cars and Other Vehicles. Your lease should have a provision dealing with derelict cars, abandoned cars, and other vehicles such as boats and trailers. Make sure your lease has a provision for such situations. Require tenants to remove any such vehicle that is clearly inoperable or has not been moved for the past 30 days (unless they have permission in advance from you for such an event). You can issue parking stickers that have expiration dates shorter than the term of the lease. This will require tenants to renew the sticker (provided their lease is current, all security and damage deposits up-to-date, etc.) or risk having their car or other vehicle towed away.

Driveway Damage Due to Oil or Gas Leaks from Vehicles. Periodic inspection of the driveways will quickly pinpoint the problems—and likely the person whose vehicle has caused the problem. Failure to stop this can cause the damage to increase, as oil and gas can be quite destructive to asphalt and unsightly on any type of driveway.

Drugs. Periodic inspections of the rented premises may disclose evidence that there is an illegal drug situation present. I once discovered beautiful green potted plants growing in an apartment I manage. Security staff staked out the place for a couple of nights and observed brisk sales of crack taking place from that apartment. Any illegal circumstance must not be tolerated. The police should be notified of your suspicions and any evidence you believe to be present.

Encouraging Pests to Breed. I do not mean the tenants will urge palmetto bugs to propagate their species. Sloppy housekeeping, however, the careless dumping of trash, feeding of pets and other animals outside the premises, and other unsanitary practices can turn a nice apartment into a roach motel.

Include pest control to the inside and outside of all rental property on a weekly basis. There is an added bonus of this weekly service. It gives you access to make a weekly inspection of the property, and whoever does the pest control spraying should have an inspection chart to follow.

To give you some muscle to deal with this problem, make sure your lease provides that tenants must remove any pest-breeding conditions at their own expense or be in default on their lease.

Extra People Living in the Apartment. Have a visitor provision in the lease that reasonably allows family members or other guests the right to visit overnight. But if extra people suddenly move in, well now, they might be guests or subtenants. Any subtenants should be required to sign a lease, and perhaps the monthly rental would increase (that's a business decision you can make at the time, or put it in the lease ahead of time). A family of 10 living in your one-bedroom rented apartment is not a nice thing, and damage is bound to occur.

Fire or Fire Hazards. Any kind of fire is something to be avoided. Periodic inspections will help you spot hazards or dangerous habits that may lead to serious problems. Burn marks on the edge of furniture may indicate cigarettes left burning; burn holes on carpets or furniture indicate a need for immediate action. Storage of combustible materials, improper overloading of electrical wiring, and other such problems can be averted by following six steps:

Six Ways to Reduce Fire Hazards

- Get a fire department inspection of the entire building on a periodic basis.
- Follow all recommendations.

- Have more than the minimum number of fire extinguishers available for tenant use, and have them serviced as required.
- Post fire evacuation routes and instructions and make sure every tenant has read the material.
- Provide smoke alarms for every apartment and test them on a regular basis.
- When making periodic inspections, make fire hazards an entry on the checklist.

Fleas.   Most animals are apt to get fleas. While those fleas may seem to go unnoticed by the pet's owner, as soon as that tenant has moved out and removed the source of food for those pests, they will live in the carpet and furniture of the premises, waiting for any unsuspecting visitor. Fleas must be dealt with swiftly and on a continuing basis whenever pets are or have been in an apartment.

Some chemicals used to kill fleas and their eggs are noxious and hazardous to humans, so use of these chemicals must follow the manufacturer's detailed instructions. Even so, the residue from such chemicals may cause reactions days after their use, so a thorough cleaning may be necessary a day or so after using them.

Things Hanging out of Windows.   Unless you are living in Naples, Italy, where it seems to be fashionable to hang things out the window, apartment buildings of any kind should have strict rules on where clothes and other items may be placed to air out or dry.

Holes in the Walls.   The lease should require tenants to repair any holes in the wall caused by them, including nail holes, doorknob holes, and so on. Periodic inspections will catch many of these problems before the tenant has moved out, and the repair can be dealt with from the security or damage deposit. As with other deductions from a damage deposit, be sure that the tenant replenishes the deposit. Problems can be dealt with from that security deposit, unless you have been lax and let the tenant use the security as the previous month's rent.

Illegal Use of Rented Space.   The lease should be specific about the use to which the rented space can be put. If you discover that the use is illegal with respect to the zoning or other laws, then the tenant would be in default. To ensure that the tenant has been given proper notice about the legality of use, spell out clearly what use is allowed: for example, "Said apartment to be used as a single-family residence only," or "Said office space to be used as private offices for an insurance company. . . ."

Improper Number of Tenants in the Facility.   Several elements need to be addressed in this situation. First and most important is the fire code dealing with the maximum number occupants in the premises. You cannot exceed this amount under any condition, and the tenant needs to know what it is. The second matter deals with the local zoning ordinances that govern the use of the space. These ordinances may have subtle restrictions such as the number of parking places that must be provided for certain use. A medical doctor, for example, may occupy 1,000 square feet of your commercial space, and the code may require you to provide a set number of parking spaces for that tenant. Based on that, you can comply with the city parking code. However, what if a month later the doctor brings in a partner and the city requires you to double the parking spaces for two doctors? Can you do it? Can you stop the first doctor from bringing in a partner? Are you in trouble? You may be.

Other city ordinances may limit the number of families that can live on any plot of land. If you have a tenant whose family suddenly grows to include several generations and distant relatives, you may have a violation caused by this tenant. Does your lease spell out the tenant's obligation to abide by the local ordinance? Or did you forget to tell the tenant what that ordinance was?

The third aspect, and perhaps the most important, is the limitations you may want to impose on your tenants. If you want to limit your tenants to single people, then address the issue by having a rental schedule that goes up for every extra occupant living in a rental unit.

Improper Parking.   See the section on derelict cars and other vehicles.

Inoperable Appliances.   It is not unusual for a tenant to move out without ever complaining about anything, and when you do the cleanup to ready the property for a new tenant, you may discover that several burners on the range do not work, the heater in the bathroom is burned out, and three electrical switches are inoperable. Why? Because the tenants damaged them and were afraid (rightly so) that you would charge them for the repair. The key is to look for these things in the periodic inspection, and whenever possible do not let tenants move out until a complete and thorough inspection has taken place.

Inoperable and/or Unlicensed Vehicles.   Your lease should have a provision that allows you to have such vehicles towed following a notice to the tenant of this situation. A reasonable time to allow the tenant to repair or relicense the vehicle should be provided.

Letting Plants Die.   This becomes a problem when you lease a home to people and they have full control over the landscaping. It is not uncommon for tenants who are paying the water charge to shut off the sprinkler system the day they move into a property. If they also have a lease whereby they agree to mow the lawn, they may never mow it at all.

The key is to provide a yard service that is given the responsibility to make periodic inspections of the sprinkler system and to ensure that it is working properly and is in fact being used. Lawn and plant trimming should also be given to this or another yard service company and should be a part of the rent, over which you have absolute control.

Periodic inspections will help ensure that your beautiful lawn and plants do not die.

Loud Music and Other Noise. See the section on barking dogs.

Missing Items. The midnight move that many tenants perform with great finesse may include taking your refrigerator, sinks, carpet (if in good condition), and even wall switches. This is theft and is punishable if you can prove the items taken were yours to begin with and that the tenants took them.

Step one is to document items on the property when tenants move in. The lease should spell out in detail what the items are and their condition. It is a good idea to get into the habit of taking photographs of the interior of a property before tenants move in (to be used in court as a contrast to the "after they moved out" photograph).

Step two is to make sure you have information that will help you track down tenants after they have moved out. This will require a detailed tenant's information sheet to be filled out. On that form should be information such as driver's license number, Social Security number, credit card numbers, banking account numbers, references, who to notify in case of accident, employment data, references, auto registration and tag numbers, and a photograph.

Nails in the Walls. See the section on holes in the wall.

Nonpayment of Rent. The lease should have strict payment schedules with penalties for nonpayment. If tenants begins to slip behind and ask you to wait for the rent, and you are willing to do so, have them sign a simple agreement that you will apply the last month's rent (if one has been paid) against the current rent due, provided they make up the shortage within an agreed-to number of days, plus a late charge. This works as long as it is not the last month of their lease, in which case you will never see a dime for damage once they skip out at midnight.

When rent is constantly late, you may want to renegotiate the lease as the first step for the ultimate solution to the problem. For example, if your tenants have a lease that is for a year or longer, their rights may be such that removing those tenants by legal means is long and costly, even when they are several months in default on rent.

When tenants are constantly late, sit down with them and negotiate a new lease that changes their rent due date from 10 days after the first of the month (as an example) to 20 days after the first of the month while at the same time putting them on a month-to-month tenancy.

When your tenant is on a month-to-month tenancy, your rights to give notice to evict through legal channels improve in your favor.

Not Keeping Yard Maintained. See the section on letting plants die.

Offensive Behavior. It is difficult to protect yourself and your other tenants from a tenant who is offensive and abusive to other people. However, such people will usually violate other more reasonable and easier-to-govern rules and regulations, such as loud noise codes.

If you have a tenant who is suspected of doing illegal things on the premises, you may want to increase your inspections.

Parking Lot Damage.   See the section on derelict cars and other vehicles.

Peeping Toms.   This is an illegal activity for which it is often hard to get legal remedy from the local authorities. If this happens, you should first check the police list of pedophiles in the area. Do not assume that such tenants have notified the authorities of a move into the state or within the community. If their name is on the list, let the police know the person is now living at the address of your property. Be sure to report to the authorities any neighbor's or tenant's complaint of any Peeping Tom activity.

Shoddy Tenant Improvements.   When a tenant makes so-called improvements to a property, it is critical that the improvements be made only after your specific approval and that the tenant obtains the required city permits. Often, tenants circumvent these steps and undertake improvements that would not be allowed by you and that have not been permitted by the city. When this happens, it can place you in the uncomfortable and expensive situation of having to remove the unpermitted construction.

There are two basic ways to approach tenant improvements. The first is to allow reasonable improvements that in your mind actually enhance the property. After all, it is your property, and if the tenant wants to make changes to the structure or layout that will later benefit you (at no cost to you), then there should be no logical reason to object. Keep in mind that any work done must be by licensed personnel and any required permits should be obtained.

The second situation is that such tenants' improvements are only good for those tenants and that when they move out (perhaps sooner than either you or they expect), you will have an expense to return the property to its original or usable condition. When this is the case, you should expect a deposit equal to the estimated cost to restore the premises when they vacate the property.

In every case, make sure your lease provides that any fixture or improvement made by the tenant becomes your property. Also, it should be the obligation of the tenant to maintain these new items or improvements under the terms and conditions of the lease, and that unless specifically indicated, the tenant may not remove the improvements or items at the termination or cancellation of the lease. The nonremovable provision is critical, because even simple removal of a piece of machinery can leave gaping holes in floors, ceilings, walls, or all three that can be very expensive to repair.

Storm Damage.   Check with your insurance agent to make sure that you have good coverage on the building; then be sure to include in the lease that tenants must insure for damage to their own windows due to storms or vandals. Some tenant's insurance will cover these items only if the lease requires the tenant to provide that insurance.

Whenever you require a tenant to provide insurance of any kind, make sure they do the following.

Four Factors with Tenant's Insurance

- Includes you as coinsured
- Covers adequate minimums
- Deductibles no greater than the damage or security deposit you are holding
- Sends you a copy of the insurance policy and evidence of each renewal payment (or new policy each year)

Theft and Other Crimes.   See the section on Peeping Toms.

Trash Accumulation.   Periodic inspections will prevent this from becoming chronic. When you spot this problem, immediately act to have it cleared up. Then follow up with more inspections to see that it does not start as soon as your back is turned.

Uncleaned Appliances.   Until you have a midnight mover leave you with a refrigerator full of rotten food and an oven that could be used as a test lab for creatures from outer space, you do not know what unclean really means.

Periodic inspections, prompt use of damage or security deposit to rectify the problem, and then replacement by the tenant of that deposit is the only way to get your tenants to clean up.

Unreported Casualty Damage.   Tenants may not report damage because they are afraid you will charge them for the item. When there is another violation at hand (e.g., the failure to maintain required insurance that would have covered the loss), tenants will be doubly wary of informing you of the damage. Inspections are the key to finding this problem before it grows.

Unruly or Dangerous Pets.   To prevent a costly legal action from another tenant who has been bitten by an unruly or dangerous pet, is scared by escaped snakes, or is sickened by piles of animal waste on the walkways, make sure you have strict pet rules and regulations. One way to put some muscle in this part of your lease is to require a special and costly deposit for pets. Use it to clean up animal clutter, repair damages to the apartment, clean carpets and drapes, and so forth.

When tenants move in and do not have pets, make sure the lease designates that any pets they acquire in the future must be approved by you in advance (you can limit the size), that they agree to the pet rules and regulations in advance, and that they will pay you the added pet deposit.

Unruly Children.   Both working and nonworking parents can have unruly children who can create havoc in an apartment complex. Restrict hours for outside play, limit the areas for such play, and promptly impose penalties for violations.

Use Not Conforming to Lease.   When you discover that tenants are using the rented space for a use that does not conform to the one stated in the lease, even though the use is legal, you should act quickly to notify them of the violation. Explain that this violation causes a breach in the lease agreement and that if the use does not cease, then they must vacate the facility.

13

How to Pay the Least Capital Gains Tax and Other Real Estate Tax Matters

107. How Does Owning Real Estate Help Me Save on Income Tax?

There are a number of ways that you can save on income tax through the ownership of real estate.

Solution: Review the following most common methods to use the IRS as a wealth-building tool.

Seven Ways Real Estate Can Reduce Your Income Tax

- Paper deductions from real income
- Untaxed appreciation
- Section 1031 tax-free exchange
- Capital gains exclusion
- Installment sale
- Untaxed benefits
- Other IRS benefits

Paper Deductions from Real Income.   The IRS term is *depreciation*, and this is a paper deduction of a portion of the value of an asset as it grows older and, likely, less valuable. Prior to 1986, depreciation was the major reason that many people invested in real estate. The goal was to shelter income, and the investments were called *tax shelters*. The idea was to use money that was going to be paid to Uncle Sam as income tax for the down payment on a property that would generate sufficient tax deductions to offset the investment. As the investor was now an owner of real property with no real cost, the investment could be rather risky, which might mean big gains. There was little or nothing to lose.

The rules for sheltering income changed, and due to changes in the amount of depreciation that can be taken, the tax shelter business is no longer the way to get into real estate risk-free.

However, depreciation still exists, and the opportunity to shelter income remains a benefit to property ownership.

Here is how it works. If you purchase an apartment building that is worth $250,000 and the land portion is worth $50,000, you would have a depreciable value of $200,000. The depreciable portion of the total value is made up of the building and its contents, as the land portion of the transaction cannot be depreciated. Because of this, it is important that the purchase agreement separate the different values into their three categories: *land*, which is not depreciable; *building*, which is depreciable over the long term; and *contents*, or personal property, which generally has a much shorter life (furniture in a hotel, etc.). Each item of the building and its contents would have a life that has economic value. (Groves and orchards, for example, have a tree life, for which there is a similar depreciation available. Also, if minerals are mined from a parcel of land, those minerals would eventually be depleted, but the basic land cannot be depreciated.)

The IRS publishes standards for the different items that make up the building, giving each a minimum number of years over which you would be allowed to deduct the total value. It is possible to spread out the depreciation over a longer period of time, say, to take a straight-line deduction of the whole $200,000 over 40 years, giving you an annual deduction of $5,000, or to separate each item into its minimum life terms, thereby increasing the early years of depreciation.

The method you chose should be designed to match your investment plan. Clearly, if you do not need the depreciation now but anticipate increased income in your later years, you would want to push the allowed depreciation to the period of time when it will be most important to your tax savings.

Depreciation as a tax shelter is, however, a temporary situation. The deduction is allowed as an expense from your otherwise taxable income, but it also decreases your tax basis (book value of the property), and when you ultimately sell the property you will have a capital gain, which will be taxable. This capital gain is the total amount of proceeds from a sale less the cost of the sale and your tax basis. Therefore, what you do not pay tax on now you will pay tax on later. However, the best part of this is that you choose when you make the payment by determining when to sell the property; if you choose wisely, the tax you pay could be less on the same amount of gain due to a lower tax bracket at the time you elect to make that payment.

The actual calculation of the value of your assets that can be depreciated and the amount of depreciation and the methods available to you can be somewhat complicated and is beyond the scope of this book. This comment should encourage you to seek competent tax advice from your accountant or tax lawyer, who, knowing both your situation and goals, can help you plan the best approach to this matter. The key is to have a good idea of your future earnings so that you can balance your taxable income by using potentially available depreciation to lower your overall annual tax level. For example, your accountant tells you that next year you can take either a $15,000 or a $5,000 depreciation on the building you just purchased, depending on which method you choose to use. If you know that you are going to have a bonus of an extra $15,000 in revenue next year, you might be wise to choose the higher depreciation. But keep in mind, this decision should be based on more facts than I have presented in this limited example, and each investor will have different goals and a different set of circumstances.

Untaxed Appreciation.   If you put $100,000 in a bank and let it appreciate through the interest it earns, you will report that interest every year as a taxable income. This is an annual event and applies to savings deposits, bonds, mortgage interest paid to you, and any other form of interest you earn regardless of whether you take it out of the bank.

Real estate, just as stocks and rare stamp or coin collections, may go up in value, and that value, unless realized (through a sale or other taxable disposition), is not taxed. Therefore, the value you invest in real estate appreciates without hindrance from any deduction for income taxes.

Section 1031 Tax-Free Exchange.   A Section 1031 tax-free property exchange allows you, under the right circumstances, to exchange your investment in real estate for another investment property. This type of exchange is greatly misunderstood and is often called a *like-kind exchange*. This term is part of the reason a Section 1031 exchange is misunderstood. Like kind does not mean that you can take advantage of this IRS-approved transaction only by swapping a farm for a farm or an office building for an office building; like kind signifies that an investment property must be exchanged for another investment property.

My book, *The Tax-Free Exchange Loophole: How Real Estate Investors Can Profit from the 1031 Exchange,* published in 2005 by John Wiley & Sons, explains this IRS technique in great detail. As with many IRS programs, it is important that you do not attempt to use Internal Revenue Code (IRC) Section 1031 without competent legal and accounting help. Not every transaction will qualify to start out, and even for those that do qualify, the benefits may not be sufficient to warrant the added cost to accomplish the transaction under 1031 rules. In addition, there is a timetable that works like this: You have a total of 180 days from the day you close on a qualified property until you must acquire the replacement investment (can be more than one property). During that 180 days, you must, within the first 45 of those days, identify to your closing agent (also called an *intermediary* or a *facilitator*) what you have chosen as a replacement property. The key here is that the entire transaction must be set up carefully in advance, and in no way can you or someone close to you (even your own lawyer) receive the proceeds of your sale.

Nonetheless, this is a powerful tool. If you, like many thousands of investors, have a large capital gain that the IRS would love to tax, and you can qualify for Section 1031 treatment, you can reinvest the entire proceeds of the sale and not have to pay any capital gains tax at all. You can also roll over the next investment using the same rules, provided the IRS does not change them, time and time again. In the end, if the final property passes on to your estate it is possible that all that gain over all those years will never be taxed.

Capital Gains Exclusion.   This is the latest IRS-designed benefit to owning real estate. It occurs only with your personal residence, and has some interesting rules attached to it. I discuss this in detail in question 51, so I recommend you turn back and review this wonderful loophole. In essence, however, it will allow you to take advantage of a capital gain on your personal residence provided you have owned it for five years (subject to some leeway described in question 51) and have lived in it for a minimum of two years during that time.

The exclusion allows $250,000 per person, meaning a husband and wife or joint tenants would have a total potential of $500,000 of capital gain excluded from tax. Say you and your wife sell your home for $1.5 million. It costed you $250,000 twenty years ago, and your capital gain of $1.25 million would have a deduction (exclusion) of $500,000, bringing the taxable portion down to $750,000 ($1,250,000 – $500,000 = $750,000). If the sale price on that same home is only $750,000, the taxable gain would be completely wiped out ($750,000 – $250,000 – $500,000 = 0).

Installment Sale.   An installment sale is a method of selling whereby you hold a mortgage for part of the proceeds of the sale. This form of sale works for any kind of real estate and is not limited to your residence, as is the one-time exclusion of $125,000 under Section 1034. Under this provision, the percent of gain to the overall price establishes what would be taxable in the sale. For example, if your basis is $50,000 and the value is $150,000, the ratio is 50/150,000 or $\frac{1}{3}$ basis and $\frac{2}{3}$ gain. If a buyer pays you $50,000 cash and you hold a $100,000 mortgage, two-thirds of the cash down would be treated as a gain, and two-thirds of every principal payment against the mortgage balance would also be gain and taxable as such.

However, nothing requires you to write a mortgage that contains principal payments, and in a situation where the seller wants to maximize interest income, an interest-only payment schedule may accomplish those goals nicely. Only when the mortgage is paid off would the gain be taxable.

Even when the mortgage has a more normal amortization of principal, it may be advantageous to the seller because it will spread the gain over several years and thereby avoid having the proceeds of the sale push that taxpayer into a higher tax bracket.

The preceding discussion shows briefly how these IRS-approved provisions work. As with any IRS rule or regulation, there are apt to be changes in the mechanics of the rule, so it is wise to check with your accountant well in advance of contemplating any tax-related event.

Untaxed Benefits.   Any benefit that you would normally pay for out of earnings on which you pay taxes becomes an untaxed benefit. For many people this becomes the single most important bonanza to ownership of real estate.

Consider the family-operated motel or small hotel. The property cannot only support wages for many members of the family, it can also provide food and housing, transportation via the company car, insurance through usual fringe benefits, and so on.

Other IRS Benefits.   In any comprehensive investment and estate planning it would be prudent to discuss current state and federal inheritance laws with your tax and estate lawyer. It seems that there are always some rules and regulations that are going through modification or enactment. It is important that any estate plans take into consideration these plans and changes of old plans.

No matter if you spent thousands of dollars setting up your future estate in such a way that your heirs will receive the maximum benefits from your own hard work, a plan enacted yesterday could have a major and detrimental effect on those plans. Review your plans annually, and instruct your lawyer to contact you if any changes in IRS and state laws, or the interpretation of such laws, will affect you and your estate.

108.   How Do I Keep Good Tax Records That Will Help Me Survive an IRS Audit?

Just the mention of those three letters, IRS, can cause a CPA's heart to flutter with anxiety, so why should you be different? The key to dealing with the IRS is simple and painless.

Solution: **Follow these seven key steps for your tax records and you will be on solid ground during any audit.**

Seven Key Steps to a Painless Tax Audit

- Know your legal situation.
- Have detailed records.
- Cross-reference checks and bills.
- Know your tax basis.
- Show changes to basis.
- Take the honest approach.
- Do not fear the IRS.

Discuss Your Situation with a Qualified Tax Professional.   With your accountant or tax lawyer, go over all details of your situation that may present tax problems or wave red flags and that an IRS agent will find interesting and may want to examine further. An IRS audit can be a time-consuming and costly event for you. Keep in mind that many accountants and tax lawyers ask this question: Should we take an aggressive approach to saving on tax obligations? Or should we take the approach that is more submissive and try to avoid any kind of red flag? The reason they will ask this is just in case you have not given them a 100 percent accurate picture of your situation. During an actual audit, the IRS agent(s) in charge can suddenly ask for far more data than you ever thought possible, and finding it might be difficult (because it went down with your yacht two years ago).

Record Everything in Detail.   The exactness of your records will enable you to get maximum deductions on all your expenses. Many people overlook small items, or they improperly document medium-sized payments. Even though those expenses are deductible, if you lack the background data to support the deductions, they may be disallowed in a nitpicking audit.

Cross-Reference Checks and Bills.   Show a clear pathway of items paid. At the time you or your accountant gets a bill, make a note on the bill, and on the check write down the details about what the payment was for. A bill with the heading "Lacore, Inc." for $2,500 without a clear notation of the purpose for the bill could be for just about anything, and the IRS audit agent may set that aside for a closer look. However, if the bill and the check both indicate "repair to office building boiler," then it is less likely to become an issue. Such cross indications will be helpful to you when you need to check on something for your own use as well, so get in that habit.

Keep a Running Adjustment of Your Tax Basis.   This is important for any kind of real estate you own because if you eventually sell it, your gain will be determined by deducting this basis from the realized proceeds of the sale. As your basis can go up and down, depending on certain factors (e.g., depreciation or demolition reduces your basis and improvements increase the basis), a separate file should be kept to support each deduction and addition to your basis.

Show Changes to Basis.   It is important that you include every possible increase to the value, even if you are not sure whether the expense at the time spent would qualify as an addition to your basis. At a later date, when it becomes essential for your basis to be accurately determined, your CPA can sift through the amounts (even years of such additions) to eliminate those that may not qualify.

An Honest Approach Is Best.   Honesty works when you understand that this approach allows you to take every cent of the deductions you are allowed, provided that you document those expenditures properly and that they were genuine.

Do Not Fear the IRS. While IRS agents may feel the power and revel in the intimidation their office can provoke, there is no reason to be frightened by them. However, regardless of how honest a person may be, some people are intimidated and sweat profusely without real cause. If you are one of those people, then make sure you do not attend an IRS audit—let your accountant go for you.

109. What Is the Tax Write-Off That Most People Overlook When Selling a Property?

The tax basis of your real estate establishes the point from which a gain is obtained in the event of a sale.

> **Solution:** Take a look at item 4 in the solution to question number 108, then review the rest of this section.

Keeping an accurate account of increases to your tax basis for any property you own makes this the most overlooked of all the available deductions. One reason for this is the fact that there is no immediate deduction at the time of the expenditure, so the record may be nothing more than a bill and the corresponding check that satisfied the account. All of that was filed away, then after a while (three or more years later) was thrown out to make room for new years of tax data and records.

Twenty years or more of improvements to a property can add up to substantial sums of investment in the property you own. All of these qualified expenditures will increase your tax basis by the same amount and, in turn, will reduce the capital gain you have at the time of a sale.

The items that add to your basis are many and include obvious capital expenditures for items such as a swimming pool, awnings around the pool, a dock on the lakefront part of the property, and so on. These are obvious and can be recorded and then placed in a separate and permanent file that you keep until you sell, exchange, or otherwise dispose of the property. However, other expenditures should end up in that file as well—some that are less obvious, such as fees to the designer who drew the plans for the pool and the gardener who removed plants and lawn to make way for the pool. Each of these costs is related to capital improvement.

You should, on an annual basis, ask the person who prepares your income tax for a current list of qualified capital expenditures that will increase your basis. If you do it yourself, ask the IRS to give you a guide on these allowable items. The following form should be completed at the end of each year, or at least, while you are preparing your income tax return for that year. When you have finished filling this out, keep a copy with that year's tax data, *plus* put a copy in a file that is just for this form. Label the file "Annual Tax Basis Adjustment Form" and keep it where it will not be put in a storage box and locked away (or thrown out after a few years).

Annual Tax Basis Adjustment Form

Year end: _____

Year purchased: _____

Property address: _____

Basis at the start of the year: $_____

Plus all capital improvements:

_____ Check #_____ $_____

_____ Check #_____ $_____

_____ Check #_____ $_____

_____ Check #_____ $_____

_____ Check #_____ $_____

_____ Check #_____ $_____

_____ Check #_____ $_____

_____ Check #_____ $_____

Less depreciation, demolition, reduction:

_____ $_____

_____ $_____

_____ $_____

_____ $_____

_____ $_____

_____ $_____

_____ $_____

New basis $_____

Special items such as partial sale

---

110.   What Is a Capital Gain?

When you sell something, in this case real estate, you either have a loss, break even, or have a gain. Capital gains are treated to special tax advantages and are one of the basic elements that enable real estate investors to profit so handsomely.

> **Solution:** A capital gain is any gain in the amount of a sale of a property that exceeds the combination of your adjusted basis and the cost of the sale.

Anything you purchase may be subject to a capital gain if the value of that property increases to an amount above what you paid for it and the added investment you have made to improve it. Because there are several ways to reduce the amount of tax you may ultimately pay, it is beneficial for an investor to plan an effective use of those reduction methods to convert earned income, which would be taxable, into a present tax-free income with a future taxable event at a lower tax rate.

Recent changes in tax law have increased the maximum tax rates for earned income, which has made the tax rates on capital gains more favorable to the investor. This is a major benefit to ownership of real estate.

111. What Is Mortgage over Basis, and How Does That Affect My Tax Liability on a Sale or Exchange?

When you have a situation where the amount owed on a mortgage exceeds your tax basis in a property, the excess sum above the basis will be treated as cash in the event of a sale or exchange.

> **Solution:** Remember my previous cautions about anything that has to do with the IRS. When you have a situation where a mortgage on your property is greater than your tax basis, the IRS will assume that you have either taken excessive depreciation or that your have refinanced your property or a combination of both. While there may be no negative consequences, you should understand what could happen. Review the following.

This situation frequently occurs when a property that has been owned for a long period is refinanced. For example: You own an office building that is currently worth $500,000. However, because you have owned the building for nearly 30 years, you have depreciated the book value down to only $100,000, which was the original value of the land under the building. Two years ago you refinanced the building with a new first mortgage of $300,000 to generate the cash you needed to buy another property (or to take a vacation to Europe; it does not matter how you spend the money).

You now sell the building for $500,000 net of all cost of sale and take $100,000 down and hold a second mortgage for the balance above the first mortgage of $300,000. The transaction looks like this:

Sales and Tax Calculation

Down payment you get	$100,000
First mortgage buyer assumes	300,000
Second mortgage you hold	100,000
Price	$500,000
Capital Gains Tax Calculation	
Price	$500,000
Tax basis	100,000
Capital gain	$400,000
Mortgage over Basis Calculation	
Mortgage amount	$300,000
Less tax basis	100,000
Amount of your mortgage over basis	$200,000

Analysis.   Because you took out a mortgage and put that cash into your pocket (even just for a moment prior to buying that ticket around the world on a deluxe cruise ship), the IRS will now want to tax you at earned income rates in the year of this sale. Why? Because at the time you got the mortgage it was not a taxable event, and you had use of the cash without paying the IRS a dime for that money. You then proceeded to depreciate the property down to a level below the amount of the mortgage by making good use of that depreciation as a deduction from other income. It is now time to pay the IRS for the benefit you had when you took out the mortgage.

Keep in mind that depreciation may have no role to play in this situation. If this original investment had been a vacant tract of land, there would be zero depreciation in the calculation. If you had purchased the land for $100,000, its tax basis would have been that all the time. Along the way, you see the value going through the roof and want to use some tax-free cash by taking out a loan on the property. Because the IRS does not calculate borrowed money as taxable income, you can take the $300,000 and do with it as you please, as in the earlier example. At the end of the sale of the land for $500,000, you let the buyer assume a $300,000 mortgage and hold a second mortgage, and the end results would be the same as before.

Here is the potential problem. Assume that your tax on this capital gain of $400,000 is $60,000, and you get only $100,000 down, thinking you would keep all of that. But you really owe an additional tax on the mortgage over basis. Say you are in a 25 percent bracket due to other income that year. The added tax on the money from the mortgage ($200,000 above your tax basis) would be another $50,000. You close the deal, and all your proceeds, plus another $10,000 out of your pocket, go bye-bye.

Check out your potential tax consequence prior to signing the contract.

112.   Should I Take the Maximum Depreciation Available?

Depreciation, that great paper deduction that can reduce your income tax, can be molded to best fit your specific investment plan. There is no absolute requirement that you take any depreciation at all.

> **Solution:**   Rely on your goals and your investment plan to be your guide. Remember, land is not depreciable, so you can simply think of every investment as land, or your accountant may say, "Let's be aggressive and postpone every tax payment to the IRS we can." The key is to know where you are going and plan accordingly.

If your investment plan indicates that your adjusted gross income will increase over the next 10 years, then it would be prudent for you to anticipate setting up a depreciation schedule that would spread out your available depreciation to use as much of it as possible when you are in a higher tax bracket.

There are trade-offs to this reasoning, such as a potential sale of the property within a shorter period of time or a tax-free exchange in the future. It is important that you have an investment goal and work toward that goal in every way. Planning to maximize your tax deductions can be an important part of reaching your goals as quickly as possible.

113. How Does Depreciation Affect My Income Tax?

First, remember that depreciation is a business or investment type of a deduction. It will not apply to your personal residence unless you have an office as a part of that residence and depreciate a prorated portion of that space from the tax basis of your residence.

> **Solution:** When you take depreciation on any investment, the deduction is treated as an actual expense during the year it is taken. Although the IRS can deal with future recapture of depreciation at the time of a sale, or because your tax basis had been reduced because of it, the immediate benefit will vary depending on your situation.

The paper deduction obtained through depreciation of your real property assets gives you instant (in the year you take it) reduction of your taxable income by the amount of the depreciation taken. For instance, a $15,000 depreciation is deducted from otherwise taxable income and slides directly into your pocket. You now have $15,000 in your pocket. But did you save $15,000? No, you saved the amount of tax you would have paid on that $15,000 portion of your taxable income had you not taken the deduction.

114. How about My Home Office? Should I Depreciate It?

Considering the trend the IRS is taking on the issue of home offices, unless the office is a substantial part of the total residence (square footage ratio) and you are able to meet all the rules that establish the office as a depreciable item, my recommendation would be not to use the home office as a possible tax shelter.

> **Solution:** Be cautious about office-in-the-home deductions for depreciation. This can be difficult to substantiate and waves red flags.

However, where office depreciation is meaningful, the tax deduction should be taken only as long as it fits the overall investment plan. When you establish a portion of your home or apartment as a commercial event, you lose other benefits that would apply to a residence only.

   The capital gains exclusion of up to $500,000 does not apply to the portion of your home that is classified as an office. All of these matters need to be reviewed prior to taking the depreciation of a couple of hundred square feet of your home. Remember, too, worst of all, the IRS considers depreciation of home offices as a possible trigger for an audit. You may not want that to happen, even if you emerge from the audit owing nothing.

115. Can I Use Techniques When Disposing of a Property to Reduce or Eliminate the Capital Gains Tax?

The key words here are *disposing* and *reduce*.

> **Solution:** There are creative approaches that can allow you to attain your goals without following the usual methods. A disposition of any asset may not require a sale. Look at some of the creative approaches you can take.

For example, you own a motel worth $800,000 and along comes a buyer who wants to buy the property at that price. All you have to do, says the buyer, is agree to hold a second mortgage for part of the transaction.

The problem with this is that your tax basis is only $50,000, so you will have to pay a major tax on the $750,000 gain of at least $112,500.

Three Methods You Can Use to Reduce or Eliminate Capital Gains Tax

1. *Use a Section 1031 exchange.* A tax-free IRS Section 1031 real estate exchange can accomplish this task if you qualify. One key to a Section 1031 exchange is to remember that if the property is an investment property, then you can find a buyer, put that buyer on hold, or close under the IRS provisions of a deferred exchange (Starker exchange), and then acquire a replacement property without having any tax to pay (if all the rules work in your favor).

2. *Use the installment sale.* Another technique that can reduce the capital gains tax due is an installment sale, which allows you to postpone some of the tax by spreading the constructive receipt of the funds over several years.

3. *Divide the property into two values.* A very creative approach would be to split the property into two different values: one value for the land, another for the building. Depending on how the values come out, you may want to sell one and lease the other to the buyer.

Assume the land was worth $50,000 at the time you purchased it and you have fully depreciated the building. In reality, you might place a value on the land of $700,000 but not sell it; instead, you lease it to the new buyer. And you put a value on the buildings of $100,000, which you sell to that buyer.

The lease proceeds to you are considered income (as is interest on a mortgage), but you have not triggered a capital gain calculation on that land portion of the deal. Your tax on the gain of the building, which has been depreciated to zero, would be the full $100,000, but that is it. At least at this point.

If you gave the buyer an option to buy the land at some other time in the future, a sale at that time might create a taxable event, or you could use a Section 1031 treatment at that time to move the value into some other asset.

116. How and Why Is Real Estate Taxed?

Your annual real estate tax as imposed by the local government can be a real shocker if you are used to renting and not owning property. As a tenant, you may not have been aware that in some tax areas of the country, rent from one out of every four apartments in a complex is used just to pay the annual real estate tax for that property. Luxury homes can amass a large tax levy, and it is not uncommon for annual real estate tax to exceed three cents per hundred dollars of the tax appraisal value of the property.

This means that if your office building is appraised at $90,000 and the taxing authority has a combined millage of 20, then the annual tax for that property would be $0.020 \times \$90,000 = \$1,800$.

A county tax bill is usually made up of the different community charges that are added together to make up any specific property tax amount. These charges can include the following.

Example of Typical Tax Bill Charges

Property Tax Bill for Rain County, Florida

Taxing authority	Taxes from this authority
County	$ 600.65
Schools (state)	40.04
Schools (county)	300.21
City	570.00
Water management	120.66
Special districts	90.31
Fire and police	40.09
Convention	20.04
Total tax due	$1,800.00

It is not uncommon for there to be a discount on the payment of the tax if paid early. The tax bill might come out in October or November of the year prior to its due date. Say you get the bill in October of 2006 but the payment date is not until March 2007. You could have declining discounts for November through February. Because you can pay the bill in either 2006 or 2007, you may pick the year that the deduction would best suit your income. This is a plus factor because real estate tax is deductible from your federal income tax bill.

As for the details on the bill, it is your obligation to understand exactly where this money charged to you is going and to be watchful of the local hearings and meetings where the public has the opportunity to voice opinions before elected officials who impose these taxes.

117. How Can I Reduce My Real Estate Tax?

As with most things dealing with real estate, there is little that is etched into stone. Much the same is true for the ad valorem tax, which is assessed against your real estate.

> **Solution:** Review this section; it will give you all the steps you need to pursue to obtain a reduction in your real estate tax.

It is possible to reduce your taxes by having the tax assessment on your property reduced. To do this will require you to take the following steps.

11 steps to reduce your tax assessment

1. *The easiest method is to engage a tax-reduction firm to handle the necessary paperwork to petition to have your taxes reduced.* You can call the local tax assessor's office and ask for the names of several such companies (often local law offices), or check the Yellow Pages, or call a couple of lawyers. You will no doubt find several such firms to call. I have gone through all the steps myself, and I now use such a firm (local law firm) and find that is the best way to go. But you can do it yourself so read on.

2. *Get a copy of the local procedures to petition for a reduced tax assessment from the local county tax assessor's office.* It might be that your state offers homestead exemptions and other exemptions that will automatically reduce your assessed value, thereby lowering your taxes. In Florida, which is a homestead state, there are several such exemptions. First is a homestead act that provides a reduction based on age, so senior citizens get a break. In addition, widows and widowers get a break, as do the blind and persons with other physical impairments. Many homestead states also have a limit to any annual increase in tax assessment, which keeps one's home tax from going through the roof. None of these homestead exemptions or limits to increases, however, affect a parcel or home that is not your residence. Rules to qualify for homestead exemptions vary, too, so check with your tax assessor.

3. *Obtain a printout of the tax assessments of all the property within three blocks of your area.* Such data can be obtained from the county property records office, your computer-equipped real estate agent, your lawyer, or the tax assessor's office. You are looking for a pattern of assessed value for property similar to yours in the same or a similar area.

4. *Obtain data on tax assessments of property similar to yours in other areas of the county.* The source for this is the same as item 2, but be sure you have specific addresses of properties that match or are similar to yours around town.

5. *Pick specific examples of similar property that illustrate your position for a reduced assessment.* Out of many different properties, pick less than a dozen to show as specific examples of similar properties that are assessed lower than yours. Double-check the dates those properties were originally purchased by their present own-

ers. This is important if your state has a cap (maximum) by which the tax can be increased in any year. The more similar the tenure of ownership, the better your case. If you are petitioning for investment property, even if it is a home you have rented out, you will want to show examples of other properties that are rented in the same area, your expenses (include management cost even if not taken), and what you end up with at year's end. Do not forget to deduct the annual tax, insurance, interest on the mortgage, and everything else that qualifies as a management or operational expense.

Base the equity value as an investment at 10 times the net you make at the end of the year, then add the amount of any mortgage (for which you deducted the interest), and show that as your gross value. If you come up with a number below the assessed value, your case is a good one. If not, go ahead anyway, because we have not discounted that value (in this example) to account for the limit on increased value if you live in a homestead state. Let the tax assessor do that calculation when he or she reviews your petition.

6. *Take one photograph of each property you plan to show as a similar property.* There is no need to show the property in its best light; the idea is to downgrade value, not to create a "For Sale" brochure.

7. *Include one or more similar properties that sold in the past year.* Do this only if that information is favorable to your position, and if so, include the sales price. A property similar to yours that has sold for less than your tax appraisal, for example, would be to your advantage.

8. *Obtain realistic estimates from two or more local real estate agents in your area.* Show the price your property would quickly sell for, as long as these numbers represent a relative reduction in value over past years or the ratio of the usual tax appraisal to market value is favorable. It is rare for the tax appraisal to equal the market value. Therefore, if you can illustrate through sales comparisons of several similar properties in your area that the norm of the tax appraisal is 70 percent of the market value, then a market value of $200,000 would suggest that a realistic tax appraisal should be around $140,000. If it is greater by a substantial amount, then this would be a favorable indication for a reduction.

9. *Build a professional-looking presentation.* Make sure it is neatly typed, put in a professional folder, and given with the required copies plus one. If you do not type, take all your material to a quick-print shop—you should find one not too far away—and let the printers help you put it all together.

10. *Indicate the appraisal you expect, and why.* If you feel the appraisal of $188,000 is too high and that your calculations point to $140,005, then indicate that, and in clear and concise terms explain why. Reference your examples of similar properties to show a pattern that will allow the examiner of your petition to have an easy way to approve your material. Avoid statements such as "You idiots do not know what you are doing . . . ," even if you strongly feel that way about it.

Do not take no for an answer, and even if you get a reduction, apply for another reduction next year.

118.   Are There Other Tax Reduction Methods I Should Be Aware Of?

Each state may have different types of exemptions from taxes that could apply to you or be made to fit one or more of the properties you own. To get a list of these exemptions, pay a visit to your tax assessor's office after making an appointment to see one of the senior tax appraisers. Some of the exemptions that may allow you to reduce or avoid tax altogether are as follows.

Six More Ways to Reduce Your Annual Real Estate Tax Bill

Homestead exemption (discussed in problem 117)

Agricultural exemption

Nonprofit exemptions

Church and school exemptions

Recreational land exemptions

Handicapped ownership exemptions (discussed in problem 117)

Of these, the best for many real estate investors is the agricultural exemption. This exemption, when available and when you and/or your property qualifies, allows property that is used for qualified agricultural uses to remain at a very low tax rate. Often the qualification is relatively simple, but you do not get it automatically. You have to check with the local tax assessor to find out all the rules that apply. There are deadlines to file, and if you miss it this year, then try again in a more timely manner. Mind you, if your property is vacant or mostly vacant there might be a way to qualify. I have been successful in getting agricultural exemptions by leasing vacant land I owned to farmers, ranchers, and once to a U-Pick-It strawberry grower.

119.   What Happens If I Don't Pay the Assessed Real Estate Tax?

In this modern world where just about anyone you do business with can check on your credit rating, you need to be very careful with nonpayment of bills, which can have a catastrophic effect on your credit as well as on the disposition of your assets.

> **Solution:** If you did not pay your assessed real estate tax, you had best take immediate steps to rectify the situation. It is possible to overlook the payment, especially if your accountant is in charge of these payments and you own a lot of real estate. Take a look at the events that are likely to unfurl if you do not pay on time.

Each state may have procedures that differ, but for the most part the results will be similar to those in Florida. To learn about the actual process as applied to your community, call the tax collector's office and ask for the delinquent tax department. Have this department give you the details for your area.

In the meantime, for Broward County, Florida, the following procedure applies: Real estate tax bills are sent out in October of the taxable year with a March due date. To encourage early payments, there are discounts for payments made prior to the month of March. These discounts are based on the March amount and are 4 percent for payment in November, 3 percent for December, 2 percent for January, and 1 percent for February. Payments made in April through the last working day of May would have a penalty of 3 percent plus a $3.50 advertising fee. After the end of May, the tax certificate is sold.

Tax certificates are documents that prove the holder has paid the tax and other costs due for a specific property. These are sold at a public auction and in Broward County, Florida, they are sold during the first week of June (usually the first Monday of June).

Florida limits the maximum interest the buyer of the certificate can earn to 18 percent. When a certificate is sold, the bids start at an 18 percent return and go down. Unlike other auctions, where the ultimate buyer has bid the most, the tax certificate is sold to the investor willing to earn the lowest yield on the amount that the investor had to pay the county for the taxes and costs due.

The holder of the tax certificate must remain in possession of the certificate for a minimum of two years and not longer than seven years. At the end of two years, the holder can petition the county for a tax deed, which will ultimately force the sale of the property unless the unpaid tax and costs have been paid prior to the sale.

Some states have vastly different views on this matter, and the actual yield minimums in your state could be much greater than the norm for Florida. If you have not made a payment for a past year's tax, you should find out your rights as soon as possible and what you may have to pay to make your account current.

The person who has purchased a tax certificate on your property can sit back and hope that the value of the property does not go down the toilet. If you sell your property, any good title company will see that there had been a tax certificate sold against your property, perhaps even one for every year you held the property.

Any outstanding tax lien must be satisfied, or the would-be buyer does not receive good title to the property. If you simply gave someone a *quitclaim deed* (erroneously called a quick claim) for the sale of the property and no lawyer or title company was involved, that buyer could have a major problem and expense on his or her hands. This is one of the many good reasons why a title needs to be checked before a sale is finalized.

120. What Can I Do if a Tax Certificate Is Sold against My Property?

In the case of Broward County, Florida, tax certificates are sold the first week of June following up to four weeks of public advertisement giving notice of this pending event. All legal descriptions and/or property addresses are advertised.

Copies of the list of all properties in question are available for viewing at the tax collector's office.

> **Solution:** If you are a mortgagee and hold a mortgage on a property in that county (or any county) you would want to ascertain whether the mortgagor has failed to pay his or her taxes and whether a certificate is about to be sold. You may want to bid on that certificate to doubly protect your mortgage rights or, if you are in a secondary position, to give you a leg up on the first or superior mortgages. Review the steps that take place.

Once the certificate has been sold, the only way to remove it as a lien on the property is to pay it off, along with the interest that is due. The interest due will depend on the amount of return the buyer was willing to accept when he or she bid for the certificate. There may be other costs imposed by the tax collector to handle the paperwork involved.

If there has been an application (by the holder of the tax certificate) for a tax deed, then time is growing short for the certificate to be redeemed. The application for the tax deed will lead to the eventual auction of the property by the county. The property owner can buy the tax certificate at any time up until the auction, but the cost increases, as the county is spending money to prepare for the auction.

Keep in mind that the chain of events can proceed quickly from the date the tax is due to the sale of the tax certificate. At that point, there is a period when things slow down (in Florida, at least), and until 22 months pass, the tax deed cannot be applied for and would not be issued for at least another two months.

121. What Happens to the Mortgage Holder When the Property Owner Fails to Make the Mortgage Payment and the Real Estate Tax Payment?

When both a mortgage and a tax liability are in default, the tax lien must be satisfied first. In the case of real estate tax, as mentioned earlier in the answers to questions 119 and 120, continued default on the annual real estate tax due will trigger the sale of a tax certificate that may lead to the ultimate auction of the real estate itself.

> **Solution:** If you are a mortgagee, it is important that you follow the mortgagor's actions as they pertain to payment of tax due and the possibility of a lien being filed against the property for any reason. This becomes more critical when you are in a secondary position behind a first mortgage, and especially so if it is a large sum of money that approximates the amount the property might bring at an auction.

Most delinquent tax departments make sure every reasonable effort is made to notify a mortgage holder of record of the pending events. This may give the mortgagee the right to foreclose on the mortgage and give the county a payoff of any tax due prior to a tax certificate sale, or at least allow the mortgagee the right to protect his or her interest in the property before the county sells the property at auction.

Even if the property went to auction, any proceeds over and above the tax and interest due (to the owner of the tax certificate), plus the advertising costs and other pre- and postsale costs, would go next to satisfy any other tax liens against the property, then to pay off recorded mortgages. Any balance is paid to the previous owner of the property.

Keep in mind that in some circumstances this pattern may not fit—for example, if the property had been confiscated by the federal marshal's office in a case involving drugs, as well as in other situations that can occur due to changes in the current laws governing these matters.

14

All about Foreclosures

122. How Do I Foreclose on Someone?

The simple approach is to foreclose only when all else fails. But first things first. A *foreclosure* is the procedure that you, as a mortgagee, would initiate against the mortgagor when the loan terms, as described in the note and mortgage, have been breached and the loan is in default. The usual term that is breached is the payment of the loan installments in a timely manner.

> **Solution:** This section will hold your hand through the steps that take place leading up to a foreclosure and ultimately resulting in the sale (on the courthouse steps) of the foreclosed property.

When the person you lent money to fails to meet his or her obligations to you, according to the terms of the loan agreement that person is now in default. Default allows you to demand immediate payment of the past-due payments, as well as to accelerate the mortgage, which would require the borrower to pay back the entire amount owed. If you are not paid as you demand, you could begin an action of foreclosure.

The action of foreclosure follows a fairly standard procedure regardless of which state you live in or in which state the property that secures the loan is located. However, as with all laws that govern property rights and actions against breach of contract, each state generally has its own specific set of laws, and these can vary among states. Nonetheless, the actual steps leading up to the foreclosure follow.

---

18 Potential Steps of a Foreclosure

- Mortgagee generally late making payments
- Lender raising subject of foreclosure
- Discussions taking place to no satisfaction
- Mortgage or loan agreement now in default
- Notice of pending legal action
- Final notice before legal action starts
- Title search by lender
- Notice of foreclosure
- Decisions on tenants
- *Lis pendens* filed
- New title search
- Final chance to halt foreclosure
- Foreclosure sale advertised
- Sale held
- Buyers bid at auction
- Right to redeem
- Deficiency judgment awarded
- Possibility of court battle as mortgagee attempts to collect on judgment

---

Mortgagee Generally Late Making Payments. Getting behind on payments is the first clear sign of a pending problem. However, it is possible that mortgagors are skipping less pressing payments (like their credit card accounts) to keep you off the scent. That will not last long, however, and eventually such mortgages will slip into arrears.

Lender Raising Subject of Foreclose. If you are the lender, you will want to jump on this situation as quickly as possible. At the same time, the borrower will also want to have some kind of understanding with you so that foreclosure does not take place. If the mortgage in question is a first mortgage, and the lender is a banking institution, the loan officers handling the collection of this loan will try to work out a solution. Banks and other such institutions hate to foreclose, as it most certainly does not make their day bright and sunny. If the borrower is cooperative and the lender can find a way to restructure the loan, there may be a light at the end of the tunnel (and not the headlight of an approaching train!).

Discussions Taking Place to No Satisfaction.   Assume that discussions and promises failed to derail the approaching train. This generally happens because the borrower is not responsive. Perhaps he or she has no real equity in the property, has no money, has just enlisted in the Nigerian Foreign Legion, or has plans to skip town. Too bad. If the lender has the borrower's Social Security number, this event will follow that person for a long, long time.

Mortgage or Loan Agreement Now in Default.   The mortgagor (person who borrowed the money) has breached the mortgage contract with the lender (the mortgagee). Usually this occurs by way of a default in the required mortgage payments, but it is not limited to those terms or conditions. Any form of breach or default can cause the lender to accelerate the mortgage and, if not then paid in full, to file for foreclosure action.

Notice of Pending Legal Action.   Notice of pending legal action is usually sent to the lender. Most lenders would rather not go through the process of foreclosure and try to work with the borrower if at all possible, so they will usually attempt to collect past payments without resorting to a foreclosure action. Lenders know that many different situations can occur that would cause a good credit risk to suddenly miss several payments, and they want to avoid the time and expense of legal proceedings. The initial notices to the borrower are usually letters, and these may come in several stages, each letter building in intensity. A collection agency or department may also call on the phone or even pay for a personal visit to try to motivate the borrower to make the mortgage current. It is important to recognize that this step may not be necessary or legally required. Some lenders may take the position that they would like to get the property back, or an investor who has purchased the mortgage may have done so for the opportunity to get title to the property through foreclosure. If this is the case, then the moment the mortgage is in default, the foreclosure process will probably start.

Final Notice before Legal Action Starts.   Final notice pending the foreclosure action is sent to the borrower. There may, of course, be several final notices, but sooner or later the lender's patience will have been exhausted and the procedure will advance to the next stage.

Title Search by Lender.   To ascertain the chain of title and to identify the interested parties, a title search is ordered by the lender. Most state laws decree that the borrower must join with other creditors of record and that all persons who have any interest in the property are made parties to the action.

Notice of Foreclosure.   Notice is sent to interested parties informing them of the initiated action. Such notice is initiated by the lender, naming them as parties to the suit and serving them a summons to that effect. This summons must be served according to the laws of the state (either in person, by proper notice and advertisement, or both), but if the lender intends to demand a deficiency judgment to collect the proceeds of a foreclosure sale that is short of the needed payoff of the delinquent debt plus expenses, the notice to the borrower must be delivered in person.

The lender need not, however, name as a party to the suit a holder of a superior lien. Such would be the case if a second mortgage holder filed suit for foreclosure action and a first mortgage existed. The rights of the first mortgage would not normally be affected by the foreclosure action of the junior mortgage, as a purchaser at a foreclosure sale would acquire the property with the mortgage in place, unless a superior mortgage has also filed for foreclosure action.

In any event, unless a junior lien wishes to dispute the validity of a superior lien, there may be no advantage to joining them as parties to the action.

Decisions on Tenants.   If there is a tenant, and the tenant's lease precedes the mortgage without being subordinated to that mortgage, then the foreclosure action may have no effect on the rights of the tenant. However, this is a function of law and the circumstances. Even if the lease was written after the mortgage or subordinate to the mortgage, the lender seeking foreclosure action may wish to keep the tenant in place, as that tenant could be an asset to the ultimate sale of the property; in that event, the lender may choose to name the tenant as a party only for notice purposes.

Lis Pendens Filed.   A *lis pendens* is filed and recorded. The *lis pendens,* or notice of the pendency of the action, is a legal device that results in the automatic joining in of any party who acquires any interest in the property after the notice is filed. This action is a legal notice that appears in the county property records and has the ultimate result of notifying anyone who may want to buy, lease, or otherwise obtain an interest in the property of a pending legal action. It would be rare for anyone to buy or rent (for a long term) under these conditions.

New Title Search.   A second title search is made to ensure that everyone necessary has been given proper notice and joined in as parties to the action. The second title search also double-checks that the owner has not made a midnight sale of the property in an attempt to complicate the matter.

Final Chance to Halt Foreclosure.   This is the final opportunity for negotiations between lender and borrower. Up until the moment of the foreclosure sale, the owner of the property may attempt to negotiate with the lender to reactivate the original loan, to obtain new and more attractive loan terms, or just to get out of the property by deeding it back to the lender by way of a deed in lieu of foreclosure.

Foreclosure Sale Advertised.   Most states require that the foreclosure sale be advertised in advance. This is to ensure that the public is given an opportunity to come to the sale and to bid for the property. These advertisements frequently appear in legal journals or professional newspapers whose subscribers are mostly lawyers, title companies, and a few investors who specialize in the many opportunities arising from legal evolvements. Many local newspapers have a legal section, often as part of the classified news section, where these notices are placed.

Sale Held.   The sale itself may be administered by the court or an officer of the court, such as a judge, a sheriff, or another party. In some states, laws allow the lender to administer the sale, but that is rarely the case. Foreclosure sales are usually an absolute auction where the highest bidder becomes the buyer. Care must be undertaken to ascertain if there are any obligations that must be assumed (superior existing debt, construction problems, city, county, or other governing agency violations or penalties, etc.).

Buyers Bid at Auction.   Anyone can show up and bid at the auction, and parties who have recorded liens or judgments can use those as value sums to bid. If there is a first mortgage of $100,000, the lender holding that lien does not have to bid at all and can wait to see if there is anyone else who will bid sufficiently to cover the cost of the foreclosure sale (court costs, advertising, etc., come off the top) and tax liens that would be superior to the first mortgage. If the highest bid seems to be settling around $80,000, which would leave $80,000 for the payback of the first mortgage, the lender would have to decide to bid and take a loss on the sale and attempt to collect a deficiency judgment from the borrower.

Right to Redeem.   The previous owner may have a right to redeem, both before and after the sale. In some states the mortgagor has the right to redeem before and/or after the sale. The period following the sale may be very short or not available at all under the circumstances.

Deficiency Judgment Awarded.   A deficiency judgment may be awarded to the lender. If the loan document called for a personal liability on the part of the borrower, then the lender may want to have the foreclosure suit include a deficiency judgment. This usually requires that a personal notice be delivered to the party or parties, and failure to make personal contact can thwart the procedure altogether. This factor is why many banks are reluctant to make loans to people who have primary residences outside the reach of such legal summons. Courts vary on their decisions governing deficiency judgments even within the same jurisdiction.

Warning: It is not wise for a property owner to play around with the potential results of a foreclosure sale. I have seen property owners threaten their lenders with statements such as, "If you can't give me a lower interest rate, then I'll be glad to give you the property." This might sound good in the movies, but does little to win friends at your favorite lending institutions.

Because of the complexity of many mortgage documents and the fact that many old savings and loans institutions are now defunct, most lenders are quicker to react, act tougher than they should, and often are so remote to the situation that there is little or no personal attention possible. These circumstances make it difficult to have that chat across the desk to work everything out.

Possibility of a Court Battle as Mortgagee Attempts to Collect on Judgment.   If you are the mortgagee and have just been awarded the deficiency judgment because of your court action, most of the time you can receive the judgment.

However, being right does not always produce positive results. In times gone by, it was possible to have debtors thrown into prison. This was unfortunate for them, of course, but did not result in restitution of the mortgagee's lost money. Today people may simply disappear, and you cannot collect from someone you cannot find. Or they may file for bankruptcy or simply hold up their hands and say, "I don't have the ability to repay you." In the case of big money, lawyers can often drag out the matter until time erodes the impact of having to make the payment. Legal actions should be avoided whenever possible.

123. If I Get Behind in a Few Mortgage Payments, What Can I Do to Keep from Facing a Foreclosure Myself?

Let's assume that you know when your mortgage payments are due, and you make the payments yourself. There is no accountant or forgetful spouse on whom to blame the lack of payment.

> **Solution:** Consider how you got into this pending circumstance. If there is a good explanation, such as sudden illness, an unexpected major expense, or a lawsuit you must defend, then sit down with the mortgagee and see what you can work out. Read on.

The steps you might consider in this situation would vary depending on the nature of the loan and the lender. Some mortgagors actually want the lender to foreclose and force the issue. This is rare and generally occurs when the foreclosure action will cause an ultimate benefit to the owner. One such event would occur when the property owner wants to refinance the existing loan that is at a high market rate in comparison to the interest rates available for a new loan, but the owner would be forced to pay a penalty for early retirement of the loan. Many institutional loans and most private mortgages have such provisions as standard clauses in their loan documents.

Even with the cost of the foreclosure action, the owner may find that route the best direction to follow. Of course, the whole ploy might be used as a negotiating tool, as many lenders would quickly negotiate for a payoff at a reduced penalty or waive the penalty to avoid a legal action where they would benefit little in the long run.

Another mortgagor-initiated foreclosure situation would be when the property is financed by municipal bonds or other public bond issues that impose restrictions on the property and the lender. These bonds may restrict the use of the property or limit the nature of tenants that can be housed in the property. Time restrictions can be binding for a minimum period of years even if the bonds are paid off early. A foreclosure may circumvent that minimum time period.

If, on the other hand, you are simply caught in an economic bind, have gotten behind in mortgage payments, and want to do everything you can to catch up so you do not face the ultimate foreclosure sale, then follow these steps.

Four Steps to Negotiate to Try to Avoid a Foreclosure

1. *Know your documents.* Get complete copies of your note and mortgage and read them over carefully. Make sure you understand all the terms and what your obligations are under those terms and conditions.

2. *Know your legal rights.* Spend an hour with a good real estate lawyer who is familiar with foreclosure actions. Have him or her advise you about your rights and exactly what you can do to prevent the foreclosure or the lien holders forcing a sale and removing you from the property. Knowing this can be essential, because this is your leverage, even if you never mention it or threaten to exercise those rights to the fullest extent.

3. *Negotiate with a decision maker.* This may be harder than you think. We live in a world of computers, and in the case of institutional lenders, service companies could not function without them. Your lending savings and loan association that made the loan might be just around the corner, but the loan service company could be 2,000 miles away.

Mortgage service companies can be very impersonal, not trained in anything other than the mundane tasks they perform. My personal experience is that they may promise you anything but not have the authority or any initiative to follow up. You may not be able to negotiate with these people, but try anyway. Sometimes their utter impersonality works in your favor.

If you still get nasty letters threatening to expose you to the world of bill collectors, then push to get to someone who actually works for or represents more closely the holder of that mortgage.

4. *Have a proposal ready.* This is an important step. Your success in any form of negotiation improves if you can illustrate to the other side of the dispute that what you are asking them to do should be acceptable to them. Be quick to explain that you want to live up to your obligation, but need assistance, time, understanding, and forgiveness from the lender. If you can then follow that up with some positive action, such as a check for one or two past payments, then you should be met with a willing response.

124. Are Foreclosure Sales a Good Buy, and Where Do I Find Them?

In general, the foreclosure market is the same as any other marketplace. There certainly will be opportunities, but these opportunities take special skills to locate and special attention to deal with. However, there are people who swear by the foreclosure market, and it is possible that your community offers some great bargains.

> **Solution:** Find yourself a real estate agent who specializes in the foreclosure properties. These will fall into two categories: those about to be foreclosed and those that have already gone through the foreclosure process. The second group are now real estate owned (REO) properties of the

lending institution that ended up with the title after the sale
on the courthouse steps.

Buying a property at a foreclosure sale may require you to have a sizable cashier's
check or a lot of cash ready for an on-the-spot deposit. You may have a short time
to get your financing in order, and if you fail, you will most likely lose your deposit.

Prefinancing qualifications with the mortgagee who forced the sale would help,
but having your own bank behind you is the ultimate answer.

Look at the list of foreclosure sources in the answer to question 125. A quick
check in your local phone directory should produce phone numbers and addresses.

125. How Can I Find Foreclosure Property?

Every institutional lender, such as banks, insurance companies, FHA, and VA, as
well as private lenders, have had experience with foreclosure proceedings, and
they frequently end up with those properties from the sale on the courthouse steps.

> **Solution:** Foreclosed properties are offered for sale under
> one of the following circumstances: (1) The lender who
> actually foreclosed on the property ended up with it at the
> courthouse sale. This happens when no one else bids
> enough to cover the lender's exposure (amount of loan plus
> lender's expenses to date). (2) This same lender may have
> made a deal with the mortgagor whereby the borrower gives
> the lender a deed *in lieu* ("instead of" going through the
> foreclosure procedure). (3) An investor like you may have
> purchased the property at the courthouse sale and is now
> looking for a quick profit by flipping his or her contract.

Every community has its fair share of foreclosed properties. If you are unsure
about getting into this area of the market, start slowly by attending a few foreclosure sales. Talk to the loan officers and department heads of the resources listed
here. You will find that almost everyone will be helpful to you in your learning
process—after all, you may buy one of their properties in the near future.

Four Places Where You Can Find Foreclosed Properties
for Sale

1. *Subscribe to the local legal newspaper.*   Most communities have one. Find out by
calling any local lawyer or title insurance company and asking for the name and
phone number of the paper they subscribe to. This is where most foreclosed properties in your area are advertised.

2. *Contact the local or closest office of Veterans Affairs.*   This association may have
a list of properties that it has taken back in foreclosure and will sell to you directly.
Usually the down payment is very low and good financing is available.

3. *Contact the local office of Federal Housing Administration (FHA) properties.*   The

FHA has its own properties it has taken back in foreclosure and, like the VA, can offer you good financing with low down payments.

4. *Institutional lenders in your area usually have departments that handle REO proper- ties.* Some lenders give these foreclosed properties interesting names, such as Special Assets or Seasoned Properties. In all cases, when the lender has taken back the property on which a foreclosure action was initiated, it is because no one bid high enough to satisfy the lender's position or because the lender took the prop- erty as a deed in lieu of foreclosure. In virtually every case, the lender does not want to own the property—it wants to lend money. Make a few phone calls to the Special Asset or REO departments of some of the bigger lenders in your area and get on their mailing list. You may also want to become prequalified for a loan in the event you see exactly what you have been looking for.

Property owners who are behind in their payments and see that they may have a chance to sell their property before that train in the tunnel catches up to them generally do attempt a last-minute sale.

The unfortunate aspect of this is they are often too embarrassed to tell their real estate agent the truth about their financial situation, and the broker, attempting to get the highest price, does not know that any price might be the salvation of the client.

Enter lenders and investors who actually go out and try to find a property about to go into foreclosure. They put up large billboards advertising that they buy any- thing, even not-so-pretty houses. They also advertise in the newspaper, and even strike up working relationships with real estate brokers and agents in the area. You can do that, too.

126. What Are the Major Pitfalls of Buying Foreclosed Property?

Any property that has an economic problem attached to it may end up having sev- eral or all of the following additional problems.

> **Solution:** Review the seven major pitfalls of foreclosed
> property.

> ### Seven Major Pitfalls of Foreclosed Property
>
> - Sudden death
> - Deferred maintenance
> - Hidden liabilities
> - Lost market potential
> - Financing problems
> - Long recovery time
> - Title problems

Sudden Death. By this I do not mean yours, although there is a suddenness if you are buying foreclosed property off the courthouse steps. There the action is fast and sometimes furious. You will be expected to have cash or a cashier's check or some other form of credit depending on the local procedures and who is doing the actual auction. In any event, do not even think of going to such an auction for the first time and bidding. Check out what goes on. Observe who is there; if you go to several, you will see a lot of the same faces. Talk with some of the ones whose bid is chosen. They may not give away any secrets, but if you say things like, "Wow, that was fantastic," and "I can't believe you are so lucky," or even, "I sure wish I knew how to do that," you might find that they will teach you.

Deferred Maintenance. One of the first things a property owner does when short of funds is to stop the usual upkeep to a property. If the mortgagor is trying to take advantage of the property, sometimes right up to the time of the foreclosure sale, you can be sure that even serious repairs may not have been done.

Sometimes lenders will attempt to spruce up a property pending a foreclosure sale, provided they have gotten some control over the property by having a receiver appointed or through agreement with the property owner (who should not object to a lender spending its own money) to increase the potential sale proceeds. Often this spruce-up procedure is just a cosmetic cover-up. Very detailed inspections are essential to protect your interest.

Hidden Liabilities. If the state law allows the mortgagor to redeem the property, then there could be problems even after the sale. Even if that is not a potential problem, this kind of sale has other latent problems that can occur. Tenants' rights can be affected, or a legal action can occur for little or no real reason other than to take advantage of your new position. Never take title to any property from a foreclosure action sale unless you have had a title company or lawyer review and agree to insure your new title and give you a written list of any conditions or exclusions in their policy. The fact that they include exclusions may not be bad, but make sure you know what they are and that you accept the risk those exclusions impose. A usual exclusion would be any potential liability that a recent survey uncovered as a potential risk. The term *recent* needs to be defined, and if the survey you are given is not recent enough, then request a current one from the court or the seller. If possible, you should strive to have all exclusions removed that create even a marginal risk for you.

Lost Market Potential. If the property is in an area where there are many foreclosed properties, the neighborhood may be depressed. Sometimes the neighborhood looks like a battle zone, with builder's models abandoned, half-finished structures with their walls open to the elements, and so on. This kind of area can breed more foreclosures, and the market there may be headed for a sharp downturn.

Financing Problems. Financing problems can start at the time of the sale itself, because your cash or cashier's check may be a nonrefundable deposit. You may not want to take that risk. Usually you are entitled to some escape provisions, such as a bad title, or a counterclaim by an interested party that will block the sale, but getting the needed financing and safeguarding your investment can be tough problems to solve.

Long Recovery Time.   If you are acquiring your dream home or the ranch you have always wanted but could never afford until now, then there may be no reason to even think about recovery. However, if you are looking at this acquisition as an investment or a stepping-stone, then the acquisition of a foreclosure should be contemplated only after you have taken a careful assessment of the time it will take for you to recover your investment and the added costs of fixing up the property for a profitable resale.

Title Problems.   In most foreclosures the title will come through pretty clear. That is, unless there was something fishy about the owner. Did he or she sell the property three days earlier? Was the title clouded (with problems) even before that owner (who was foreclosed on) bought the property? Because of the sudden death, which was the first item of this list, you may not have a lot of time to get to the bottom of any such issue. Be sure you have a title company check the title and seek legal advice prior to entering into any binding real estate contract of any kind.

15

Buying and Selling through Auctions

127. How Does a Real Estate Auction Work, and How Can I Benefit from It?

"Hello, eBay, here I come." Auctions can be great fun, as well as places for genuine bargains. However, woe to the person who tenders a bid for something about which he or she knows nothing.

> **Solution:** Never go to an auction with the intention to bid on anything there unless you (1) have more money than brains, (2) immediately recognize that the painting being auctioned off is that of your long lost grandfather, (3) are just checking out the action to see what you can learn about auctions, or (4) already know enough about the items you plan to bid on not to make a mistake. Pick one of these, then read the balance of this section.

Virtually every manufactured product can end up at an auction at one time or other, and for many items the auction may produce the highest price possible. On other occasions, the auction can be a marketplace for real bargains. The key is to know how the auction process works and to take advantage of the bargain if it fits your plans. All real estate auctions follow a format similar to the following.

Four Stages of a Property Auction

1. A property is put up for sale through an auction format because of a foreclosure action, a tax deed application, a court-ordered sale, provisions in a contract, a divorce resolution, a provision to satisfy the needs of an estate, a dissolution of

a partnership or trust, or because the owner chooses the auction as a means to quickly dispose of the property.

2. The auction rules are established and the category of the auction is determined from one of the following:
   a. Absolute auction, in which the highest bidder will get the property regardless of how low that bid might be.
   b. Absolute auction after a minimum bid is reached.
   c. Subject to withdrawal at any time by the seller. When the seller does not like the amount of money bid, the seller can bid for him- or herself or withdraw the property outright from the auction.
   d. Silent or sealed bid, in which bids are made in advance and submitted for review. No one knows what anyone else is bidding.

3. In the case of a foreclosure or other court-ordered sale, state laws generally establish a period of time over which the property must be advertised prior to the sale. This serves several different goals. The most important is to give ample notice to draw prospective buyers. The other main reason for such announcement of the auction sale is to give all interested parties sufficient time to react to protect their interests. However, even with advance notice and advertising it is rare for an auction to draw many prospective buyers.

4. At every real estate auction the prospective buyer has been given some reinsertion rights. The inspection period is usually shown in the advertising material, but not always. Direct contact with the administrator of the auction is frequently needed to arrange personal inspections.

Once you understand how the auction works and what signals are accepted for a bid, then you need to ask yourself: Is this for me? It can be fun to bid and it can be costly. Never bid because you get caught up in the fever of the moment. Some auctions can be very intimidating, like car auctions that go at such a fast pace, and the person conducting the auction (and his or her helpers) can spot a novice a mile away and will ensure that the novice gets the car no matter how much the guy (rarely a girl) pays.

128. What Are the Most Important Steps I Should Take before Bidding at Any Auction?

Let's assume that you have checked out the action on several previous occasions. Also, let's assume that you have a good working knowledge of the procedure and have some experience in judging the values of the property or items on which you will bid.

> **Solution:** Understand that auctions work because people love the idea of getting one thing that other people also want. React only to what you want and are willing to pay for (even if it were not a bargain); predetermine the maximum price you will pay and then stick to that plan.

There are many different kinds of auctions, but there are only three kinds of people who go to them:

Three Kinds of People Who Go to Auctions

- People who go to buy and know what they are doing
- People who go to watch
- People who buy when they should not have

To make sure you do not fall into category 3, review the five steps outlined here.

Five Steps to Follow When You Bid at a Real Estate Auction

- Review your goals.
- Look for properties that serve those goals.
- Make thorough inspections of the property.
- Preset the maximum amount you should bid.
- Never exceed the maximum you set.

129. Why Is the Absolute Sale Auction the Best to Attend?

When a property is offered for sale at an absolute auction, the audience can anticipate that the property will be sold no matter what happens. In auctions that are not absolute, bids not meeting a preset level may subject the property to being withdrawn from the sale. If you have to incur an expense to go to the auction, make sure that your time, money, and effort are spent wisely.

130. Which Government Agencies Hold Regular Auctions?

Most government agencies hold auctions of one kind or another. Some, such as the U.S. Postal Service, can be interesting if you are in the market for delivery vans, jeeps, and other vehicles used by the post office.

The customs department frequently has auctions to get rid of unclaimed items left in customs warehouses (e.g., the duty exceeded what the recipient wanted to pay) or items confiscated by customs officers.

The U.S. Marshals Service frequently auctions off property taken because of drug busts or other illegal activities. These properties often include some very expensive real estate.

Government agencies and departments that hold auctions generally advertise extensively in advance of the event. Look for these advertisements in your local "legal notices" publication and national financial newspapers.

131. How Does a Court-Ordered Auction Differ from a Seller's Auction?

A court-ordered auction is the last resort to resolve the problem. Triggering events can be a defaulted mortgage, a contract dispute, or some other legal action involving title or ownership of a property that could not be resolved without a forced sale.

The seller's use of an auction as a tool to move a property is an attempt to bring a large number of prospective buyers together. Because motivation becomes collective with a large group, some buyers end up owning something they would not otherwise have thought of buying.

Nonetheless, many properties are sold in court-ordered auctions as a method of resolving disputed ownership, property seized during a crime, and other such events.

132. Why Does a U.S. Marshals' Drug Property Auction or Sale Offer the Least Bargain?

When in the hands of a master auctioneer, and given sufficient advertising funds and the draw power of an absolute auction, the auction is likely to draw a very large audience. With this and the fact that some of the items are apt to be in demand by other drug dealers, the prices at the auction can skyrocket.

However, these auctions can be very interesting to watch. Be careful not to scratch your head or you may have just bought a speedboat capable of traveling 150 miles per hour!

133. How Can I Select an Auctioneer to Auction Off My Property?

Auctions are like any other service you hire. Some are great; some are moderately good; and others are horrible at reaching your expectations.

> **Solution:** Review the following steps to best select an auctioneer.

10 Steps to Follow to Select the Best Auctioneer for Your Property

1. Attend two or more different auctions.
2. Find out who the insiders are among the auction attendees.
3. Ask the insiders which auctioneer is the best.
4. Contact two or more of the recommended auctioneers.
5. Attend at least one auction of each prospective auctioneer.
6. Meet with your final choice of three.

7. Explain your investment goals to them.

8. Outline your expectations of the auction.

9. Ask their advice and proposed plan to auction your property.

10. Review your findings and make a choice.

134. Can I Use the Auction as a Tool to Sell My Own Property?

The auction can be an effective method of selling property, so it seems logical that a voluntary selection of this technique might produce a beneficial result to a property owner who has not been able to sell a property that has been on the market for some time.

The decision to use an auction to sell your property should come after you weigh the local market conditions very heavily. If the real estate market in your area for the type of property you own is soft, and there are few takers for what you have to offer, then the auction could be a disaster.

On the other hand, if your property can be offered at a bargain price and your motivation to sell strong enough to allow the auction, let it proceed as an absolute auction. This kind of auction draws more people because they know the property will be sold to the highest bidder, regardless of how low that price may be. When there is a strong turnout of prospective buyers, a well-run auction and a strong auctioneer may whip the crowd into a buying frenzy and entice a prospective buyer to pay more for the property than if he or she were the only buyer looking at that property.

16

Real Estate Finance Made Easy

135.   What Makes U.S. Real Estate Financing So Great?

Americans take real estate financing format for granted. So much so, in fact, that they fail to appreciate the fact that everything about financing real estate in the United States is unique.

Let's start with the lending institutions and work down to the actual borrower to see just how great it is. Lending institutions are found everywhere, and if they are not on the next corner, you can get dozens to respond to your borrowing need with a few clicks of the mouse on your computer. Internet lending is massive, and it has created incredible competition between lenders, some of whom may be a thousand miles away in a distant state.

Lenders take money from a series of sources and pass that money into the commercial flow that makes this country so great. Where does that money come from? There are many sources; likely you are one of them just by having a checking and/or savings account at a local savings and loan association or bank. These lenders also conduct business that causes a flow of funds to be channeled through their doors. This money is often parked in a bank or other such institution for a few days, and during that time, the institution earns interest in addition to its fees for the transaction undertaken.

Lenders also borrow from each other and from the federal bank that provides working capital to them. Of course, these lenders also pay interest to their depositors, and in the end, they make a profit from the spread between what they pay for the use of money and the interest they earn for lending funds to people like you and me.

However, what about the lending process? Is it different in the United States? Let's look at this. In many parts of the world a loan is made by a lending institution or company based on a rather short payback term. A long-term loan in many places is 5 to 10 years in duration. A 30-year loan is almost unheard of in most parts of the world. If you had to pay back a $500,000 loan over 10 years, it would total $50,000 a year (for 10 years) just to pay back the *principal* portion of the loan. Interest, at the usual 15 percent, would make the first year's payment $125,000 (principal of $50,000 and interest of $75,000).

Then someone created a mathematical formula for the amortized loan. This single simple-to-use but hard-to-come-up-with formula has revolutionized the entire lending business. How so? Let's take that same $500,000 loan that you might need to acquire a tract of land on which you can build a warehouse. The lender might offer you a 30-year amortization schedule but ask you to pay off the loan by the end of the twenty-fifth year of the loan term. That payback term could be negotiated and might be as short as 15 years, but during those years the payments would be established at an amount that would not change at all and would include a blended sum of interest and principal.

If the interest is set at 6 percent for the duration of the loan, the interest amount for the first year would total $30,000 (0.06 × $500,000 = $30,000). If the term is 30 years, an equal payment of principal each year would be $16,666.67 per year ($500,000 ÷ 30 = $16,666.67). If we added the interest and principal together, the total for the first year would be $46,667.67. But wait, if we use this magic formula to give us a monthly payment that will be exactly the same each month at the same 6 percent interest rate, we end up with a monthly payment of $3,000 and an annual total of only $36,000.

This may not sound like magic, but little by little the interest portion of the mortgage payment will decrease as the principal owed is eroded a tiny bit at a time.

Okay, so far we have a business that is happy to make loans, in fact, hundreds and thousands of such businesses all competing for the right to give you money, and they are willing do this for a very small profit spread between what the money costs them, and what they charge.

But wait, there is more. These people, whom you may never see and who may never see you, give you money and let you make money on it by investing in real estate. That real estate becomes occupied by tenants who gladly give you money that you can use to pay back the lender. That is how "double-dipping" other people's money works.

Some person gives you money (the mortgage), and some other person gives you money (rent) so you can pay back that mortgage.

136. When Is Negative Leverage Okay?

The simplest example of leverage is a teeter-totter. You know what I mean. As children, most of us played on seesaws. If two people of the same weight sit at the opposite ends of a board that is stretched over a low wall or some other object, the two people are suspended the same distance above the ground. However, if one weighs more than the other, the heavier person goes down and the lighter person goes up.

Using leverage with money works in much the same way. If you rent your apartments so that you take in $300,000 a year and the cost of operation is $150,000 per year, you have a net operating income (NOI) before debt service of $150,000. If your total debt service is greater (heavier) than the NOI (say, $160,000) you sink to the bottom and lose $10,000 that year. That is negative leverage.

On the other hand, if your debt service is $130,000 for the year, you have $30,000 on the positive side, and you rise to profit heaven. That is positive leverage.

In financing we talk about leverage as getting money from one person at a cost that is less than what we can make with it.

It might appear that negative leverage, which can leave you without any cash at the end of the year, is a bad thing. That is not entirely so.

> **Solution:** Some real estate investments do not produce any revenue, or at least not enough to meet operational and debt expenses. This can be the result of an investment that has yet to be converted into an income-producing venture. If the property value is increased by your efforts, or simply by time, that ultimate profit nullifies the earlier negative leverage.

Early in my career I formed a number of investment groups that invested in vacant land. Every venture proved to be successful, and profits ranged from 200 to 800 percent return on our invested capital. In every instance, however, there was virtually no cash flow, and although we have excellent seller financing in all situations, there was no positive leverage present. Yet the investments were great.

137. What Is the Best Way to Calculate Mortgage Payments?

The real insiders, that is to say, mortgage brokers, real estate brokers, and others in the financial end of the business, frequently rely on computers to print out amortization schedules, or else they are proficient in using a financial calculator.

> **Solution:** Purchase an easy-to-use amortization calculator, buy a book of tables, or learn to use Internet programs for quick and easy calculations. But remember, when calculating equal monthly payments of principal and interest combined, some calculators are programmed to round off to only two decimal places, and therefore large mortgage amounts will be less accurate when using that kind of a calculator.

There are several great, and not too expensive, calculators that will serve you very well to obtain exact answers quickly for virtually all kinds of mortgage calculations. Some of the most economical financial calculators are made by Texas Instruments, and several of its models can be found in most discount office product stores for less than $30. No matter what your profession, there is no need to spend more than that to get adequate results.

For quick and easy answers, there are two great publications that you may want to invest in. They are *McGraw-Hill's Interest Amortization Tables*, which is commonly referred to as the "red book," and *McGraw-Hill's Compound Interest & Annuity Tables*, known as the "blue book," both of which are compiled by Jack C. Estes and Dennis R. Kelley. These books offer the real estate investor a fast way to determine the answers to many real estate problems. It is helpful when using these tables to have the additional help of an inexpensive calculator, but the only calculation you will do will be to add, subtract, multiply, or divide. You can order these and any other McGraw-Hill publications by calling 1-800-2-McGRAW.

In several of my books I have also provided amortization tables, which are very comprehensive and can be useful in a number of ways you might never have thought about. The next time you are in a bookstore, check them out. Try the *Real Estate Finance and Investment Manual*. There are instructions on how to use the table I have worked out, and by following the easy-to-use formulas, you can find the right payment for a mortgage, calculate the balance due at any period of the mortgage, arrive at a new yield you will earn if you buy a mortgage at a discount, determine the interest rate when you know only the term and payment amount, and more.

138. How Do I Calculate the Yield on an Income-Producing Property?

Yield is the term used to describe the amount you earn from an investment in relation to the amount you have invested. For example, if at the end of the year you have $8,000 left over after all expenses have been paid, including your mortgage principal and interest payments but not including any income tax you might owe to the IRS, then $8,000 is your cash flow.

If you have invested $100,000 as a down payment on the specific property in question, that cash flow amount of $8,000 represents an 8 percent cash flow yield. This is found by dividing the yield by the return ($8,000 divided by $100,000 equals 0.08, or 8 percent).

> **Solution:** The calculation to arrive at a yield or percent of return has just been described. However, there are many different forms of yield, and they are not all equal. It is important to understand which kind of yield the seller is talking about when he or she offers an 8 percent return. Read on.

Yield is an important measure of what an investment is going to produce, or has produced, for the investor. Several different terms refer to yield, which can be confusing or if improperly used and can convey a very misleading picture of the actual events.

Cash on cash return is the most basic of all yields and is often used as a guide to the immediate benefits of any investment. A cash on cash return, however, is not as informative to any specific investor as would be the *after-tax spendable return*, in which the income and other taxes have been deducted from the cash flow.

Say you have $50,000 to put down on a property. Let's assume that amount represents 20 percent of the total purchase. Therefore, the total price would be $250,000. If at the end of the first 12 months of ownership, you have $4,000 left over after paying all the expenses and debt service (full principal and interest amount) and your year-end income tax, you would have a spendable cash flow of $4,000, which represents 8 percent of the cash down. In this situation you have earned 8 percent as your *spendable cash flow return.* Your yield is 8 percent of your invested cash.

Yield Points and When They Are Calculated.   A yield can be calculated at different points or times. Each separate type of yield is important, but if you get them confused you can easily make a faulty apples-versus-apples comparison between two or more properties you are considering purchasing. Because of this possibility, let's look at some of the different yield terms and examples that you can face when talking to a broker or seller. Let's look at the three different time periods at which a return (or yield) can be calculated.

Net Operating Income Return (or Yield).   Net operating income (NOI) is found by taking all collected income and deducting all actual cash outlay for the operation of a property. Not calculated at this point would be depreciation or debt service. In the true sense of the word, NOI does not take into consideration any mortgage on the property or any depreciation. NOI is a reflection of cash flow before income taxes with a 100 percent investment and no shelter from depreciation or leverage through financing.

Calculation to Arrive at Net Operating Income

Total collected revenue	$100,000
Less actual cash expenses	50,000
Net operating income (NOI)	$ 50,000

If the property is purchased at a cost of $500,000, it does not matter in the NOI calculation whether a mortgage is used to finance the $450,000 amount above your down payment of $50,000.

Net Operating Income Yield Calculation

Value = $500,000
NOI = $50,000
NOI yield = 10 percent   (NOI is divided by value)

The NOI yield is also called the *cap rate,* which should always be calculated at the NOI point. Note I said *should* always be so calculated. Many people do not calculate a cap rate this way, so when talking about cap rates be sure to qualify that it is the NOI cap rate, which, while redundant, is sometimes helpful to keep everyone on the same page.

Cash Flow before Income Taxes Calculation.   This is the next point at which a yield can be calculated. Cash flow takes into consideration debt service. By *debt service* I mean the total payment to service the debt, including principal, interest and any other charges (penalties, insurance, whatever).

Total collected revenue	$100,000
Less actual cash expenses	50,000
Net operating income (NOI)	$ 50,000
Less total debt service	
First mortgage	30,500
Second mortgage	10,000
Cash flow before IRS tax	$ 9,500

Cash flow before IRS tax takes into consideration the mortgage cost. To arrive at the yield now, we need to know what the investment is. Assume that the investor puts $50,000 down and has a mortgage for the balance. We do not need to know what that balance really is to calculate this yield, but naturally that would be something you would like to have when reviewing properties. Because we are now entering a calculation that will also measure leverage, a mortgage that has an unrealistically low interest rate or one that is well above the market rate could distort the debt service and not give a realistic result. No matter what the actual debt service on any property you plan to purchase, it is important to run the calculation based on the amount of debt you will need to service and the terms you can realistically obtain in the present market.

Net operating income (NOI)	$ 50,000
Less total debt service	
First mortgage	40,500
Cash flow before IRS tax	$ 9,500 = 19% yield on $50,000 down

The cash flow yield is therefore based on the cash invested, which in this example is $50,000. The cash flow yield is found by dividing the amount of the cash flow by the amount of the investment ($9,500 divided by $50,000 equals 19 percent yield on the cash invested of $50,000).

If the best you can do in financing the $450,000 you need is a debt service of $46,500 per year, your cash flow before IRS tax would be $3,500, with a cash flow before IRS tax of 7 percent yield.

Net operating income (NOI)	$ 50,000
Less total debt service	
First-mortgage annual payment	46,500
Cash flow before IRS tax	$ 3,500 = 7% yield on $50,000 down

Cash Flow after Income Tax.   This is the final step in the yield process, and it takes into consideration not only debt service but also any shelter that may come from depreciation. Because depreciation is a calculation only, that is, not an actual cash payment or expense, it should be reviewed separately from any real cash-paid expense.

Net operating income (NOI)	$ 50,000
Less total debt service	
First mortgage	46,500
Cash flow before IRS tax	$ 3,500
Less depreciation allowed	8,000
Taxable loss for the year	($ 4,500) (loss is shown in parentheses)

To consider this stage in the return (or yield) calculation, we have to make an assumption. Assume that there is $8,000 of actual allowable depreciation on this investment for the time period being reviewed. That amount of depreciation is greater than the cash flow, so it will wipe out any income tax liability on the sum of $3,500 and actually create a loss of $4,500. In the earlier example with a cash flow before tax yield of $9,500, depreciation of $8,000 would leave a taxable sum of only $1,500.

In any event, the shelter here is important, because the investor may have other income that will also be sheltered, or perhaps the loss will be carried forward to shelter part of next year's income. Assume the investor is in a 20 percent tax bracket.

Cash flow before IRS tax	$ 3,500	$ 9,500
Less depreciation allowed	8,000	8,000
Taxable loss for the year	($ 4,500)	$ 1,500
Tax due	0	300
Spendable cash flow after tax	$ 3,500	$ 9,200
Yield after tax	7%	18.4%

In the examples shown in this section thus far, we have seen how debt service has leveraged the return from a 7 percent NOI yield to a 19 percent cash flow before income tax yield. This is the effect of leverage by virtue of a debt service payment (combination of principal and interest) that is less than the NOI yield. This fact makes the NOI yield the most important factor when comparing different properties. Why? Because your ability to structure new financing or restructure existing financing will be one of the critical elements you will have to face in improving the overall investment.

Leverage worked its magic because, of the total purchase price, only $50,000 was the investor's money. The debt of $450,000 was other people's money. In the initial debt situation, the debt service of $40,500 per year equaled only 9 percent of the total debt. As the debt-free NOI yield showed a 10 percent yield, the spread of 1 percent between the NOI yield and the total debt service on the $450,000 (which was $40,500) allowed the investor to earn an extra 1 percent on the full amount of $450,000. In refinancing the debt that resulted in a debt service of $46,500 per year, this put the cost of that debt at 10.3333 percent of the amount of the debt. That small margin of 0.333 percent shows you how important the little things are in real estate.

Analysis of the Two-Debt-Services Effect on Yield

Amount invested $50,000 × NOI yield of 10% = $5,000
Amount earned from leverage 1% × $450,000 =   4,500
   Total yield in first example $9,500

Amount invested $50,000 × NOI Yield of 10% = $5,000
Amount due to negative leverage of debt × .3333%   (1,500)
   Total yield in second example $3,500

139. How Can I Increase Spendable Cash Flow from an Income Property?

One of the greatest dilemmas of property management is the mystery of increasing the bottom line of a rental property. The finesse needed to accomplish this task is less difficult if the work is broken down into the individual elements that make up the truly important bottom line—the spendable cash flow.

> **Solution:** There are only seven ways to increase the spendable cash flow of a property. Review them carefully and see how they can be used in combination to improve the bottom line.

The first step is to see the bottom line in its most important definition: spendable cash flow. Spendable cash flow is the amount of money that is left at the end of any given year, after deductions have been made from all income. This is the amount of money that the property owner can spend once everything, including operating expenses, fixed charges, debt service (interest and principal), and all taxes have been paid.

Keep in mind that the term *bottom line*, when used by itself, can mean NOI, cash flow, or other accounting results that may vary, depending on the specific investor. Spendable cash flow is relative to the specific investor whose circumstances match the assumptions made for tax bracket and depreciation, because to arrive at this amount, income tax must be deducted from the cash flow.

Here are the seven ways to increase the spendable cash flow.

Seven Ways to Increase the Spendable Cash Flow

- Increase rental rates.
- Decrease vacancies.
- Decrease expenses.
- Reduce debt service.
- Add rental units.
- Decrease tax liability.
- Convert to another use.

Increase Rental Rates.   It is often taken for granted that rental rates will continue to go up and that property values will increase accordingly. Anyone who has owned rental real estate during the 1970s and 1980s knows that this is not an absolute truth, nor is this a function of the condition of the property. Rental rates vary widely for many different reasons, but in general, the greatest effect on the amount of rent a property will bring depends on the level of vacancies in that specific rental category. Low-priced rentals in an area may have a high vacancy factor, while upscale (higher rents and/or better clientele) rentals may have a negligible vacancy factor.

All rental properties fall into rental categories within every market area. It is possible for two identical buildings to have rates that vary 30 percent or more because of the location, condition, ease of access, and tenant makeup. Because of this, one of the best long-term approaches to increasing rental rates is to upgrade the rental category of the property if at all possible. This may take concentrated effort and expense.

If a property owner is able to increase the rents by as little as 5 percent and hold firm all other costs and expenses, an increase from $100,000 to $105,000 will have the bonus of increasing the value of this property by an additional $50,000. How so?

The value of income property is based on the ultimate return that property will generate. A rental property that generates a 10 percent cash on cash return may be considered a good investment. That extra $5,000 reflects an additional cash investment of $50,000 (10 percent of $50,000 equals $5,000).

Decrease Vacancies.   Astute property manager investors look for rental properties with high vacancies that can be reduced by good management practices and capital improvement. Because value has a direct connection to the yield, a property operating at only 70 percent of its maximum capability will be valued accordingly. If the investor can decrease the vacancies while holding the rental rates steady, then an income boost from 70 to 90 percent can cause a sudden and very dramatic increase in the NOI of the property.

For example, a 20-unit apartment building with quoted rents of $600 per month would have a gross rent roll potential (if 100 percent occupied) of $144,000. At 70 percent occupancy, it would have an actual rent roll of $100,800. If during a one-year period the vacancy factor could be reduced from 30 to 10 percent, the new rent roll would be $129,600. The increase of $28,800 in revenue would reflect a value increase of $288,000 or more.

Decrease Expenses.   Logically, any decrease in expenses should increase the bottom line, and this is often the first place investors look to concentrate their efforts for an increased bottom line. There are many opportunities to decrease expenses, and the astute property manager knows how to bring about those decreases. However, most sellers are less than 100 percent accurate about their expenses, and it is not uncommon for even an astute property manager to acquire a property with the belief that the expenses can be reduced only to find that they go up instead—often dramatically.

This is likely to happen with some of the larger expenses. Real estate taxes, for example, are likely to continue to rise. However, even this may sometimes be mitigated if you discover that the present owner never challenged the tax assessor's imposed assessment. That is correct, even assessors make mistakes, and not generally in your favor. Make a habit of challenging the tax assessor every year. Hire a firm (usually a lawyer) to handle the paperwork. These firms are usually paid only if they save you money, and then they get a percent of that amount. More on this later.

Insurance is another area where the cost is likely to go up. Pay close attention to ways to get the coverage you need at a reduced cost. Not all insurance companies charge the same amount, so shop around.

When it comes to the nitpicky kind of expenses that you are likely to find on the rise, one of the nastiest is neglected property maintenance. Neglected property maintenance is often the culprit that needs to be tackled early, as it's easy to cut back in this area, especially if the previous owner has planned for some time to sell the property and meanwhile is milking it for every dime it can produce. A buyer looks at the income and expense report on the property and finds several expenses that seem too high, such as travel and promotional expenses. These should be easy to cut back on, the buyer thinks. But there is not enough attention given to the fact that over the past five years the amount of money dedicated to repairs and replacements has been pitifully low or nonexistent. This property is going to need repairs and replacements to bring it to the level it should be. These expenses cannot be overlooked.

Many weekend property owners sell because they can no longer keep up with the maintenance costs. At first they did the work themselves: a little paint here, an unplugged toilet there, and so on. But now they do not have the time, and to hire it out for a small rental property is too expensive. If you want to own this kind of property and can either do the work yourself or have enough units to justify hiring a full-time person or crew to do the work, then your expenses can be reduced tremendously.

Buying a job is a good investment, and many foreigners coming to the United States have begun their fortunes by buying a property or business that not only gives them a job but provides jobs for their whole family. Properties that are management- and employment-intensive, such as hotels, motels, and restaurants, are good examples of this kind of investment. While this aspect does not decrease overall expenses, it has the benefit of keeping the cost within the family.

In the final analysis, when it comes to cutting expenses, it could be that the right thing to do is not to cut expenses but to increase them. The key with these seven factors is how they relate to each other. It is clear that deferred maintenance by the old owner needs to be dealt with, but how about upgrades? One of the best ways to increase the value of a property is to increase the amount of money you can charge the tenants, and that might mean more than a new coat of paint.

The key is to have a plan and to estimate how long it will take you to recover the cost of upgrades by way of increased rent.

Reduce Debt Service.   If a property has NOI of $144,000 and total debt service of $100,000, the cash flow will be $44,000. If the demand rate is 10 percent, the value of this property may be assumed to be $440,000 plus the amount of the debt. If there is a first mortgage of $1 million on the property (with an annual debt payment of $100,000), then the property value would be $1.44 million. However, the debt service of $100,000 may not reflect the true value of the property. For example, if the outstanding first mortgage is $500,000 at 13.75 percent interest and would fully amortize in just slightly over 8.5 years, the annual payment would also be $100,000.

The NOI yield indicates that value is there. Based on the NOI yield, a 10 percent demand rate on $144,000 would reflect a value of $1.44 million and not the combination of $500,000 plus $440,000. Yet the cash flow does not support a greater purchase price unless the debt service can be reduced. Refinancing the high interest rate would be the logical solution.

Add Rental Units.   When a property has untapped potential, the logical step is to find out what it is and then obtain it. In the case of rental properties, this untapped potential may be additional units that can be added or created by remodeling the existing building.

Start by finding out what you can do. The first step in discovering this untapped potential is to review the building codes, ordinances, and zoning for the subject property. This will tell you exactly what the current laws allow for that property given your existing situation. It is possible that you may already have more than the currently legal number of rental units and that, although you are grandfathered in, there will be little opportunity to add more units without first having the whole building conform to the current laws. Even if this is the case, however, it may be worth doing, so do not overlook any possibility. If your ultimate goal is to sell the property at a profit, the exercise to find out all the potential options may help you sell to someone else who wishes to follow up.

Decrease Tax Liability.   Real estate tax can be a substantial part of total expenses. It is not uncommon for the ad valorem tax on a rental property to exceed 25 percent of the total expenses. Any reduction in the real estate taxes can result in a substantial jump in the spendable cash and property value (see question 117).

Convert to Another Use.   Economic conversion is the technique of taking a property and converting it to another use. This does not mean that you need to make any physical changes, but only that the new use will give you an economic benefit following that conversion. A small apartment building may be converted to a college fraternity house if a university is willing to pay you more in rent than apartments would bring and if zoning laws allow that use. An office building may be simply and more subtlety converted to a medical center by catering to doctors only. Economic conversion can also be a long-range goal, as might be the case in purchasing a rental apartment complex with the idea of converting it to condominiums within 10 years.

140.   What Is the Loan-to-Value Ratio, and How Do I Calculate It?

The *loan-to-value ratio* (LTV) describes the relationship between the amount of a loan and the value of the property that is security to that loan.

> **Solution:** Learn how to calculate the loan-to-value ratio by reviewing this section.

If a property worth $200,000 has a $150,000 mortgage on it, the LTV is 75 percent. If the mortgage is $180,000, the LTV is 90 percent. This percentage is found by dividing the amount of the loan by the value of the property. For example:

- $150,000 ÷ $200,000 = 0.75; thus, $150,000 is 75 percent of $200,000.
- $180,000 ÷ $200,000 = 0.90; thus, $180,000 is 90 percent of $200,000.

This ratio is important to both the lender and the borrower, as it establishes the level of risk for the lender. Because the lender will adjust his or her interest rates according to the risk of the loan, a higher LTV will usually carry a higher interest rate for the borrower to pay back.

Some lenders set loan rates to specific LTV levels. The prospective borrower would be advised to find out what those levels are and to review the result of reducing the LTV of a loan requested to obtain the lower rate. It is possible that other terms in addition to the interest rate could affect the borrower favorably with a greater equity position.

It would be logical that 100 percent minus the LTV would be the borrower's equity. While this is the theory, in reality this is not always the case, and a lender should be careful to examine the real value of any property that is mortgaged as security to a loan.

Be wary of values that have been artificially established to suggest a value greater than a fair market would deliver. For example, in-house transactions can create leases showing income that, while actual, is temporary and unrealistically high. That high income would reflect an equal value. If a prospective lender is offered an LTV of 70 percent on a loan request of $700,000, one would expect the property to be worth $1 million. A lease to a retail enterprise that produced a triple net (all costs covered by the tenant) to the property owner of $100,000 would suggest a value of $1 million at a demand rate (interest the investor demands on his investment) of 10 percent. If, on the other hand, the real market rate for rent in the building is only $65,000 triple net, then the real market value of the property could actually be less than the requested loan of $700,000. This could be a classic example of a property owner trying to pull the wool over the eyes of a lender. This borrower would have no actual equity in the property, and the property would have zero equity above the mortgage.

However, not all zero-equity transactions are bad. A builder clearly manufactures equity in a property; even when he or she borrows 100 percent of the funds needed to acquire a property and to construct a building on it, the final result should represent a value in excess of the loan. The term *value added* is what a person or other entity brings to the total equation. Real estate investment trusts (REITs) have borrowed this term to the extent that the day after major privately held owners, like shopping centers, become REITs, they can say that as publicly traded real estate investment trusts they (the founders) have added value to their portfolios. Is that possible? They think so, and as long as people believe them, I guess it's true.

141.   What Are the Different Ways to Calculate Mortgage Payments, and Why Is Each Important?

The typical mortgage that is obtained from a lender is usually based on an equal monthly payment for the whole term of the mortgage, or at least equal payments between adjustment periods for changes in interest rates. However, there are other ways to calculate these payments.

Eight Common Methods to Calculate Mortgage Payments

- Equal constant payments of interest due plus principal
- Equal constant payments when short-interest principal increases
- Equal constant payments of interest only
- Zero payment with principal increases
- Equal principal plus interest payments
- Adjustable rate mortgage
- Graduated rate mortgage
- Reverse mortgage

Equal Constant Payments of Interest Due Plus Principal.   This is the most common method of calculating a mortgage, and in this type of mortgage the monthly payments are fixed at the same amount for the term of the mortgage (or term between adjustments of interest rate). A mortgage made at 10 percent interest for 20 years would have a constant rate of 11.58 percent. A constant rate is a rate that combines interest and principal. If you had *McGraw-Hill's Interest Amortization Tables* (the "red book") you could calculate the constant rate by finding the payment rate under 10 percent interest for 20 years, which would be a monthly rate, taking then the 1,000 repayment rate and multiplying that by 12, moving the decimal one more place to the left in the result. Therefore, a $60,000 mortgage would have a monthly payment of $579 ($60,000 × 0.1158 = $6,948 ÷ 12 = $579). This mortgage would then be paid out over a period of 240 months (20 years) at a constant rate of $579.

The formula to get this payment takes into consideration that each month's payment will be made up of two separate amounts of money: interest and principal. Of these two amounts, each year the total interest paid will be less than that of the previous year because of the slowly increasing deductions to the principal.

These mortgages can have a balloon payment or an adjustment in interest rate that would cause the amortization schedule to be changed to reflect the new balance owed and the altered interest rate. When these adjustments are made, the new payment schedule changes from the previous schedule.

The important characteristic of this kind mortgage is that the principal owed will decrease slightly every month until the mortgage is paid off. If there is no balloon payment, then the mortgage will eventually amortize itself fully with this payment.

Equal Constant Payments When Short-Interest Principal Increases.
Some mortgages are established with a constant mortgage payment but have a flexible interest rate that can be adjusted at periodic times. This type of mortgage differs from the first in that although the payment remains constant during the term of the mortgage, the amount of principal may (and generally does) increase.

The principal owed actually increases because the mortgage payment does not fully cover all the interest due. This may not be the case in the first few years of the loan, but as interest rates are adjusted upward, the amount due for interest is greater than the monthly payment. This deficit is added to the principal due. As the principal due increases, more and more interest would be due, but as the payment does not increase, the continuing short-fall increases. It is easy to see that this kind of mortgage can cause a fast growth of principal outstanding.

These mortgages can build up principal owed very quickly and should be carefully reviewed before accepting this form of repayment. A critical aspect of this kind of mortgage would be the ability of the borrower to pay principal at any time. If the loan does not allow that, or imposes a penalty for principal payments during the term of the mortgage, then the loan should be rejected.

Equal Constant Payments of Interest Only.
A mortgage of payments that are interest only and do not include any principal will have the same monthly (or other period of time) payment during the term of the loan. The final payment would, of course, include all the principal due.

If the interest rate can be adjusted by the lender, the payments would remain constant and equal only for the term between adjustments.

Zero Payment with Principal Increases.
Often, as an inducement to a buyer, the seller will agree (or the buyer will insist) that the seller hold a zero-payment mortgage for a period of time. This provision can be incorporated into any mortgage at any period of time during the mortgage. In this situation, the borrower makes no payment at all, and the principal owed is increased each month (or other period) by the amount of interest for that period. For example, an $85,000 loan at 12 percent interest per year with zero payments for the three years and then seven

annual payments of a constant equal payment of principal plus interest would have the following repayment schedule.

End of Year	Total	Payment Made Interest	Principal	Principal owed
1	$ 0	$ 0	$ 0	$ 95,200
2	0	0	0	106,624
3	0	0	0	119,419
4	26,166	14,330	11,836	107,582
5	26,166	12,910	13,256	94,325
6	26,166	11,319	14,848	79,477
7	26,166	9,537	16,630	62,847
8	26,166	7,542	18,624	44,222
9	26,166	5,307	20,859	23,362
10	26,166	2,804	23,362	0

This mortgage, while it has zero payments during the first three years, shifts to an annual amortization payment for the next seven years.

Equal Principal Plus Interest Payments.   This payment schedule is similar to the previous schedule, but with a significant difference. Here the principal payment remains the same, say, for example, $8,500 per year for a $85,000 loan. This would retire the debt in 10 annual payments. If the interest rate is 10 percent, the interest owed would decline each year as the amount owed is reduced.

End of Year	Total	Payment Made Interest	Principal	Principal owed
1	$17,000	$8,500	$8,500	$76,500
2	16,150	7,650	8,500	68,000
3	15,300	6,800	8,500	59,500
4	14,450	5,950	8,500	51,000
5	13,600	5,100	8,500	42,500
6	12,750	4,250	8,500	34,000
7	11,900	3,400	8,500	25,500
8	11,050	2,550	8,500	17,000
9	10,200	1,700	8,500	8,500
10	9,350	850	8,500	

Notice that the total payment for the first year is nearly double that of the last year.

Adjustable Rate Mortgage.   This term, often abbreviated ARM, is any mortgage that has a method of adjustment to the interest rate built into the mortgage payback terms. This form of loan is very attractive to lenders, as they are not locked into any fixed interest rate over any period of time. The mortgage can also be attractive to borrowers, who may guess correctly that interest rates will go down rather than up.

   ARM mortgages are generally adjusted to U.S. Treasury bills. As there are several different types of Treasury bills, the variation of rates between different lenders can vary accordingly. This type of mortgage should be carefully selected from among several lenders, and all the different terms should be considered. One of the most important terms is the maximum that the interest rate may be increased during any period and over the term of the loan.

Graduated Rate Mortgage.   The graduated rate mortgage (GRM) starts with payments that are below the amount needed to pay interest, and in this respect it functions like any other mortgage where the deficit is added to principal owed. This mortgage, however, has scheduled increases in payments so that eventually the payments will begin to amortize the loan fully. This form of loan is attractive to a young property buyer who anticipates a steady increase in income to handle the higher-than-usual payments that come with this kind of mortgage.

Reverse Mortgage.   This kind of a mortgage is touted as a very effective tool for retired people who need additional income to sustain their lifestyle. My personal opinion of this form of lending is Shakespearean: "Neither a borrower nor a lender be." In any event, I am often asked questions about reverse mortgages, so here is some information that should help you get started in your quest to decide whether this kind of mortgage is for you.

Reverse Mortgages and Whether They Are Good or Terrible

- They are available for people over 62 who live in their own home.
- Such persons generally must live in the home most of the time.
- Some loan programs accept up to four-unit buildings.
- Generally, no repayments are required as long as you live there.
- The payments to you can be one lump sum or periodic payments.
- You continue to be responsible for taxes, insurance, repairs, and so on.
- These loans come from public and private sectors.
- They are not recommended by AARP or Jack Cummings.

Home Equity Conversion Mortgage (HECM), offered via HUD, is the only such mortgage that is federally insured. Rules and requirements vary, as do rates.

The lowest-cost mortgages are made by state and local governments. Costs start out high then taper off. Outlive your life expectancy, and these loans are great. Die early, and you may have zapped your estate.

Warning: Be careful of potential tax consequences. See a tax lawyer before signing on. These mortgages can affect your Medicaid eligibility. Read the fine print carefully. Penalties can lurk inside legal jargon. Two great sources of helpful data, as well as a place to complain if you feel you are being unduly pushed to accept a reverse mortgage, are www.aarp.org/revmort and www.hud.gov/offices/hag/sfh/hecm/rmtopten.cfm. You can navigate each of these sites for up-to-date information.

142.   What Is Subordination, and How Is It Used?

Subordination is a term that literally means to "fall behind" or, in reality, "to allow your rights to become secondary to another's rights." It is a very important term often used in land leases and seller-held financing; however, it can also occur in other real estate transactions.

> **Solution:**   You need to question every possible risk when the term *subordination*, or another form of this word, appears in any contract to which you are a party. Anytime you allow someone else to exceed your rights there can be substantial risk. Review the rest of this section for more details.

Subordination with a Land Lease

If you enter into a land lease whereby you give a developer (or investor) the right to lease a parcel of land you own, say a 100-acre commercial site, and the developer's idea is to build a shopping center on that site, subordination will likely enter the picture. Assume the developer proposes a 99-year lease, for which she will pay you a substantial annual rent. You might like this idea because it provides you with annual income, and your estate may end up with the property at the end of those 99 years. A nice legacy to leave to your family.

However, the developer is not going to spend $100 million of her own hard-earned cash to build this center; the developer would want to borrow the funds from her usual lender (e.g., an insurance company or pension fund), and that lender would likely want to hold a first mortgage position as security on the lease-hold interest of the property.

This first position would exceed your right as owner of the land and would require you to agree to "the subordination of your rights" as owner to the first mortgage position of the land lease.

Where Is the Risk?   If something goes wrong at any time during the lease and the lender takes over the property (by foreclosure), then unless you are able to protect your interest in the land by taking over the mortgage yourself, you can lose your land.

What Can You Do to Limit That Risk?   First of all, make sure you have a very good lawyer. Then go over all the different kinds of protection you can build into the deal. This will include, but is by no means limited to, the following:

- Require the developer to pay several months of mortgage payments ahead of schedule throughout the entire life of the mortgage. This can give you a clue about problems ahead of the actual "the well has gone dry" moment.
- Have a substantial security deposit from the developer that allows you to dip into it to meet any shortfall due the lender.

- Have notice provisions that all parties, including the lender, agree to. This means you receive copies of any notices sent to the borrower and that notify you of any pending default on the loan.

- Have the lender agree that you can step into the shoes of the borrower in the event of a default and that there would be no automatic foreclosure proceedings filed.

- Require all development to be bonded with a sufficient bond to complete the project should the developer last be seen boarding a flight to Rio.

- Have release provisions that require unused land, often called *out parcels* which shopping center developers would leave undeveloped until a later date. This would keep those parcels out of the hands of the lender and yet the developer would have the right to obtain your future subordination if and when they were to be developed. If the developer intends to sell the out parcels, then you may want to have a substantial portion of the proceeds of the sale go to you. Predetermine the formula for such a division of the out-parcel sales proceeds.

- Have the developer pledge other assets as additional security in return for you giving up your rights to the lender.

Subordination Used with a Sale

This occurs when you sell outright the 100-acre commercial site but do not get 100 percent of the proceeds of the sale. Say the developer or investor gives you 25 percent down, and you hold a five-year mortgage that pays you interest only per year (or any other acceptable terms) and then pays out in full at the end of that term. The developer, just as with the lease example shown earlier, wants to borrow a massive amount of money to construct the center, knowing that on the final draw from the lender he or she will get enough money to pay off the balance owed to you.

Where Is the Risk?   The risk remains the same as with the lease, and your protection is also the same. The only advantage this situation has is that the risk is reduced, because you want it to be very clear that the final draw is enough to pay you out and that the lender knows this and has agreed to this arrangement.

143. What Is a Balloon Mortgage, and How Is It Used?

A balloon can burst, and then it no longer exists in its original form. So it is with a balloon mortgage.

> **Solution:** In the example of the subordinated sale in question 142, I mentioned a five-year loan that paid interest only for that term. When a mortgage has terms of any nature that do not amortize the loan fully within the term of the mortgage, and there is a call date (payoff time) when the mortgage must be paid off, it is called a *balloon mortgage*.

This situation occurs quite often, even though the term *balloon mortgage* may not appear in the documentation. The most common use is when the lender gives the borrower a long period of amortization for calculation purposes, which has the effect of lowering the amount of each monthly payment.

For example, a $500,000 amount borrowed at 6 percent interest for 15 years with full amortization during that term will have a monthly payment of $4,220.83, which amounts to $50,649.96 a year. This represents, by the way, a loan payment with a constant rate of 10.13 percent ($500,000 × 10.13 percent = $50,649.96). Because this is a direct deduction from the NOI of the property, the cash flow will be reduced by that same amount. On the other hand, if the lender offered a 30-year amortization with a call (balloon date for payoff) at the end of the fifteenth year, we would see a monthly payment of $3,000 and an annual total for debt service of $36,000, which is a 7.20 percent constant ($500,000 × 7.20 percent = $36,000). The difference between the cash flow of the property with this debt service is an additional $14,649.98 a year.

From the investor's point of view, this can be a substantial increase in the yield of the property and would make that loan very attractive over the shorter, fully amortized loan.

Naturally, both loans end at the same date, and in the case of the second situation there would be a sizable balloon of the outstanding principal still due. How much would that balloon payment be? Solve this by asking how many years it would have had to go. The answer is 15 years. The interest rate remains 6 percent, so how much principal would a payment of $36,000 a year (in monthly installments of $3,000) pay off? We already know that the 15-year loan had a constant rate of 10.13 percent. If the formula is the amount remaining times 10.13 percent equals $36,000, we would then divide $36,000 by 10.13 percent. Remember, when calculating percentages in math, move the decimal two places to the left. Therefore the remaining principal due at the end of 15 years is $355,380.05 ($36,000 ÷ 0.1013). As you can see, there is a trade-off between getting greater cash flow with the balloon mortgage versus the quicker payoff of debt. Look to your investment goals to see which of those two scenarios you would want to use.

144. How Does a Wraparound Mortgage Work to Benefit Both the Buyer and the Seller?

The wraparound mortgage is a technique of secondary financing whereby the mortgagee incorporates existing debt into the mortgage structure to effect a payback schedule that can leverage up the return to the mortgagee of the wraparound funds while establishing an overall rate and payback program that is satisfactory to the borrower.

> **Solution:** A wraparound mortgage takes several mathematical events into play and gives the holder of the mortgage an advantage over the interest yield of the original or subordinated mortgages. It can also provide some

protection to the holder when senior mortgages (such as a
first mortgage) hold secondary positions in a sale.

Wraparound Mortgage Example

Assume you are the seller of a 6,000-square-foot office building that has a fair market value of $360,000 and is supported by the $38,000 NOI that the property honestly reports each year. Against this value you own two existing mortgages:

$120,000   First mortgage at 8 percent interest, 10 years remaining. Monthly payment: $1,455.90.

$80,000   Second mortgage at 7 percent interest, 10 years remaining. Monthly payment: $928.90.

This gives you a total existing debt service of $2,384.80. Along comes a buyer who is willing to pay your price, but who wants to invest no more than $100,000 down and expects to earn a cash flow of $10,000 (demand rate of 10 percent) each year. Current market rates for this type of property are at 9.5 percent interest.

Conventional Solution.   The buyer goes to a local lender and refinances the loan for a new mortgage of $260,000, providing all the funds to pay off the existing debt and to pay you the difference of $60,000. That, plus his $100,000, closes the deal. At 9.5 percent over a 23-year payout, his debt service will be $27,860.80 per year, and without any increase in the NOI his desired return of $10,000 seems to be preserved.

Problem with the Conventional Solution.   The cost to the lender can be as much as $8,000. In addition, many current lenders will not consider a payout over 23 years, and many want a balloon at the end of 7 or 10 years.

Wraparound Mortgage Solution.   As seller, you agree to hold a wraparound mortgage in the amount of $260,000. This amount takes into consideration the existing debt, which consists of $200,000 and the new money portion of the wraparound of $60,000. The terms you establish are 8.75 percent interest with an amortization based on an 18-year schedule with a balloon at the end of 10 years. As this is a wraparound mortgage, you will continue to make the payments for the existing first and second mortgages out of the money paid you from the buyer. The buyer need be concerned with only one mortgage schedule and one monthly payment of $2,394.30.

A quick check of the combined payment on the first and second mortgages will show that these mortgages total $2,384.80, so there is not much of a difference each month, so little, in fact, that for the rest of this example we will forget about the $9.50 left over.

However, at the end of seven years you will no longer need to make the payments on the second mortgage, so that $928.80 starts to stay in your pocket and does so for three years.

At the end of the tenth year, your wraparound will balloon and the owner will have to pay you off. The balloon payment will be $164,888.20, all of which will stay in your pocket because the existing first mortgage has self-amortized and has been paid off. Here is a summary of the total benefits:

$9.50 each month for 120 months	$ 1,140.00
$928.80 each month for 36 months	33,436.80
Final balloon payment	164,888.20
Total benefits and payback	$199,465.00

All this is your return on the new money portion of the wraparound mortgage that was originally $60,000.

The primary benefit for the lender is the leverage over the existing debt, as the interest rates on both the first and the second mortgages were less than that of the wraparound. As the borrower paid 8.75 percent on the total of $260,000, he was in essence paying 0.75 percent overage on the first mortgage of $120,000 and 1.75 percent overage on the second mortgage of $80,000.

The primary benefit to the borrower is the relative ease with which this transaction can proceed to close and that his overall payment, mortgage terms, and interest rate are below the current market rate.

145. How Does the Cost-of-Living Adjustment Work?

A cost-of-living adjustment is calculated in leases as well as in some mortgages. Its purpose is to keep future payments level with changes in the cost of living. Different indexes can be used to calculate this adjustment.

> **Solution:** Whenever a stream of future payments is to be collected, the use of indexing tends to keep those payments in line with changes in everyday expenses and potential currency devaluation. As the alternative to such indexes is short-term leases that tenants must renegotiate each period, indexing gives tenants the security of having a set long-term lease to count on.

Cost of living is a term that is primarily used as a basis for adjustment of leases and purchase contracts. The U.S. Department of Labor maintains a series of indexes that keep track of the cost of living. These indexes are published with specific references to different areas of the country, and by sending in a request, you can be put on the mailing list to receive both the national and local indexes. Send your request to the U.S. Department of Labor, 1371 Peachtree Street, N.E., Atlanta, Georgia 30367.

Example of Cost-of-Living Adjustment

Look at Figure 16.1. Assume a lease provides for an annual adjustment to any increase in the cost of living All Items Index for All Urban Consumers and was

12 Months Percent Change

Series Id: CUUR000OSAH, CUUSS000OSAH
Not Seasonally Adjusted
Area: U.S. city average
Item: Housing
Base Period: 1982–84 = 100

Year	Jan	Feb	Mar	Apr	May	June	Jul	Aug	Sep	Oct	Nov	Dec	Annual	HALF1	HALF2
1995	2.4	2.3	2.3	2.4	2.4	2.5	2.6	2.5	2.5	2.7	2.7	3.0	2.6	2.4	2.7
1996	2.9	2.9	2.9	3.0	3.0	2.8	2.9	2.9	2.9	2.9	3.0	2.9	2.9	2.9	2.9
1997	3.0	3.0	2.8	2.6	2.6	2.8	2.5	2.3	2.5	2.4	2.5	2.4	2.6	2.8	2.5
1998	2.1	1.9	2.1	2.4	2.4	2.4	2.3	2.5	2.4	2.3	2.3	2.3	2.3	2.2	2.3
1999	2.2	2.2	2.3	2.3	2.1	2.2	2.2	2.2	2.3	2.2	2.2	2.2	2.2	2.1	2.2
2000	2.6	3.0	3.1	3.0	3.1	3.4	3.6	3.6	3.8	4.1	4.1	4.3	3.5	3.1	3.9
2001	4.9	4.5	4.5	4.5	4.6	4.5	4.1	4.2	3.5	2.9	3.1	2.9	4.0	4.6	3.4
2002	2.0	2.2	2.1	2.3	2.2	1.9	2.0	2.1	2.3	2.7	2.4	2.4	2.2	2.1	2.3
2003	2.6	2.6	2.9	2.6	2.7	2.5	2.6	2.4	2.4	2.4	2.2	2.2	2.5	2.7	2.3
2004	2.2	2.1	2.0	2.3	2.4	2.7	2.7	2.7	2.8	2.9	3.1	3.0	2.5	2.2	2.9
2005	3.0	3.0	3.3	3.2	3.0	2.7	3.0							3.0	

tied to the 1982–1984 index, which was set at 100 for that start time. Every new index from 1984 forward will have a different index number for the month and year you are comparing. As the index, or the cost of living reflected by that index, increases, the numbers will increase slightly. If the cost of living goes down (which it rarely does), the number will decline.

Look at the index for U.S. City Average All Items 1982–1984, which has monthly index numbers from January 1995 through to June 2005. Such a provision may require the adjustment to be on an annual basis or any other period of time.

Refer to the price index shown in Figure 16.1. Look at the January index for 2003, which is 181.7, and for the same month in 2005, which is 190.7. Here's how to calculate the increase.

Step 1. What is the actual increase between January 2003 and January 2005? The index shows 2003 to be 181.7, while 2005 is 190.7. This indicates an increase of 9 ($190.7 - 181.7 = 9.0$).

Step 2. Calculate the percent of increase by which 190.7 exceeds 181.7.

$$CPI\% \times 181.7 = 9$$

$$CPI\% = 9 \div 181.7$$

$$CPI\% = 0.0495321$$

Rounding this number will give you approximately a 4.953 percent increase between January 2003 and January 2005.

Step 3. Assume a lease began January 2003 and had its first cost-of-living adjustment two years later. A base rent adjustment of a lease that started at $3,000 a month would be increased by this CPI adjustment as indicated:

Old base rent	$3,000
CPI increase	× .04953
Actual increase	148.60 (rounded up)
New base rent (until next adjustment)	$3,148.60 ($3,000.00 + 148.60 = $3,148.60)

146. What Is a Sliding Mortgage, and How Does It Work?

A sliding mortgage is rarely used, mostly because not too many people know when and how to use it. It can be a lifesaver, however, when used in the right circumstances.

> **Solution:** Discover the magic in a sliding mortgage. Its purpose is to retain the negotiated terms obtained from a seller (or other lender) by having preagreement from the holder or subsequent holder of the mortgage that the security to the mortgage can be replaced by another property.

The Sliding Mortgage Defined. You purchase a commercial building and the seller agrees to give you a mortgage to aid in your purchase. This mortgage could be a first, a second, or any other rank—any mortgage can be used in this event. Remember, however, if there is any debt below that, it will move up a rank when you slide the mortgage to another security. Assume here that the mortgage to the seller is a first mortgage in the amount of $300,000 and is interest-only at 5 percent for 15 years with a balloon at that time. The property in question is a vacant lot worth $400,000, so the seller is paid $100,000 and holds a mortgage for the balance.

These terms fit the seller's goals because it gives him some additional income for 15 years and will balloon the year he plans to retire. Your idea of what to do with the property is unclear, so you ask the seller to agree to allow you to move the mortgage (i.e., slide it) to another security at any time in the future. You agree to certain provisions and protections to the seller (e.g., the new security must have a minimum of $400,000 of appraised equity above any existing debt).

A couple of years later you have the opportunity to exchange the lot for a motel in Vero Beach, Florida. The owner of the motel is willing to take the lot at your quoted value of $700,000 free and clear of any debt. The motel is worth $3 million, so you will owe the seller $2.3 million. You ask the seller to hold a second mortgage of $200,000 behind a new mortgage of $2,100,000. He agrees to this.

But wait. What about the $300,000 you still owe to the seller of the lot? You estimate that the new equity in the motel after this transaction will be as follows:

Value of the motel	$3,000,000
Less debt	2,300,000 (first and second combined)
Equity in this property	$ 700,000

To make the lot free and clear you now slide the lot mortgage over to the motel.

Value of the motel	$3,000,000
Less debt	2,600,000 (all three combined)
Equity in this property	$ 400,000 (which the seller of the lot agreed would replace the security)

This results in your saving the low-interest-only $300,000 mortgage and allows you to avoid having to overleverage the property with the primary lender. If the seller would not agree to hold a second mortgage, you would have to renegotiate the price down a bit and the new first mortgage up a bit to make the numbers work.

147. What Are the Most Important Steps When Making Income Projections?

A projection of any kind requires a lot of research, comparisons to past trends, and some luck.

> **Solution:** Prospective purchasers should review the following eight steps prior to making any purchase. The first three steps should be maintained in a ready-alert status; that

is, investors should continually update these three steps so that they recognize genuine opportunities that arise and that fit their goals.

Eight Steps to Making Meaningful Income Projections

- Know your investment goals.
- Review the levels of risk acceptable.
- Know the standards for the area.
- Make general assessments quickly.
- Tie up the property.
- Complete due diligence.
- Keep projections realistic.
- Have an exit strategy in place.

Know Your Investment Goals.   Every investor should have a clear set of goals. These goals become the focus of everything the investor does. For every property considered, the following question should be answered in the affirmative: "Does that property move me closer to my goals?" If the answer is maybe, then additional time should be devoted to study the possibility, but if the answer is a clear no, then no more time should be spent on that property and the investor should move on.

Review the Levels of Risk Acceptable.   Two elements determine acceptable risk. The first is the investor's ability to handle a specific property. By *handle*, I mean the ability to deal with everything about the property. If the investor is comfortable owning and operating small apartment buildings, that does not mean that same investor should buy a 200-unit complex. The second element that determines acceptable risk is financial capability. If the transaction is marginal and the complexity of the property at the upper limit (or above) of the investor's ability, then risk increases substantially.

All investors need to make continual adjustments to decrease risk by expanding their abilities and capabilities. Management, accounting, legal, and building trade skills, are all factors that can be learned to advance investors' comfort with any specific type of property. As this learning progresses, investors can take on larger and more complex properties without increasing their level of risk.

Know the Standards for the Area.   Every local area has its own standards for income and expenses. While there may be similar comparisons among different areas of the world, the data going into income and expense calculations can vary widely. You will be able to learn the standards for your area by getting the facts firsthand from real estate insiders. The real estate tax accessor's office often has information that can be used to build your own file of standard income and expenses. Often, that department publishes its findings that give rather detailed information about income and expenses for different kinds of rental property.

Make General Assessments Quickly.   Many prime opportunities are lost because the prospective buyer has spent too much time making studies of the property only to find that another buyer has snapped it up. The key to successful acquisition of real estate is to see the opportunity and buy it before someone else does. It is a very simple and absolute concept. If you can do that, you are bound to succeed.

Tie Up the Property.   After the general assessment, if the property fits your goals and is within your acceptable risk level, then tie up the property so that additional studies can be made without fear of losing the property.

There are many different techniques that investors can use to tie up property with little or no risk of capital. Letters of intent that lead to formal contracts can be accomplished without any initial deposits, and sometimes the deposit itself can be a promissory note (promise to pay), or the contract may be a real estate exchange proposal that does not require any deposit at all.

Once the property has been tied up, the investor should move to the next stage.

Complete Due Diligence.   The key to good due diligence is to know the limitations of those making the inspections. Home inspectors may not be qualified to inspect a warehouse or high-rise office building, so seek the inspection team (or teams) that have the expertise to properly inspect the property in question. Be sure you know what will *not* be inspected, as this is often overlooked when you okay standard-looking forms and pay for services.

The title work, which is a critical part of the inspection of a property, should extend to the actual survey. I have seen many transactions close only to have later problems due to the failure of a lawyer, a title agent, and even an owner to recognize that the dimensions on the survey do not match those they see on the ground.

Keep Projections Realistic.   You will only kid yourself if you think that there is hidden cash you can pocket, just like the seller said he or she was doing. Make sure you have anticipated increases in things like taxes and insurance, which are likely to go up.

Have an Exit Strategy in Place.   This might be a plan or an idea, but have something already thought out about how you are going to ultimately dispose of this property. This kind of a plan can and should go through constant rethinking as events change. Never fall in love with a property to the extent that emotions get in the way of making decisions. Stick to your goals in this respect. If you love it, be ready to keep it.

17

Insider Secrets for Creative Investing Techniques

148. Are Those Get Rich Quick TV-Offered Real Estate Programs a Realistic Way to Learn Real Estate Investing?

I have seen them all and have even been asked if I would put my own program together: "If Cummings can do it, so can you." However, the reality is that real estate investing is so personal and so local and the keys to making money are so simple, I believe anyone who really wants to invest in real estate is better served by picking good books on the subject and following the tips and guides of those of us who are knowledgeable.

> **Solution:** The task of becoming a successful real estate investor cannot be learned from any single source. The quest to become a true insider is a constant learning process. Remember, real estate is an eyes-and-ears-open plus hands-on proposition. But do not just listen: see and touch. It takes a lot of doing and profiting from your own mistakes and those of others to fine-tune your abilities to see what isn't there (yet) and to have exit plans ready when you start.

True insiders in the real estate investment game have learned the secrets to success by becoming experts in their comfort zone.

Any program that begins with the premise that all you have to do is buy right and then sell for more than you paid has missed the target. While learning techniques can be very helpful in structuring a creative deal, the fundamental truth about real estate is that you will be successful because you recognize the opportunities within your comfort zone. You reduce risk by knowing what not to buy, and you ultimately buy because you see the clear path to a profit before you close the deal. The problem with most of the TV get-rich-quick real estate programs is that they teach you techniques that can actually help you buy real estate. However, using a technique without knowing where and when to use it can create economic disasters. The guy who teaches you how to buy without using any of your own money is taking advantage of you. The key to success is not necessarily buying property without using your own money, but buying the right property for you.

To build your wealth to the point where you achieve financial independence is a worthy goal that you can attain. The road to that end is not possible overnight. It requires time, effort, and the willingness to overcome obstacles, expand your sphere of reference, and make sacrifices. You will need to follow the examples set by those who have made similar choices and succeeded. You must strive to develop your own comfort zone. The steps to achieve this are available from masters who have spent their lives experiencing it, and these masters make this knowledge available to you in their books, which are free to borrow in any well-stocked library in America. Take advantage of those sources and that kind of experience instead of paying big bucks to use a get-rich-quick plan or program that will work only by accident.

Build your own library of material from authors who have written their experiences for you to learn from, and dive into the world of real estate. You will soon become an insider yourself. The effort must come from you.

149. Is There at Least One Easy Way to Invest in Real Estate without Risk?

Risk comes with almost everything you can do. However, there are many ways to reduce your exposure to it. It is like flying an airplane. If you do not have a clue how to make it go up or how to land it, you are in tremendous trouble. But if you are patient and take the interim steps required to learn how to fly an airplane, then you will have eliminated the great majority of risk that goes with flying.

My recommendation to all first-time real estate investors is to attempt to satisfy their most basic of needs while at the same time moving closer to their overall goals. For most people this means acquiring a place to live. If you are now renting, you are actually in a loss situation every month. There is no equity being built up, no appreciation, no tax write-offs, and so on. All the benefits of real estate are in the hands of someone else: the person you pay your rent to every month.

The United States is full of small rental properties that are affordable to millions of first-time buyers. If you are able to acquire one of these income properties, you can satisfy your housing needs while at the same time using other people's money (OPM) as your ally in the investment game. Using OPM instead of *being* one of those other people who pays will enable you to build your wealth.

It might be true that your first small apartment building will not be in the neighborhood where you eventually want to own a home, but it will move you closer to your goal of financial independence than if you continue to pay rent.

150. When Using Other People's Money, What Are the Most Important Questions I Need to Ask First?

In my McGraw-Hill book, *Investing in Real Estate with Other People's Money*, I have devoted nearly 400 pages to this one subject. Other people's money, or OPM, is one of the essential elements that has made real estate investing as dynamic as it is.

> **Solution:** Getting and using OPM requires two important abilities. The first is the willingness to go into debt, and the second is to discover how to get other people to pay off your debt.

Using OPM gives all investors the opportunity to acquire something that they would not be able to afford otherwise. However, OPM does not grow on trees, and the use of someone else's funds is not free. The overall price for a mortgage, for example, can be more costly than the property or the investment can support. Many investors end up in deep trouble with debt they cannot pay back.

Part of the solution to this problem is to know what questions to ask before you obligate yourself to any mortgage, and to know how to evaluate the answers you get. The following are the 21 most important questions you should have the answers to before you go into debt.

---

21 of the Most Important Questions to Ask before You Go into Debt

- What are the current market rates for similar mortgages?
- Who are the lenders?
- Has the lender or the lender's agent asked for a nonrefundable deposit?
- Are you required to sign personally on the note?
- Are cosigners required, and what does that mean?
- Does the lender ask for cross-collateralized security?
- What will you lose if you cannot repay the debt?
- Can the debt be assumed by a future buyer or other party?
- What are the repayment terms of the debt?
- Can the interest rate go up?
- Is there a balloon payment?
- Does the lender have any equity kickers in the loan agreement?
- Is there a penalty for early repayment of principal?
- What are the notice dates and why are they so important?
- Can you substitute security to the loan?

- Does the mortgage require the lender to subordinate to other debt?
- Is any part of this mortgage a wraparound?
- Do you have any releases of security from the mortgage?
- Do you have the right to obtain secondary financing?
- Are there provisions that trigger sudden payback of the debt?
- Can I meet the obligations of this debt?

Market Conditions for Debt Are One of the Guides to Successful Property Negotiations.   If you are in the middle of a heated offer-counteroffer situation, the transaction may hinge on how the debt is structured. When you are asking the seller to hold debt, you need to make sure that you do not overpay for that debt. At the same time, you should be aware of the cost of the usual charges to obtain market loans so that you appreciate and take into consideration what you are saving by using seller-obtained or other less expensively obtained debt.

Who Are the Lenders?   It can be helpful to know who you might have to deal with should you need to make a change in the repayment terms. A mortgage held by a previous owner, for example, can have far more flexible terms than one held by an insurance company. The larger institutions may not be accessible to discuss even the simplest of mortgage terms with you. Private parties generally are more motivated to keep the loan in place or to seek an early payoff at a discount. However, when you discover who the lender is, find out if this person (or company) has made a habit of selling and then foreclosing on the same property. This does happen, and you do not want to be the next victim.

Nonrefundable Deposits before the Loan Has Been Committed May Be a Clue to Move On.   Many lenders ask for an application fee to run a credit check or handle some basic paperwork. However, when lenders or persons who represent themselves as agents for the lender ask for a substantial nonrefundable deposit, beware. Mortgage agents, people who pretend to be mortgage brokers, and even companies that claim to be genuine insurance companies, banks, and other sources of money exist and make their living (and a very good one at that) from the deposits they take for loans that never are obtained—loans that never were intended to be obtained.

A very simple way to avoid this problem is to ask for references, check with the Better Business Bureau, and ask reputable lenders in the area for verification. (Do all three.) If you cannot get references because the agents "never give out the names of their clients," then move on and do not give them a deposit.

Many Loans Require Personal Signatures.   Your personal signature on a loan may not increase your immediate risk to the transaction, but it can place a burden on your ability to obtain other credit.

Virtually all savings and loan mortgages and similar institutional loans will want your personal signature. If you can acquire a property subject to another loan without having to assume it or to give your own personal guarantee, that fact may make the property easier to sell.

Nevertheless, even though lenders would like to have a personal signature, that does not mean they will insist on it. If you are experienced in development and have a great track record in completing successful projects, lenders will consider that aspect being as important as, if not more important than, personal signature saying that you will be responsible for the loan. Strive to attain the status where lenders look to your professionalism as being critical to the entire process.

Cosignatures May Be Needed If Your Credit Is Weak.   Some first-time buyers discover that the lenders want additional security to make the loan, and one way to obtain that is to have a partner, friend, or relative co-sign. This is a risky situation for the cosigner, who may want (or be entitled to) an interest in the property or some other consideration. As a cosigner to a mortgage, you want to know what you stand to lose if your friend, partner, or relative does not make the payments.

Cross-Collaterization Gives Lenders an Additional Property or Other Item of Value as Security.   Lenders may ask what you can add as security to a loan because they are not satisfied with your ability to repay the loan and they do not want to be at risk without additional security. When you give some other valuable item or property, the loan becomes cross-collateralized, and that other property or item of value is locked into the loan until it is repaid or until the borrower obtains a release of that security.

What Do You Risk If You Cannot Repay the Loan?   Many borrowers do not put this question in the proper time frame. For example, if you buy a property with $25,000 down and get plenty of help from friends to fix it up, remodel it, and rent it, do you have only $25,000 at risk? No. The correct answer is that you have a lot more at risk because of the invested time and effort. If you increase the value to double what you paid for it, then the new value is still not all that you have to risk because you may also be personally responsible for eventual payback of the loan. At the time you bought the property, your total net worth may not have been substantial, but what about ten years down the road?

What if the seller holds the mortgage and there is a balloon payment and the whole amount you borrowed comes due and payable at a particular time? At a future point in time, your increased fortune can be at risk to early decisions. It is important for you to look at the level of risk over a period, particularly as the due date of any balloon payment approaches.

Assumption of Debt by a Future Buyer or Other Party Is Important.   If you assume an existing loan on a property you are buying, you save the cost and time it takes to go out and get a new mortgage. Better yet, including a provision in your loan obligation that allows a new owner to assume that loan increases your opportunity to sell the property in the future. This occurs because the loan you have when you close might have a much better term and interest rate than will be available in the future, even the near future.

Be careful of loans that appear to be assumable but are not. Some lenders give the impression that their loans are assumable by incorporating phrases such as "This loan may be assumed by a future party on approval from the lender." The lender may mean that a new buyer will have to apply for assumption as though he or she were taking out a new loan (with the additional expense of points and other costs). That kind of assumption is very misleading.

Every Borrower Should Know All the Repayment Terms.   This means carefully reading the mortgage and the mortgage note. Do not rely on what the lender tells you about the loan, as the lender's representative may not know what the loan provisions actually call for. This is common today, as many savings and loans institutions sell their loan portfolios to other lenders, some from other states. The loan documents may vary among lenders, and the exact details contained in the document itself are important. Read and make sure you understand what it says.

Adjustable Interest Rates Are Common, but How Adjustable Are They?
Adjustable rate mortgages (ARMs) are very common for both institutional and private loans. The amount of adjustment and how the adjustment is made can vary greatly, and you should be aware of all the details that pertain to those calculations. If the loan interest rate can be adjusted up, why not down, too? You should insist on the following provisions:

Adjustments that can go down as well as up, tied to the same criteria

A maximum that the rate can be adjusted in any one year

A maximum that the rate can adjust upward over the life of the loan

Balloon Payments Can Sneak Up on You.   When the mortgage has a balloon payment, which is a scheduled repayment of some or all of the principal owed, you must be very careful to keep track of these due dates. Some loans have a call date that gives the lender the right to require you to repay the principal or to renew the mortgage for another term at an adjusted interest.

If the lender decides not to renew, then the mortgage has a sudden balloon. Other balloon payments are planned, and when used properly can be an effective technique for the buyer to obtain an easy payment schedule for a period of years leading up to a refinance of the property. Smart borrowers make efforts to refinance their mortgages a year or two in advance of a balloon payment to ensure they have sufficient time to get the needed financing.

Some Leaders Require Equity Kickers to Increase Their Return.   Often, these are provisions that give lenders a percentage of the income over and above a set amount or that give them a percent of the profit on a future sale. Whatever the kicker, make sure you understand the exact formula that is used to calculate it. Many buyers use equity kickers as a tool to entice sellers to give good terms or accept a lower price. As with most financing terms, offering kickers can be beneficial to both the borrower and the lender when used correctly.

Prepayment Penalties Often Exist.   When lenders want to make sure that they will have a set return for a minimum period of years from the loan, they may insert a prepayment penalty in the mortgage document. This can cause many problems in the near future if you suddenly are able to refinance at a much lower rate or have a buyer who wants to pay off the high-interest mortgage. If you find such a penalty, do not automatically assume that the lender will impose it. If you are assuming a mortgage at a closing, attempt to get the lender to remove that provision.

Mortgages Often Contain Notice Deadlines That Can Cause Havoc If Not Met.   When a mortgage has a provision that requires a specific notice be sent to the lender, it is critical to make note of the deadline dates. For example, if the mortgage allows partial repayment of principal at a specific time (say, every January of every other year) only if notice is sent 60 days earlier, failure to send the notice could make it impossible to repay without penalty until the next eligible period. Other important notice dates may trigger mortgage extensions or releases of security.

Substitution of Security Allows You to Move the Mortgage to Some Other Property.   This great buyer's technique is the magical ability to slide a mortgage from one property to some other element as security to the loan. Most home mortgages or other institutional mortgages do not allow you to replace one security with another, but within private seller-held financing, this can be a good tool to use. The right to pledge a different property as the security to the loan could allow you to take advantage of the good terms of a seller-held second mortgage while refinancing the property with a new mortgage that might not otherwise be possible without first paying off the second. If you are ever asked to give this provision to a loan you are holding, make sure you have the right to approve the substitution property.

Subordination of Debt to New or Other Debt Is a Good Buyer's Technique.   This provision allows you to refinance or obtain additional financing without having to repay the existing debt. When lenders subordinate their position, they give up their place in line to the security pledged on the loan to another. A simple and very common form of subordination occurs when the owner of land that is leased to a building owner agrees to subordinate to a first mortgage. In this situation, the first mortgage now has a right to the land ahead of the property owner, even though the lease may have been in effect prior to the loan.

Wraparound Mortgages Should Be Reviewed Very Carefully and All Underlying Mortgages Read and Understood.   Remember, in the wraparound mortgage the holder of that mortgage becomes the intermediary between the new owner of the property and the old debt that is part of the total wrap situation. When there are existing or new wraparound mortgages on a property, the buyer's contract may show obligation to make the wraparound mortgage payment only, with the underlying mortgages being paid by the seller (who now holds the wraparound mortgage).

However, if the seller does not make the payments on the underlying mortgages, then the buyer can be in default and lose the property even though all required payments on the wraparound have been met. One way to solve this problem is to make sure that the wraparound mortgage sets up a trustee or other collection agency that takes the required payments from the buyer and before giving any money to the seller makes the necessary payments to the underlying mortgages.

For example, if you buy an office building and are obliged to make a $20,000 per year payment on a $180,000 wraparound mortgage, make sure that the collection agent (title insurance company, escrow agency, real estate agency, or lawyer) takes your money and then pays out on the existing first mortgage of $80,000 and the second of $40,000 before giving the seller any return on his or her new money portion of the wrap ($60,000). Then you can be sure that the first and second mortgages do not go into default.

Releases of Security, Critical in Land Deals, Are Important Whenever Multiple Security Is Given. The typical release of security is when a land developer buys a tract of land and then sells off or builds on individual lots he or she carves out of the tract. Without the ability to release those lots as part of the overall security of the mortgage, the mortgage would have to be paid off, or the new buyer would have to accept the risk that if the developer did not continue to pay on the mortgage, the lot could be lost.

In the case of a loan where the lender had originally required a cosigner or cross-collaterization, you should insist on the right to release that additional security once the loan has been paid down to an agreed-to level.

Secondary Financing Can Be Helpful, Now or in the Future. However, some loans have provisions that do not allow you to increase the amount of debt against the property. If this is the case, make sure you understand the full ramifications of this provision, and seek to limit its scope or to have it removed completely.

Acceleration of Payback Can Mean Disaster. Most loans have provisions that allow the lender to accelerate the repayment of the debt. The usual situation is a *due-on-sale* clause that gives the lender the right to call the loan if you sell the property. Other provisions can be tied to long-term leases, exchanges, sale of partial interest, replacement of management, and other conditions that the lender believes important when the loan is originally made. A default on your part of any of the mortgage terms may also give the lender the right to trigger this demand for payment, so it is important to look for any provision that ties one clause of the mortgage document to another.

Can You Meet the Obligations of This Debt?   Do not view this as a border-line situation where you might be able to pay if everything goes well for you. What I am talking about is the absolute ability to make payments when due. If you lose a few nights' sleep thinking about the debt, odds are you are going to lose much more sleep worrying about making those monthly payments until the day you lose the property.

If the mortgage is on non-income-producing property, then you will need other income or savings to draw against to meet the payments. This is okay if it fits your goals and the plan to reach those goals. If the property you are buying produces income, then that income plus your other income sources will be at risk. Can you handle it, or are you on that thin edge that comes with highly overleveraged investments?

If you are on that edge, have some inside information, trust in the luck of the Irish (if your name is O'Hara), and have a silver spoon tucked away somewhere; then you are okay. Otherwise, go back to the drawing board and reconsider this investment and the debt you are about to go into.

151. How Can I Maximize My Negotiating Leverage with Any Seller?

Savvy buyers learn negotiating techniques that work for them. What you do may be different from the next successful buyer, but your overall strategy will be improved if you keep the following 14 steps in mind.

14 Key Steps to Negotiating with Sellers

1. Have your real goals firmly in sight.
2. Remember that sellers are not the enemy.
3. Learn all the facts you can about the property.
4. Attempt to discover the real reason why the property is for sale.
5. Meet with sellers on their own turf, and be observant.
6. Let sellers know your goal is to help them reach their goal—which is to sell the property, hopefully to you.
7. Have insulation between you and sellers by having a qualified broker represent you.
8. Make an informed offer.
9. Do not respond quickly to negative reactions from sellers.
10. Make sure sellers fully understand your proposal.
11. Do not appear anxious.

12. Let your intermediary be anxious and willing to help a seller make a deal.

13. Be ready to give and take to close the deal.

14. Close the deal on small items, never big ones.

152. What Are the Key Steps for Negotiating with Buyers?

There is an art to good negotiation techniques, especially when they are successful in helping you acquire property at a price and terms that ensure a future profit.

> **Solution:** Remember foremost that any prospective buyer is a path to your goals (as a seller) so grasp their offers, no matter how low, with the sincere goodwill. At least they have made an offer. Think how many millions of people do not think enough of your property to even do that.

Buying and selling real estate is an essential part of making real estate a source of income and wealth. The smart seller knows how to deal with buyers to move property in tough times and how to make deals that work and do not fail. The following 10 steps will improve your chances of being a more successful seller.

10 Key Steps for Negotiating with Buyers

1. Have your real goals firmly in sight.

2. Remember, the buyer is not your enemy.

3. Do not be insulted by any offer.

4. Use the broker as a buffer between your frustration and the need to sell.

5. Look for the smallest meeting of the minds.

6. Build on every positive agreement.

7. Do not accept or decline any segmented offers.

8. Do make counterproposals.

9. Be open to creative ideas.

10. Keep your social activities with the buyer to a minimum.

153. What Is a Letter of Intent, and When Should It Be Used?

A letter of intent is a simple proposal, drafted in the form of a letter, to a seller from the buyer or the buyer's agent outlining the basic terms and conditions under which the buyer would enter into a contract with the seller. The letter is not a binding contract and does not cover all the legal aspects of a contract. It generally deals only with the most important points of a purchase.

> **Solution:** Because you can draft a letter of intent yourself without using a legal (and sometimes intimidating) lawyer-oriented document, it is possible to move quickly to a mutual understanding and agreement between the parties regarding the business elements of the deal. Factors such as price, amount of down payment, deposits, due diligence periods, and closing date are generally the principal elements that need to be decided. Once decided and mutually agreed to, the parties can then move to the formal purchase agreement with their lawyers leading the way.

A letter of intent is effective in many situations ranging from very complicated and very expensive acquisitions to simple deals that may not involve more than a few thousand dollars. Advantages and the disadvantages of this format follow.

Six Advantages of Using a Letter of Intent

Quick and easy to find out what the seller will really do

Not binding

Deals with important issues only

Not in legal language

Easy to respond to

Less costly than formal legal proposals

Three Disadvantages of Using a Letter of Intent

Might be a plate of mashed potatoes thrown against the wall to see what sticks (risks offending some sellers)

Not binding

May delay the actual formal contract

A Sample of a Simple Letter of Intent

The following sample letter of intent is a proposal to acquire a 50-unit apartment building. The seller is asking $1.65 million for the property, all cash to a first mortgage of $300,000.

Letter of Intent

Dear Mr. Seller,

This letter is to express my interest in purchasing the Sutton Hill Apartments located in Plantation, Florida, which you own.

To speed up this process, I have outlined below the basic business terms, which I believe would be fair. I know that there may be special circumstances you might like to discuss with me about this sale, such as date of closing, time you may need to find a replacement (tax free) investment, and so on. I will be most accommodating in working with you on any aspect of this transaction.

If the basic terms are acceptable to you, please get back to me so that I can have a formal agreement of sale drafted for your review. Naturally, if any of the terms are not acceptable to you, I suggest you let me know what might be acceptable and perhaps we can work out the details. Understand that this letter does not constitute a binding agreement on either your or my part, and such a binding agreement will occur only after mutual acceptance of the formal purchase agreement.

Basic Terms and Conditions

Price: $1,450,000

Deposit: $50,000 on signing of the formal agreement with another $150,000 on approval of inspections and due diligence.

Payment Terms: (1) a total of $700,000 to you at closing; (2) assumption of the existing debt of $300,000; (3) a second mortgage you would hold amortized at prime plus 2 points, over ten years, in the amount of $450,000.

Kindly direct your reply to my Fort Lauderdale office, and should you have any questions, please call me anytime.

Sincerely yours,

Jack Cummings

The preceding letter of intent may seem to be very simple and basic, but that is the whole idea.

When Would You Use a Letter of Intent?

The usual application of this format is for a more complex transactions. The deal in question need not be a purchase, as the letter of intent works just as well for leases, exchanges, and so forth. One word of caution: most real estate brokers and salespeople do not want to use the letter of intent because they are trained to get the buyer and seller to sign on the dotted line. That kind of sales procedure works very well with contracts that become binding the moment they are signed, but not too well for letters of intent.

154. What Is a Standard Deposit Receipt Contract?

The word *standard* sends shivers up and down my spine. Any teenager with a smattering of computer smarts can turn out a document that may look like it was purchased at an office supply store.

> **Solution:** Know which standard contracts are frequently
> used, and read them very carefully. Every time you are
> presented with something that appears to be a "standard"
> document, make sure you read it very closely. It just might
> not be the "standard" you remember.

Standard contracts can be found in just about every office supply store and many well-equipped drugstores, and they can cover everything from a lease to a power of attorney. However, you should avoid the standard real estate contract sold at office supply stores. Instead, pay a visit to the local board of Realtors or any Realtor's office and pick up a copy of the most recent board of Realtors–approved real estate contract.

Board of Realtors' contracts are drafted and approved by the state or local bar association members and are designed to take into consideration all the factors that govern real estate matters specific to the laws of the state and the peculiarities of that region.

Having a contract that is generic but totally comprehensive is important because it will speed up the formal contract stage of any purchase or sale. It is a good idea, however, to make sure that the terms and conditions within this standard contract are exactly to your liking. Just because the contract is standard does not mean that you must agree with the terms and conditions it contains. If you are the buyer, then you can dictate what you want to offer and the terms and conditions you want to be obligated to or expect the seller to live up to.

It is a good idea to have your own lawyer make suggestions for changes or additions to this standard form so that it fits your special and unique needs. If you begin with a truly comprehensive standard form, the customized one should contain substantially all the same provisions, and therefore it should not be quickly rejected by the other party as being overly obscure. The best part of following this procedure is that by minimalizing changes to the standard contract, you should be minimalizing your cost as well.

Warning repeated: Not all so-called standard forms are standard. With the advent of modern computers has come the ability to print out forms that appear to be standard, but that have been altered by a few words here and there to change the meaning of whole paragraphs. For example, one simple typo can change the word *not* to the word *now*. Every contract you sign should be read aloud by you. If there is anything you do not understand or that sounds strange, then do not sign that agreement until you have a full and comprehensive understanding of what is written and you accept and agree with everything.

155. What Is the Best Investment Technique I Can Use to Reduce Risk?

There are many investment techniques that an investor can use to meet the demands of the seller and to structure a deal to fit the goals of the buyer, but one technique is by far the very best at reducing risk in a transaction.

> **Solution:** The best single technique real estate investors can learn to use is the *option*. When the option is used to its maximum potential to reduce risk, buyers option a property that they already know they are going to purchase. The option period and the option funds are buying time . . . time that will allow other things to occur and that will limit the expenses normally incurred to carry the debt on the property.

The option is a very flexible technique that is used in many creative transactions. The basic option is a simple promise from a prospective buyer that if that buyer is allowed to buy (or lease or exchange) a property owned by a prospective seller, then in payment for that option the prospective buyer will give up some valuable consideration.

The advantage of using the option is that you have 100 percent control of the outcome of the situation. For example, if you pay a property owner $5,000 for the option to buy his or her lot at the end of 12 months, the property owner has given you the right to buy that property and cannot sell it to anyone else (except subject to your option). Best of all, if your agreement allows the $5,000 option money to apply to the purchase price, then you truly benefit. If the value of the property goes up within that year, then you will get the benefit of that value increase.

The option can give you time, and in real estate time can be the best factor to have on your side. Within the time of your option, you may be able to cause something to happen (e.g., new zoning, property improvements, erecting a building next door), or something favorable may occur (proposal for a new highway, plans for a new hospital a block away, etc.). Options give the informed investor the opportunity to leverage a very small amount of money with a very limited risk into great gains.

156. Can I Use Sweat Equity to Acquire Real Estate with Zero Cash Down?

Sweat equity is the added value that you create by doing something to improve the value of the property you want to purchase. For example, if you paint the property, that cosmetic improvement will likely increase the value.

Solution: Virtually every investor is capable of adding value to a property through some form of sweat equity. To make the best use of this, you need to assess what talent you have that you can use to this end. Can you paint, plant, simply clean up? All have their place in sweat equity improvements.

Sweat equity is the added value you create whenever you buy a property and do something to improve its worth. At times you can capitalize on that sweat equity by using it as all or part of the down payment to acquire the very property for which you create the value. Follow six key steps to maximize your chances of using sweat equity as a tool to buy property.

Six Key Steps for Achieving Maximum Results with Sweat Equity

- Know your sweat equity talents.
- Find goal-oriented situations that fit those talents.
- Have a plan to implement your talents quickly.
- Be confident when you make your presentation to the owner.
- Demonstrate your sweat equity benefits to the owner.
- Show how this win-win plan can help both of you reach your goals.

Know Your Sweat Equity Talents. First of all, you may have talents that you never thought you had, so the first step is to find out what those might be. Start by reviewing everything that can be done to increase the value of a property. If you have no talent with a hammer, a paintbrush, or garden tools, do not stop looking, because your real forte might be doing the paperwork to get a property rezoned. Keep in mind, too, that sweat equity need not be limited to effort specifically oriented to real estate—it can also be effort that the seller will find valuable and satisfactory as a down payment. If you install swimming pools for a living, for example, you could offer to construct a swimming pool for the seller's house.

Find Goal-Oriented Situations That Fit Those Talents. Look for property that will work to move you toward your goal and at the same time allow you the opportunity to use your sweat equity talents. This does not mean that you buy only this kind of property, because other opportunities will come up that do not require sweat equity.

Have a Plan to Implement Your Talents Quickly. Stress the areas that give quick results and are positive value producers. These generally will be centered around economic conversions, but they are by no means limited to that technique.

Simple fix-ups, new paint, a new front door, minor (but quality) repairs, new or redesigned landscaping, a new rental theme, a zoning change, or a building variance can boost the value overnight.

Be Confident When You Make Your Presentation to the Owner. Selling your sweat equity talents can require you to be a good salesperson, but even if you are not, be sure that you are confident in what you are doing. Often the low-key approach works well, and if you have examples of your work, then show it off. Use photographs of homes you have painted, pools you have installed, and landscaping you have cut or planted, even if the work was not done for properties you were buying. The end result is to show the seller that he or she can have confidence in your abilities because you do.

Demonstrate Your Sweat Equity Benefits to the Owner. You have to show that what you are offering the seller has positive benefits. For example, you and the seller come to terms on the price and the payout but have yet to agree on your down payment and the closing date. Offer to repaint the entire building, rebuild the broken gate (if there is one), and do other odds and ends that likely would have a value of, say, $10,000. For this, ask for an option to purchase the property at the price and terms you and the seller have already agreed on . . . except that the closing date will be 8 to 12 months from now.

The seller gets the benefit of all this improvement at no cost and dreams at night that you will not be able to come up with the needed cash down to close. What the seller does not know is that you will be working with your mortgage broker to get the needed financing, showing off the property's new look from the added value that you have given to it. In the end you triumph.

Show How This Win-Win Plan Can Help Both of You Reach Your Goals. If you agree to fix up the seller's apartment building, redo the landscaping, paint the walls, and so on, and all the seller has to do is supply the material and give you an option to buy the property at the end of 18 months at today's price, what does the seller have to lose? The seller loses nothing except some time, and he or she is well paid for that time by the effort you are going to expend. This is just one way to show a win-win situation to the seller; each situation will vary, but each can be a positive experience for both sides. Show that you are ready to risk your time and effort to increase the value of the property.

When you increase the value of the property, you are doing so because you want to borrow funds to buy the property or to warrant the seller holding 100 percent of the financing. When the situation fits, anything is possible.

157. How Can I Use My New Sweat Equity to Acquire Other Property?

Sweat equity works well when combined with one or more creative deal-making techniques.

Solution: Never stop looking for a way to skin the cat (poor cat), because not every method you might think of will work for all situations. Sweat equity is taking hard work and applying either the work itself or the added value that the work has provided and leveraging it into another transaction. If one thing does not work, try another.

One of the best techniques is the option, mentioned earlier. The following is an example of how one investor used sweat equity and an option to start her real estate investment portfolio.

Jan owned a small garden shop that employed a team of landscapers to take care of yards around the neighborhood. She had never thought of using these talents and facilities as a base to acquire real estate until it was suggested to her by a Realtor friend who presented her such an opportunity.

The property was a large old home that was well located near the center of town. It was on a large lot that was zoned such that in addition to single-family use, professional offices were permitted. One of the best features, and the original reason the Realtor had thought of Jan in the first place, was that around the house were several dozen large Canary Island date palm trees. These trees, plus other mature landscaping around the home, had all but overgrown the lot and nearly hid the house from the street. With one look at the lot, the trees, and the neighborhood, Jan realized she was looking at a good opportunity, if she could manage it.

The talent matched the opportunity. She knew she could sell most of the mature landscaping around the lot, retaining a few of the Canary Island palms but moving virtually everything else. What she would get from the sale of that plant material she could spend fixing up the building and converting it into law offices.

The situation was ideal for her talent. All she needed was a plan that would enable her to convince the owner to sell her the property with nothing down. Together with her Realtor friend, she formulated the following:

- A price was agreed to that was fair for both parties.

- She developed a plan for fixing up and remodeling the lot and the home that would involve completely new landscaping, repainting, and restructuring the home into large office suites that could also, if the rental market shifted, be used as residential apartments.

- The seller was to grant her a lease option on the home that would give her 24 months free rent based on the fact that she would do all the work outlined in the plan. At the end of that period she would have the option to buy the property at the agreed-upon price. If she did not buy the property for any reason, she could continue her lease by paying the monthly rent, plus an increase based on the cost of living.

Jan was risking her time and effort, but little else. A few months into the project she moved into one of the first suites that had been remodeled, which saved her the rent she had been paying for an apartment across town. In the end, she sold all but one of the Canary Island palms, and the proceeds from those and the other mature plants more than paid for painting the building and the other repair costs. Before the end of the first year the property was finished.

The building showed off beautifully once the landscaping opened up. Shortly thereafter, several law firms were interested in renting the whole building.

At that point Jan could simply have sold her option at a big profit. She had more than doubled the value of the property because what was once a dark, gloomy, unrentable old house had become a well-located, stately site for the headquarters of a local law firm. However, selling her option was not in her plans, and instead she negotiated a great long-term lease with one of the interested law firms. With the lease as the basis for her collateral and the newly improved property as the security, she obtained a first mortgage that more than paid the full purchase price she had negotiated a year earlier.

One added bonus to this deal was that while all the work was going on at the old house, she had a large sign out front advertising her landscape business as the company doing the work. That sign brought additional work to her business. The combination of the well-done work and extra business added to the reputation of her firm, and the solid experience of using sweat equity plus an option to acquire property led Jan into other, similar transactions.

158. Why Do Real Estate Exchanges Work?

Real estate exchanges are hot items in any market because they enable a buyer or seller to deal without the need for money.

> **Solution:** This situation points out the importance of being able to mix and match your investment techniques. Exchanges do work, for a vast variety of reasons. They can be structured using anything from sweat equity (see questions 156 and 157) to almost anything that is tangible or intangible. The investor does not even need money to make it work.

This is important, not because the seller shuns money, but because the seller can actually *receive* money in the exchange, but not necessarily from the buyer. Exchanges function in both small and enormous transactions all the time, and they do so for one or more of the following reasons.

Five Reasons Real Estate Exchanges Work

- Tax savings
- Way to move you closer to your goals
- Face-saving transaction
- Accommodation to the deal
- Because it is the best offer you've had

Tax Savings.   The IRS allows certain real estate exchanges to be tax-free and other kinds of transactions that involve a swap or change from one property to another to have tax-saving opportunities. The IRS rules are covered in IRC Section 1031. (Review the IRS 1031 tax-free exchanges discussed in this book.) If your property qualifies for 1031 treatment, it is possible for you to exchange your equity into other investment properties and never to pay the capital gains tax. Not ever.

Way to Move You Closer to Your Goals.   Any exchange that moves you closer to your goal is a good exchange. Notice that I did not say the *best* exchange, but it is important to understand that you should make decisions based on your available options, not wishful thinking. Many sellers overlook the difference between these two factors and hold out for an unattainable desire rather than taking a positive move in the right direction, even though that move may not take them the full distance they want to go.

Face-Saving Transaction.   Some real estate exchanges work only because they enable the seller or the buyer to finalize the deal. When the seller is highly motivated, an exchange property added to the offer as a sweetener by the buyer might be that "mystery box behind the curtain" that allows the seller to save face and execute the deal at the same time.

Because many real estate exchanges do not show values of either property, but only the differences (mortgages assumed or given, cash paid, etc.), there is the added face-saving benefit that the sellers need not admit (even to themselves) they took a loss on the deal.

Accommodation to the Deal.   Often, a big deal or an important transaction is closed on an exchange. This might come following a long negotiating process in which the buyer offers something as a counter to a seller's proposal. To attain the main goal and make the bigger deal, many sellers will accept something they actually do not want and would not otherwise buy. Of course, they may turn around and exchange that same property or item in another deal or give it to the broker as part of the commission owed.

Because It Is the Best Offer You've Had.   Okay, so no one has offered to buy your run-down motel, and you are going nuts trying to keep it open while you sell it. Then along comes someone who offers you something as a down payment equal to 20 percent of the value. All you have to do is take this thing and the buyer will take the motel off your hands, assume the $12 million mortgage that is eating a hole in your bank account, and set you free. Why not?

159. How Can I Use Exchanges, as Both a Buyer and Seller, to Invest in Real Estate?

Not every real estate market is universally hot. Los Angeles might be a buyer's market, which means there are fewer buyers than sellers and buyers rule the roost, while at the same time Chicago is a seller's market. What causes this to happen? It is simply the local nature of real estate, and it is another reason for you to avoid thinking of real estate as a commodity that is sold in the great supermarket called the world.

> **Solution:** Look for investment techniques that allow you to become proactive. When it is a buyer's market and you are having trouble selling your property, jump into a phone booth (like Clark Kent) and change into your Superman costume. Or in this case, change into a *buyer*.

Two basic approaches to real estate exchanges work well for investors. All investors should be aware of these approaches and should strive to learn how to use real estate exchanges as a method to build wealth.

Two Basic Approaches to Using Real Estate Exchanges

- Exchange as an aggressive buyer.
- Use exchange as a tool to attract buyers.

Exchange as an Aggressive Buyer.   All sellers should look at their situation and determine whether they can use the property they have for sale as a stepping-stone to move into another real estate investment. For example, Marilyn has two apartments in New York City. The one she lives in has a $100,000 mortgage, and the other is free and clear. She has decided to sell the mortgaged property and move into the unmortgaged apartment. However, it is a buyer's market, and the few offers she has had on the mortgaged apartment have been way below her bottom line. What should she do?

Marilyn should consider exchanging for a better investment. In fact, she might discover that by using both apartments in the deal she can move her equity into a truly meaningful real estate investment that could change her life by giving her the income to become financially independent.

Best of all, by becoming an aggressive buyer, she can actually turn the market around. She is now not really a seller at all: she is a buyer in a strong buyer's market.

Use Exchange as a Tool to Attract Buyers.   When no decent offers are coming in, sellers can offer their property for exchange, or at least partial exchange. This aspect may entice a buyer to show interest who otherwise may have avoided that property.

Many sellers do not offer exchanges because they think, "If I exchange, I won't get the cash I need . . ." This is far from the truth. First of all, it is possible to exchange and get cash, as the following example shows, but more important, what do you need the cash for? If the answer is to buy something else, to move to Chicago, or to go on a trip around the world, then the exchange might produce that end result just as easily as, or even easier than, a sale that has yet to happen.

For example, Oscar has a mountain cabin for sale. He has not used it for five years and is tired of renting it out and having to deal with the problems of owning rental property a full day's drive away from home. The cabin is offered for sale and is free and clear of debt. Oscar wants $70,000 cash.

What is he going to do with the money? At least $40,000 is going to go to pay off the first mortgage on his existing home—that is, if a buyer comes along. But the problem is that no buyers seem to be interested in his cabin.

Oscar runs an advertisement in the local paper offering to accept an exchange for up to $20,000 in value. He gets several offers from out of the blue: a late-model car, a boat, a vacant lot nearby, and so on. In each case the potential buyers want to pay the balance over a period of time at a good interest rate.

In the end, Oscar realizes that his original goal of paying off his home loan is not exactly reached, but he does end up with a nice vacant lot that he thinks will go up in value and a first mortgage on the cabin that is at a higher interest rate than the one on his home. The payments made to him by the new owner of the cabin give him more than enough to meet his mortgage payments, and he has some cash left over. His exchange moved him closer to his goal.

Think about Oscar's situation for a moment. Did he really need to pay off the mortgage on his home? Or did he simply need someone else to pay it off for him? Think outside the box and look to the results you want to attain, not the method you believe is your only choice to follow.

160. How Can I Use Barter to Acquire Real Estate?

Barter is the original method of acquisition. I give you two apples and you give me a handful of salt. It is still the way of life in many parts of the world, and communities can thrive on this simple give-and-take approach.

> **Solution:** Barter deals require you to look beyond your wants and needs to examine what else will satisfy the circumstances. If you are being pressed to get rid of something and there is but one person in line for what you have, then be flexible. But do not hold onto those apples in search of a person with salt who does not ever come.

What if you don't have a handful of salt? What if you instead offer me a fish you just caught? That depends on how much demand I have for my apples. After all, I have to review my apples and guess how long I can hold out waiting for salt before my apples go bad. A fresh fish might sound pretty good with that in mind.

Barter is the oldest known method of commerce. It is also a very active way of doing business in the world today. Countries barter millions of dollars of goods for the goods or services from other countries. Businesses use barter as a way to exchange goods and/or services that would go unused or unsold for items or services that allow them to expand. These sources for bartered items are much like sources for borrowing money (banks and other lenders) that lend you other people's money (OPM). In this instance, instead of money, you exchange your own goods or services or to obtain something more to the liking of a person you are attempting to do business with. I call these sources "other people's barter" (OPB). Companies that do bartering are open prey if your services are such that they constantly use those services anyway, or if you can offer them benefits in return for their bartered items.

Airlines are just one of the businesses that barter frequently. Following are some of the OPB businesses that make considerable use of bartering.

16 Sources for Other People's Barter (OPB)

Airlines

Art galleries

Cable networks

Cruise lines

High-end fashion clothing

Hotels and motels

Insurance

Jewelry manufacturers

Local newspapers

Magazines

Nonproperty rentals

Printing companies

Radio stations

Restaurants

Special travel programs

Television stations

If you own or work for such companies, you are an insider in knowing how to make a deal with them. If you are not, you should not worry; perhaps you can work out a deal for their services or products that can be used as a down payment. You promise to give them something in return, such as renting one of the apartments in your new apartment building.

Barter need not be all there is to any deal, but every time you can incorporate some barter into your transaction you are moving closer to the maximum use of your services. Even the seller who agrees to accept a cruise around the world worth $50,000 as part of the sale of his $500,000 office building can be the result of a beneficial barter. All you have to do is contact a travel agency, find out which cruise companies pay the highest commission, and then offer that cruise as a part of your deal. If your cut of the commission is $10,000 (it could actually be even more), that is only 2 percent of the purchase price; however, if your purchase price requires only $100,000 down, you may save a full 10 percent of the down payment.

161.   How Can I Use Pyramiding as an Investment Tool?

Pyramiding is another form of exchange, but instead of offering a property in exchange for another property, you offer a mortgage on a property you own (or are going to acquire, or that is owned by a friend).

> **Solution:**   Review this section and open your eyes to one of the most creative methods of exchanging. Remember Oscar's example in question 159. People will take what solves or relieves their problem when other solutions have not materialized.

Pyramiding is a technique of acquiring a property by offering a mortgage on another property as the down payment. For example, you own a home in Texas worth $200,000. There is a first mortgage of $115,000 on that home, leaving you with $85,000 of solid equity. You want to buy a small apartment complex in Alabama and offer the seller a $40,000 second mortgage on the Texas home as a down payment. This is the basic form of pyramiding:

You own a home worth	$200,000
You owe the bank	115,000
This leaves you equity of	$ 85,000
You create a second mortgage	40,000

Because you have control in this situation you can create this second mortgage at terms and interest that fit your financial capability. In short, the alternative might have been for you to go to a bank and ask, "Please give me $40,000 in cash so I can buy this small apartment complex in Alabama. . . ." Such a request puts the bank in charge, not you.

Instead, you point out to the seller of the apartment complex how solid this mortgage is, that it is one point more than he would get at the best savings and loan in the country, that it is interest-only to him for 10 years (after which it might balloon), and that he will have some ready cash in his pocket every month.

One of the advantages of using this technique is that by not adding secondary financing to the property you buy (at least at this stage) it might be possible to generate cash in a short-term refinance of the property once its value has been increased. To make more elaborate use of the technique, it is helpful to understand the five key steps that make this interesting tool work.

Five Key Steps to Real Estate Pyramiding

1. *Understand the greener-grass syndrome.*   It is natural for people to look across the fence and think the grass is greener on the other side. It is much the same with real estate. Many sellers are more inclined to hold a mortgage on another property than on their own property. This factor can be used successfully by investors who want to use pyramids to increase their real estate holdings.

2. *Get control over the first property before you move to the second property.* It is essential that before you offer a mortgage against one property as the down payment on another, you must either own the first or have it firmly in your control.

3. *Use your knowledge of the area to demonstrate value.* This is where your comfort zone pays off. You should already have done the homework to back you up on the values and on how to further increase those values.

4. *Move the other party closer to his or her goals.* This is just logical negotiating. Whenever you can help the other party in the transaction move closer to his or her goals, you have also moved closer to finalizing a deal.

5. *Never let anyone question your success.* Your research and your facts should speak for themselves, and your confidence should be unshaken. The seller does not have to take your deal; that is the seller's right. But one of the pitfalls with the pyramid technique is that the buyer may be put on the defensive about the value of the property being offered as security. Always be willing to support any statement you make, but in the end, suggest that the seller is welcome to make an independent study or appraisal to justify your values and leave it at that.

162. How Can I Form a Real Estate Syndication?

A real estate syndication is an investment technique or program in which one person, the syndicator, finds a property to buy, then brings in other people to join in the purchase. To be successful at this requires knowledge of the best procedure to follow.

> **Solution:** Know the law (both federal and state laws can dictate steps and procedures you need to follow), and learn the best approach to follow.

It is not uncommon for several people to get together to purchase a property as co-owners. This is a form of syndication, and if you spend a couple of hours with a lawyer who understands the legal steps you need to be aware of, the approach can be very rewarding.

The legal elements are important. Have your lawyer answer the following questions as they relate to your state and to current federal laws, so that you do not inadvertently violate them.

- At what point do you need to register your purchase as a security? This threshold can be the number of investors you are allowed to contact or to have as co-owners. It may also relate to the amount of capital that is raised in the investment process.

- What information do you need to disclose to the would-be investors? The safe thing to do, whether you register or not, is to disclose everything that pertains to your involvement in the deal: your past record of participation in such events, how you discovered the property, fees you are getting, whether you receive a management salary, whether you collect a piece of the action without any capital investment, and so on. The answers to those questions are not as important as the consequences of not disclosing something.

- Can you contact someone who is not in the state where you and the property are located? How can you contact that person, and what is it that you cannot do in contacting someone?

- What is the best legal entity to use for holding the property?

Other important elements may come to light because of the kind of property in question and how the purchase agreement is to be drafted. Whatever you ultimately do, be sure to use a lawyer to draw up the agreements, and make sure that your investors are qualified both mentally and financially to enter into this investment venture.

16 Key Steps to Successful Real Estate Syndications

1. Look for property you want to own.
2. Be able to justify the potential for profit.
3. Have an exit strategy with a timetable.
4. Get control of the property.
5. Have your ownership format ready to use.
6. Demonstrate why the property is a good investment.
7. Know what the state and federal laws will allow you to do.
8. Have strict investment rules with hefty penalties for backsliders.
9. Offer the opportunity to others.
10. Limit the time for their response.
11. Take backup applications.
12. Check out every prospective investor carefully.
13. Choose the investors you want.
14. After a short wait, offer their money back.
15. Close on the deal.
16. Enforce your investment rules with an iron fist.

From my own experience in forming or investing in syndications, I can tell you that there are five categories of potential investors to either avoid or at least consider very carefully whether you want them in the syndication:

Retired lawyers

Retired anyone else

Medical doctors

Widows

Family members (especially in-laws)

163.   How Can a Syndication Be Used to Acquire Property?

A syndication is a very flexible use of OPM. Not only are you using OPM to buy what you want to own, but you can actually get paid for doing it.

> **Solution:** To become a syndicator it is best to build a track record. This means that you start with a small investment and then go on from there. Follow the key steps shown in question 162, and keep your investors' interests ahead of your own.

Say you find a 50-unit apartment building that is worth $3.95 million. You know that by offering a down payment of $500,000, you can buy the property for around $3.5 million. In your opinion, this is a great buy. Why? Because you have been looking around for smaller apartment buildings (the size you could afford), and you know what is available on the market, what rents can be charged, and what the trends are. You know these things and you recognize this opportunity. All you have to do is to get some other people to agree with you and put up the cash. How much cash should you ask your investors to contribute?

It is important to anticipate your needs over the first year of ownership. In the case of an income-producing property, cash flow will help to cover or will fully cover operational expenses and debt service. But there may be some hidden expenses, higher expenses, or newer expenses than you counted on. You need to have a nest egg set aside to help or to fully cover those added costs along the way. You and your accountant might estimate that an additional $100,000 should do nicely. Okay, then you need to show up at the closing with $600,000 and the balance of the deal already arranged through either seller financing or new institutional financing.

Disclose your role in the syndication as the "managing person." Avoid the word *partner*, because you never want to suggest that you and the other investors have formed a partnership unless it is a limited partnership. If it is a limited partnership, then you would likely be the general partner in the deal. Whatever you expect to get as remuneration is okay, as long as the rest of the investors know this and have joined you in this venture because you are the controlling person.

With this in mind, you can invest some of your own money as though you are an outside investor, then receive the benefits of being both an investor and the managing person. First, you should tie up the property, and then proceed with the steps outlined in the answer to the question 162.

164.   What Is the Secret to Land Speculation?

Investing in vacant land, or already improved land, for the land value alone has been a great source of profit, and many huge estates have been forged through land speculation.

> **Solution:** The solution to profiting through buying land is
> not as simple as it might sound. You profit by keeping your
> eyes and ears open to potential opportunities, and you
> always test the political water before diving in.

Does that sound too simple? The key to profiting through land speculation is to buy or tie up land that is destined to go up in value. But which land is going to go up in value first? Land goes up in value because of what is happening around it. Almost everything positive that happens in real estate does so with a long lead time. You need to know where to find that lead time, which can be slowed down or accelerated due to local, state, and/or federal politics, all of which can throw roadblocks in the way of your profit.

Keep your eyes open and be observant of all those events that are taking place within your comfort zone that may affect the long-term values of land. You can see and hear what you need to see and hear by attending local commission and planning and zoning hearings. The agendas for these meetings are often posted on the city or county Web site, or they can be obtained through the mayor's office. Read them. If nothing is planned that looks important, you might just skip that night and read about the trivia in the next day's newspaper. But make sure you understand the agenda; otherwise, an important project might be either passed or turned down, leaving you uninformed because you didn't recognize that it was scheduled that night.

The local newspaper is a good source for news as projects get close to becoming a reality, but by then it might be too late to capitalize on what is going on. Still, it is often better to be late than never to follow the path that these trends are setting. The vast majority of people don't believe (or know) the new superhighway is coming until they see the black asphalt before their very eyes. Learn to spot the events that lead to higher values.

14 Events That Are the Prelude to Increased Land Value

New highways

Road expansions

New turnpike or expressway exits and entrances

New public works

Increases in commercial or industrial infrastructure

Airport expansion in the area

Expanded public utilities to new areas

A negative impact in another area

New employment centers planned

New entertainment centers such as parks and playgrounds

Hospital and school expansion and growth

New bridges or removal of old bridges

Dwindling land available for purchase

Reduced development politics in neighboring cities

When any of the preceding events are in the talking stage at the local planning office or are being presented before the city council or county commissioners, it is time to start looking for land that will benefit from this proposed event. You can even start to talk to prospective sellers about their properties.

The idea is to position yourself to make a move on property in the areas likely to go up in value as soon as you can pinpoint where the positive impact will take place.

165. How Can the Land-Lease Technique Be Used to Acquire Property?

A land lease occurs when someone separates newly created improvements on a tract of land from the land itself. Generally, this situation occurs when a developer or investor leases a vacant lot and then erects a building on that land. A growing trend, provided you own both the land and the improvements on that land, is to separate these two elements and sell or lease each separately. These sales or leases can be to the same person or to other investors.

> **Solution:** Using a land lease as an investment technique maximizes profit centers that outright sale or outright lease without the separation of the two elements (land and improvements) cannot. Review how this works.

In this example, let's start with a vacant lot that you own. You have been trying to sell it for $500,000, which you feel is a fair price, but the highest offer you have had is $350,000. However, you know the value is there and decide to wait for the right buyer to come along. After all, you've held this land already for 20 years, and you paid only $50,000 for it back then.

A Realtor friend of yours suggests that you stop trying to sell the lot and look for a user for the property who will pay you rent. You might even consider building to suit if such a user is a good credit risk, or simply rent the land and let that user build his or her own building.

The Realtor lists the lot and checks the zoning to determine allowable uses for the property and whether different zoning might be obtainable. The Realtor makes a long list of possible uses, and then starts looking for either a build-to-suit tenant or a land-lease client.

The marketing effort, which includes a couple of ads in the local newspapers and on Web pages that cater to Realtors and directly contacting select potential tenants, produces results. Before long, several users express interest in the site, one of which is a national drugstore chain that is moving into the state in a big way.

Like many large public companies, this chain likes to lease properties rather than to own them. Real estate is expensive, and having assets tied up in land and buildings may not suit a company's balance sheet. Because this kind of tenant is a good credit risk, your Realtor tries to negotiate a situation where you build the drugstore and lease the land and building to the parent company.

However, say this tenant has its own management company, personally owned by the founder of this public drugstore chain, who likes to own the properties that his public company rents. He offers to pay you $450,000 for the land. You think about this for about three minutes and jump at the chance.

A couple of years pass and the founder of the drugchain, and by now proud owner of the hottest drugstore in town, decides it is time to retire. The rent he is getting from the drugstore is $250,000 a year. The only cost is the debt service on the existing mortgage of $500,000, which represents 100 percent of the cost of the improvements. This mortgage costs $60,000 a year in principal and interest and will fully amortize in 24 years.

The owner's retirement plan is to get out of managing his real estate holdings. He knows that one of the best retirement investments you can own is a triple net (NNN) land lease. *Triple net* means that the lessee pays the lessor a base rent plus all other expenses (taxes, insurance, repairs, maintenance, etc.) of the property just as if that lessee were the owner. Because the lessee pays 100 percent of those expenses, the actual base rent is the same as spendable cash flow before income tax.

This about-to-be-retired founder puts the drugstore on the market at $1.5 million, subject to a land lease. The land lease, of course, is an instant creation, as it did not exist prior to this moment. Let's say he makes it a 65-year lease, with the following terms: $90,000 per year with a cost-of-living provision to keep it steady and at par with the increases in the cost-of-living index. The buyer of this drugstore will collect $250,000 in rent and pay the now-retired seller $90,000 per year plus annual increases. In addition, for the next 24 years the buyer will make payments on the existing mortgage, which costs him another $60,000 a year. This reduces his cash flow to $100,000 per year.

The buyer paid $1 million plus assumed the existing $500,000 mortgage on the property, so he is making a clear 10 percent on his invested cash.

The retired founder is paid $1 million in cash and, in addition, has income for the next 65 years in the amount of $90,000 plus any cost-of-living increases. At the end of 65 years, if he (or his estate) still owns the land (which is leased to the owner of the building), everything comes back to him or his estate.

He can sell the land at any time, subject, of course, to the lease.

This transaction could have taken several different turns, depending on how the separation between building and land was valued. Had you, the original owner of the land insisted that the drugstore company lease the land and build its own building, you would have gone from land owner to income property owner in a near instant. Because your original cost of the land was only $50,000, ending up with a $90,000 lease on the land would have been a major windfall. But think how this might relate to the price you eventually accepted, which was $350,000. At that price you had a $300,000 capital gain, on which, if you did not use a 1031 (tax-free) exchange for a replacement property, you would have paid at least $45,000 in tax (based on a 15 percent capital gain rate, which could have been higher depending on other circumstances). After tax and other expenses you might have ended up with a total of, say, $300,000 from the $350,000 sale. If you wanted to reinvest that cash into an annual income stream, you would be hard-pressed to find a return as high as you could have generated by leasing the land instead of selling it.

If you can convert a property subject to a potential capital gain tax into a cash cow of an investment property, why sell? Shouldn't you just lease? The answer to this is that land leases present some unique problems to both the lessor and the lessee. Let's take a look at the land lease from each side of the coin.

Lessor's Risk Factors When Leasing the Land Instead of Selling It

- The transaction may require lessors (the owners of the land) to subordinate their interest in the ownership of the land to a lender. This means that if lessees want to borrow money to erect buildings on the property, the lender is likely to want a first position on the land. In this circumstance, Atlantic Federal Savings and Loan (or whoever) wants to know that if it has to foreclose on a borrower (also the lessee in the lease situation), it can do so. This clearly can create a risk factor for the land owner. The amount of the risk will vary, depending on the amount of the loan in relation to the value of the land. As an example, assume the land is truly worth $500,000 and the annual lease the lessee is willing to pay is $50,000 a year for the next 99 years. If the mortgage amount is $500,000, the risk to the land owner might be tolerable based on the potential cash flow from the improvements on the land. Why? Because if the bank has to foreclose, the land owner would want to step in and protect his or her interest by taking the property instead of letting it be foreclosed by the lender. On the other hand, if the mortgage is $15 million to construct a 300-room hotel on the site and the lessee goes broke in the middle of construction, or gas jumps to European rates of $6.00 per gallon and motels across the country begin to dry up, then there is a great risk to the land owner. The risk that comes with subordination can be reduced by setting a limit on the amount of a loan. But anytime there is subordination of your rights, you stand in line behind the person or entity you allowed ahead of you.

- The eternity of a long-term lease can present future problems, which cannot be foreseen at the time the lease is created. Because the lease has separated the property into two values, one being the land itself (which is leased) and the other the buildings, what happens if the buildings burn down? That situation can be partially or even completely covered by insurance, but what if the improvements simply become obsolete? Have you ever seen a dark box? This is a term for a big-box store (e.g., a very large super-mega-supermarket) that has closed. Empty and dark, it often sits that way for a long time until someone figures out why the store went out of business and what might replace it that will *not* go out of business. In the meantime, who is paying the rent? Would you, as a lessor, be able to step in and take over the property ahead of the lender? If not, then do not lease your land.

The Lessee's Risk When Leasing the Land Instead of Buying It

- Even the most lessee-friendly land lease may present problems to the lessee when compared to an outright purchase of the land. In essence, why lease the land for $50,000 if you can buy it and own it forever for only $500,000? The answer to this question should be obvious: you lease land at a location you truly want (or even desperately need) when the owner will not sell it to you; you will also lease it if you don't have the cash to buy it, or if you have an option to buy it in the relatively near future.

- When there is an abundance of low-cost mortgage money available, most users would rather simply buy the land using cheap financing. In essence, they would finance the new building they plan to construct and the acquisition of the land at the same time. Take that $50,000 a year that would have been set aside for the land-lease payments, add it to the debt service, and in 25 or so years you have paid off the land part of the deal and own everything.

Okay, so the major stumbling blocks to a land lease are subordination and the cost of the lease in comparison to the cost of financing a purchase. Still, land leases exist, and they have a solid place in investment strategy. The key factors that make them a good deal for both parties is found in the strategy in which the lease is used to help finance the overall project.

Often the structure of the transaction comes down to the overall structure of the financing. Because the land lease has several attractive features for the seller, these aspects can be used by the buyer to an advantage. The two main benefits to a seller are tax benefits and the intrinsic value of land.

By Not Selling the Land, There Is No Capital Gain. If there is no capital gain, then there is no tax to pay. This can be a great benefit to the seller who has a low tax basis in the property and who would have to pay a high tax in the event of a sale. Whenever this kind of situation is present, the seller should consider the land lease as an alternative to outright sale. Buyers may want to propose the land lease as a buyer's tool to increase the overall amount of financing.

Land Ownership Is One of the Most Fundamental Human Aspirations. Because of this, it is often easier to get a property owner to hold a land lease at a lower cost than a second mortgage for the same principal amount. For example, if the land under a building is valued at $200,000, the seller may be better off taking a land lease at $16,000 per year than a mortgage at $16,000 a year in a direct sale.

Why? Because the mortgage is ultimately paid off, and the seller may have a large tax gains to report over the life of the payback of the mortgage. The seller may, in fact, be so motivated by the land lease that he or she would rather hold a land lease than receive $200,000 in cash (if the gains tax is 30 percent, the seller would be left with only $140,000 after tax and would be hard-pressed to make a $16,000 return on that.

166. How Does the Lease-Option Technique Work to Maximize Values?

In a lease option, the owner of a property leases it with a provision that the lessee has the option to purchase the land at a future date or dates. The leased property may include both the land and improvements or only the land (while the improvements are sold).

> **Solution:** The keys here are to maximize the values of the property while at the same time enticing the prospective buyer into the deal by making it easy for that buyer to acquire the property.

The lease-option technique is widely used in the acquisition of many different kinds of properties. A basic example follows.

Using a Lease-Option as a Buyer

You are interested in buying a vacant lot on which you would like to build an office building. The seller has fairly priced the land at $200,000, but you do not want to buy it right now, mainly because you do not have the $200,000. You know that once you have found tenants for the building and get them to commit to leases prior to your actually constructing the building, you will be able to obtain the needed financing to acquire the land and build the building, so you need to buy time. You estimate that it may take you a year to get approval from the local building authorities to construct the building, another six months to a year to prelease it, and then eighteen months to construct. We are looking at what might be three and a half years of time. To give yourself some additional time, in the event you start the construction without 100 percent of the building leased, you add another two and a half years to this equation. Six years in all.

You offer to lease the lot for a period of six years at an annual rent that begins at $5,000 for the first year and increases every year thereafter by an additional $5,000 per year. You believe that you will actually exercise the option within those six years, but in the proposal you show this to be a 35-year lease. This is a negotiation tactic, as you will see in a moment. For now, you indicate that at the end of the sixth year the rent will jump to $40,000 a year and become tied to a cost-of-living index so that it will continue to increase. You make your initial offer using a letter of intent, which gives you the freedom of making an offer that is not binding. By using this nonbinding approach, you are able to negotiate the major elements of the ultimate deal without resorting to long legal documents now. These will be used later when the formal purchase and lease-option documents are drafted.

Depending on the situation, you may elect to make no mention of an option to buy in the initial offer, saving it as an afterthought in a counterproposal after the seller reacts to your original offer.

Eventually, you will propose that the lease contain a provision that enables you to buy the property at a future date—say, anytime after the third year. The price of the land will be whatever you can negotiate. One method is to set the property's current value, say $450,000, as the minimum amount, then tie it to a formula that allows it to increase. The longer you keep the lease in effect the greater the purchase price. This makes the lease look attractive to the land owner, who sees this as some form of protection for the increased value of the land over time.

Both parties should keep in mind that an option is not the same as a promise to exercise that option. This is the lessee's option, and allows the lessee the right to buy or not to buy.

The seller may very well accept a lease even though the original goal was to sell the property. Why? Well, one very good reason might be that no one has offered to buy it yet. As long as the option price is satisfactory to the seller and he or she does not view the lease as a hindrance to the ultimate sale of the lot (if you do not buy it), this kind of deal should be quite workable.

The problem of subordination might be handled between the lessee (buyer) of the land and the lender with an agreement that at the end of the construction of the building, the option to buy will be exercised and the land paid off by using additional funds borrowed from the lender.

The advantage to investors is that they can tie up a property for a small amount of capital and have absolute control over it for a sufficient time to prelease the building.

167. As a Property Owner What Should I Know before Getting Involved in a Joint Venture?

A joint venture is a transaction in which several different investors join together to mutually invest in a project. Often, one of the players is the original owner or part owner of the property at the heart of the investment. This owner may be approached by the others and enticed to throw in the property, while the other players bring cash and or financing to the transaction.

> **Solution:** Joint ventures can be structured in many different ways. Be sure you know or check out all the players to the deal and have absolute faith in the proposed end results. If financing requires you to subordinate your property, your risk may jump to an unrealistically high and unacceptable level.

Joint ventures can work well for certain real estate investors. However, you must weigh five simple factors prior to getting into business with anyone as a joint-venture partner.

> ## Eight Items Pre-Joint-Venture Checklist
>
> - How do your goals differ from those of the other partners?
> - Are you required to subordinate your property to a lender?
> - What security do the other players provide to your interests?
> - What are the weak links in the partnership?
> - What are your liabilities?
> - Who will be in control?
> - Do you trust the person in control?
> - What is the exit strategy if things go wrong?

How Do Your Goals Differ from Those of Other Partners? This is important because if everyone has vastly different goals, it may be very difficult to fit the investment to these diverse goals. Decisions that are motivated because of income-oriented goals, for example, may not work for growth-oriented goals.

Are You Required to Subordinate Your Property to a Lender? I have already touched on the aspect of subordination. This is usually the case when a property owner puts his or her property into the joint-venture pot. More often than not, the other player is a developer who is going to bring expertise on how to do the development or operate the business and who has the clout to arrange the financing. However, he or she arranges the financing using your property as the fundamental security to the debt.

Some joint ventures are structured in such a way that the risk to the property owner is reduced by paying some of the value of the property up front. The funds may go to the property owner, or they might be applied to the initial development costs that occur during the planning stage. Other ways to soften the risk would be to limit the amount of any debt, to require personal signatures on the debt by the other players, and/or to make partial payments to the land owner out of construction draws so that by the time the project is completed, all or substantially all of the value of the property will have been paid to the property owner.

A quasi–joint venture might also solve some of these problems. One such structure would be to have the venture, of which the property owner is a part, sell the property at a soft price and good terms to the venture. The purchase agreement by the venture could allow the needed time without initial payments and a low carrying cost during the development. To compensate for the soft price, the property owner could be given a bonus in the deal over and above the profit that would ordinarily go to the property owner as a member of the venture itself. For example, if this were a condominium apartment complex to be constructed on the property owner's land, the bonus might be a percentage of each apartment sale, or even ownership of one or more of the actual apartments in the complex to be built.

What Security Do the Other Players Provide to Your Interests? One such security was already mentioned: personal signatures by the other players. This might be very hard to accomplish, however, so what other elements of value might be pledged to the transaction? Perhaps the property owner would be satisfied if the other players put up other assets and bound them to the transaction. This would not cost the other joint-venture players any money as long as the project is a success. But if things go south, then there would be a sharing of the pain and suffering between all the players more or less equally.

What Are the Weak Links in the Partnership? Is it you or the mechanics of the operation or venture? Look around and make sure that if there are any weak links there will be a solution to circumvent the difficulties bound to occur, or else stay out of the deal from the beginning. One of the problems with multiplayer joint ventures is that some players are stronger than others, which means there will be some weak links. The way to overcome that is to make sure that players who do not live up to their original promised duties can be removed from the venture.

What Are Your Liabilities? Your liability may be limited to your investment, but not always. If there is any possibility for personal liability because of an accident or other loss, make sure that the venture has provided insurance for each partner. There are many different legal entities that can be used to structure a joint venture. A limited partnership is one of the better entities to use, but it may not fit the situation. Because of this, it is important to seek the advice of a lawyer who is comfortable and experienced in the type of business or development plan at hand.

Who Will Be in Control? Control issues should be decided before the venture partners put up their money. However, be aware that control can change along the way, and if there is a change, it may go against your wishes.

Do You Trust the Person in Control? Trust is relative and is often tied into risk factors. However, how well do you know those in control? Have you checked their backgrounds? Have they been honest with you? You may never know until you thoroughly check them out, after which you may have a different opinion. Along with trust will be your ability to check their backgrounds. Ask questions of their references and find out how these references came to know the people you are about to join with in a venture you may know very little about. Past success does not mean that any future venture will be successful.

What Is the Exit Strategy If Things Go Wrong? Every real estate transaction and every business plan should anticipate problems. The abilities of those in control will be critical when and if things go wrong, and generally something *will* go wrong along the way. Ask questions and have your lawyer and accountant ask questions in a "devil's advocate" scenario. If you or your team feel uneasy about the answers you get, then bow out of the deal.

168. How Does the "Keep Some, Sell Some" Technique Work?

In this situation, when you are ready to sell something you own, instead of selling the entire item, you sell only part of it and keep the balance for yourself. This might mean selling only a portion of your tract of vacant land to a developer, not the entire tract. Or perhaps you turn that condo you own in Vail, Colorado, into a "private" time-share by selling 10 shares equal to 30 days each to 10 friends and keep the balance of the time for your own use.

> **Solution:** The sum of the parts can easily exceed the value of the whole. This concept works with just about everything, from a ton of coffee divided into 2,000 tins of java to a sailboat divided into manageable rental periods. Investing in properties that can be so divided can be a path to instant profit while at the same time providing benefits for yourself and your family.

The idea of contracting for something and then keeping part of it as you sell off the rest can be a very easy way to build wealth in a hurry. Here is how it works: You find a property you would like to own, say a golf-course-view villa in Hilton Head, North Carolina. The villa would be ideal as a weekend or holiday home. The problem is that the purchase price is more than you can afford, and the maintenance and other costs to carry it for 12 months and then use it for 2 months is more than your pocketbook can bear. However, if you could get several friends together who would like to get in on a good deal, you can use their money to buy your interest in the property.

This is a type of private time-share in that you take a residence and apportion the use among several owners. To compensate for your expense and effort in putting the deal together, you would be entitled to an interest in the deal. No one will object to that as long as you follow the usual rules of the game.

Do you want to own some getaway land that is in the general path of growth? Why not purchase a 600-acre tract of land and subdivide it into 60 parcels of 10 acres each, often called *ranchettes*. Sell enough of the 10-acre tracts to cover all your investment costs, even to put some cash in your pocket, and keep the rest of the land. If you play your cards right you might even be able to buy some time by having a long period for due diligence, perhaps even a one- or two-year lease with very modest rent (not uncommon with farmland) that gives you the time to get everything ready to subdivide. You might even sell all the parcels prior to having to close on the deal. Why not just close on the land in the morning and close with the new owners of the smaller parcels that same afternoon?

Take a good look at the solution to question 160 and follow those suggestions.

169.   How Can I Exchange Something I Do Not Own for Something I Want to Acquire?

Investors in the stock market do this all the time. They sell something they don't own with the hope that prior to having to deliver it (corn, for example) they can purchase it at a lower price. In real estate this also happens all the time. It might be the condo or home that you contract to buy, knowing that it might be a year or longer before you have to close on it. Six months into the deal you flip your contract to another person and make a profit.

> **Solution:** The idea of a future exchange or sale works nicely when the market is booming. Right now, as I write this, the real estate market is in that mode across much of the United States. Prices are going up at a rapid rate, and it isn't uncommon for people to double their invested cash in a year or so. But this is trendy and unpredictable, and I have seen people get caught up in the fury of the market with poor results. The solution is to contract for something you either (1) know you can sell or exchange at a profit or (2) are prepared to keep.

One sure way to be successful is to attempt to acquire a property that the owner indicates is not for sale. What? Hold on, "not for sale" doesn't mean the owner won't consider exchanging it for the right replacement property. Ask that owner, "What would you take?" The owner smiles and then whips out a list of properties that would be acceptable.

When you have a shopping list of other properties, it is possible that you can enter into a three-way exchange to achieve your desired goal. The following is an example of a three-way exchange.

Use a Three-Way Exchange to Acquire Property That Is Not for Sale

You have found that golf-course-view villa on Hilton Head Island that is perfect for your needs. Only Donna, the seller, doesn't want to sell it. You discovered that when you offered her $350,000, a fair price for the villa. She says the price is okay, but she doesn't need the money. "Isn't there anything you would rather own?" you ask.

She thinks about that question for a few days and then tells you that she would like to own some land somewhere between Savannah, Georgia, and Charleston, South Carolina. "Something worth up to $250,000," she confides to you. "The balance I'll take in cash and go on a round-the-world cruise." You are now given a doable task. Two of them, in fact.

She has given you two things that you can work on: the vacant land and the round-the-world cruise. Knowing you would pay $350,000 for the villa gives you the financial target to locate several tracts of land that fit her needs and wishes.

You might even choose to acquire 200 acres and carve it into two tracts: 30 acres for you, which is your profit in this deal, and 170 acres for Donna. All you have to do is make an offer on the land, and tie it up first before you tell her about it.

What about the second doable task? Round-the-world cruises can be expensive, and the cruise lines often pay whopping commissions to travel agents. Well, you aren't a travel agent, *yet*. Make a deal with one in return for a cut of the commission. Get some brochures on the cruises offered and send them to Donna as a package deal: 170 acres plus a round-the-world cruise. If you want to, you can even throw in a couple of cases of expensive champagne.

170. What Is the Quickest Way to Become a Real Estate Insider?

No matter what your goal is, you will reach it quicker by associating with those people who have already achieved their goals. A student of any trade learns from the professional. The key in real estate investing is to find the insider and to learn from that person. This is not as hard as it may seem, because the real insiders are clearly visible if you know where to look for them.

> **Solution:** Emulate success and it will come to you. Do what other successful real estate investors do. After all, they are the members of this insider's group. There are five different kinds of real estate insiders. Learn how each group operates and what you can learn from them. Then practice what they do.

Five Basic Groups of Real Estate Insiders

1. *Those who directly affect property values.* These people run the decision-making side of real estate: the local political figures who decide when a new road is to be put in or how large to expand the school system or hospitals in the county. They are elected and appointed officials, and their actions or the trends they establish influence whether a community will be development-friendly. You will find these people simply by attending commission meetings and planning and zoning sessions. Get to know the building department officials and what they do and how they do it. These people can help you discover what is going to happen or what is not going to happen long before the average investor is aware of it.

2. *Those who serve as intermediaries.* These are the lawyers and architects and the vast world of development and the mountains of people who help the decision makers make decisions. These people may never profit from what they know, but they can share that information with you. Become their friend.

3. *Those who directly affect value and are able to maximize profit.* This is the club you want to reach. It is made up of different levels of players in this real estate game. They are the developers and the investors who find value, then add to it

with their own unique talents. They might be land speculators who tie up large tracts of land, then spend a year or more taking that land from its present use to the potential of a higher-value use. They are easily found because they are highly visible at the planning and zoning meetings. Often they are sitting behind or next to their lawyers and architects or consultants at those meetings, so learn to distinguish the workers from the employers. Discover where they are investing and in what, and spend some time checking out the surrounding area. They know how to turn dirt into gold, so hang onto their coattails and they will lead you to your own gold mine.

4. *Those who read the trends and know the values in their comfort zone.* This is the first level you should strive for. You will attain it by getting in touch with the first three groups of people and by building your own comfort zone. Opportunities are around you all the time, just as are pitfalls. Your ability to differentiate the opportunity from the pitfall will develop relatively quickly. But more important, the talent to determine which opportunity you should jump on first will begin to emerge. The more you know about your comfort zone and the more focused you are to your own goals, the more successful you will become.

5. *Those who have the ability to reduce or remove risk from their decisions.* These insiders either have exit strategies built into the deal or know something that others have not yet seen coming. I have discussed the concept of risk a number of times in this book thus far. The major element that allows you to mitigate your potential for loss is *time*. If you act quickly but close slowly, you maximize the use of time. How so? Look back at this whole opportunity issue. You may see five different real estate investments that seem like a good opportunity. But are you sure there are five? What if there are only two, perhaps only one? What do you do? You analyze the deal to death, and all five are gobbled up by other investors who acted quickly. Did they risk anything by acting quickly? No, but you lost the opportunity by acting slowly. Tie up the deal first, then use your time to think it through, knowing you have the opportunity to decide in comfort.

18

Finding Money for All Your Real Estate Transactions

171. What Basic Mortgage Definitions Do I Need to Know?

What is a mortgage? What is a mortgage note? Who is the mortgagor? Who is the mortgagee? You should clearly understand these basic terms.

The Mortgage

A mortgage is a document that spells out the details of a transaction in which a lender provides money (the loan) to you in return for your pledge of certain assets (e.g., your real estate) as security should you default in payments to the lender. You get money from a bank (or other lender), which then holds the mortgage until you pay back the loan plus interest. When you or someone who has assumed your mortgage obligation has repaid the principal plus interest to the lender, the lender will give you a mortgage satisfaction to prove that the loan has been repaid, that there is no further obligation to the lender, and that the lender no longer has any rights to put a lien on the property (i.e., the security listed in the mortgage document).

The Mortgage Note

This is a separate document, attached to the mortgage document, that spells out the precise details of how the borrower will repay the lender. It has elements such as payment due dates, payment amounts (or a formula to calculate the amounts), interest rates charged, and penalties levied if payments are not timely. It also shows exactly who is responsible to repay the loan. In some parts of the world it is common for a mortgage loan or an unsecured loan (no mortgage) to contain a series of notes. These notes are for single payments, perhaps one for each month or each payment period over the life of the loan. In Europe, for example, lenders often trade (buy and/or sell) these future notes among themselves. In the United States and some other countries, major lenders such as savings and loan associations and banks bundle their mortgages and sell them to other investors (e.g., insurance companies, Fannie Mae, Freddie Mac).

Who Is the Mortgagor, and Who Is the Mortgagee?

There is a very simple way to remember which party is the *mortgagee* and which is the *mortgagor*. The key is the last two letters of each word. The *or* and the *ee* establish who is the lender and who is the person who must pay back the loan. But first let's make sure you understand the routine of getting money and giving a mortgage.

Real estate financing generally involves a combination of two different financial obligation instruments. The primary financing obligation is the mortgage note (sometimes called the *bond*). This note is really a promissory note, and, as I explained earlier, this document describes the details of repayment, such as the amounts due, the method of payment, the interest rate charged, the grace period, and so on. The mortgage is the document of the financing obligation and is the pledge of property as security to the debt. Each of these two instruments are given to the lender. Because the person borrowing the money gives the note and mortgage to the lender, you can see that you do not go to a bank to get a mortgage, but to get money and to give in return a mortgage to the bank or other lender.

Now, back to the two differentiating letters at the end of the words. The *or* found at the end of mortgag*or*, grant*or*, less*or*, and so on distinguishes that person as the party who gives something. Thus, a mortgagor gives the mortgage document to the lender. The *ee* found at the end of mortgag*ee*, grant*ee*, less*ee*, and so on distinguishes that person as the party who receives the document or item. As the mortgage is the document showing the security pledged, the lender gets the mortgage and gives money.

The word *mortgage* is formed from two Old French terms: *mort*, which means dead, and *gage*, which means pledge. I will leave it up to you to decide whether the true meaning is "you're as good as dead when you pledge it," or once paid off, "it is a dead pledge."

172. What Are the Most Common Types of Mortgages?

Remember, the mortgage is the document that has the mortgage note attached to it. The combination of these two create the pledge of security and the promise to pay the loan and interest to the lender.

> **Solution:** There are many different types of mortgage repayment programs, and each has its own merits to be considered when you are shopping for a loan. However, there are nine basic mortgage formats that make up the majority of loans.

> ### Nine Common Types of Mortgages
> - Fixed rate mortgages
> - Adjustable rate mortgages
> - Graduated payment mortgages
> - Growing equity mortgages
> - Reverse annuity mortgages
> - Shared appreciation mortgages
> - Blanket mortgages
> - Balloon mortgages
> - Conduit mortgages

Before reviewing each of these nine mortgages in detail, keep in mind that interest rates, points, closing costs, and payment schedules can vary from lender to lender based on the total payout term and the period of installments. There is no set standard deal, and each loan offered should be compared only with another loan of the same payout schedule. Monthly, quarterly, semiannually, and yearly payments are the usual periods of installments, but these can vary within the same document.

Fixed Rate Mortgages. These mortgages have a fixed rate of interest for the term of the loan. In general, the loan terms quoted range from 15 to 30 years, but may have a balloon payment at an earlier date. A loan of $100,000 to be repaid over a 30-year term at 9 percent interest would have a monthly payment of $804.66. This payment would fully amortize this loan over a full 30-year period. If the loan had a balloon at the end of 10 years, the unpaid principal would become due and payable at that time, although most lenders take this provision as an opportunity to renew the loan at new interest rates.

Adjustable Rate Mortgages. Adjustable rate mortgages (ARMs) are very popular mortgages because they give the lender the opportunity to adjust the mortgage on a frequent basis, usually annually, to keep the return to the lender current with the market rates. This type of loan repayment schedule can be good for the borrower if interest rates remain unchanged, or even go down, as they did in the early 1990s. However, when interest rates in the marketplace move up, these loans become more costly for the borrower. There is usually a maximum interest rate to which an ARM may be adjusted, and adjustments can be tied to one or more of several different national rates, such as the average yield on 15-year Treasury notes over the past 12 months, the prime rate, or the price of gold.

Graduated Payment Mortgages. Graduated payment mortgages (GPMs) have an adjustment in the monthly payment over a period of time. These mortgages often begin with monthly payments that are less than what interest-only payments would amount to. When this is the case, the total principal owed will grow by the amount of unpaid interest. A $100,000 mortgage at 9 percent interest per year may be set up as a GPM at $500 per month for the first two years. Clearly, the monthly payment is now less than interest-only (9 percent of $100,000 is $750 per month). The result of this mortgage would be that at the end of two years the principal would have increased in value by that shortfall between the $500 payment and the interest due (which would increase slightly every month as the principal grew).

The mortgage payment could then graduate to a higher amount, say $800 per month, then $900 per month, and so on. The advantage is that the early, lower, payments are designed to help a first-time investor by moving the obligation of the debt to later years of the repayment.

Growing Equity Mortgages.   The growing equity mortgages (GEMs) plan is an interesting approach to the repayment of a loan because, although the monthly payment increases over the term of the loan, it does so in such a way that the entire increase is allocated to the repayment of principal. In this way, what starts out looking like a 30-year schedule (based on a fixed rate method of repayment) can suddenly decrease to around 12 years, depending on the increase in payment. This method of repayment is an excellent choice for a buyer who wants to repay the loan in a hurry and knows that he or she can handle monthly payments that may double over the next 10 years or so.

Reverse Annuity Mortgages.   This is a very controversial form of lending that is not exactly a mortgage. In the reverse annuity mortgage (RAM) the borrower is given a line of credit that results in a loan amount that must then be repaid. Instead of the borrower getting a lump sum at the start of the mortgage, the lender pays monthly installments to the borrower over a period of time until the amount paid, plus interest due, has accrued to the maximum line of credit. I share in the growing objections to this kind of loan because it can place a major burden on borrowers at a time when they can least afford more burdens.

Shared Appreciation Mortgages.   This type of mortgage is also called a *shared equity mortgage*. The basic format of this method of mortgage payback relies on the fact that two or more borrowers enter into the mortgage agreement. Generally, one of the parties actually lives in the property. The original shared appreciation mortgages (SAMs) provided that a percentage of any appreciation in value at the time of a sale would be given to the lender. This has changed, however, and new SAMs are far more conservative. The FHA has a SAM program that requires co-borrowers to be related, which has given this mortgage another title, the *call-your-dad* (CYD) mortgage, as parents are more often than not the co-borrower.

This type of loan differs from simply having a cosigner to a note and mortgage in that the co-borrower actually shares in the ownership of the property. As it is likely that only one party will actually make the payments (the one living there), any increase in value would ultimately be earned by the co-borrower, who has allowed his or her credit to be used to secure the loan.

Blanket Mortgages. These mortgages have more than one property as security to the loan. They can take on some of the same repayment schedules as any of the mortgages discussed here, but will always have two or more separate properties as security. Some blanket mortgages have provisions that allow the borrower to remove one or more of these added properties from the obligation as security. The lender may release these properties at any time, of course, but a borrower will attempt to have such a provision built into the original mortgage. This is a common event with a development loan for a subdivision, where the developer would need to release lots or other properties for sale or other development purposes.

Balloon Mortgages. I have discussed the balloon mortgage in earlier situations, and any mortgage with a provision that lump sums of principal are due earlier than the scheduled amortization rate would provide is called a *balloon mortgage*. The borrower could say that the mortgage balloons at a certain date. These dates may call for all or only a portion of the principal outstanding to be repaid at that time.

Conduit Mortgages. These mortgages can take many different forms but will generally contain several provisions that are common to conduit loans. The repayment schedule is generally softer than a market rate loan, and it likely will have a long amortization period but balloon earlier. These loans also have a yield management provision and a nonrepayment provision. These two provisions protect the lender from having the borrower refinance the loan when or if interest rates go down. The yield management provision means that if the loan is repaid and the lender gets back the outstanding principal but cannot relend at the same rate, then there will be a penalty to the borrower to make up for the lost revenue. These penalties can be substantial.

The nonrepayment provision is a period of time when the borrower is prohibited from repayment of the loan. There may be a way around both of these provisions that, although costly, can be used. Basically it requires the borrower to replace the security with an annuity that returns to the borrower the same monthly installments and balloon payments as called for in the conduit documents.

173. How Can Wording in the Mortgage Make a Big Difference in How the Mortgage Is Paid Back?

A mortgage and its mortgage note are generally drafted by the lender's legal department. Those who wish to can get a copy of a recorded mortgage from public records, copy the document word for word, and end up with an effective legal document. Or they can copy *nearly* every word, change a few along the way, and end up with what looks like a standard or commonly used document, but might not be one.

> **Solution:** Every note and mortgage should be very carefully
> read and understood. Even so-called standard mortgage
> forms can contain provisions that can be misleading to

> professionals, so if you are not fully comfortable in
> understanding the terms contained in any contract (a
> mortgage is a very important contract), follow the simple
> tactic of asking the loan officer or closing agent to go
> through the agreement step by step.

Take, for example, the following two paragraphs that describe the repayment of a first mortgage of $100,000 over 20 years at 8 percent interest, with monthly payments.

1. "Payments are to be 240 equal monthly principal installments, together with interest, at 8 percent per annum on all unpaid principal outstanding. This repayment schedule will fully amortize this loan by the 240th month."

2. "Repayment of this loan shall be over a term of 20 years in 240 equal monthly installments comprised of principal and interest, at 8 percent per annum. This is a fully amortizing loan."

At first glance, many investors and even some smart real estate lawyers will come to the wrong conclusion that each paragraph describes the same monthly payment. How do they differ? See the following calculations.

Paragraph 1.   The loan amount is $100,000. Equal monthly installments, numbering 240, will be $416.67 per month. This is found simply by dividing the loan amount of $100,000 by the number of monthly installments (240). To this monthly installment the interest on the declining loan principal must be added.

The interest for the first month would be 8 percent times the principal owed, with the result divided by 12 to find the monthly equivalent of the annual rate.

$$0.08 \times \$100,000 = \$8,000$$
$$\$8,000 \div 12 = \$666.66$$

We already know that the principal portion of the monthly repayment is $416.67, so by adding the first month's interest of $666.67, we have a total payment (for the first month only) of $1,083.34. The second month would be reduced by the interest on the reduction of principal outstanding.

As each month has a reduction of $416.67 of principal, each of the remaining payments would be reduced by the interest portion due on the principal reduction. Therefore, the amount of each reduction would be $1,083.33 less 8 percent of $416.67 divided by 12, or $2.7778. This would result in a second monthly installment of approximately $1080.55, and the third payment would be $2.78 less than that, and so on (rounding off $2.7778 to $2.78).

Each month, however, the mortgage payment will decline because although the principal portion remains constant, the interest will be less. At the end of 10 years, a total of $50,000 will be paid off ($5,000 per year, rounded off). So the 121st payment would be $416.67 plus interest on only $50,000 remaining, which is $333.33, or a total of $750.00 per month. This payment continues to decline until the final payment, the usual $416.67 principal plus $2.78 interest.

Paragraph 2. This is a standard form of repayment based on the same amount each month that is calculated to amortize the loan over the 240 months. Check any amortization schedule and you will find that the yearly payment would be $10,370. Divide that by 12 to get the monthly payment of $864.17. The difference between these two payments of $219.17 at the outset could be more than the buyer anticipated.

Solve the problem by including the exact amount of the monthly payment part of the agreement. This is easy to do—just use a rate-constant table and calculate the monthly payment, or let the agent calculate it with his or her computer (if the agent does it, ask for a full amortization schedule that will break down each payment into principal and interest on a calendar basis. The first and last years of the repayment schedule will rarely be a full 12 months, so keep that in mind. This type of printout will be helpful later when you need to calculate your annual tax deductions for interest paid.

174. How Do You Set Up a Wraparound Mortgage for Maximum Protection of the Mortgagor?

A wraparound mortgage is any mortgage that is created in such a way that the principal amount to be paid back to the holder of the mortgage (the wrap mortgagee) is made up of principal due on prior existing mortgages plus a new amount of principal due.

For example, Judy wants to sell her home to Bob. They have agreed on a price of $300,000. Bob has a provision in his purchase agreement that he must obtain new financing in the amount of at least $225,000 at an interest rate not to exceed 7 percent. Judy asks him if he would agree to an interest-only payment that would balloon in 10 years. He agrees. Here is why she asked that question. An existing private first mortgage on the home was created by the original owner when he sold the home to Judy. It was set up as an interest-only mortgage for 25 years, with a balloon payment that is not due for another 10 years.

The principal owed will remain the same as from day one, $100,000 until the balloon payment. The interest rate was set at 5 percent. Because this is such a soft payment mortgage, Judy wants to leave it in place and use a wraparound. Bob has already agreed to close if he can get a $225,000 mortgage at 7 percent interest. He has also agreed that it can be an interest-only mortgage with a 10-year balloon. Judy says "great" and will hold that mortgage as a wraparound.

At closing, Bob executes the proper wraparound mortgage that says he will pay Judy interest only (in monthly installments) at 7 percent of $225,000. This means he will have a monthly payment of $1,312.50 per month ($225,000 × .07 = $15,750 ÷ 12 months = $1,312.50). Judy gets this sum, but must pay out $416.67 to the person she purchased the home from some years earlier. So she keeps the balance of $895.83 per month, which totals $10,749.95 a year. As her portion of the wraparound is $125,000, Judy is earning about 8.6 percent interest on the $125,000 equity she has in that mortgage. As an added bonus to Judy, this transaction would also qualify as an installment sale, because she did not receive the gain portion (if any) of the $125,000 amount. This 8.6 percent return is pretty good.

Solution: The wraparound mortgage can be complicated to understand, but is relatively easy to set up. There are a number of "safe guards" that protect the mortgagor and the mortgagee that are essential. They are discussed in this section.

When you are the buyer and you give a wraparound mortgage to the seller, there are several important factors to consider and three important steps to take to get the maximum protection on the repayment of the underlying mortgages.

Potential Wraparound Mortgage Problems

In the following situation Marilyn owns a triplex that you want to buy. Your plan is to live in one unit and pay off the purchase mortgage(s) partially with rent from the other two units.

You have negotiated a fair price of $180,000, but she has two existing mortgages on the property. One is a first mortgage for $60,000 that pays out in 12 years at 8 percent per year. This mortgage has a monthly payment of $649.45 per month (check a constant-rate table for 12 years at 8 percent).

There is a second mortgage for $50,000 that pays out in 10 years at 9 percent per year. This mortgage has a monthly payment of $633.38 per month (check a constant-rate table for 10 years at 9 percent). If you assume the total debt, you are obligated to a combined monthly payment of $1,282.83, which seems high for only $110,000 in debt. However, these mortgages are amortizing quickly and will be paid off in 12 and 10 years, respectively. Yet you have only $30,000 cash to invest, and that means that you have to finance a total of $150,000 or pass up the deal. If you were to give Marilyn a third mortgage of $40,000 at 9.5 percent interest for the 15 years she has said she will take, that would mean an additional monthly payment of $417.70. Added to the first and second payments, this gives you a grand total of $1,700.53, which may be much more than you can afford, even with rent from two of the units.

A wraparound mortgage is set up to facilitate your down payment and repayment schedule. This mortgage is in the amount of $150,000, with a 28-year amortization schedule at 9.75 percent interest, with equal monthly installments. The payment is $1,304.75 per month, or just slightly more than the combined total of the first and second mortgages. Marilyn agrees to this only if you agree to let the wraparound mortgage balloon at the end of the twelfth year. At that time, if you still own the property, you will likely be able to refinance the loan and pay off the balloon, which would total $126,623.53.

The wraparound mortgage is set up so that Marilyn is to be obligated to continue the payments on the first and second mortgage out of the funds you pay her on the wraparound mortgage. Each mortgage is treated separately as far as the amortization schedule is concerned. The important and critical factor to keep track of is that you do not owe $150,000 plus the first and second mortgages. The wraparound mortgage consists of the first mortgage of $60,000 and a second mortgage of $50,000 plus the new money, or a difference of $40,000.

Marilyn accepts this deal for any of several good reasons. It might be because she does not need the money now, but can see the benefit of letting the loan build up so that at the end of the 12 years she will have a nice nest egg. Of course, when the first mortgage is paid off at the end of six years, she will get to keep the money that had been going toward that monthly payment. Another reason she accepts the deal could be because it solves her primary motivation: to sell the triplex.

Three Factors That Concern a Buyer in a Wraparound Situation

- That the wrap mortgagee makes the payments on the underlying mortgages
- That if the mortgagee defaults on those payments, there would be an immediate opportunity to step in and make the payments
- That failure of the wrap mortgagee to meet the obligations on the existing mortgages would constitute a default by the mortgagee and allow the buyer to recover costs

Establishing a Collection Escrow to Protect the Mortgagor's Rights

All three of the preceding factors can be properly taken care of if, as a part of the contract, or at least at the closing of the sale, a collection escrow agreement is set up to ensure that all the payments you make on the wraparound mortgage are properly channeled to meet the underlying debt. Only then should any leftover funds be paid to the seller.

Set Up a Third-Party Collection Agent.   It is important that the collection agent not be your own or the seller's accountant, lawyer, or best friend. Instead choose a third party, such as the closing agent, a real estate management firm, or some other party agreed on by you and the seller.

Give the Collection Agent Fixed Instructions.   The collection agent must have detailed instructions about what to do with the funds paid by the wraparound mortgagor. These instructions should require prompt notice to the seller should payments from the mortgagor be late so that the seller can protect his or her rights and interest in the property by making the underlying mortgage payments on time.

Sellers Need Special Provisions to Protect Themselves.   All sellers who take back a wraparound mortgage on a sale will want the collection agreement to contain provisions that allow them to promptly step in when the buyer defaults on any payment. Because the seller relays the payments made by the buyer to meet all underlying mortgage obligations, it is recommended that very short grace periods (if any) be allowed for the buyer to make payments due. Stiff penalties for late payments should correspond to the necessary paperwork and added cost that may be needed to cover late payments on the underlying mortgages.

175.   What Provisions Should I Include When Using a Blanket Mortgage?

A *blanket mortgage* is a mortgage that pledges more than one property as security to the debt. See question 170 for additional data on blanket mortgages.

Solution: When you give this kind of mortgage, you should include five key provisions.

Five Important Blanket Mortgage Provisions

- Release of security clauses
- Assignable to a new owner
- Substitution of security provisions
- Clear and concise position of security defined
- Repayment terms covered

Release of Security Clauses.   This enables you to remove some and eventually all of the extra security or property you have pledged to the loan as the loan-to-value ratio decreases. The change in loan-to-value ratio occurs through the continual paying of the principal owed or through the increased value of the property that secures the loan.

Assignable to a New Owner.   If the current mortgagor sells the entire block of security to the mortgage, will the mortgagee let the new buyer assume the blanket mortgage? This is a business decision that should be examined. If the mortgage is not assignable, then that might require the new owner to pay off the entire balance. If you were the mortgagee, would you want that to happen? Perhaps not, at least not just then.

Substitution of Security Provisions.   This is also called a *sliding mortgage provision*. This will allow you to release one property (that you may want or need to sell or refinance) and to replace that lost security to the blanket mortgage with another property. This flexibility will allow you to deal with your portfolio in a more responsive way than if you were tied into a static situation.

Clear and Concise Position of Security Defined.   If there are any limitations to the position you are giving up when you add a property to the security, those limitations must be carefully spelled out in clear and concise terms. For example, if you put up a vacant lot you own as additional security, but you want the right to build a home on that lot and to obtain a first mortgage of up to 50 percent of the combined value of the home and the lot, then that limitation should be absolutely clear. For the other party, such a limitation may not actually reduce the value of the security, because the 50 percent value remaining could be greater than the value of the original lot.

Repayment Terms Covered.   Repayment schedules of any mortgages should be carefully outlined, but when the mortgage contains releases of security, or substitution of security as often is the case in a blanket mortgage, the mortgagor should have some flexibility in splitting the different segments of the added security. This would require separation of the blanket mortgage into one or more blanket mortgages that would maintain the principal owed, but divide it from one large mortgage into two or more smaller ones.

For example, a developer puts up several vacant lots as security to a $200,000 loan to construct a model home. As sales occur, the builder may want to construct a second model home and at the same time start construction on five presold homes. To build these five homes would require a release of five lots from the blanket mortgage, but in turn the builder agrees to split the original $200,000 into two $150,000 loans on the two models (the original and the new one) and at the same time add $100,000 in cash equity to generate the extra $200,000 needed to build the second model home.

176. What Is Novation, and Why Is It Important?

How tricky can lenders get? Remember assumption? When a lender allows you to sell a property that has an existing mortgage on it by letting the new buyer assume the mortgage as the seller, you may think that you are completely off the hook for any further liability on that mortgage. Sorry to tell you this, but unless the assumption agreement also contains an agreement of novation, you are still tied into the mortgage.

When the lender agrees to execute a novation, the lender is agreeing that the former mortgagor is no longer obligated to the loan and that the new mortgagee (who was approved for assumption) is the party now obligated.

When selling a property that has an FHA mortgage, make sure that the assumption contains novation.

177. What Key Problems Need to Be Answered to Protect Both the Buyer and Seller When There Are Releases from the Mortgage?

When you buy anything that you plan on subdividing (land, apartments, timeshares, etc.), and you owe a lender (seller or third-party lender) on the mortgage you gave when you purchased the property, you will want to have the ability to release parts of the security as you develop or sell it. Without this ability you (as the developer) will have to repay the entire loan to get individual releases.

> **Solution:** Both the mortgagee and the mortgagor need to
> have a release plan or schedule prior to funding the

> mortgage. Generally, this is accomplished with a fail-safe
> release program that allows the developer to release the
> property from the underlying debt in large blocks. At any
> time during this process, the parties may agree to smaller or
> more random releases if it appears to be mutually beneficial
> to both parties.

When you hold a mortgage on a property that can be divided into separate parts, such as an apartment complex, vacant land, or an office building, the buyers may want you to give them the right to release portions of the original security from the remaining balance of the mortgage.

This situation is most common when an investor buys a rental apartment complex with the idea of conversion to condominium or cooperative apartments, or when a land developer acquires a large tract that is to be subdivided into lots. The land developer may wish to sell off lots, or to build homes and sell the lot and home together, prior to the repayment of the mortgage on the purchase of the land.

Before agreeing to a provision like this, you should have clear and agreeable answers to four questions.

Four Questions to Be Answered Before You Release Security from Mortgage

1. *Is there quality control of the buyer's use of the property?*   If the project is to take a 500-acre farm and subdivide it into a residential community, as long as there is a mortgage on some of the land, that mortgagee would want to know what kind of community is to be built. Builders often paint a far more rosy picture of the end result than it turns out to be, so as soon as that pretty picture has been described, the mortgagee should ask the developer to build in some safeguards to ensure that the development will continue to improve the value of the remaining property. The mortgagee can do this easily by putting in deed restrictions that restrict or limit what the buyer (and subsequent buyers) can do on the land. You can, for example, establish minimum lot size and minimum building size, designate that all residential construction contain an enclosed two-car (or three-car) garage, forbid flat roofs and black asphalt driveways, have setbacks greater than the local rules require, and so on. Naturally, mortgagees do not want to be so repressive that they completely tie the hands of developers, but most of the truly magnificent residential subdivisions in America have very specific deed restrictions that some thoughtful land owner or developer agreed would have a beneficial long-term effect.

2. *Have you established release prices and minimums to ensure the buyer's equity?* When the lender agrees to releases, the actual release price should be greater than par. For example, if there is a mortgage of $500,000 on a 50-acre tract of land on which a developer plans to construct a "manufactured-housing project" (the new name for a trailer park), par would be $10,000 per acre ($500,000 ÷ 50). The lender's release price to the developer should be a greater percentage than that, often 125 to 150 percent of the par rate. At 125 percent, the release price per acre would be $12,500 per acre.

3. *Is the remaining security adequate for the balance of the loan?* As was mentioned in item 2, the remaining security can be increasing due to an above-par release payment. If there is a $100,000 mortgage on a five-acre tract of land, and the developer wants to build warehouses on half-acre lots, each half-acre lot would be at $10,000 par (an equal share of the mortgage found by dividing the mortgage amount of $100,000 by 10, which is the number of half-acre lots within the five-acre tract). If the release price were 150 percent of par, the developer would have to pay down the mortgage by $15,000 per lot to have them released. By the time five lots were released, a total of $75,000 would have been paid off, leaving only $25,000 to cover the remaining half of the land. The seller's situation would be improving if the release pattern did not leave undesirable lots remaining.

4. *In case of foreclosure, would you be satisfied with what you get back?* Random releases or ill-advised release patterns can use up the desirable property and leave the lender with property that may appear to be above par in value but in fact may be well below it. Such would be the case if the property is released in a way that uses up all the road frontage first. When you agree to a release pattern, it is critical that you determine the absolute maximum situations under which you would be willing to hold a mortgage. You can limit or hold back road frontage until the final release, for example. Other provisions to increase your security would include the following:

No unreleased land can be surrounded by released land.

No unreleased tract can be less than a specific size.

Developer infrastructure (water, sewers, roads, etc.) must be brought to all property before releases.

When the developer needs to have land released from your mortgage (to sell it, for example), the mortgagee can require a minimum amount of land be released at any time. This is negotiable, of course, but it should be established according to the type of development the builder anticipates. In the case of a trailer park, the release may be in five-acre minimums. An important factor to consider is to keep all the land in each release package in one block. In essence, if the developer must take at least five acres at a time, all of those acres would be within one boundary. Most developers will want purely random releases, that is, releases that can be scattered all around the development. This gives them the maximum salability of the product, but can be the least attractive method of release from the mortgagee's point of view. Lenders generally want to provide a release pattern that starts with the least valuable land and works toward the more valuable land (e.g., start at the rear and work toward the road frontage).

In the final contract there is apt to be some give-and-take to allow the pattern to fit the project while offering some protection to the seller. A random release provision with minimum sizes that must remain together can be a good compromise.

If the release provision is at 150 percent of par, it is easy to see that as the land is released the amount of land remaining is at a lower loan-to-value ratio, which increases the lender's security.

A word of warning to sellers holding purchase money mortgages with releases: Read the wording of any release provision very carefully to see how the release value is calculated. For example, you sell 500 acres of land for $1,000 per acre. You get

$100,000 down and are holding a first mortgage for the balance, which is $400,000. Your intention is to allow the buyer to release land from the mortgage on the basis of 150 percent of par in 5-acre minimums. Par would be found by dividing the $400,000 by the acreage (500 acres).

Thus $400,000 divided by 500 equals $800 per acre, and 150 percent of that would be $1,200 per acre. Since you have established a minimum of five acres per release, you believe the buyer must reduce the mortgage by $60,000 (5 × $1,200 = $60,000) for every five acres. The buyer's lawyer or agent draws up an agreement that includes the following provision:

> . . . and it is further agreed that the Buyer shall be entitled to releases from the purchase money mortgage (originally set at $400,000) for every principal payment of $60,000 toward the purchase price. Releases need not be taken on each payment, and Buyer may accumulate credits toward releases, which may be taken only in increments of five acres or more.

This might sound like it does the trick, but if you caught the buyer's slick wording you will realize that as the original down payment is a principal payment toward the purchase price (not the purchase money mortgage), the buyer would already have credit for more than five acres. With an additional payment of $20,000 of principal, the buyer's total payment to you would be $120,000, which would give the buyer a full 10 acres to be released from the mortgage.

However, your understanding of the agreement between you and the buyer was that by the time the buyer got 10 acres you would have received the original down payment of $100,000 plus $120,000 for the two five-acre releases, or a total of $220,000, not just the $120,000.

178. How Does Subordination Affect the Security of a Mortgage?

Subordination, as we discussed earlier, means giving up rights to someone else that puts you at risk when you are the mortgagee. In essence, if you hold a first mortgage and allow the mortgagor to refinance for some purpose, say to erect a new building on the land, you no longer have a first mortgage position if there were to be a default.

> **Solution:** Be very cautious if you are asked to subordinate your rights to a new mortgage. There are things you can and should do to reduce your risk if you decide to go ahead with a subordinated interest in the property. Seek very competent legal advice.

There was a time when less-than-ethical developers would contract to buy your property subject to your agreement to subordinate a large purchase money mortgage to new financing. For example, you would sell a hotel for $1 million and agree to hold a second mortgage of $500,000 behind the existing first mortgage of

$300,000. This gives the developers an equity at this point of $200,000 (they paid you that amount, exchanged something else, or whatever). You subordinate your interest to a new first mortgage because they say they want to remodel the property and return it to excellent condition and income potential.

What happens if a big mortgage is slapped on the property and the developers walk away from it? This does not sound too good, does it? What if the buyers go out and borrow $2.5 million on the property and pledge the property as the security—ahead of your second mortgage—and then promptly stop making any payments? In essence, they walk away from that loan (so it may appear). The lender calls you up and informs you the property will be foreclosed and asks whether you want to protect your $500,000 interest by paying off the new first mortgage. What then?

A superior mortgage can wipe out your second mortgage. Bad news can get worse. Not only did the buyer walk from the mortgage, the improvements that were to be made from the mortgage funds were never finished (or even started). As the buyer did not do anything to the property, there is no reason to expect additional income, so it will clearly not support that kind of debt presently on it. You stand to lose your interest in the hotel because you are behind a first mortgage that is greater than the value of the property. You do not want to start making payments, so in the end your second mortgage is wiped out and the lender then takes over the hotel (deed in lieu of foreclosure). Later, if you are lucky, you may discover that the original buyer and the lender who took over the property were actually one and the same, but dealing under different corporate names. Why did they do this? Because they acquired the property with only $500,000 invested instead of $1 million.

Subordination is the act of moving behind an existing or future lien, so whenever you agree to step aside in this way, you are at risk of losing your entire position. There are ways to protect yourself to some degree. The following are examples of things you can do to increase your security in the advent of subordination. You should use combinations of these protections rather than just one or two of them.

---

10 Things to Improve Your Security When You Subordinate Your Position to New Loans

Get cosigners.

Get blanket security in the form of other property.

Get assignment of rents from other properties.

Have a letter of credit as additional security.

Insist on advance principal payments during subordination.

Insist on a completion bond in the advent of new construction.

Limit subordination to a specific period of time.

Limit new loan terms and amounts.

Limit subordination to clearly defined institutional financing.

Require personal guarantees.

179. What Is Substitution of Collateral, and Why Is It Considered an Insider Technique?

Substitution of collateral is a provision that creates a very flexible situation for the mortgagor because the mortgagee agrees to accept, at a future date, another property as substitute collateral or security to the loan. The lender may agree to a specific property or a formula of value replacement. This is in essence what occurs in the sliding mortgage technique described in question 146. The following are two different provisions as examples.

1. The lender agrees that anytime following the first anniversary of the mortgage, provided the mortgage is current, the mortgagor may replace the security to the mortgage, described as the site herein, by either of the two properties described in exhibit A hereto attached.

2. In substitution for the all or part of the security pledged to this mortgage, as described in paragraph A of this document, the mortgagee agrees to accept any property that meets the following criteria:

   Is free of any debt or liens

   Has a recent certified appraisal showing its value to be equal to or less than two times the outstanding balance of the loan at the time of the replacement

   Is located within a specific geographic area

   Is not under any moratorium of use, subject to impacts or assessments for use

   Is not in violation of any code or ordinance

Example 2 might sound restrictive, but it still provides considerable flexibility to the property owner. Why would the owner want such flexibility? Take a look at the following example.

Frank's Substitution of Collateral

Frank has acquired a large apartment complex that consists of 48 apartment units. The complex consists of eight 6-unit buildings in a beautiful garden setting. The price was $2 million.

There is a first mortgage of only $200,000, and the seller agreed to a second mortgage of $1.7 million based on the agreement by Frank to pay the seller $100,000 down and spend another $250,000 for immediate repair of the property. The seller-held mortgage amounts to just over $35,000 per unit.

The seller also agreed to allow substitution, in all or part, along the lines of the provisions in example 2. In addition, the seller agreed to release each building from the second mortgage for every principal payment or substitution of $240,000.

This allows Frank to do some major restructuring of the project to free up some units to sell off. Here are just a few of the things Frank can do:

- Give the seller a substitution of collateral of $480,000 to release two buildings from the second mortgage, or 12 units in all.

- Sell condo units in the buildings, and with the proceeds from a few of the sales pay off the existing first mortgage and pay down the second mortgage to get more releases.

- Get releases for the remaining units by substitution of collateral by pledging the newly remodeled units from the first four buildings that have been released, but as individual units. This can actually make it easier for Frank to sell the units, as financing will not be in place for a buyer to assume.

These insider techniques help to make real estate interesting. There are many ways to make deals work that are all ethical, aboveboard, and exciting.

180. When Is a First Mortgage Not a First Lien?

A mortgage document is a pledge of security by the mortgagor to the lender. The pledge cannot extend a security position that the mortgagor does not have. For this reason, mortgages obtain their rank (first, second, third, etc.) in accordance with when that pledge has been legally recorded. In essence, what is the time stamp placed on that document? This time stamp is essentially the time of day and date on which the document was duly recorded in the public property records of the county where the property is located.

The security position is determined by the order of recording, not anything written to the contrary, and it is critical that you not be persuaded into believing otherwise.

> **Solution:** Title and mortgage documents should be recorded simultaneously and only after one last check of title shows that (1) no other title or mortgage has been recorded that would invalidate yours, and (2) any prior mortgages that are not supposed to remain on the property have been satisfied.

If the mortgage and mortgage note are not recorded in a timely fashion or are recorded in the wrong property records (in California instead of Florida, in the wrong county, etc.), then any subsequent mortgage that gets recorded will jump ahead of what was intended to be a first mortgage. Such would be the case if the buyer took out a second mortgage to help pay for closing costs and down payment, and this second mortgage got recorded ahead of the first mortgage. Guess what? The second mortgage is really the first mortgage and the first mortgage (but only if recorded) is a second mortgage.

Closing agents know all about this and generally insist that prior to releasing funds at closing, they run a postclosing title check to make sure that the seller did not actually take out another loan (and not tell anyone) a day or so before the closing. Then, after the documents have been recorded, some closing agents double-check yet again to make sure that the loans were properly recorded in the right order.

This is critical for obvious reasons and points out a very good reason to use qualified closing agents, whether lawyers or title insurance or escrow agents, who are professionals in this task. If you are contemplating buying a first or second mortgage at a discount, you must double-check to ensure that the mortgage is exactly what it is supposed to be.

Some investors make big returns by buying "second" mortgages at a discount once they discover that the recorded first mortgage has actually been paid off or is at such a low loan-to-value ratio that for all practical purposes the second mortgage will soon be a first mortgage.

Keep in mind that unless the mortgage has a subordination provision that would allow new financing to be placed ahead of it even after superior mortgages have been paid off, all mortgage positions move up in their lien position when superior mortgages are paid off (e.g., a second mortgage becomes a first when the previous first is paid off).

181. How Do I Get the Best Mortgage Terms from the Seller?

Motivated sellers are usually the best source for a purchase money mortgage as well as other, more creative financing techniques. After all, sellers have other motivations that need to be satisfied, and if you can pinpoint the goals they need to achieve and can show them how your proposal will advance those goals, then the other aspects of the contract to sell become secondary.

> **Solution:** Stress the fact that you are solving their primary goal, which is to sell the property. Dwell on the other benefits they get, too, such as possible tax savings or postponement of the tax, a good and safe return from the interest you will pay, and the freedom to move forward with other plans they might have.

The key is not to stress the mortgage terms but to dwell on the benefits the overall agreement achieves. This may require some creative thought on your part, or at least proper orientation to focus sellers on creative options available to them.

For example, a seller is anxious to sell his or her home in order to move to Texas where a new job awaits. The seller may be convinced that to achieve this move his or her property must be sold for cash so the cash can be put toward a new place to live. The reality is that the seller need only obtain something that can be used as a down payment for a new place to live. Cash works fine, but if that is not available, then a buyer who offers a well-secured second mortgage (cosigners, a blanket mortgage, etc.) may be able to show the seller that there will be other sellers in Texas who would be glad to allow a pyramid to work (i.e., sellers hold the mortgage on another property when they sell theirs).

Sound complicated? Not really. All it takes is the simple understanding that when people need to sell, you should help them find a solution, not what they believe to be the solution.

182.   How Do I Shop around for a Lender?

The availability of capital varies, just as real estate cycles change. In general, however, financing is either strong or week in a very broad-reaching way. This differs from real estate cycles, which can vary from location to location. Because financing is critical for a boom time to continue, the downturn of a major sector of funding can put a screeching halt to a seller's market. When there is easy money from the banks and institutional lenders, buyers don't mind paying higher prices, because in the long run they are operating on other people's money.

> **Solution:** Keep your eyes and ears alert to the status of the lending market. If money starts getting scarce for one type of real estate, check to see if this situation is spreading to other kinds of real estate. You may have to change your investment strategy to different locations or categories of real estate to stay in the stream of easy money.

It's worth it to shop around for both private and institutional lenders. Start with the institutional lenders, as they are easier to find: banks, savings and loan institutions, thrift institutions, credit unions, insurance companies, mortgage real estate investment trusts, and pension funds are the major institutional sources. Some of these, mainly the first four, can be approached by you directly. Alternatively, you can seek out mortgage brokers, who may be found an ample supply in most communities by looking in the Yellow Pages under Mortgages or Mortgage Bankers and Brokers.

You want to avoid putting up nonrefundable deposits, and when dealing with mortgage brokers and bankers, make sure you check their references. Remember that some lenders are oriented toward certain kinds of loans and prefer certain types of security. If you are turned down, perhaps you chose the wrong lender for your situation. Ask up front what kind of loans and what types of security a lender prefers. If your plan is to build a hotel and the lender you are dealing with does only shopping centers, say good-bye.

When you find the right lender, feel free to mention loan quotes you may have gotten from other lenders. Often the best approach is an honest face and a straightforward statement: "You know, First Federal offered me $200,000 more without any closing costs. Can you beat that?"

183. What Is the Key to Getting the Best Loan Amount and Terms Possible?

Let's start with a most important three-point cliché. Look confident; act confident; and demonstrate your self-confidence by knowing what you are doing. This trio puts a real sparkle into any presentation (or any first-time meeting, for that matter) and rubs off not only on the loan officer, but also on those who work with you. Above all, have a goal that you can visualize. Goal-oriented people are able to focus on the end result and are less likely to become emotional about the interim step. At least that is the way you should think about it. If you find that you are more emotional about getting to the destination than the destination itself, then it is likely you do not have a clearly defined goal or destination in your mind. Work on that. Check out question 188 and review the tips contained there as well.

184. What Is an FHA Mortgage, and Where Do I Get One?

In 1934 the Federal Housing Administration (FHA) was formed out of the Department of Housing and Urban Development (HUD) of the federal government. FHA is primarily a loan insurance program that works through institutional lenders. This insurance guarantees the upper portion of the loan made, which increases the security to the lender and allows the loan to be made at a competitive market rate, even though the required down payment may be well below the conventional market.

The down payment allowed may be as low as 3 percent for an acquisition of $50,000 or less, and only an additional 5 percent for purchase prices above the first $50,000.

As the FHA does not actually make loans, its programs are made through local lenders that specialize in FHA programs. The easiest way to find these lenders or their representatives is to call the FHA office nearest to where you want to invest. Check with your phone company for the listing of the Federal Housing Administration.

A quick glance in the Yellow Pages under Mortgage Companies, Brokers, and Bankers, may show large ads for companies that advertise their specialty in FHA and VA loans.

185. Who Can Qualify for an FHA Loan?

There are over 15 different types of FHA loan programs, and each program has slight variations that can affect qualification. However, the good news is that all FHA programs are designed to help first-time buyers acquire their own property.

Once you find a lender in your area who is experienced in making FHA loans, sit down with that person to discover which of the FHA programs may best suit you and exactly what you qualify for in the way of price and type of property. Keep in mind that FHA loans are not limited to homes or apartments, as small income-producing residential properties can also be purchased if you or a shared appreciation mortgagor will live there. The loan officer or mortgage agent will want to know the following information.

Seven Important FHA Questions You Will Need to Answer

Your and your spouse's combined earnings

Type of job and tenure

Total debts

Scheduled monthly payments for that debt

Rental payments (car and furniture, but not living quarters)

Court-ordered payments for outside support

Outside expenses you pay for others (parents, children, etc.)

The loan officer will review these items with you and will establish the levels that FHA will insure. There are some guidelines and rules of thumb, but there are also exceptions to those rules, so it is best to have your specific circumstances reviewed to ascertain exactly what you qualify for.

186. What Is a GI Loan, and How Do I Get One?

At the end of World War II, Congress approved the Serviceman's Readjustment Act of 1944. The common term for this new program was, and still is, "the GI Bill of Rights." The purpose was to give the hundreds of thousands of GIs (general infantrymen) a new start and to ease their expenses in civilian life by providing them with a variety of medical benefits, bonuses, and low-interest loans. Title II (one of six sections of the original bill) was dedicated to giving the GIs an opportunity to buy their own home or other real estate.

> **Solution:** Prior to applying for a GI loan, you will need to request a Certificate of Eligibility for VA Home Loan Benefits. To do this you need to complete VA Form 26-1880 together with proof of military service. To find the proper address to send this to, call toll-free number 1-888-2446711. You can also check online at NCELIGIB@vba.va.gov for current information about VA loans.

These loans are not directly made by the Department of Veterans Affairs but are insured by it, and they work much the same as do FHA loans. However, GI or VA loans can be 100 percent of the purchase price.

Who Qualifies for GI Loans?

One of the most misunderstood parts about GI loans is finding out who qualifies. Following are the basic qualifications; however, as with most anything that has to do with the government, if you seem to qualify but are not sure, then contact the nearest VA office by using the preceding phone number. You can also look in your local Yellow Pages under Loans and you will discover lenders who process and specialize in VA or GI loans. Here are the general qualifications.

Veteran Loan (GI Loans) Qualifications. This list applies to service men and women who served on active duty during the following periods for the number of days indicated.

September 16, 1940, to July 25, 1947	90 days
July 26, 1947, to June 26, 1950	181 days
June 27, 1950, to January 31, 1955	90 days
February 1, 1955, to August 4, 1964	181 days
August 5, 1964, to May 7, 1975	90 days
May 8, 1975 to September 7, 1980 (enlisted)	181 days
May 8, 1975 to October 16, 1981 (officer)	181 days

Service after September 7, 1980 (Enlisted), or October 16, 1981 (Officer). If you were separated from service that began after the preceding 1980 or 1981 date, one of the following must apply:

1. You completed 24 months of continuous active duty or the full 181 days for which you were ordered or called to active duty and were discharged under conditions other than dishonorable.

2. You completed at least 181 days of active duty and were discharged under the specific authority of 10USC 1173 (hardship) or 10 USC 1171 (early out), or you were determined to have a compensable service-connected disability; such individuals may also be eligible if they were released from active duty due to an involuntary reduction in force, certain medical conditions, or, in some instances, for the convenience of the government.

Gulf War: Service during the Period That Began August 2, 1990. If you served on active duty during the Gulf War, one of the following must apply:

1. You completed 24 months of continuous active duty or the full 181 days for which you were ordered or called to active duty and were discharged under conditions other than dishonorable.

2. You completed at least 181 days of active duty and were discharged under the specific authority of 10USC 1173 (hardship) or 10 USC 1171 (early out), or you were determined to have a compensable service-connected disability; such individuals may also be eligible if they were released from active duty due to an involuntary reduction in force, certain medical conditions, or, in some instances, for the convenience of the government.

Active Duty Service Personnel. If you are now on regular active duty (not active duty for training), you are eligible after having served 181 days (but only 90 days during the Gulf War), unless discharged or separated from a previous qualifying period of active duty service.

Selected Reserves or National Guard. If you are not otherwise eligible, you may be so if you have completed a total of six years in the Selected Reserves or National Guard (member of an active unit, attended required weekend drills, and two-week active duty for training) and were discharged with an honorable discharge; or were placed on the retired list; or were transferred to the Standby Reserve or an element of the Ready Reserve other than the Selected Reserve after service characterized as honorable service; or continue to serve in the Selected Reserves.

Note: individuals who completed less than six years may be eligible if discharged for a service-connected disability.

You may also be determined eligible for the following reasons:

If you are an unremarried spouse of a veteran who died while in service or from a service connected disability.

If you are a spouse of a serviceperson missing in action or a prisoner of war.

If you are a U.S. citizen who served in the armed forces of a government allied with the United States in World War II

If you are an individual with service as a member in certain organizations such as Public Health Service officers, cadets in the U.S. Military, Air Force, or Coast Guard Academies, midshipmen at the U.S. Naval Academy, officers of National Oceanic & Atmospheric Administration, merchant seaman with World War II service, and others (check with the local VA office to ascertain this full list).

If you are a surviving spouse who remarries on or after attaining age 57 and on or after December 16, 2003, you may be eligible for the home loan benefit.

Note: As time advances, the rules for new veterans will change. Not being covered by any of the preceding qualifications does not automatically exclude you from coverage. Double-check with the VA office nearest you, or go online and search under VA Qualifications to determine your own unique status.

187. What Are the Eight Most Asked Questions about Veterans Affairs Loans?

1. *What if I was in the reserves and not on active duty in the regular army or other service?* The VA or GI loan is not for you, but FHA has a program that is called the FHA/VA loan [203(v)]. This is similar to other FHA programs that are available, but for the qualifying reservist the down payment requirements would be lower.

2. *How does the VA guarantee to the lenders work?* The VA insures 25 percent of the loan, which acts as protection for the lender making the loan. The maximum

amount is subject to some variation. For example, in most states the maximum insured portion of the loan is $89,912 and that 25 percent would put the total loan at $359,650. However, in Hawaii and Alaska the insured portion is as high as $134,868, which would make the top loan there $539,475. Still, if more than one eligible person were to join together (a husband and wife who are both eligible, two or more friends, etc.), then the total amount of the insured portion could, in some instances, go up to 40 percent of the total loan). The actual amount of the loan is not tied to this guarantee but is a function of what the lender is willing to do. VA loans do not require a down payment.

3. *Can you get a GI loan on a manufactured home?* Yes, although the maximum loan guarantee will be less, resulting in lower loan maximums.

4. *If the entitlement was already used, can a qualified veteran get requalified for a VA loan?* Yes. The entitlement for the full amount available can be used again, even if the original entitlement was much less. After a loan is paid off, you qualify for renewed entitlement only when you sell the property. However, if you sell your property and the buyer assumes the loan, the buyer must qualify as a veteran and submit a Certificate of Eligibility to the lender, or you must obtain a release of liability from the lender. If the buyer cannot qualify as a veteran, you will not get a release of liability, and the amount of your entitlement used to guarantee that loan remains tied into that loan until it is paid off. The solution here is to make sure that you sell to an eligible veteran or that the buyer refinances the loan and the VA loan is paid off.

5. *What is the biggest danger when a veteran sells his or her property and the buyer assumes the loan?* Unless you get a release from liability, not only is your entitlement locked into the loan, but you are also the primary guarantor to the loan. In case of a default (even years in the future), the lender would look to the VA for coverage, and either the lender or the VA could look to you for recovery of any deficiency in a foreclosure.

6. *How long is a VA entitlement good for?* Once you qualify, that qualification lasts as long as you or your surviving spouse lives or until that rule is changed. What can a VA loan be used for? You can buy a home (including a townhome or condominium in a VA-approved project), build a home, buy and remodel a home, or buy a manufactured home and/or lot, and purchase a multifamily property of up to four units. You can also join with other eligible veterans to acquire a multifamily property larger than four units.

7. *Does the VA make any loans directly to eligible veterans?* Yes, but only to Native Americans on trust land or to supplement a grant for a specially adapted home for certain eligible veterans who have a permanent and total service-connected disability.

8. *Can the property covered by a VA loan be outside the United States?* That depends on what you define as the United States. All property covered by a VA loan must be located in the United States, its territories, or its possessions. This includes all the states, plus Puerto Rico, Guam, the U.S. Virgin Islands, American Samoa, and Northern Mariana Islands. Most VA lenders, however, are more specific about which of those areas they exclude from their lending practices.

188. What Can You Do to Increase Your Chances of Getting Any Kind of Loan?

Is there a simple list that will get you through almost any kind of a problem safely and successfully? Yes, there is, and if you follow the advice contained in this section you will be leaps and bounds ahead of your competition. Jump back to question 183 for additional information on getting a loan.

> **Solution:** The following steps work wonders for many different situations. Whenever you are to meet with someone who has some control (even the very slightest control) over something you want, follow these nine steps.

Nine Steps to Increase Your Chances at Nearly Everything

- Look and act successful.
- Be prompt and courteous.
- Have an appointment to meet the head person.
- Articulately explain what you need.
- Meet the head person's secretary and ask for help.
- Have the secretary set up your appointment with the loan officer.
- Have the secretary remind the person of your appointment.
- Let the secretary prod the person for you later on.
- Be sure to send thank-you notes to everyone.

Look and Act Successful.   This is so obvious that unfortunately many people take for granted that it is unnecessary. But mind you, this does not mean that you dress up in a suit and tie if the successful people in your field spend their life on a construction site. Look like you are successful in the business you are in. You will act successful by knowing what you are talking about and learning how to get the other person to talk. Some of the most articulate and brilliant conversationalists are those who are good at getting you to talk about yourself. Funny, isn't it?

Be Prompt and Courteous.   About the worst thing you can do, especially if you are trying to obtain a big loan, is to give the impression that you are always late and then blame it on something lese. "Sorry, there was a big accident on I-95 and my cell phone was on the blitz." This prompt and courteous stuff goes double when the person you are dealing with comes to you and not the other way around.

No one wants to drive across town (or fly there, either) for an important meeting (like checking out the person who just applied for a $10 million construction loan) only to be kept waiting in the lobby: "Sorry, Mr. Banker, but Mr. G is on a conference call. It shouldn't be more than an hour longer. Can I get you some coffee?"

Have an Appointment to Meet the Head Person.   This is not difficult to do and will pay off. In the situation involving a mortgage, the head person would be the president of the bank or lending institution. To meet this person, write a letter on your own high-quality letterhead and ask for an appointment in the relatively near future. Mention that you are planning to invest in the area and would like to discuss several items of mutual benefit. Prior to the appointment, make sure you have spoken with the head person's secretary. You might call one day to double-check the address or ask which floor the office is on or some other plausible question. Ask for his or her name, and thank him or her by name (but never use the first name by itself no matter how many times he or she says you can do it).

Articulately Explain What You Need.   The saying goes, "Ask and you shall receive," but are you capable of presenting your case in a way that maximizes your chances for success in attaining the desired objective? Your odds for success increase when you first have a clear understanding about that objective. If you need a $2 million loan to acquire a hotel, are you sure you can be successful in that venture? Have you anticipated what information the lender will want before making the loan? If you are confident in your abilities and have anticipated the data a lender will want from you, then practice your explanation of your needs to a friend or associate before meeting with the lender.

Meet the Head Person's Secretary and Ask for Help.   You have talked with the secretary by phone, but have not met face-to-face. You can do this on the day of the appointment, or if convenient, drop by the office a few days before the appointment and introduce yourself. Be sure you are dressed in your most successful-looking business apparel. A good approach is to have an envelope that has a clipping about the institution from the newspaper. It would be good to mention something about the head person. Least effective and something to avoid is talking about yourself.

Have the Secretary Set Up Your Appointment with the Loan Officer. Here is how you work this. You have an appointment with the head person and you keep it very brief. You do not ask for anything, but spend the whole time asking about the bank or institution. How long has it been in business, how the head person got started, what is the future of the company, and so on. The idea is to make the head person sell services to you. You are there as a prospective client of the bank, not as someone off the street who wants a loan.

During the appointment, tell the head person you are going to be in touch. The head person might suggest that you talk to someone important, like the mayor or some other person. Say that you will do so and will let the head person know how it turns out.

A few days later, drop the head person a note, and let him or her know what happened. Even if nothing positive occurred, you have established a small seed of truth or integrity in that you did what you said you were going to do, and you did it right away.

Before you drop this note in the mail, call and ask the secretary to tell the head person that you have followed on that person's suggestion, and ask the secretary to thank the head person for you. Do not mention what the suggestion was. You are giving the impression that you and the head person share information that the secretary may not be privileged to know.

If the conversation goes well, or the next day, mention that you would like to talk to the "best" loan officer to discuss some business with the bank regarding single-family homes (or apartment buildings, or the type of property you want to deal with). Make sure you make it plural, as in homes, apartments, or buildings.

When the secretary suggests someone, ask about that person, just to get some background information. How long has this person been with the bank? What kind of loans is he or she experienced in? Again, put the onus on the bank to sell you on its people and services.

Now ask the secretary, almost as an afterthought, if it would be possible for him or her to set up an appointment for you . . . and oh, yes, what would be the best day next week? You are suddenly in a hurry: "Oh, I have a call from London. . . . Please set it up for me. I'll check with you in the morning. Absolutely anytime on Thursday or Friday next week is fine. Bye."

The secretary will call the loan officer (or employment director, or head of the purchasing department, or whoever is important for your visit). The person who gets the call from the secretary of the head person will assume that the call was directed by the head person, and another subtle seed is planted.

Have the Secretary Remind the Person of Your Appointment. When you call to check the details on the appointment, thank the secretary. Then write a quick note, thanking that person again, and in the last part of the note ask if the secretary would mention that you will try to be a few minutes early just in case your person could see you early, but there is no need to get back to you.

Be sure to show up a few minutes earlier than you mentioned. By now the person with whom you are meeting may think you are the head person's brother or someone even more important.

Let the Secretary Prod the Person for You Later On. If the person you met with needs a subtle push, as in the case of a loan officer and your pending loan, look again to the head person's secretary. Call the secretary and suggest he or she let that person know you will stop by the next day to see how things are going. Be very sparing in this, and do not use it unless necessary.

All this might seem to be overkill, and in some situations it could be. However, the effort is not difficult, and if you are establishing yourself as a potential real estate investor you want to be making contacts with head persons (and their secretaries) all over town.

Be Sure to Send Thank-You Notes to Everyone.   Start with a note to the head person. Thank him or her for everything, call attention to how much you appreciated the advice (even if there was none), and compliment that person on the great staff working at that institution.

189.   Do the Mortgage Reduction Plans Really Save Me Money?

Sure, but are the savings worth the cost? Does this sound like a paradox? First take a look at the way most mortgage reduction plans work: If you pay down the principal of a mortgage faster than the scheduled repayment, you will shorten the repayment time.

> **Solution:**   Remember, time is money. This applies to both the money you earn and the money you pay. In real estate, most of the return you get is from other people paying off debt you got from yet other people. The cash flow you put into your pocket can, of course, go to reduce your debt so that you end up with free and clear property sooner rather than later. On the other hand, taking some of that cash flow and plowing it back into improvements (rather than debt reduction) might give you a greater return. Which is better? To own a run-down property that is free and clear, or to own a sparkling gem that brings in three times the rent as the run-down property?

This statement is the basis for the repayment program and is the simple fact for which someone would be willing to pay several hundred dollars if it were packaged as a "sold on TV" financial program with the title "How to Save Over $160,000 in the Repayment of a $250,000 Loan."

Assume that you have a 30-year repayment on a $250,000 loan at 7 percent interest. The monthly payment for a typical mortgage would be $1,795.50 per month over the full 30-year term. In essence, 360 months times $1,795.50 gives a total (add up all 360 months) of $646,380 over the 30 years.

If you add only $300 per month extra to your mortgage payment, this same mortgage will be paid off in about 17 years and three months, or 207 months. As the original loan schedule still has 129 months to go, you might say (correctly) that by following the "Cummings Prepayment Plan," you would save having to pay the original monthly payment of $1,795.50 × 129 months = $231,619.50.

So far, so good. By paying an additional $300.00 per month for 207 months, you paid in $62,100 earlier than you needed to. At first it might appear that by deducting that amount from the $231,619.50, you would come up with the real savings of this plan, or $169,519.50. Is this your real savings? No. Based on the information at hand, not only have you not saved anything, but this plan may have cost you money. How so?

This mortgage is at 7 percent interest. If you can get more benefit from the $300 per month than 7 percent, then you would be better off not making the added payments. Notice I used the word *benefit* rather than *return*. Many people have consumer loans or credit card charges that cost them a great deal more than 7 percent interest per year. Some of these charges exceed 18 percent.

On the other hand, if you have money in savings that you do not need as a security blanket, and it is earning less than 7 percent, it might be better to pay off the loan. But even here there is something else to consider.

What is your plan for this property? If the plan is to keep the property for a few years and sell it, then the mortgage in place can be an important factor to help you sell this property.

It is certain that supposedly saving money simply by paying off a mortgage early is not true. As this example shows, it can cost you money on one hand, and even if there is a positive effect due to interest rate differences, the overall disadvantage of building equity in a property you plan to sell may not be to your advantage.

As with every investment, look hard at your goals before you take any shortcut that leads to a dead end.

190. What Are the Insider Tips for Negotiating the Best Mortgage Terms?

In general, lenders seek to reduce their risk wherever possible. However, as risk goes down, it is an accepted financial reality that so does the yield on the investment. Because of this, lenders seek a balance where they can leverage their deposits up to a portfolio of loans that create a blended return for an acceptable risk.

The blending comes from a mix of high-return, high-risk loans such as automobile, aircraft, boat, credit card, and similar financial transactions. The lower-risk loans are the high-equity real estate transactions given to proven risk-free clients. In their quest for loans that will not end up in foreclosure, bankers and other lenders want their files to contain loan requests and applications with as many gold-star items as possible. Gold-star items point to successful loans, and they are the opposite of red-star items, which point to their own failure to make good loans. Lenders want to avoid red stars.

Solution: Bring gold-star items to your lenders. Look at the following list of three surefire gold-star indicators.

Three Surefire Things That Increase Your Chances for the Best Loan Terms Possible

- Have a professional loan presentation.
- Show a proven track record.
- Decrease the loan-to-value ratio.

Have a Professional Loan Presentation.   Keep in mind that lenders will have their own loan application and format that they like to follow. You will want to adhere to that format, but you should also be creative in adding other material to the package that enables them to make a decision based on the assumption that they had material in their hands to support that decision.

Loan officers are, after all, not giving you their own money. They are giving you the bank's money. This means that a risk they might take with their own cash might not be acceptable with the bank's money. On one hand, the bank depends on them to make loans, and to make a lot of loans every week to ensure the needed incoming revenue to keep the bank in business. On the other hand, the bank also demands that the loan officers not make mistakes.

One of the worst mistakes a loan officer can make is to recommend or push for a loan and then have that loan fail. That results in a big red star against that loan officer in his or her personnel file. If there are too many red stars, the loan officer can be terminated.

So, when you meet with loan officers, provide more than enough material to support these three elements: the value of the property, your ability to do everything you say you will do (including meet the repayment terms of the loan), and why their approval of your loan would be a sound move. A professional approach such as a good loan application or project presentation is a great big gold star and, as such, can deflect any fault away from that loan officer should the loan go south.

Show a Proven Track Record.   If this is your first loan for your first real estate investment you may have to be creative about your track record, but always be honest. Track records are other great big gold stars. Look to success you have had in anything else you may have done. Your job and your personal life will do if there is nothing real estate–related to use as evidence of success. Remember that it is not what you say you did that is really important, it is what you *do*. To prove this, make demands on yourself and then live up to them. Even doing this for a very short period of time can have a major impact on your self-confidence. Be prompt for appointments and have everything the loan officer asks for, on time or early, and you will build the loan officer's confidence in you, too.

Decrease the Loan-to-Value Ratio.   If you can demonstrate that the value of the property is even greater than the price you are paying, then you can show the lender that what looks like a 110 percent loan-to-value ratio is really closer to a 70 percent LTV. For example, if you have a contract to buy a vacant warehouse for $300,000 and you want to borrow $325,000, the loan officer might tell you that your chances are zero. However, if you can show that the real value of the property is $460,000, you are in good shape.

I was involved in a situation exactly like this, where the buyer got a bargain price from the seller because the buyer was the sole tenant who planned to move if he could not buy the property for $300,000. All the buyer had to do was show that because his own company would agree to pay rent, the value was clearly established at $460,000. He substantiated that with some independent opinions and got enough money to pay off the seller plus some extra cash to cover legal and closing costs.

191. As a Buyer, Just How Creative Can I Get with Mortgages?

Short of usury and being involved in some other illegal act, you can be very creative with mortgages in a contract. Taking into consideration honesty and ethical dealing, a contract between two people that is discussed openly can be very flexible and creative.

> **Solution:** When it comes to real estate transactions, there are many different ways to solve problems. The most flexible and therefore potentially the most creative lender will always be the seller. However, institutional lenders are becoming more creative, too, so don't let the image of a stoic banker stand in the way of your suggesting something truly new.

The following techniques can be incorporated into mortgages to give you the edge, to help make the deal, to save on taxes, to increase cash flow, to shift income, or just to help out relatives in their first real estate purchase. All of these techniques and more can be used in various combinations to create an endless supply of creative opportunities.

27 Creative Techniques That Can Be Applied to Mortgages

Adjustable rate mortgage

Assignment of payments for benefits you receive

Balloon payment

Blanket mortgage cosigner

Deed in lieu of foreclosure

Discounted mortgage

Friendly foreclosure

Gift of interest in the mortgage

Graduated payment mortgage

Interest-only payment

Lease-option conversion

Limited liability divided between partners

Moratorium of interest

Option as a security

Pyramid mortgage

Release of security

Repayment by barter

Repayment by return of benefits

Selling of an interest in the mortgage

Shared appreciation mortgage

Subordination of interest

Subordinated lease to mortgage

Substitution of security

Unsecured note

Use of mortgage as security for a loan

Wraparound mortgage

Zero-coupon payment plan

192. What Can I Do to Get around a Nonassumable Mortgage?

Many mortgages have provisions that make them nonassumable, or even when they appear to be assumable they have the same restrictions on the new mortgagor as on a buyer taking out an application for a new loan. Because of this, many buyers want to assume the existing loan while at the same time avoid added cost. However, the nonassumable provision is often very clear and precise about what might trigger the borrower to be in default, which may stop the sale of the property.

> **Solution:** When an existing mortgage contains provisions that do not allow it to be assumed, there are two things you can do. The first is to attempt to renegotiate with the mortgagee to allow the loan to be assumed. This may be productive, especially if the new mortgagor has good or better credit than the original one and if there is some added benefit that can be given to the mortgagee. The other thing you can do is simply ignore the provision that says mortgagees have to approve any such assumption. Once title is transferred, they are likely to change their mind about this assumption thing anyway. Naturally, if they get nasty, the owner of the property (would-be mortgagor) would have to pay off the loan.

193. What Is a Starker Exchange, and What Are the Pitfalls I Need to Avoid?

Once upon a time there was a tax case involving a delayed 1031 exchange. Remember that the IRC 1031, also called the tax-free exchange, allows you to postpone or even completely avoid payment of any capital gains tax on your qualifying real estate investments (see questions 73 and 74 for more information on this subject). The defendant in a related tax case was named Starker, and thus the historic name that reflects a host of rules and regulations governing exchanges that start as a sale and end up as an exchange.

> **Solution:** The Starker tax case has opened the doors for all investors to plan for maximum growth of their real estate investments through the avoidance of paying capital gains taxes. This comes about through the Internal Revenue Code, Section 1031, the tax-free exchange, which should become a good friend for you in your real estate investment life.

What is a Starker? Here is a very simple example. Alice owns a vacant lot she wants to dispose of so she can invest the proceeds in a small motel she would like to own. She has tried to effect a 1031 exchange, whereby she would swap her equity for that of a motel and, if the accounting worked out right, avoid any gain on the lot. Her problem, after all, is that the vacant lot is worth $500,000, but she paid only $50,000 for it 20 years ago. A taxable gain of $450,000 is not a pleasant event when it comes to tax payment time.

However, no direct exchange seemed possible, yet several buyers were ready and willing to pay her price. What should she do? She should follow the rules and guides of a Starker and beat the IRS at its own game.

Here's how it works. As long as Alice meets the IRS guidelines, she can enter into a contract to sell her lot. She must set aside the cash she gets from the sale within very strict rules that do not allow her to use the money but that permit her to look for and place under contract another property to her liking. If this property qualifies for a 1031 exchange, and if Alice abides by all the IRS rules and regulations, she will not have to pay any capital gains tax that might otherwise have resulted from the sale of her lot.

In essence, this is a 1031 exchange as described earlier in this book, but with one major and very important twist. It is not really an exchange. It is a *sale*, and with the proceeds of the sale it becomes a purchase.

Keep in mind the true importance of this statement. If Alice sold her lot for $500,000 and paid the tax on the capital gain of $450,000 (which could be $150,000 or more), she might end up with only $350,000 to reinvest. However, if she can meet the requirements of a Starker exchange, she can reinvest the entire amount (less commissions and cost of the deal) into another property.

Warning: When it comes to actually doing this kind of transaction, you are urged to seek the advice of professionals who can clue you in on the latest information, tax rules, and legal ramifications as they apply to this type of real estate deal. This is not something you should try to learn from this or any other book. When it comes to the IRS, you had best stick with those professionals who are 100 percent current, which no book can be.

Remember that a 1031 exchange must be a like-kind exchange, and therefore a Starker exchange must also meet that rule. Like for like does not mean farm for farm or office building for office building. Like for like is based on the intent of ownership. What we are talking about is investment real estate. If what you want to dispose of is investment real estate, then it will qualify for a 1031, and also a Starker exchange, provided that you acquire investment real estate.

Key to the Starker is precise documentation of the transaction. You must follow some very strict rules that will, in their finality, allow you to close on a sale of your property only as long as you do not have use of or access to the proceeds of the sale. Any cash must be tied to the acquisition of replacement property or you will fail the test for 1031 tax benefits.

The rules of the delayed exchange require that within 45 days of the date you close on the sale of your property (the day someone else takes title to your property), you must identify a property you will acquire in its place. Fortunately, you can identify more than one property (because you do not know whether you can actually take title or close on a given property at that time).

The rules also require that you take title to your new property no more than 180 days from the date you close on the sale of your property or the due date of your tax return for that year, whichever comes first. It is here that problems start to arise, and you should be well represented by experienced tax and legal counsel, because whenever you mess with the IRS, you flirt with the devil.

There are many pitfalls with the Starker, and the most common is falling into a trap that only one property need be identified. As you have only the first 45 days following the closing of title on your property to identify the new one, failing to locate more than one property may lock you out of a successful 1031 tax treatment if the one property you select cannot be delivered. Real estate titles are often hard to transfer, sellers sometimes lie about their situations, and many transactions fail at the closing table due to undisclosed problems. A problem that might be cleared up a year from now will not help you, because you will have run out of time under the rules of this kind of tax deferment.

Because there is a limit to the number of properties (generally, three are considered within the safe harbors, which are simply guidelines the IRS considers acceptable), it is wise not to identify them until the very last moment. But do continue to look for your replacement properties right up to that time. In fact, you can even go to contract and start due diligence investigations without identifying the property. Thus, if you discover that there are title problems that cannot possibly be cleared up in time to close, you can drop that one and move on without putting your list of identified properties in jeopardy.

194. What Critical Factors Should You Be Aware of before You Hold a Mortgage on a Property You Sell?

It is possible that there will be unique situations that can make other factors even more important than the ones that follow, but for the most part it is essential to answer all of these questions.

Solution: Pay close attention to the answers you get when asking these following seven questions. Do not rely just on the answers that come from the mortgagor. Run a credit check; get references and check them out; find out what other property the mortgagor owns and has sold.

Seven Questions You Need Answered before Holding Financing When Selling Property

1. *What is the value of the security?*   The real value is what is important, not the price. You have to consider that there will be costs in the event of a foreclosure and that the property may ultimately be returned to you in a distressed condition and with a lower value than at present. You have to start with adequate real market values and discount those.

2. *What is the record of accomplishment of the mortgagor?*   This can be simple to discover, but not without some effort and willingness to make personal calls. References are a start but are only truly effective if they give you leads to other people or places to contact. If you come across something strange or anything that leaves you with an uncomfortable feeling, then dig deeper.

3. *Can the loan be reasonably repaid?*   Some sellers take pride in selling property they know they are going to get back. If you do not want to get the property back (which is the right approach), then you should never take a mortgage that is clearly a burden to the mortgagee of the property.

4. *Can you get notice of default from superior mortgagee?*   Remember that to foreclose on your mortgage you must either have a direct default made on your mortgage or have the right to call your loan in default when superior or inferior loans are in default. The first mortgagee may be six months in arrears and you may not know about it because this mortgagee does not even know about you. One step to solve this is to have periodic estoppel agreements from the other lenders regarding the status of the loans. Keeping track of this may be difficult and time-consuming, but could be worth the effort.

5. *Will the buyer send you copies of canceled checks he or she has paid to lenders who are ahead of you in this property?*   If this is an obligation of the buyer and a part of the contract and the mortgage the buyer signed with you, then failure to send you this proof of payment would be evidence of possible default. If a buyer will not agree to do this, then you should think seriously about saying no to the loan.

6. *Can you reasonably serve notice to the mortgagor?*   Take, for example, the mortgagor who lives outside the United States and whose address is unknown. If you cannot get service to that person, then you may have a problem with any legal action. One way to solve this problem partially is to insist that the mortgagor designate a local agent for such service. Make sure that your lawyer sets this into both the contract and the mortgage and that the local agent has the authority and power to act as the legal agent for the mortgagee.

7. *Can you reasonably collect on a judgment?*   Getting a judgment and collecting on one are two different matters. Even if you can serve the person's local agent, that person may now live in another state, or even in Rio, and your ultimate cost to get a judgment may not be worth the effort.

The bottom line is that whenever you hold a mortgage you must do your homework to ensure that the person obligated to repay the loan is likely to do so. If you are comfortable in that, then be satisfied that the equity in the deal is adequate, and keep on top of the repayment.

19

Reducing Cost and Avoiding Problems at Closings and Deed Transfers

195. What Happens at the Real Estate Closing?

The term *real estate closing* refers to the actual event when the title transfers hands. This occurs when all the documentation is completed, papers, affidavits, mortgages and mortgage notes, deeds, bills of sale, and so on are all signed and executed, and the mechanics of the transfer of title or other real property interest takes place. This moment can be a simple, smooth, uneventful happening, or it can be a traumatic, emotion-filled episode. In either case, it is sure to be something you will remember for a very long time.

To increase the chances that the closing will be simple and smooth, review the following series of events of a transaction that has only a few snags, none of which threaten the deal.

38 Possible Steps to a Real Estate Closing

1. The property is offered for sale. Property owners meet with a real estate agent and sign an exclusive listing agreement, and later that day a "For Sale" sign goes up on the lawn.

2. Time goes by, and despite some action and a few offers that were too low, the property remains unsold.

3. The sellers reduce the price.

4. The sellers reduce the price again.

5. You come along and make an offer below the newly listed price.

6. The sellers reject the offer, saying they are insulted at such a low regard for their property value.

7. Their agent gets them to make a counteroffer to you.

8. You counteroffer, accepting their price, but making a change in the terms, asking them to include the furniture.

9. A final counteroffer is proposed, as the sellers agree to include some, but not all, of the furniture.

10. You accept, and there is now a deal, subject to your approval of inspections.

11. You have the right to inspections that (as usual) allow you to check for termites and structural, electrical, plumbing, roof, pool, retaining wall, and environmental problems, review contracts, leases, and other property problems including the status of the title. The contract has a provision that the seller is to correct any problems up to 3 percent of the price of the property.

12. The inspectors discover that there is termite damage and active infestation, that there are roof leaks, and that other minor repairs are needed. An estimate for repairs is obtained.

13. The sellers object to your inspector's results and hire their own inspectors, and there are some back-and-forth arguments about the actual extent of the termite problem and the cause of the leaks.

14. In the meantime you apply for a new mortgage to refinance the sellers' old financing.

15. You shop around at three lending institutions, fill out the necessary papers, meet with the loan officers and wait.

16. Two weeks go by and you are contacted by one of the lenders, who offers you a loan commitment that spells out the terms of the loan from that lender.

17. By the end of another week all three lenders have responded.

18. You go to the other two lenders and ask if they can better what you have been offered.

19. One of the other lenders comes up with a slightly better loan package for you and you accept.

20. Both buyer and sellers have agreed to the cost of repairs according to the inspections.

21. It is agreed to set funds aside to cover the cost of repairs rather than to actually do the repairs now, because you want to close and move in.

22. A closing date one week away is set; you fly back to Toronto and have the movers pack up everything in your rented apartment in Canada, and the vans start for Arizona and your new home.

23. The closing agent (your lawyer or title insurance company) discovers there is a problem with the title. An improper deed transfer several transactions earlier

had apparently been overlooked when the current owner purchased the property. The sellers may not have a clear title to pass on to you.

24. The closing is postponed while the lawyers work on the problem.

25. You have to find storage for your furniture.

26. You move into a motel.

27. The lawyers discover several more problems with the title.

28. After a week, and the sellers running up costs to clear title of several thousand dollars, everything is set to close.

29. The lender says, "Wait just a minute. Where are the financial reports you promised to send?"

30. You call your accountant in Toronto. "Sorry," he says, "I forgot to send them," but does so that same day.

31. The morning of the closing you wake up with a migraine.

32. The morning of the closing, one of the sellers is in a serious car accident, and the closing is postponed for three weeks or until the accident victim recovers.

33. You have to return to Toronto, but you go to the closing agent's office and sign everything you need to sign, put up the balance of the money, and execute the loan papers. All of the money and paperwork is to be held by the closing agent in escrow pending the sellers' delivery of the title.

34. While you are in Toronto the sellers complete their part of the deal, and it finally closes.

35. The closing agent now takes all the documents that must be recorded (mortgage documentation, deed, bill of sale, and other items that are related to the transaction and required to be recorded or that either party wants to be recorded) to the proper authorities so they can be recorded.

36. The closing agent checks the title just before the recording and then following the recording to make sure that nothing else is recorded that would cause a change in the intended order of the transaction.

37. Several days following the actual date the documents are executed by both the buyer and sellers, the recording has been accomplished and the closing agent releases the funds to the seller and delivers the deed to the buyer.

38. For a period of time following the closing, the sellers are obligated to certain warranties specific to the contract, such as "all appliances are guaranteed to be in good working order for a period of X months," or to certain warranties that are controlled by state law. Both the buyer and sellers know what these warranties are.

The important message in these steps that lead up to the actual closing is that you should anticipate that there will be snags. It is rare for everything to run completely smoothly, with no bumps, so anticipate glitches and allow yourself ample time to deal with them. The buyer or seller who sets the closing date six weeks in advance and expects it to occur without any problems is overly optimistic.

196. Should I Use a Lawyer at the Closing?

To consider representing yourself, you should be an expert in all real estate procedures from both the buyer and seller perspectives . . . or should seek out professional help in dealing with the potential problems that can occur. Oh yes, even the
experts already know they need to use a lawyer.

> **Solution:** Since you will be using lawyers your entire real
> estate investment life, why not make sure you have a good
> one? Interview lawyers just as you would anyone else you
> might hire. You need to be impressed with their knowledge,
> reputation, and ability to communicate well with you. You
> can judge professionals pretty well by the questions they
> ask you, and not just by the answers they give to your
> questions.

If one side is represented and the other is not, then it is possible for things to occur
that will not be in the best interest of the unrepresented party. However, representation at a real estate closing need not be through a lawyer. Many buyers look to
other professionals to represent them at the closing.

In some states, such as California, escrow agencies are designed to function as
closing agents for both buyer and seller. Around the country, title insurance companies provide title insurance and at the same time take care of all the required
paperwork, recording, and so forth.

Why would you use a lawyer? The answer is easy. The closing of the title transfer is apt to be the single most important financial transaction that you will ever
make. Your lawyer should be involved right from the very start to ensure that the
contract has been properly executed and that it contains all the provisions necessary to protect you. It does not make any difference whether you are the buyer or
seller, make sure you are properly protected.

In the final analysis, there are no disadvantages to using a lawyer, provided you
have one who understands your goals and financial abilities and is competent to
deal with real estate in the area where the property is located. The cost difference
between using a lawyer or a title insurance company should be minor as long as
you do not have a very complicated contract; if you do, then the lawyer is needed
anyway. But be sure that you have a good relationship with your lawyer and other
professional advisors. They should be there to advise you, not make decisions for
you.

197. As a Buyer, How Do I Keep My
Closing Costs to a Minimum?

There are many costs when buying real estate. You have lawyers and accountants to advise you; there are inspection fees, loan application fees, title insurance, closing costs, and a mountain of small things, but it all adds up. What do
you do?

> **Solution:** The first step to keeping costs down is to know what the normal costs are for a similar closing. This is information you will want to shop around for before you make an offer. How do you find this out? Simple—you make a few phone calls, and you also ask the real estate agent to get several price quotes for you.

Title insurance companies and/or escrow agencies may offer services similar to those of lawyers for closing, and these are your first source for the needed price comparisons. Armed with data, you can then ask your lawyer, or several different lawyers, to quote charges for a package deal, which should include the following items.

The Five Most Important Things a Lawyer Does for You

- Reviews and make suggestions on the actual offer to purchase
- Reviews the final contract document before signing it
- Discusses the potential hazards of the agreement with you
- Provides title insurance
- Handles all the closing documentation and recording

Because most lawyers who practice real estate law are associated with an insurance company that sells title insurance, it is likely that they will match or nearly match the prices of title insurance companies. But you may have to ask them to do that.

Most insurance companies that insure title give a price break on policies that are issued on properties that have had previous insurance. This insurance need not have been with the same insurer, but because it did exist, the discount can save you as much as 25 percent of the cost of new insurance. You must make sure that you find out whether the sellers had obtained title insurance when they acquired the property; even though that may have been dozens of years ago, you can still save now.

198. What Are the Key Steps to Keeping the Seller's Closing Costs to a Minimum?

There is an adage: "If you buy right, you can sell right." This can apply to just about every aspect of a real estate transaction, including the closing costs.

> **Solution:** Review the following key steps that will help you keep your closing costs (as the seller) at a minimum.

Six Key Steps to Keeping the Seller's Closing Cost to a Minimum

1. *Have the buyer pay for the survey.*   Make sure that when you purchased the property you got a recent survey paid for by the buyer if he or she will agree to that (after all, it is for their benefit and use, not yours). This will save you money when it is time for them to sell.

2. *Make sure you qualify for a title insurance discount.*   Have your former title insurance policy handy. It can also save you money or allow you to save the buyers money (and then let them pay for something else).

3. *Pass on other costs to the buyer.*   Get the buyers to agree to pay for as much as you can. All that goes into the contract, so there is nothing common, and what is in the agreement sticks. Many of the new Realtor contracts have little boxes that can be checked to designate who pays for what. Sellers want the buyers to pay for everything. However, remember that buyers want sellers to pay for everything, too.

4. *Well-maintained property brings a top price.*   Keep up with continual property maintenance. Good maintenance will not only help you get a higher price for your property when you go to sell it, but it will help you have a smoother closing. One approach is to look at your property from time to time as would a property inspection team. Find the problems that are developing and get them fixed.

5. *Promptly solve preclosing problems.*   One of the keys to keeping small problems from growing into big problems is to tackle them right away and solve them. This is very important, because it is a matter of attitude more than anything else. First, anticipate that there will be problems, then have the mental attitude that when they come up you tackle them aggressively and solve them. Sometimes you cannot easily solve the problem, but the very fact that you are promptly and diligently making an attempt to do so can smooth rough waters.

6. *Be very cautious about getting bogged down with a problem.*   Often, closing agents show a lax attitude about common problems and forget that your motivation is to get the deal closed. Keep on top of everything that is going on, and while there is no need to hyperventilate when something comes up (because it will), deal with it when it does.

199.   What Are the Dos and Don'ts I Should Know When I Am Getting Ready for the Closing?

There are many things you should be aware of that can happen between the moment you sign a contract and the actual closing. Of these, nine seem common enough that you should become specifically aware of them.

> **Solution:** Review the following preclosing potential nightmares and be ready to deal with any of them if they strike your deal.

Nine Preclosing Nightmares and How to Deal with Them

- Personality conflict between the parties
- "Coldfeetitus," the seller's remorse
- "Backoutitus," the buyer's nightly cold sweats
- Confusing advice
- "I've been suckered" syndrome
- Termite delight
- Legal problems
- Money problems
- Renegotiation time

Personality Conflict between the Parties.   It is not uncommon for the buyer and seller to be at odds somewhere along the route from contract to closing. The deal may start out that way the very first time the prospective buyer walks into the house and says, "My goodness, who in the world picked out the hideous color of that carpet?" Who? The seller, that's who. The seller who is standing right in front of the prospective buyer. This is bite-your-tongue time if you are the seller.

Of all the problems that arise, personality conflicts are the most difficult because emotion, not logic, causes people to react. No seller should ever be insulted by any buyer's offer. After all, at least the buyer likes the property enough to make an offer.

However, because emotion can get in the way of a signed contract or a smooth closing, all experienced real estate agents know that sometimes it is much better if the buyer and seller never even meet face-to-face. It is possible, in fact, to go all the way to closing and never have the two parties come together in the same room.

"Coldfeetitus," the Seller's Remorse.   This almost always happens. The usual situation occurs a few days following the signing of the contract when the seller tells a friend, neighbor, real estate agent (not the one involved in the deal), or some other party (hairdresser, bartender, etc.), about the sale. Here is how the conversation starts: "You idiot, you've been taken."

From that little seed, "coldfeetitus" spreads quicker than bubonic plague, and in a few days the seller starts thinking of ways to get out of the deal. Fortunately, this often passes. There is little a buyer can do to deal with this problem, and usually it is up to the agents involved to satisfy the seller that the original decision to accept the contract was the right move.

"Backoutitus," the Buyer's Nightly Cold Sweats.   I do not know any buyer who has not had second thoughts about the deal. In this case, "backoutitus" often starts with a comment from someone (it could even be the seller), who says something like this: "Why, if you'd held out one more day, I'd have accepted $50,000 less." The nightly sweats begin.

Buyers often need to be reinforced that they made the right decision, and often the only person who can do this is the real estate agent who participated in the sale.

Confusing Advice.   Both parties can become confused by advice that begins to filter in as the closing nears. Sometimes the buyer is setting up the seller for the final problem or the renegotiation of the contract, or the seller could be playing mind games to pressure the buyer to speed up approvals of inspections.

When one party or both parties become confused by the situation, usually all they need to do is to slow down and meet with someone who can fully explain what is going on and what can be done about the perceived problem, and then they should relax. Often, the confusion has been caused by a misinformed advisor—sometimes their own lawyer.

"I've Been Suckered" Syndrome.   This is almost exclusively an exchange problem. It is similar to the seller's remorse or the buyer's "backoutitus," and when it occurs the deal is doomed unless some major renegotiation can put the transaction back on track.

In an exchange, one or more parties swap properties, often in a three- or four-way deal in which no one actually gets the property of the person who gets theirs. In this kind of transaction, the parties may have painted an inaccurate picture of what they were offering, and that information was embellished along the way. In the end it is like a whispered phrase that goes around a circle of people and ends up being so far from the original statement that the property is not what the taker believed it to be.

I have known people to take property in an exchange without ever looking at it, accepting the giver's word, and then exchanging it with someone else, and so on, with no one ever reviewing what finally ends up on the table of a deal where the final taker actually goes out and tries to find that beautiful, wooded mountain paradise.

In the real estate game, try to learn who to trust, but make sure you double-check everything.

Termite Delight.   That is what I call this problem in Florida and in other termite-prone areas. In your area it might be something else, like swamp gas or sinkholes or earthquake faults. This refers to any problem that the present owners most likely knew about but did not mention. You may never prove that they withheld this information on purpose, and it may matter only a little. But it matters nonetheless, and like any untruth that seeps through the crack of integrity, it may just be enough to cast doubt about all the other statements that are behind the dam.

Legal Problems.   Real estate is a sea of legalities: deeds, mortgages, satisfactions, liens, judgments, foreclosures, *lis pendens*, leases, notices of eviction, and so on, all of which can cause anything from a minor headache to a major (and expensive) day in court. One legal element that seems to be surfacing more often these days is the problem of code violations. Most code violations deal with very minor things, such as fire extinguishers that have not been serviced according to the date stamped, signs that do not meet code, that sort of thing. But what if the code violation is something major, like "Who added that second story to the building without a permit?" Ouch, big problem. As a buyer, you cover your asset by having the city make a preclosing code violation survey. Most people never do that, and, boy, are they surprised when they get the notice of code default.

This does not mean you need to lose sleep over these problems, but that you should make sure you have very good lawyers and other professionals to deal with these legal situations.

Fortunately, when a legal problem does arise, it can be dealt with promptly, and most of the time you may never know about the steps the closing agent took to solve it.

Money Problems. The biggest money problem occurs when the buyer cannot get the mortgage needed to buy the property. The loan commitment does not come through as quickly as everyone thought (or was told) it would (or doesn't come through at all). This might be because the buyer didn't fill out all the necessary forms, or didn't submit documents to the lender, or just that the lender is dragging its heels on the loan request.

One way to solve this problem is to be prequalified for a loan. Many buyers understand this procedure and take the steps to build their contacts with lenders early in their investment career. Some lenders will even process your material to ascertain just how much of a loan they would make to you before you present the application for a specific home or other property.

Renegotiation Time. This is the point when the buyer has finished the inspections and now wants to sit down and fine-tune the deal. In essence, the buyer attempts to renegotiate the price and/or terms, because, according to the buyer, the property needs more attention, does not have the income promised, has deferred maintenance, requires painting, or whatever. All of this may be true, but then perhaps it is not and the buyer is just testing the water to see what the seller will do.

If you are the seller and want to find out whether the buyer is just attempting to negotiate a better deal (but will close on the old one), determine whether the buyer will commit to walking away from the deal. Ask the question in writing and request a written answer: "If we cannot agree to a modification in the agreement, do we understand that you are electing to cancel the agreement under the provisions in the contract?"

If you have other buyers, then you, as the seller, may be more hardheaded in these renegotiations. On the other hand, if the present buyer is your only hot prospect, you should not let the deal slip away without an effort to close it. It may be that buyers want minor, unimportant changes in the agreement that would be acceptable to a seller. On the other hand, if major revisions are suggested, then every factor needs to be looked at all over again.

One good tactic is to be willing to entertain new contract proposals only if the buyer agrees to cancel the first contract completely.

200.   How Can the Seller Legally Back Out of the Deal?

Virtually every real estate contract has a provision whereby the buyer has a period for due diligence, during which time the buyer can make different inspections of the property. These inspections can be anything from the roof to the plumbing and everything in between. During this period, the buyer can notify the seller that the inspections prove to be unacceptable and therefore the buyer withdraws from the deal. Okay, but what about the seller? Is there a way that the seller can back out of the deal?

> **Solution:** If the buyer asks the seller to hold financing, the seller has every right to include a provision in the contract that the seller must approve the buyer's credit. Other escape clauses can also give sellers the opportunity to pull back from the deal if they want to. Here are three such ways.

1. *Site plan or development plan approval.*   If the buyer is purchasing real estate for the purpose of building something or developing something, the buyer may include a clause that gives the seller the right to approve the project. Why? Because the seller owns other property nearby, or perhaps just because the seller wants to be able to get out of the deal if a better offer comes along. Buyers would be very cautious entering into a deal like this, so they would insist on a very quick approval time, long before the buyer starts spending money to advance the project.

2. *Release provisions can also give the seller an out.*   Large tracts of land with release provisions and a seller-held mortgage likely mean that the buyer and the seller must come to agreement on the release provisions of the deal. Failure to come to an agreement would naturally kill the deal.

3. *Delivery of important documents.*   Often, the buyer will request documents from the seller that are important to redevelopment or other purposes. These might be environmental studies that took months to obtain and that are very expensive. The buyer does not want to redo something that the seller has already done, but since the friendly handshake at the signing of the contract, things have changed. Suddenly the seller cannot find those documents: "Gee, I was sure my lawyer had them."

The term *legally back out* can be misleading, however, so all buyers should be aware that if a seller is determined to get out of the deal, it can become very expensive on the part of the buyer to force the seller to a closing. Even though the buyer may have every right to compensation for damages or for costs and the right to sue for specific performance breaches (where the court would ultimately order the seller to transfer title according to the terms of the contract), such legal actions are rare. Why? Because buyers generally prefer to move on to something else rather than be tied down in a long battle over a property they now no longer want because of the bad taste in their mouths from the deal.

Why would a seller want to back out? There can be as many answers to that question as there are dollars in the new offer that came in yesterday.

201. Can the Buyer Legally Back Out of the Deal?

Hey, this is America, and anyone can do whatever he or she wants to do, so is there anything you can do if the buyer decides to back out of the deal? You betcha.

> **Solution:** Solution: If your contract says the buyers can make and approve inspections and can wave a silk handkerchief and say good-bye if they do not approve of them—then make sure that they actually do the inspections or whatever within the designated inspection period. In addition, make sure they do them in earnest and with the intention of purchasing the property.

Because of the multitude of problems that can be latent in any property, buyers should make sure that they have an inspection period that gives them one or both of the following options:

1. If for any reason the buyer does not approve of any of the inspections to be accomplished, then the buyer may elect to withdraw from the agreement and promptly have refunded any and all deposits.

2. If any damage is found in the building, fixtures, or structure, if any manual electrical or mechanical device or apparatus is not in good working order or is in need of repair or maintenance, if any code violations are found (current or soon-to-be enacted building codes, city codes, or other governing ordinances), or if any defect, cloud, or other problem with the title occurs, then the seller shall promptly correct said findings or, at closing, credit the buyer with sufficient funds to correct the same.

Naturally, the buyer can simply elect not to close. In this event, the seller may have some rights to legal actions against the buyer to recover damages and costs; however, in reality such legal actions often prove to be very costly and drawn out. Generally, the only source of pressure to the buyer comes from the at-risk money the buyer has placed in escrow pending the closing. Deposit monies are generally put up by buyers, and these deposits are at risk (buyers lose the money if they do not close) after the inspections have been completed.

A buyer determined to get out of a deal may reach that point the day of the closing when something new comes to light that changes the whole picture of the transaction. This might be something relatively simple that was overlooked during the inspections, such as an addendum to a lease from tenants in the property that gave those tenants the right to extend their lease for another 99 years. Ouch, that means the buyer cannot move into the property. Or the buyer may want out because he or she discovered that the seller (or anyone else for that matter) knew something very important and damaging about the property and was required by law, or at least by ethics, to disclose that fact to the buyer, but did not.

Many situations occur where the agents are blamed, and often they are at fault for misrepresenting the property. "Why, Mr. and Mrs. Buyer, you can rent out this vacant space for $30.00 per square foot anytime you want." However, the agent forgot to say that to get this kind of rent you would first have to build a 500-bed hospital across the street.

202.   What Can I Do If the Property I Bought Is Not Everything the Sellers Told Me It Would Be?

The term *caveat emptor* means "let the buyer beware." In many parts of the world it is the rule that governs most transactions between two or more people. But with real estate transactions in the United States (at least), buyers have many different safeguards working for them to ensure that the property purchased is exactly what has been presented.

> **Solution:**   Often, buyers wake up in the middle of the night and recognize that something the seller said about the property they closed on that very afternoon was not right. There were not really 540 units in the hotel, but only 330, or the monthly NOI was not $56,000, but only $36,000. Are we dealing with typos, or are we dealing with downright crooks?

Let's look at some of the postclosing problems and go from that point forward. Every day, dissatisfied buyers wake up to realize that the property they now own is less than they expected it to be. What happened in between the moment that the seller signed the deed over to the buyer and this distasteful moment? Well, many things could have gone wrong. Look at some of the problems that can arise and their possible solutions.

12 Not-So-Unusual Problems That Surface after the Closing

- You purchased the wrong property.
- The lot size is different than reported.
- The survey is very, very, wrong.
- The barn belongs to someone else.
- The tenant has a 50-year lease at $35.00 per month.
- There is a second mortgage no one told you existed.
- There are no live termites—only 500 million dead ones!
- The seller's "dead" wife shows up and moves into "her" home.

- Other people claim they paid the tax so they own the property.
- The rental potential is half what you were told.
- The sellers dig up the landscaping and take it with them.
- The property was built in 1891, not 1981.

The Solutions to Most Pre- and Postclosing Problems

The real solution is to check and double-check everything. This does not mean that you have to do all the work yourself, because if you are using a professional closing agent he or she should do it as a part of the normal closing procedure. Note the words *should do it*. There are often big cracks in the procedure. The following checklist will help you close them up.

The Buyer's Pre- and Postclosing Checklist

1. *Have all parties execute the agreement.* Make sure you have an approved contract executed by all the legal owners. Just because the home seems to have only one occupant, that does not mean there is just one owner. The only way to be sure is to check the title in the property records. One quick way to check is to ask for the past real estate tax bills (go back a couple of years at least). If several names show up as owners, then you know you may need other people to execute the contract. Divorces, separations, and murders can account for confusion. By the way, proof of who has been paying the real estate taxes can help remove the risk of any possible squatter's rights from people who may claim title by adverse possession.

2. *Get a copy of the seller's title insurance policy.* This will give you a lot of important information and can provide you with a discount off the title insurance when you close. Some of the important information contained in the seller's policy would be possible exclusions to the policy, which would be specific situations or items that the insurer (when the seller purchased the property) would not insure. These situations or items may still exist, and, though acceptable to the buyer then, they may not be acceptable to you now. Make sure that the seller clears them up.

3. *Obtain a recent property boundary and building survey.* In a title insurance policy there is often a simple statement such as this: "No item or situation shall be covered by this insurance that would have been disclosed by a recent property survey." Some of the problems that can come back to haunt you years after you close could be that the property had and still has latent legal problems such as encroachment of buildings onto neighboring property, easements, or rights-of-way that haven't been used yet, but plans are under way (new train track down the middle of the land, high-tension power lines, road to the back 40 acres, etc.). One of the worst problems is that when you see the recent survey you discover that the property is not actually what you thought it was, or even *where* you thought it was.

4. *Having a survey is great, but one of the most important things you can do is to walk the boundaries of the property.*   Find the corner markers; be sure the buildings are well clear of any setbacks; check out everything. Most closing agents never actually go to the property, so looking at the survey in a closing office 10 miles away is little help for those kinds of problems.

5. *Get every lease, contract, mortgage, and other document that has anything to do with the property from the seller.*   Be sure that the seller signs a statement that the documents given to you constitute all relevant documentation. Then double-check the property records to make sure there are no other documents recorded that would prove otherwise. Leases, mortgages, judgments, tax liens, and so on may exist, even without the seller knowing about them.

6. *Make sure that there is a detailed inventory of all items you are to acquire.*   Often this inventory list is a part of the buyer's approval process, as sellers rarely have such a list ready the moment they sign a contract. When the list is made, make sure that a phrase is included along the lines of the following: "In addition to the items mentioned above, all landscaping material, underground and aboveground sprinkling equipment, and other items that are affixed to the buildings or other structures, or embedded in the ground shall be a part of those items being acquired by the buyer." When many different valuable items are to be included, sometimes it is important to take photographs of those items; rather than listing the ones that are included, specify which items *are not* included.

7. *Be specific about times for inspections and rights to withdraw.*   This works for both parties and can help solve problems that occur simply because people drag out the inspection process.

8. *Be there when the inspections are made.*   Actually, this is good advice for both the buyer and the seller. This is important, because the inspectors will be far more careful to do a thorough inspection under the watchful eyes of at least one of the parties to the contract. The more important reason, however, is to be able to question every problem that the inspector finds. Get the inspector to probe a little deeper into the problem to see whether it can be fixed easily or whether more comprehensive and expensive repairs are needed.

9. *Give yourself ample time to accomplish the preclosing things you need to do.* Remember, you do not want to limit your cost until you are absolutely sure you approve of all the items that are being inspected. If it takes three weeks to get financing approved and three weeks to do and review the inspections, then having a six-week period until closing might be too tight of a schedule.

20

Planning Your Real Estate Insurance Needs

203. Do I Need to Insure My Real Estate?

One of the costs to owning real estate is the insurance you should carry. You generally have several options when dealing with insurance. The first to ask: Is insurance a must? The answer to this question is determined by your own circumstances, and here's a related question: What do you stand to lose if you do not carry insurance?

Insurance covers you against a casualty or liability loss. There are many different points of view in the discussion about insurance, but five key factors demand that you insure your real estate.

> **Solution:** We live in an age when doctors have stopped taking out malpractice insurance. Instead they have a poster in the lobby of their office that says: "Doctor no longer carries liability insurance." What it does not say is, "Don't bother to sue, because all the doctor's assets are buried in a family trust in Zaire. Okay, but what about your real estate? There are too many scary things out there in this big world that can damage it, burn it down, wash it over a cliff, or . . . well, lots of things. Not only should you insure your real estate, but once a year, review the coverage you have and consider improving it.

Five Key Factors Demand That You Insure Your Real Estate

- Lenders insist on it.
- People are quick to sue.
- Defense can be very expensive.
- Repairs may not be allowed.
- The more assets you have, the more you risk.

Lenders Insist on It. It is logical that a mortgagee of a large first mortgage is going to insist that you carry ample insurance to protect the asset that secures the mortgage. Some lenders build this insurance into the mortgage payments and float the insurance through their own in-house insurance company. If this is the situation with any mortgage you currently are obligated to, find out whether you can buy your own insurance. If you can, then shop around for a better price. You can often lump all your coverage with one company and get a break on the annual premium.

People Are Quick to Sue. If no one ever sued, would there be need for insurance? Yes, there would. After all, there will still be storms and other casualty damage. But just the thought of having some hotshot just-out-of-law-school advocate ready to take you for every dime you own can give you some sleepless nights. Sue? Sure they do. Worse than that, they win, and they can win big. Juries have been known to return awards that can make the value of the property you own seem insignificant.

Defense Can Be Very Expensive. Even if you are 100 percent in the right, the very act of having to defend yourself can be the single most expensive lesson of a lifetime, wiping out your hard-earned savings. Lawyers know this. If they are defending you, they will recommend an early settlement; if they are opposing you, they strike for the jugular. Even when you have insurance, your insurance company will seek to settle whenever it is more practical than winning an expensive battle.

Repairs May Not Be Allowed. Some property owners take the posture that they will self-insure. This often is a rationalization of not wanting to pay high insurance costs, but they overlook a growing problem with casualty damage. Will the local building codes allow the property to be repaired at all? Most cities have a ratio of damage to value that can cause the property to be reevaluated to see whether it will meet the codes as though it were a brand-new building. Many older properties no longer meet the current codes, and if the property sustains damage sufficient to require full compliance to the current building regulations, major remodeling, or even complete demolition and 100 percent new construction, may be required. Self-insurance under these situations can prove to be the wrong choice.

The More Assets You Have, the More You Risk. This is a fact that saddens the richest of people. The people who have the most also have the most to lose. Worst of all is that when there is a liability claim, the amount of the claim demanded may be determined by how deep your pockets are. If you have nothing (including no insurance), then your risk is greatly limited.

Many wealthy investors seek ways to limit their own exposure to any claim. For this reason, some lawyers and accountants specialize in finding ways to shelter wealth, not only from taxes but from liability claims from others.

Corporations, limited partnerships, trusts, and so on each have some advantages to some people. If you have what you consider to be a valuable portfolio now and anticipate that it will be growing, it would be a good idea for you to spend an hour with a professional dedicated to reducing exposure to such risks. Insurance is an alternative approach.

204. What Is Casualty Insurance, and How Much Should I Buy?

There are two basic categories of property insurance: *casualty* and *liability*. Casualty insurance will insure you against a loss due to a variety of different calamities, both natural and artificial. In each situation the insurance is tailored to repay you for some or all of a loss you may have as a result of a specific event.

> **Solution:** Casualty insurance covers potential damage or loss due to a multitude of events. Unlike liability insurance, which is not tied to the value of the property and doesn't limit a judgment against you, casualty insurance is directly connected to the value of the actual loss. In essence, what will it cost to replace this building? If there is a mortgage on the property, you will have to insure in accordance with the lender's demands. In short, seek to get as much insurance as you can afford.

Every insurance policy is written so that not every item is covered, and not every cause of loss is a covered cause. If this sounds redundant it is not. This means that it is possible for a policy to appear to cover everything but does not, and there will be some events (an act of war, a flood, or some other situation the insurance company excludes) that occur for which you have zero coverage, no matter what your loss.

When it comes to casualty coverage, you should weigh the risks against the costs. To cover 100 percent of the replacement cost for every possible insurable loss can be very expensive. Because of this, insurers offer coverage that can be much like that on a car. There are deductibles, which you can increase to nearly any level you want. The greater the deductible, the lower the cost for your annual insurance policy.

Another provision that is often added to such insurance is a loss-of-business provision. I can tell you from personal experience that this can be a very worthwhile provision to include. I know several hotel owners who made more money the year their hotels were destroyed by hurricanes than they ever made during normal operations.

Three Factors to Consider for Casualty Insurance

1. *How much insurance should you get?*   Take a five-unit apartment building, for example. Assume that the current market value is $370,000, divided as follows: land = $65,000; building = $235,000; fixtures and appliances = $70,000.

In a total loss of the building and contents of the building, you would lose $305,000 in value. But is it likely that you would have a 100 percent loss? You can insure for that possibility, but you might save a lot of money by taking a small risk that your actual loss would never be that great. Because of this, most people insure their real estate against casualty loss below the full replacement value. However, the insurance company may set a level below which you cannot insure. These are your deductibles. To make this decision you need to review your needs with your insurance agent. The agent will have data that will show the probable risks.

2. *Your insurance agents can help you decide.*   Once your insurance agents know your situation, they have guides to help you establish the percent of value you need to insure, and they can suggest some of the extra kinds of insurance that may be important because of the high risk for your part of the country or location in town.

3. *Some insurance may be available only in a pool.*   If your property is in a high-risk area for certain coverage, such as a flood or earthquake area, your only chance for coverage may be through an expensive insurance pool set up by the state insurance commission. While expensive, at least you can get the insurance if you feel you need it.

205.   What Are Some of the Special Types of Insurance Available for Real Estate?

If it can happen, then you can probably insure against it. This is the rationale that allows boxers to insure their fists, movie stars their smiles (and other body parts), and ships at sea their cargo. Insurance is all a matter of risk and cost.

> **Solution:** Review your insurance needs with an insurer qualified for the kind of property you want to insure. Agents for such an insurer will know what unique risks that you need to anticipate. Not all insurance agents are capable of this kind of experience. Your lender may help direct you to the right one.

When there are no massive insurance claims, the insurance companies ride a crest of easy profits . . . but nature has a way of turning around very suddenly, as history proves again and again. Heavy claims that require enormous amounts of cash payments get lots of press, and increased media attention draws attention to the need for insurance. This has advantages and disadvantages for insurance companies. On one hand, they hate to pay out such great sums of money, but on the other they can now raise their insurance rates. The heavy coverage of catastrophes in television and other media actually encourages and promotes more people buying more insurance. Fear is one of the strongest of all motivators.

What are some of the kinds of insurance you can get for your real estate? Take a look at the following partial list of items that may be necessary or available in your area.

Things You May Need to Insure Against

"All perils"	Lava flow
Airborne ash	Lightning
Aircraft	Loss of business
Avalanche	Mud slide
Dishonesty	Negligent work
Drought	Riot or civil commotion
Earthquake	Seeping water
Electrical surges	Sinkhole
Explosion	Theft
Fire and smoke	Tornado
Flood	Vandals
Freezes	Volcanic eruption
Hail	Windstorm

Remember, this is only a partial list.

Warning: It is not unusual for an insurance policy to *exclude* some of the preceding events. To get coverage for excluded events, you may have to purchase special insurance. Specific limitations to coverage may also exist for different events in that you think you are covered 100 percent, but you are not. It is a good idea to read a sample policy of what your coverage will be before you buy it. By shopping around for insurance companies, you may find better coverage, with fewer restrictions and exclusions, for less money.

206. Why Do I Need Liability Insurance for Real Estate, and How Much Should I Buy?

You may be liable for any bodily injury or property damage that occurs on your property or as a result of your actions. If you own anything, or expect to, some amount of liability insurance may be needed. If you own real estate, then liability insurance is essential.

> **Solution:** The deeper your pockets the greater the amount
> of insurance you need to carry. It does not matter whether
> you are insuring a 150-story high-rise office building or a
> carryout pizza place. Look at what you have that someone
> can take. Also seek ways to legally insulate yourself from
> being sued. Read on.

Liability coverage may be included with a general "all perils" insurance policy, or
it may be a separate form of insurance. Generally, there is a maximum coverage
you can get, which varies with different insurance companies, but by obtaining an
umbrella policy (expanded coverage), you can increase the amount virtually as far
as you want to and are willing to pay for.

The most important aspect of liability insurance is that the insurance company
will pay for the defense of a claim. This can be misleading, however, because the
company is really defending itself and not necessarily you. Most insurance policies allow the insurance company to settle a claim and pay off the claimant even
though you are in the right. Also, once the limit of your coverage has been reached,
the insurance company will no longer represent you. Because of this, you should
obtain your own lawyer in addition to any help the insurance company provides
whenever a claim is to be decided in a court of law.

There are many ways to insulate yourself from legal actions, which might
involve setting up trusts, putting assets in limited liability corporations, and other
such steps. If your pockets are deep then, it will be worth your time to sit down
with a good corporate tax lawyer to examine such steps.

207.   What Is Title Insurance, What Does It Protect, and When Can It Be Dangerous?

Title insurance is supposed to insure that the title you have taken in a real estate
transaction is good. This insurance is much like a liability insurance in that it will
pay your cost to clear some title problem that may surface after you close on the
property. In general, it is a very profitable insurance for insurance companies
because they are insuring you for things that they should have uncovered before
they issued the insurance. Does that make sense? It's like covering a hotel against
hurricanes that hit last year. However, sometimes things do pop up unexpectedly
that even the best investigative insurance company missed . . . things that can take
away property that you thought was yours.

> **Solution:** Fortunately, title insurance is not very expensive,
> and most lenders will insist on it anyway. It will protect your
> newly purchased real estate against everything except what
> the insurance excludes. These exclusions are dangerous,
> because the insurance company will try very hard to connect
> the cause of big claims to one or more of the exclusions. You
> do not have to accept the exclusions, so do not buy insurance

from a company that fills the pages with exclusions that seem innocent and or unlikely. Get a price quote from another insurance company.

One such provision common to a title insurance policy is a phrase that reads something like the following:

> . . . and any other claim, cloud on the title, or title defect, as a result of any action prior to the issuance of this insurance policy shall be excluded and not covered if the basis for the claim, cloud on the title, or title defect would have been disclosed by a recent boundary survey and building location survey at the time this insurance policy was issued.

This paragraph sounds okay, right? Wrong. There is one major "gotcha" word there. It is the word *recent*. Many people do not get a recent survey at the time they close on a property. However, if you put a provision in the offer to purchase that the seller is to provide this survey and that all property boundaries and building corners are to be marked on the survey, with iron pipes in concrete at property corners, you will have a document that can be updated cheaply in the future when you plan to sell.

How to Get a Discount on Title Insurance

There are two basic and simple methods that will generally ensure a discount on your title insurance.

The first and most common way to get a discount on your title insurance is to ask the sellers whether they had title insurance when they purchased the property. Don't wait until the day of the closing to ask this question; in fact, you can list the "former title insurance policy" in the contract along with any other due diligence items (such as survey, environmental studies, code violations, etc.). If there was an earlier title insurance policy, then the present insurance company generally gives a discount off the new policy.

The second way sounds silly, but it works nonetheless. If you are not able to use the first method, then shop around for title insurance. Most lawyers, even the one you use, belong to a group of insurance companies that offer such insurance. Because most of the premium goes to the commission (or fee) of the person or company you are dealing with, many lawyers and title insurance companies will do the closing free if you buy the insurance through them. Let me put it this way: They will charge you for their work at the closing but give you a discount on the insurance. The key to getting a discount in this way is to ask for it.

208. If I Rent, What Insurance Do I Need to Carry?

This may depend on the type of property you are renting. This can be important, because you may overpay for insurance that is a duplication of existing insurance.

Solution: Review the following five steps to get the most out of your renter's insurance.

Five Steps to Buying the Best Renter's Insurance Possible for Maximum Coverage

1. *Get a copy of the existing property insurance policy.*   There may be more than one policy that covers the property. For example, if the building is a condominium or cooperative, there will be an association policy that covers certain elements of the building and sometimes some of the contents. This is often a function of state law. The owner of the specific space (condo or co-op) may also have interior insurance that would cover items not covered by the association policy.

2. *Have a qualified insurance agent explain the state law.*   State law often requires insurance companies to insure certain items or parts of the property even though the policy may not specifically indicate it. There may be very fine lines that occur when laws change in the middle of a policy term, so each situation and each policy must be reviewed. You cannot assume that a situation last month with another unit in the same complex also applies to the property you are anticipating renting.

3. *Find out which factors qualify for discounts.*   Extra security features, storm-proof and break-in-proof glass windows, extra locks, fire safety equipment, and the like may qualify your building for some major discounts on insurance. Be sure to ask the insurance agent.

4. *Make a list.*   List everything important you plan to have in the apartment or space. This is important regardless of what kind of rental you have. Whether this is a business or residence, be sure you have an up-to-date list of items that you add or replace during your term as a tenant.

5. *Shop around with several different insurance companies for the best deal.*   If you have insurance on other property (cars and/or other real estate), one of the best places to go for a quote will be your current insurer. This is not difficult to do and can save you money. It is not unusual for a different insurance company to quote you a lower premium. First-year premiums are often the lowest you will ever see, so make a change from time to time whenever you can save money. *Warning:* If you ask for a quote from another company, make sure you get quotes on the same amount of coverage you now have. Overzealous insurance agents may want your business so much that they leave out a few risks that ought to be included in your coverage ("After all, your building is not going to be hit by a flood").

209.   Should I Keep All My Insurance with the Same Insurer?

Yes, unless you can save sufficient money by dividing your coverage between companies to make it worthwhile.

One hazard that can easily occur if you have more than one insurance company is that you are apt to have some overlapping insurance, or worse, you may have some gaps that expose you to some risk you could have covered at a small added cost or no cost at all by staying with one company.

210. How Do I Determine My Insurance Needs before I Buy the Policy?

If you have never purchased insurance for your real estate (or anything else), it is a good idea to get a copy of an insurance policy and read it. It will be boring, but it will acquaint you with the terms and provisions contained in those policies. That will help you when you move to the next step.

> **Solution:** Before you sit down with insurance agents, it is a good idea to be ready to answer their questions and to have an idea of the valuables you may want to insure. The following steps will help you prepare for that task.

Eight Steps to Adequate Insurance Coverage

1. *Make a detailed list of items to be covered.* A simple chart that groups items together is okay, such as furniture, clothing, and so on. Do not overlook any contents of your residence or office. Homeowner's policies generally cover your personal property even if it is not at your home at the time of a loss.

2. *Determine whether you have elements that will qualify you for discounts.* Many different factors can contribute to a substantial savings in the cost of insurance, so find out what those items are. If you don't already meet the qualifications for such discounts, learn how much it would cost to meet those qualifications. You might be surprised that to upgrade certain safety features might save you more money than it costs. Especially if you spread that cost over two or three years.

3. *Assess the replacement value of each item.* In many cases you will not be able to prove the actual cost of an item, so put down your estimate of replacement cost.

4. *Determine whether you would replace the item.* This is for your own eyes only. This will help you determine whether the coverage is necessary. If the item is automatically covered, then in the event of a loss you can keep the cash settlement and not replace the item at all.

5. *Take detailed still photos and videos and show scale.* This is important, both to give the agent an idea of what you want to insure and to prove you actually had the items in the event of a loss. When taking photographs (still or video) have some reference point that will indicate the size of the items. A ruler is the best way to establish the approximate size, and it should be placed alongside the item being photographed.

6. *Review different coverages available to you.* The cost of insurance can vary much more than you might realize. The coverage within the same company can vary greatly depending on the actual location, elevation, type of construction, age of the construction, intended use, proximity of firefighting services (including hydrants), and so on. The deductible you accept can mean great savings to you if

interest is to cover the major loss and self-insure minor losses.

7. *Be sure you ask what is not covered, and what limitations there are to what is covered.* When you are making comparisons of two or more policies, be sure that you know how they differ. It is unlikely that two standard policies (from two different companies) will be identical in coverage, exclusions, and limitations.

8. *Find out what additional coverage you can add.*   This is something for the future and can make a difference if you plan on adding additional property or want to build onto the existing structure. Know what you are buying and where you can go with it.

211.   What Steps Can I Take after a Fire or Other Casualty Loss to Get the Maximum Insurance Benefits?

We had a fire in one of our office buildings some years ago. It was one of those insipid fires that really is more thick, greasy smoke than anything. Smoke, smell, soot, heat, but little fire. Apparently, a computer meltdown started the fire, but the major damage began the moment the fire department broke through the plate glass windows at the ground floor of the building and entered with high-pressure hoses of water that blasted everything into a soggy mess of terrible-smelling goop. However, they did save the building and everyone inside.

> **Solution:**   A fire in a building is terrible enough, but when it is where your business is conducted and where all your files and other data are stored, it can become a nightmare. One of the worst parts of this very bad dream is what you have to go through with the insurance company. Learn from the lessons of others and be quick to follow the suggestions here about what to do. Do it even before the embers have cooled.

Your 14-Step Fire Emergency Checklist

1. *Have the following items in a safe place you can get to even if the building burns down.*   Make a list of everyone who might be in the building; copy your insurance documents; take an inventory of important and/or valuable items in the building. Also look at question 227, which deals with any catastrophic event. Turn this list into your Emergency Fire Checklist. Post it everywhere you might need it when this emergency calls at your door.

2. *The first item on your Emergency Fire Checklist should be all the phone numbers that you will need.*   These numbers include police, fire department, insurance company, and a lawyer who specializes in dealing with insurance companies. It is a good idea to duplicate emergency numbers for any tenants or employees who are in the building at the time of the fire. First things first.

3. *Call your insurance agent as soon as possible.*   This is important, but actually kes second priority to step 4. If the casualty has been a major one that aft...

other people as well as you, anticipate that it may take some time before you can get your insurance agent on the phone. The disaster of Hurricane Andrew in 1992 taught the insurance companies many lessons about such problems, and Hurricane Katrina reinforced those forgotten lessons. You may have seen the plight of people whose homes were destroyed. Many such homeowners were so frustrated in their attempts to reach an insurance adjuster that they painted the company name and policy number on the side of their homes in hopes that someone would see it. Do not do that, as some very dishonest people wrote down those numbers and collected "cash on the spot," money from claims adjusters who were trying to help their policyholders over the worst of the storm's aftermath.

4. *Do not enter the building after the fire until the fire department says it is okay.*   I do not care what secrets lie buried under those fallen timbers and burning wallpaper. Do not go in there. It is a nasty place to be.

5. *Get the insurance people out to the site as soon as possible.*   You do not want to start moving things around until they see how terrible it really is. Do take photos as soon as you can, lots of them. The best way is to do a very slow video pan around every room. Have lights turned on. If there are none, then rent some. This is very important, so do it immediately.

6. *Salvage whatever you can.*   You should make every effort to save whatever you can, but do not do so at further risk to yourself or your property.

7. *The first chance you get, reread your insurance policy.*   This may give you some additional steps to follow that are peculiar to your particular policy.

8. *Have your agent explain all the "recoverable" damage or loss you may have before the adjuster's appointment.*   When you eventually get your agent on the phone, an appointment will be set up for the adjuster to inspect the damage. It is a good idea to know ahead of time exactly what your policy covers.

9. *Get a second opinion of the amount of the loss.*   The adjuster may give you his or her estimate, but remember, it is only an estimate and not something that is etched in stone. No matter what you think the repairs or loss should cost to fix or replace, get another estimate from a professional who will actually do the work or replace the items. The adjuster will probably increase the amount of the award on the claim if you can support the additional amount.

10. *Get advice from your lawyer before signing a release.*   It may be unusual to have a continued dispute over the amount of the loss, but if you are at all uncomfortable that the insurance company is pushing too hard for you to sign a release for an amount less than what you feel is right, then see your lawyer. Be sure to ask your lawyer about outside adjusters in case you need one to rebut the insurance company's figures.

11. *Consider using an outside adjuster to review the insurance company adjuster's estimate.*   In the case of a major loss, it is a good idea to hire an outside adjuster or a company that specializes in acting as your intermediary with the insurance company. These people know how insurance companies work and how to get the most of what your policy allows. These people also know the state insurance laws

extremely well. This is important, because the state law may require the insurance company to provide you coverage that is not specifically outlined in your policy.

12. *Take more photographs during the follow-up repairs.*   This gives you a record of what is going on. Date the photographs by having them processed quickly; usually the processors will date them, or ask them to and pay the extra charge.

13. *Do not sign a release until all loss and cost has been covered.*   You need to wait until everything that could show up does. Some damage is latent and may not actually appear until several weeks later. Mildew is a good example of such delayed damage. Water-soaked walls can look like they have been fixed. After all, the hole in the roof has been patched and the walls repainted. Oh, but what is that smell? Mildew!

14. *Review your insurance coverage for future needs.*   Now that you have experienced a loss and the problems that can come with it, take immediate steps to shop around for new coverage. If you can find the same coverage from another insurance company (the same agent may represent several companies, or shop around and see other agents), then you may want to switch. Why? One very good reason is because now that you have had a claim with your existing company, you may be on the "raise their rate" list at the first opportunity. Worse, you might be on the company's "cancel" list, and you will want to jump the gun and leave that company before it brands you as one who must answer yes to the question: "Have your ever been denied insurance for any reason?"

21

Avoiding the Major Pitfalls in Real Estate Investing

212. Can Being Overly Demanding or Too Soft Kill a Deal?

One of the most difficult problems to overcome in contract negotiations is how to walk the fine line between being overly demanding and too conciliatory. Either of these postures may kill the deal because they can send wrong signals to the other side.

> **Solution:** There is a narrow path, at times, that buyer and seller must traverse to get to the closing table. Sometimes if one side is too tough, the other side turns and walks away from the negotiation table. If someone is too soft, the other side may take that as a sign of weakness or as being overly anxious to make a deal and attempt to take advantage of that situation. Read on to discover how to play this game with a win-win strategy.

Nine Tips for a Win-Win Strategy

1. *What happens when you are overly demanding?* When buyers push for every inch they can get, the final straw will eventually be reached. When that happens the other side may throw in the towel and walk away from the bargaining table. Granted, all buyers want to get as much as they can for as little as possible, but when there is too much pushing for everything, sellers may eventually get the idea that the buyers are just playing around and not serious. Or, worst of all, the sellers will act in such a way to lock out the buyers for future dealing, even to the extent of dealing with someone else at a lower price, just to keep the first buyer from getting the property.

To play hardball effectively in any contract negotiation, the buyer runs the risk of killing the deal. This tactic is not an incorrect method of negotiation if the buyer does not care whether the deal blows up. "I'll buy it on my terms or not at all" does occasionally produce a deal, but rarely if there are other qualified buyers in the bidding for the property.

In any circumstance, it is counterproductive for buyers to give the impression that hardball tactics originate directly from themselves. On the other hand, buyers can still push . . . as long as there is an impression or feeling of genuine cooperation evident in the negotiations.

Top negotiators know from experience that reaching a satisfactory conclusion in any negotiation depends on the parties satisfying most of their goals, but not necessarily all of their goals. The key to this statement is that it is not necessary that they satisfy *all* their goals.

2. *Get the tough decisions settled early.* A major error that many buyers make is to leave the really tough decisions to the end. This occurs when the buyer continues to push for more concessions, making it harder for the seller to see a reasonable solution to his or her own goals. The deal ultimately explodes in everyone's face when the buyer asks for one item too many, and often that "one more thing" requests a major concession on the part of the seller. Transactions should be closed on small items, not on big ones. A good salesperson knows not to ask the following question: "The buyer rejects your counteroffer of $500,000 and wants you to drop the price another $50,000. Will you do it?" The better approach is: "The buyer accepted every condition of your counteroffer with a modification of the price to $450,000, and she says she will close next week if that is okay. Do you agree to close by the end of next week?" Both buyers and sellers must concentrate on the positive actions of the other party. Many deals are lost because one or both parties reacts to a negative element in an offer or a counteroffer that is not all that significant. Remember, if you gain 95 percent of your desired goal or benefit from the deal, that might be the best you will achieve.

3. *What about being too soft in the deal?* Either side can become too agreeable. If the mood is too conciliatory too soon, it can undermine the credibility of the party. A buyer who is too eager to please may give the impression that he or she is not sincere or is just shopping around. On the other hand, a seller who is too eager to please may invite an offer that is too low to ever move to realistic values.

4. *Pick the middle of the road as the best approach.* As a buyer, the best approach is to be candid with the seller, or at least as candid as you can without giving away unique ideas about the property. Clearly, you would not let the seller know that you wanted to convert the old home into stately offices for an insurance company, or some other great idea that would tip your hand and the price you might have to pay.

5. *Compliment the property owners for what they have, and let them know you would like to own it.* This approach is based on the understanding that most sellers want

to sell their property to someone who appreciates what they have to sell. Buyers whose attitude is, "This is crap, but for a price I'll take it off your hands," may end up with a deal here and there (usually because it really was crap).

6. *Flattery works in any seduction.*   Take a look at the buyer who approaches every deal with a positive approach designed to make the seller feel good: "I think your property is absolutely ideal for my needs. You should be commended on the wonderful landscaping [or some other clearly seller-caused value point]; that was one of the features that sold me on this property over all the others I've been looking at this week." Do you notice some very subtle and very positive elements in that statement? The "absolutely ideal for my needs" lets the seller know that the buyer is unique.

Not every buyer's needs may be suited by that property. There is the clear buying signal "sold me," with the caveat "over all the others I've been looking at," which indicates there are other properties out there. The clincher is "this week," which lets the seller know that there have been and will be other weeks and other properties. Despite these messages, the buyer and seller relationship can progress in a positive manner to the final stages of agreement. "Mr. Seller, I love your property and my wife loves your property and I know this home is just the right place for our five children to grow up, and you have sold me right down to the core. Gosh, if you and I can just work out a way for me to buy this wonderful property, why, my wife June and I will name our next child after you." That is overkill, but the right idea.

7. *Learn that the other side of the table is not the enemy and deal accordingly.*   The real key to continued success in buying and selling real estate is to keep reminding yourself that the other side of the table is not your enemy. They are, after all, the very vehicle that will help you reach your goal. You want to buy or sell, and they want to be on the other end of that action. If you are selling a property that they want, the major battle has been won. While you can still lose the war, your task is not to sell anymore, but to close the transaction.

8. *A buyer in hand is worth . . . something at least.*   As a buyer, your task is to convince the seller that you are worth holding onto and that your immediate value of being in a position to close is worth some ultimate concession. However, you should not let that ego trip stand in the way of losing a property you would truly like to own.

9. *Use an intermediary to absorb the heat of the deal.*   Both buyers and sellers can benefit by using someone who can maintain contact with the other side of the transaction without giving the wrong buying or selling signal. Brokers and other negotiating partners in the transaction can be worth their weight in gold in closing transactions. An intermediary, such as one of the brokers in the deal, should understand the benefit to both parties of a third-party buffer. Let the sales agents be the anxious people. Neither buyer nor seller should risk giving the other party a chance to feel insulted or turned off in any way. Brokers are paid when deals close, so implore your broker to do his or her best to close the deal.

213.   What Should I Do if Someone Claims to Own My Property?

Squatter's rights occur when someone has acquired title by adverse possession (also called *title by prescription*). In the broadest use of this right, a person who has no original legal claim to a property can enter it, even though illegal, and take possession of the land. If this possession meets certain criteria prescribed in state law, then the actual title to that land or property can ultimately be vested to the interloper.

> **Solution:**   Review the following conditions that can lead to the loss of your property to someone else by way of adverse possession. The key factor in this situation is that the effort on the part of interlopers must be openly adverse. This means they know they do not own the property, enter it, and start living on it openly so that anyone who came to the property would likely see them or evidence of them. They must also pay the real estate tax on the property. These circumstances do occur, and people do lose their property rights to squatters. You can stop this from happening simply by making sure that (1) no one is living on your property without your permission, and (2) no one is paying your real estate tax. If you discover someone on your property, take immediate steps to have that person removed. In the case of large tracts, especially with wooded areas, fence the property and post it against trespassers.

The law of squatter's rights exists for the benefit of a community, or at least that was originally so. When a property is owned by someone who never uses it or hardly knows it exists, the community may benefit by having someone there on the property who will use it. This encourages the use of the land. There are certain conditions that most states require to be met for title to be acquired by adverse possession.

Five Conditions That May Lead to Adverse Possession

1. *There must be actual possession that is open and visible.*   Possession should occur in such a way that the owner would reasonably be able to see the possession. A fence, a sign "Jack's Place," rows of cultivation, buildings, or other structures are all evidence of such occupation, especially if your name isn't Jack.

2. *Possession should be hostile to the owner's rights.*   This would be usual in just about every such case except where there was some relationship between the parties to indicate that an adverse event was not taking place.

3. *The claim to title should be notorious.*   This means that the claim should be made public. One simple way to do this is to run an ad in the legal section of the

local newspaper. It might say, "I hereby make an adverse possession claim to all land located between the Atlantic Ocean and Interstate I-95 north of Indiro Road and South of Hastings Blvd. in the County of Saint Johns, State of Florida." What are the odds you would see such an ad for a property you own?

4. *A continuous claim of possession should be evidenced.*   This does not mean 100 percent of the time, nor does it mean that the squatter must live on the property 100 percent of the time. If the property is a seasonal property or if some other part-time use would be reasonable for any owner, then such part-time use, when maintained for a period of time as is defined by the laws of the state where the property is located, will qualify this aspect of the claim.

5. *Possession must be exclusive.*   This means the claimant must preclude the use to anyone else, even the rightful owner.

214.   What Are the Most Common Pitfalls to Avoid When Investing in Vacant Land?

Vacant land can be one of the best sources for ultimate wealth. Many of the richest people in the world owe their wealth to the vacant land they once owned. Often, that land is now the site of shopping centers and other commercial or residential projects. This fact does not automatically mean that the guaranteed path to wealth is through vacant land. There are many pitfalls to be aware of when contemplating the acquisition of vacant land.

> **Solution:**   Review the following common pitfalls that can occur when you invest in vacant land.

The 12 Most Common Pitfalls When Investing in Vacant Land

- Zoning ordinances do not permit your intended use.
- Local politics is antidevelopment and in favor of no growth.
- Everything you have counted on turns out to be a lie.
- A negative future is already planned.
- Moratoriums prevent advancement.
- There's a negative community attitude toward development.
- There are hidden problems underground.
- Deed restrictions stop you cold.
- Heavy fees are onerous.
- No municipal services are planned.
- There is no interim use for the land.
- The local authorities file eminent domain proceedings against you.

These pitfalls are all avoidable, or else their impact can be substantially reduced. I will briefly discuss the solutions to each pitfall.

Zoning Ordinances Do Not Permit Your Intended Use.   This is an example of what happens when you do not do effective due diligence. You might even have looked up the zoning in the *Zoning Manual* that the seller or broker handed you. It showed that you could indeed build that hotel you wanted to construct. Only, guess what, the zoning manual you were looking at was out of date, or it applied to the adjoining city. Never take anyone's word for what you can do until you hear it from the head of the zoning department. Then, once he or she says it is okay to build a hotel there, ask this question: "Great, but is there any zoning in progress or other rezoning or new land plan or anything that is being discussed that could, within a reasonable time, change that zoning before I could submit my plans for a hotel?" You might find that, indeed, there are exactly such events going on. Why did you think you got such a good buy?

Local Politics Is Antidevelopment and in Favor of No Growth.   The saying goes like this: "I got here before you did so I don't want you or anyone from the country of Canada coming down here and telling me it's okay to build another 5,000 condos in my backyard." The thing about a democracy is that those living in a place get to vote on local issues. They generally become very protective of their privacy and the right to build the way they want to, and they do not like young families coming in, because that means children, and children mean schools, and that drives real estate taxes through the roof. Never invest in land with the hope of its value going up because it is in the path of progress unless you know that the so-called progress you are counting on will be welcomed.

Everything You Have Counted on Turns out to Be a Lie.   This likely should be the last item on the list, but let's put it here. Some people tell lies not because they are malicious but because they do not know the truth. Sellers do this; politicians do this; and salespeople do this. You can avoid this situation by thinking that whatever you have heard may not be true, so double-check everything. It is safer that way.

A Negative Future Is Already Planned.   Most events that can affect the value of real estate are public knowledge long before they actually take place. A new highway, for example, does not happen overnight; it has been in planning stages for months, even years. This event can increase some property values and decrease others. Road widening can take away needed frontage, limited access can make it hard to get to a site, and new noise levels can turn a beautifully quiet residential zone into a nightmare of "For Sale" signs.

Even though most of these future events are known well in advance, knowing they are in the works is not always as simple as opening the morning paper and reading about them. This is where the buyer's efforts to become an insider pays off. No property should be purchased until the buyer has found out what, if anything, is planned that is likely to have any impact on the area.

Moratoriums Prevent Advancement.   Any kind of community moratorium can have the effect of stopping development. This can cause buyer interest to dry up overnight. Moratoriums can be put into effect rather suddenly and, it appears, unexpectedly, but this is not the case. They are a community's reaction to a festering problem. Too much demand on utilities and too little capacity to serve that demand can force the water department to put a moratorium on new hookups. The same can be said for sewers, fire protection, and so on. Every public service department has some influence on a governing body to stop new proceedings while the matter can be studied. Often the study takes years to complete and the end result of that study is that the authorities agree that another study is needed.

How do you deal with this kind of a problem? One way is to look at the basic services and question each government department to see whether a problem now or in the near future could cause a moratorium that would affect an area of interest. The following items are the basic services or departments that should be on the due diligence list. Often there are several levels of service that need to reviewed: city, county, state, and federal.

Roads

Traffic

Bridges

Rail crossings

Water and sewer services

Fire and police protection

Garbage and trash

Schools and education

Health services

Parks and recreation

There's a Negative Community Attitude toward Development.   Some communities develop an attitude that is antidevelopment. These communities may be "old money" areas that have grown stately and do not want any change to occur, or they can be relatively new areas that still have a lot of growth potential through vacant land in the area, but the residents living in the community do not want any one else to enjoy what they currently have. Either of these groups can present many headaches to the investor looking to make a fortune, or even just a living, by investing in vacant land.

Fortunately, the mood of a community is easy to test. Attend one building and zoning meeting and one city council meeting and you will get the picture. If there is still doubt, then talk to some of the architects in the area—they will know which cities in their work area are easy to deal with and which are tough as nails. Avoid tough-as-nails communities if you have a choice.

There Are Hidden Problems Underground. That beautiful pasture or straw-berry patch may look very picturesque and may in fact be right in the path of everything good and wonderful. But what might lurk under those ripe berries? What could those cows be hiding?

A host of problems can lie underground, and you need to know about them before becoming the owner. Farmers have been known to store drums of fuel oil and gasoline for their tractors in the fields, and those drums could have been leaking for years. Other pollutants and waste can be there, giving those strawberries a bright red glow (in the dark!) and a large hole in your pocket when, as the new owner, you must have tons of soil dug up and sent 1,000 miles away to be dealt with properly.

The solution is to have the land tested and inspected by qualified experts. If there is reason to believe there might be a problem, or if the present use suggests that a problem is likely, make sure that the seller pays for the test.

Deed Restrictions Stop You Cold. Any seller can lace a deed with restric-tions. That can establish a higher level of restrictions than those of the local ordi-nances. It is possible that a deed that is several transfers back includes the restrictions that everyone forgot about; after all, the land is just a vacant lot. Why is it a vacant lot? It could be that someone put in a restriction that effectively pro-hibited a use that would be warranted for the area. A detailed review of the chain of deeds will reveal what deed restrictions, if any, may still be in effect.

Some states have enacted laws that limit the time a deed restriction will still be in effect, even if the deed restriction uses terms such as *forever* or *99 years*. Courts have also taken a more practical approach when dealing with illogical deed restrictions that no longer serve the area as intended or that are outdated for the current needs. However, many deed restrictions or restrictive covenants may be in place that are legally enforceable and highly restrictive to the use of the property.

Impact Fees Are Onerous. Many communities have a novel approach to pay-ing for their lack of services or expanding services: make developers pay for them. They do this with impact fees that can be very expensive. These fees can be admin-istered at several government levels, too, making them all the more costly. The fol-lowing are just some of the possible impact fees or costs that can come with development.

- You may pay utility impact fees to hook up to water or sewer lines.
- You may be required to donate to parks and recreation areas for the added impact on those services from people who may live near or use the newly devel-oped property.
- You may pay costs or donations to relieve traffic congestion. This can be the most expensive of all. Not only can the government take part of the land (with-out payment to you), but it can require you to build new roads or bridges or contribute to a fund for such works.

- You may pay into a schools fund. You can be forced to pay a fee to a general fund or, if your project is big enough, to set aside land for public schools.

- You may be required to contribute to other funds such as fire, police, public health, water management, environmental studies, wildlife areas, and so on.

What can you do about all this? Know what you will be asked to pay before buying the land. Once you own land you must become active in local affairs to make sure that the local residents do not shift the cost for their added infrastructure onto you.

No Municipal Services Are Planned.   If you buy too far ahead of development, you might own farmland for a 100 more years. This is okay for farmers. The septic tank or outhouse works fine, the windmill pumps up plenty of nice clean water, and the 100-amp electrical service that just barely makes it from the main line a mile away runs all the electrical appliances at the farm, but not all at once. Forget the new housing project unless you plan to put in your own public services. By the way, new cities are often formed by developers doing exactly that.

There Is No Interim Use for the Land.   If the land is costly and expensive to hold onto, then an interim use for the land is essential. It is always a good idea, and when possible it can be a criteria to consider when deciding between two or more properties. Back to the great wealth of the world: many of the wealthy families of the world got their riches from land, but not always because of the original purpose to which the land was put. Farmland became oil fields; oil fields became cities, and later shopping centers and residential subdivisions.

Modern investors should seek to find some use for the land they own that will help pay the cost of taxes, insurance, and mortgage payments. "U-Pick-It" farms, landscape growing and sales yards, flea markets, boatyards, used-car lots, storage lots, and so on are all good examples of such use.

The Local Authorities File Eminent Domain Proceedings against You. Local government has always had the right to take private land for the good of the public. Okay, I can understand that widening roads, building bridges, and razing houses for a new hospital can be considered good for the public. But recently, courts have ruled that "good for the public" might also mean removing your shopping center so that developers can construct affordable housing, which they then sell for $500,000 and up per apartment. You need to watch this trend and, if it starts to get out of hand, speak out. Your rights to use your property are important . . . not necessarily to use it any way you want, but within the legal structure of the area where it is situated. Fight back.

215.   What Can Go Wrong with My Zoning, and How Can I Be Affected?

Remember the three most important words related to investment real estate? Okay, here they are again: *location, use,* and *approval.* They generally will appeal to an investor in that order, as a start. In essence, where do I want to invest? Where can I build my fast-food restaurant? That sort of question should be answered first or the investor would simply throw a dart at the map and go from there. The use that is allowed (or can be obtained through rezoning, variances, and other local politics) is a critical step in this process, but more and more communities, and especially those that are against growth and development, seem to find ways to block some developments even though the zoning ordinance permits that use. What can you do?

> **Solution:** Be extra cautious when investing in communities
> where the planning and zoning board and the city and/or
> county commissioners have demonstrated a dislike for some
> kinds of development in certain areas. Some cities will fight
> a developer tooth and nail if the proposed project will cause
> an increase in public services. Build 5,000 family homes just
> because the land is zoned that way, and school, fire, and
> police services might increase to unacceptable levels. If the
> politics are against you, but the law seems to be on your
> side, then carefully examine the time and money you might
> spend to prove you are right. Instead, look to a political
> environment in another city that welcomes you and your
> 5,000 single-family homes. Look at some of the ways cities
> fight growth through zoning changes.

Four Ways Cities Manipulate Zoning Rules to Limit Property Owners' Rights of Use

- An adverse change to a different zoning
- More restrictive use of your existing zoning
- Moratorium of use in your category of zoning
- Use of vague rules that have more than one interpretation

An Adverse Change to a Different Zoning.   This can happen whenever the local city or county decides a master plan needs to be revised or that zoning for a specific area needs to be changed for some other reason. The change of zoning can destroy years of plans by creating restrictions for intended development. For example, you have saved up to buy a beautiful site where you hope to build your new restaurant. After 15 years of paying off an expensive mortgage, the city changes the zoning to a category that prohibits any commercial activity.

More Restrictive Use of Your Existing Zoning.   The continual tightening of restrictions is the more common adjustment that is made to zoning. Take multi-family zoning as an example. The usual adjustments are to reduce the number of units that can be constructed on a site. The original zoning might allow 25 units per acre, but the city changes that category and limits units per acre to 10. Commercial zoning may also have more restrictive changes. Sometimes the changes are subtle, and at first may not appear to have the ultimate economic impact that they do. For example, zoning that previously allowed a building to be constructed no more than 70 feet in height is changed to reduce the height to no more than 50 feet. This difference of two stories of construction can mean a loss of gross building area, which may reflect a reduced income potential from the building. It is important that you be aware of this, but if the highest and best economic use would be a two-story building, then the reduction of height would have no effect. This is critical because the present owners may have had their dreams squelched if they had purchased the property with the idea of building a seven-story apartment building, and five floors just will not do.

Another method of reducing use without even changing the zoning is to pass new building codes. Setbacks can be increased, and parking lots can be redefined so that parking space is no longer adequate for the building the zoning will allow. Fire codes can also play a role in reducing what can go on the site. No matter what, the present owners may discover that the property no longer has its investment potential to suit their needs, so the land is put up for sale. Along you come, ready to buy the land because two floors are ample for your restaurant.

Moratorium of Use In Your Category of Zoning. Moratoriums that halt building are an obvious disadvantage to increased value of property. The long-term effect may be that the moratorium benefits the community, because it gives the city leaders and their employee's time to rethink, replan, or just catch up to the level at which the community service should be. However, in the short term, there is no development, and there are no buyers.

Use of Vague Rules That Have More than One Interpretation. In a recent revision of the planning and zoning codes in Fort Lauderdale, the person drafting the code (a city-paid lawyer) was working on a section that dealt with what kind of building could be constructed at any specific location. The issue was not to define the use, because the zoning was already locked into the master plan. But let's see, could the lawyer write code with such potentially vague meaning that the land planners and commissioners could interpret the words to their own satisfaction? Yes. Okay, the idea is to allow redevelopment of old areas of town. This is only logical, and anyone would agree that without such ideas slums are born. In order not to appear antidevelopment and pro-slum, the lawyer wrote something to this effect:

> . . . and it shall be the responsibility of the Planning and Zoning staff to review the plans of the intended development to ensure that the new project is compatible with the community as a whole.

Excuse me? Does that mean that in a slum area (or an area that might become one) all new buildings must look like the old 1950s stuff that really needs to disappear?

Well, the staff and the commissioners have been using this "compatible" issue to block development that otherwise would be allowed. Another property right bites the dust.

216. Can a Building Moratorium Really Reduce the Value of My Vacant Property?

A building moratorium is another antigrowth tactic and can be used to slow or even stop development for considerable time. There are times, however, when it is essential that something be done to stop a potential hazardous or dangerous situation from occurring. Examples of that kind of development might be a proposed manufacturing facility that could have dangerous and even hazardous waste products. The need to do something about the horrible traffic in and around the city might require a traffic study, and so on.

Yes, it is possible that such moratoriums can reduce the value of your property. The simple reason for this is moratoriums generally result in studies that lead to new zoning and/or building ordinances being formulated. These new ordinances are generally more restrictive and costly for developers to deal with.

Building moratoriums are usually imposed by local authorities as a step to stop development. This can be the result of several different events. The two most common are to give time to review changes in zoning and to allow public services time to catch up with demands created by overdevelopment. In any event, the moratorium can have the effect of cooling off a prospective buyer who is interested in building now, not at some yet-to-be-determined date.

Remember, there may be exceptions to every rule. If a moratorium has been put into effect that seems to have stopped development in your area, there may still be hope. Sit down with the local building officials and have them explain the exact details of the moratorium. Ask about the possible avenues you can follow to obtain building permits despite the moratorium. Will a change in zoning help? It might, as the moratorium may be directed toward a type of development. To solve problems like these, you can call on your newly found insider friends. If you do not have any yet, ask the head of the building department to recommend a good lawyer who deals with these kinds of problems.

217. What Is Grandfathered Use, and Why Is That So Dangerous?

A *grandfathered use* is a nonconforming use that does not meet the current codes or zoning regulations but is allowed because it existed before the current rules and regulations. This does not mean that every prior situation is allowed to continue when a zoning rule or other law is changed, because many are not; but when they are allowed it is critical that you understand the dangers of acquiring a property with a grandfathered use. It is essential that you do not underestimate the problems with nonconforming grandfathered use. If you do not take this seriously you may discover that the property you purchased (e.g., an 18-unit apartment building) may exist only because it was built prior to new zoning or building code changes. If the new codes allow only 10 or less units, an 18-unit building could be an unattractive investment. The grandfathered provisions can be eliminated for many different reasons, the most common being a code change that cannot be grandfathered because it dictates that a fire code or some other lifesaving measure must be brought current. Most cities have provisions that when a certain percentage of a building's value (or sometimes square footage) is damaged or remodeled, it must meet the new codes without exception.

> **Solution:** Every building you purchase may at a future date become nonconforming to changed building rules and regulations. Because of this, it is not the end of the world if property you want to purchase is presently nonconforming. The key is to know exactly what the nonconforming issue is and then to make an educated decision whether that issue should stop you from acquiring this property.

10 Examples of an Allowed Nonconforming Use That Can Backfire on You

- Buildings have less than currently allowed setbacks from property lines.
- A recent zoning change now prohibits the current type of business activity.
- Building height is taller than current building codes allow.
- Hallways are too narrow to meet new construction codes.
- No handicapped facilities exist.
- There are fewer parking spots than the current code demands.
- Green area is less than the current building-to-lot ratio allows.
- Structural requirements to meet storm codes have changed.
- The land area required to be set aside for retention of rainwater is increased for any new development.
- Number of apartment units on site is greater than current code allows

Where the Dangers Lurk

When you buy a property with a nonconforming use that has been grandfathered in, you run the risk of not being able to make major repairs in the event of a major casualty loss. Even worse, your casualty insurance may not cover you for such loss.

If you want to make any changes to the structure, the local building department may require you to conform to all the current building codes and restrictions. This may be a task that is very costly to do and that would greatly reduce the value of the property.

218. What Are the Major Pitfalls to Mortgage Financing?

The use of other people's money (OPM) is one of the great advantages of real estate investment. Investors who could not even qualify for a car loan are able to buy property worth hundreds of thousands of dollars and owe mortgages equal to 80 or 90 percent of that amount. How? Because they either assume an existing mortgage or the sellers are willing to hold the paper themselves. However, not every cloud has a silver lining.

> **Solution:** Understand that lenders rarely give you their own money. They either work for an institution or are salespeople (mortgage brokers) who arrange mortgages as a living. In any free-market enterprise, the only thing that is free is a promise to deliver what you want at a price you are willing to pay for it. Remember *caveat emptor* (buyer beware)? The same is true for borrowing money.

Six Pitfalls That Await a Borrower

1. *Paying for mortgage commitments that do not come.* The Bank of Stark (purely fictitious) was a great place to get a "throwaway" loan commitment back in the early 1970s. What made this bank attractive was that the officers would commit to an end loan that would ultimately be used by the borrower to replace a construction loan. The end loan is significant because it is separate from the construction loan. Many lenders like to make construction loans, because the yield is higher than for long-term loans and the term of years is relatively short. If a project will take two years to build, the construction loan may be for a maximum of three years. Construction lenders get in and out of deals quickly, but not the end lender, who makes a long-term loan that may have a 15- to 30-year payback schedule.

When construction lenders see that an end loan commitment is already in place, they relax and make the construction loan.

Enter the Bank of Stark (and other mythical banks and bankers). Pay $50,000 and the bank will grant you a $2 million end loan commitment. Sure, the interest rate may look high—prime plus 6 points or more—but this is just a throwaway commitment. The borrower wants the construction loan only to build and sell the building and does not need the end loan. Or perhaps the borrower hopes the lending market will improve so much and the building will look so valuable (all rented, of course) that the expensive end loan from the Bank of Stark will not be necessary.

The success of the Bank of Stark and other lenders like it hinged on the fact that most of its loans never had to be made. The mortgagors were able to sell or find other financing—until one could not. That is when the walls came tumbling down: there was no Bank of Stark.

The moral of this is that you should be very leery of paying up-front commitment funds to mortgage brokers, bankers, and other lenders who promise something that they later cannot deliver. Ask for, get, and then check on their references.

2. *Excessive penalty for prepayment ahead of the schedule.*   It has become relatively common for lenders to offer mortgages that are set up on a long amortization schedule, even interest-only, with a sizable balloon of the principal less than halfway into the term. Say the original schedule is 30 years but the loan balloons in 12 years. The difficult part of these loans is that they may also have restrictions on early repayment. Lenders may want such a restriction because they fear or believe that the market rate will decline and that borrowers will be encouraged by other lenders to pay off an existing loan through a refinanced mortgage to reduce the interest they are paying. To enforce this no-early-repayment provision, the lender imposes a substantial penalty if the loan is repaid early. These penalties can be sufficient to make it difficult, if not impossible, to sell the property due to the excessive penalty charged to pay off the loan.

3. *Getting low ARMs that have no caps for interest increases.*   Many lenders offer very low "entry" interest rates for ARMs. This entry interest may be in place for a few months, even for the first year, or however long it's needed for the lender to drive off the competition. However, after that entry period the interest starts to go up until, like Fourth of July fireworks, it reaches a point of economic explosion. This does not mean that ARMs are to be avoided—quite the opposite in fact. ARMs can be a great way to take advantage of adjustments in the interest rates when they are already high and seem to be headed down. All of this requires some mathematical thought to work out the probable interest rate over a period of time. If the lender will hold the increases to levels that will not allow the interest rate to climb above the market rate for fixed-rate mortgages, then ARMs can be attractive.

4. *Balloon mortgage payments.*   A balloon payment has the tendency to sneak up on you and hit you right in the wallet when you least expect it. The advantage of a balloon mortgage is that it usually allows a softer payback schedule leading up to the balloon. Some mortgages are scheduled on a 25-year amortization, for example, but balloon at the end of the first seven years. The problem is, what do you do at the end of seven years? Go out and get a new mortgage? What if you cannot due to a tight mortgage market or because interest rates have gone through the roof? This can be a very difficult situation.

The answer is simply to avoid any balloon mortgage unless you have some assurance that you will be able to deal with the debt obligation when it comes due.

5. *Mortgages that are not assumable.*   Unfortunately, most institutional loans are either not assumable or are assumable with full qualification (almost the same as unassumable). Generally, only private mortgages held by the seller (purchase money mortgages) can be negotiated to be fully assumable.

When you buy a property and end up with a mortgage that will not be assumable by a buyer you want to sell to, then you suddenly have a balloon mortgage when you do not want one. The only way you can effectively deal with this is to either choose not to buy property with nonassumable mortgages or to anticipate the consequence well in advance of your need to sell such property.

6. *Lenders not approving a buyer to assume your mortgage.*   Even when your mortgage is supposedly assumable, it may not be, as mentioned previously. Why?

Because the lender turns down your buyer. This is an everyday occurrence in the industry, and many buyers seek to use creative techniques to hold their deals together.

More than one seller has had his or her hair turn gray after having a buyer turned down by the mortgagee. Some sellers are able to hold the deal together by keeping their name on the paper (in essence, remaining at risk as a cosigner to the debt) or by getting the buyer to put up other security as additional collateral to the loan. But many buyers simply walk away from the deal when this occurs.

219.   Is There an Easy Way to Avoid All the Possible Pitfalls That Await Real Estate Investors?

No, not unless you plan on renting and never owning real estate. Avoiding pitfalls in any endeavor requires a wide-awake approach to everything you do. It takes effort and dedication to the task. It demands that you learn to do and understand the things you cannot do and do not fully comprehend. It insists that you learn from your mistakes and attempt to build on what you have learned.

The positive aspect of real estate investing is that virtually everything that can happen has happened before. You can follow historical trends because similar events in the past have produced similar results to what is going on now.

220.   What Is a Quitclaim Deed, and Why Can It Be a Very Risky Form of Title Transfer for the Buyer?

A quitclaim deed (*not* "quick claim") is a deed to convey only a present interest a person may have in a property, whether or not such an interest actually existed. Famous uses of quitclaim deeds have involved properties such as the Empire State Building, the London Bridge, and so on. They are valid deeds, but are only as valuable as the interest they actually transfer.

When a quitclaim deed is given, there is no representation or warranty of title made. This kind of deed is helpful in clearing up clouds on title, such as previously unknown liens or defects in former transfers that may cause legal problems in future ownership or transfer to another party.

Danger! Be wary: Because the quitclaim deed does not represent or warranty the title, taking such a deed as payment or security for something may prove to be a mistake.

221.   What Is a Trustee's Deed, and What Are the Limitations in Protection It Gives the Buyer?

A trustee's deed is a conveyance of a property by a trustee of a property. This can result from several different situations, the most common of which is when a property owner establishes a trust to hold title to property. In so doing, the title is placed in the name of a trustee: The actual trustee may be the same person or another party, depending on the type of trust established and the laws governing that kind of entity. When the property is sold or otherwise disposed of, the trustee executes a deed in favor of the new owner. This deed is a trustee's deed.

The problem with a trustee's deed is that it transfers only that title that the trustee has rights to. If the beneficiaries of the trust have reason and rights to contest the transfer, or if the trustee violated the trust agreement, then a cloud can appear on the title.

Read the trust agreement and obtain ratification of the transfer by the beneficiaries. One sure way of dealing with a future problem is to nip it in the bud. Even though the trustee has a legal right to give the buyer a deed, the buyer can insist on verification and assurance that the deed is going to meet the qualifications of a general warranty deed.

222. What or Who Are Phantom Deal Makers, and How Do I Deal with Them?

Phantom deal makers are like the little ghosts in the comic strip who are all named "Not Me." In essence, phantoms can be either your adversary or your friend, but in reality they do not exist.

> **Solution:** You never let the other side believe that you know (or have good reason to believe) that the phantom is not real. You play along with the game, because that phantom might just turn out to be your best friend.

Here is how the events go. The seller looks you in the face and says, "A couple came by yesterday and said they would offer $400,000. That makes your offer of $250,000 look silly, don't you think?" Or a buyer looks you in the face and says, "Yeah, well, see that bigger house across the street? The owner said she would sell it to me for $245,000." In both cases, the buyer or seller's story is based on the statements or decisions of someone who does not exist.

How to Deal with the Phantom

Whenever I am told about some phantom, I shift into a two-step process. You can do the same.

1. Ask the other party if he or she would be more comfortable if you withdrew from the negotiations so he or she can work with the other interested parties.
2. Continue with your negotiations as though you never heard anything about the phantom and that you had never even asked the question in the first step.

Phantoms take many shapes. "My brother," says the seller, who is an only child, "said that he would not agree to less than $2 million. But I think I just might get him to agree to $1.2 million. What do you think?"

I have dealt with them all. The brothers or sisters who did not exist, the father-in-laws, the partners, the parole officer (well, not a parole officer, but just about anyone else you can think of). Oh, when does the phantom become your friend? No one likes to admit they were wrong, right? Well who better to blame something on than someone who doesn't exist? "My father-in-law is such a ditz," the seller says the day after he told you that the lowest price they could take was $2 million for their office building. "But," he continues, "my wife and I beat up on him and if you okay $1.45 million, I can just about guarantee we have a deal."

What do you say? "Gee, I'd love to tell you that $1.45 million is the magic number, but my fortune teller told me last night that the most I should pay is $1.35 million. Do we have a deal?"

223.   How Can I Know Whether a Property I Want to Buy Has a Defective Title, and Why Is That So Important?

Let's start by examining just what a defective title is. The title of any property is held by someone or some entity. If the chain of that title is clear of any problems (called *clouds* on the title), then the person or entity holding that title has "good title" and can transfer the property to a new owner without the potential of someone making a claim on that title. If the past hundred owners all passed on good title to the next owner, and none of them owed on a mortgage that never was satisfied or had an IRS lien or some other form of judgment against the person or the property, then there is a good chance that everything is okay.

Nonetheless, there could still be problems. What if a child was the true heir, and yet the deceased owner's sister sold the property by way of a trustee's deed to the person who sold it to you? Do you have good title? Perhaps, but perhaps not.

It is unlikely that you would know whether a property has a defective title without a detailed check of the chain of title transfers. As every legal judgment against a person and his or her property will eventually become a matter of record, a review of the property records and other public documents should resolve the matter. However, judgments are not the only items that have to be checked to verify that title has transferred correctly from one party to another along the way.

If there has been an improperly prepared document in the chain of title, it is possible that a document can create a cloud on the title. For example, a property owned jointly by a large family may convey title, but for some reason the wife of one of the members did not sign the deed, or there was no witness, or the deed was not dated. Even if that event took place several owners ago, the problem might just now surface and the heirs of that woman can cause a problem.

Every title should be checked and verified by qualified professionals trained to perform that task. Most buyers add to that by purchasing title insurance to defend their rights should a cloud or claim appear in the future. When you buy property and are shown that the present property owner acquired title insurance when the property was purchased, that does not guarantee that there are no possible problems; however, it does give you a good starting point that, if there are any problems, they may show up in what the title policy excluded. Pay close attention to any exception or exclusion of coverage, and seek to have those problem areas removed before your taking title.

These exclusions of coverage can be tiny "gotchas" that can give you a bad day, or they may loom larger and give you a bad year. After all, title insurance that you take out when you close (never close without it), may not cover every possible event in the world. An episode I went through proved that to me with a jolt to my pocketbook. A property I had purchased some 15 years earlier, and for which I purchased title insurance, ran into a problem: the property owners next door suddenly claimed that they owned a large part of my property. They said they had been paying tax on that part of the property and that their sewer septic tank was there to prove it.

I called my title insurance company and said, "Okay guys, protect me from these people and defend my rights." Six weeks later, after they investigated the situation they told me that the whole case was based on a faulty survey done 15 years before I purchased the property. They determined that the septic tank was important, but as I had not had a recent survey at the time I purchased the property, and as their exclusion paragraph relied on a survey, they opted out of defending me.

I won the case in the end, but it cost me thousands of dollars. My continued argument, that a survey would not have shown the septic tank in any event, fell on deaf ears at the insurance company. Oh well.

224. What Is an Encroachment, and How Does It Affect Title?

An encroachment occurs when some improvement or object from one property crosses the boundary of an adjoining tract. There are two kinds of encroachment: *visible* and *hidden*. A visible encroachment is one that is obvious to the eye, whereas a hidden encroachment is underground or not clearly visible because of some obstruction.

When there is an encroachment, and when appropriate and timely steps are not taken by the property owner whose boundary has been encroached upon to remove the encroachment, an *easement by prescription* may develop. It is possible that in some instances the actual boundary of the properties may change in favor of the encroaching party.

The innocent party can seek legal remedy, when the encroachment is discovered, to have the encroaching object removed. In such cases the court generally reviews the cost and benefit of such removal and may rule that the encroaching party must pay damages, but does not have to remove the object.

On the other hand, there are examples where people have constructed a building in the wrong place to the extent that the building was completely on another property, which amounts to a gift to the other property owner.

Hidden encroachments usually occur underground; basements, water, electric, sewer, various other such connections, and septic tanks have all been known to encroach below the ground onto adjoining property. These encroachments can be the most damaging because they may not show up in a survey. As most title insurance policies will not defend a claim against a title where the problem would have been discovered by a recent survey, the decision then is whether the survey should disclose both aboveground and belowground encroachments.

Not all "clearly visible" encroachments are noticed, either. This happens because the property boundary is not clearly marked or is assumed to be somewhere other than where it really is. This can be the result of negligence on the part of the surveyor or a simple lack of a survey and the reliance on the statements of a previous seller. Some metes and bounds descriptions that are measured by distances to an "old oak" or by a meandering river or stream can be altered by removal of the old oak or by reengineering a river's flow.

An encroachment does affect title, and if there is an easement by prescription or the taking of some of the land because of adverse possession, property values can be greatly affected.

225. What Are the Most Important Steps I Should Take before I Consider Buying Real Estate?

One of those steps you have almost completed, and that is to read this book. The most important factor about this book, and others like it, is that it will give you a solid look at how you can avoid mistakes that frustrate many would-be investors. It is easy to make a mistake in either the approach you take to solve a problem or in the decision you make based on information you believe to be true but which a little more digging shows to be false.

> **Solution:** Take a look at the following nine items, and apply them to your approach to investing in real estate.

Nine Steps to a Successful Pursuit of Wealth through Real Estate

1. *Establish attainable and measurable goals.*   Ask 1,000 people if they are goal-oriented, and most will say they are. However, their goals are usually misdirected and rarely clearly attainable within a timetable, and no measure of progress is possible. The goal "to be rich" is such an example. It sounds great, but is like starting a journey for Anatolia and having no idea where it is or how to get there. Only by having a well-defined goal that is attainable can success be reached, and ultimate success is reached only by working down a path of attaining one goal after another. Success breeds contempt for failure.

2. *Review your abilities and limitations.*   Now that you have a target, an ultimate goal, take stock of what you have to do to get there. In every endeavor, having the right tools is important, and if your tools need to be enhanced, then take steps to do that. This might require an adjustment in your goals or the need to establish some intermediate stepping-stones (e.g., an adult education class in bookkeeping, hotel management, or landscaping) to help build depth in your future dealings in real property.

3. *Establish a plan that builds on your abilities and strengthens your limitations.* Only you and your partners need to know about this plan or, for that matter, what your abilities and limitations really are. The only important thing is for you to work to improve. Many people are complacent about their abilities and limitations, and they get into a rut when they are functioning at the maximum of their abilities because they are walled in by their limitations. Escape that trap by expanding your abilities. Begin to build your comfort zone. The area you choose to invest in is your comfort zone. You need to learn all you can to become an expert in that area.

4. *Establish yourself as a local real estate insider.*   This task is obtainable by anyone who has the determination to learn, some time to devote to the task, and the ability and willingness to play the role.

5. *Open your eyes to the opportunities in your comfort zone.*   As you learn what is going on and start to see how past trends are a guide to future events, opportunities that escape most people will suddenly jump right out of the neighborhood. At first you will assume that everyone else sees them too—but soon you begin to realize that the average people in a neighborhood do not even know the names of those who live nearby, nor do they see real opportunities around them.

6. *Make offers.*   One of the secrets to success in buying real estate is to make offers. You make offers to learn how to deal with people; you make offers to learn about the property you might like to own; you make offers because that puts you in contact with other insiders; but most important, you make offers because sellers do not know what they will do until presented with a written offer.

7. *Periodically adjust your goals.*   Your long-range goal should rarely change. That focus can be fine-tuned, and once in a while, as you get closer to it, you may more clearly define it. But the intermediate goals, those short-range stepping-stones, need to be constantly adjusted. This is important and necessary, because events around you change and you must be flexible so that you can adjust with them. New technology is developed and new techniques are found that are better than old ones, and this demands that you continually expand your opportunities by being able to see them when they appear.

8. *Learn from your failures.*   After all, failure is nature's way of telling you that you are doing something wrong and that corrections need to be made to your plan. However, most people fail because they have no plan, and by lacking a focus and an original direction there is no clear way to know what should be changed. One of the very first failures to learn from is the frustration that comes from continually batting your head up against a wall trying to get over it, when in reality that wall is blocking a path you should not have tried to follow in the first place. By looking at yourself and trying to be objective, you may discover that what you really want is different than what you thought you needed. Learn to take all your failures seriously; examine what went wrong and why. Always ask yourself these two questions:

Did I have my heart in what I was trying to do?

Was my attitude primed for success?

Often, the turnaround from a failure to a success is to answer these questions as honestly as you can. Once done, do everything you can to change your own approach to the task, or seek a different task toward which you can develop a more positive approach.

9. *Build on your successes.*   There is nothing sweeter than overcoming adversity and achieving success. Even a small success can start a growing process wherein other successful ventures seem to fall into place. This is not luck; this is the way a well-thought-out plan that is carefully implemented should work. This is the fruit of your efforts and the demonstration to yourself that you can do it.

226.   To Be Continually Successful as a Real Estate Investor, What Should I Do Every Day?

It has been my experience in observing both successful and unsuccessful real estate investors that there are trends that each seems to follow. Clearly, by the results that occur, one trend works while the other does not. Interestingly, these trends are such that in retrospect I cannot say whether a person used the trend improperly or whether the trend itself was improper for the goals chosen.

For example, the basic structure of a comfort zone and the factors that work for prospective investors who follow them establish the format for people to apply their own talents to get the most out of that structure. What seems to occur is that some people see the structure but do not apply their talents to it at all. Real estate is something that must work by the numbers, but you must have the vision to see the opportunities in order for them to manifest themselves.

Without the ability to see what can be and not what is, you will never recognize that the 10-story, 50-year-old hotel down the block from where you work is really a new J. Alexander's restaurant waiting to happen. That is, unless you know that there is a need for such a business in the area, that the property is the right size, that the demographics of the area will support the restaurant's need for customers, and that the zoning will allow it (or could be changed to allow it).

> **Solution:** Follow the tips contained in this book as they relate to your goals. Set a timetable that is directed to building a comfort zone in which you will become an expert in zoning, the politics of the area, values of property sold and rented out, and potential uses that may have gone unnoticed.

Four Things That Successful Real Estate Investors Do Every Day

1. Read your written-down goals. Do not rely on a memory of what you are looking for. When you look at your goals daily, you keep yourself tuned in to your future.
2. Check the actual progress against your earlier planned and estimated timetable.

Time is the most important factor, and only experience in how to best use it will give you a mastery over it.

3. Make adjustments in your plans that allow you to keep your original goals firmly in sight as your beacon to follow.

4. Adjust your goals only when you have already achieved them or if they turn out to be too optimistic for your abilities. Be cautious about downgrading your goals simply because you have not obtained them. First ask yourself, "Have I done everything I can to achieve what I started out to do?" If the honest reply is no, then find out why and correct that situation.

227. How Do I Prepare for a Catastrophic Event?

This item is at the end of this book for several important reasons. First, it will be easy to find if you need it in a hurry; and second, if it is the last thing you read you may relate to it by reflecting on certain events that have already passed through your life experience.

Catastrophic events come in many different forms: fires, earthquakes, sandstorms, drought, pestilence and epidemics, volcano eruptions, mud slides, tornados, tsunamis, hurricanes, civil unrest, terrorist attacks, vandalism and looting, and so on. Each such event may be unique to your area or even absent altogether. But when disaster strikes, the result can be far more than the loss of property. The result can be like a fuse that burns on and on, disrupting life as you knew it, perhaps for the rest of your life.

Insurance is important in these matters, but insurance will go only so far to dull the impact of the event. Pay close attention to your insurance needs, and make sure that copies of those policies are kept in more than one location in the event one of those locations is destroyed. The company name and the policy number should also be kept in a safe place so that the policy itself can be obtained (although sometimes not quickly) if needed.

As a volunteer worker for a local Catholic church in South Miami following Hurricane Andrew, I witnessed firsthand just how important policy numbers really were, having seen them painted on buildings that had been all but totally destroyed.

You can prepare ahead of time in many practical ways that involve careful thought and a plan. Read and implement the following critical factors.

Nine-Stage Plan to Help You Survive a Catastrophic Event

1. *Be aware.*   Be aware of potential events that might occur. This is important for the area in which you live, but even more important if you travel to distant places. A tornado in Kansas is far different from an earthquake in Japan or San Francisco. Know your "enemy." If you are traveling to the middle of a jungle, think about what sickness you might catch, and prepare by taking preventive measures.

2. *Be able to communicate.*   When things truly shut down and communication

becomes difficult, we realize how much we took it for granted. Simple things such as having a phone card or a cell phone might mean the difference between being in touch or remaining isolated. Having phone numbers with you can put you in touch with someone who can relay messages to other family members. Lack of communication creates unbelievable stress on family and friends worried about your safety. Because there may be a lapse of time between the event and your ability to make contact of any kind, you need to have a line of communication preestablished.

3. *Prepare for your own personal safety.*   Whether you are at home or traveling, identify your potential escape routes. Do you have an escape plan for your house or apartment? Have you practiced it? Can you get to the roof of your home or building? Are escape pathways open to the outside, or will the door be locked? When was the last time you went through an escape stairway to check? Well, I did after we moved into a hotel following Hurricane Katrina and discovered that the door at the bottom of the stairwell was locked and that the doors leading back into the hallways of the hotel were one way only. (Once you entered the stairwell, you were stuck; I had to use my cell phone to call the desk for help.) Personal safety means preparing for your own personal needs—from the lull after the event to the time when things return to normal. The remaining items are things you can do in advance to prepare for such events.

4. *Have cash.*   Travelers checks and credit cards may do you no good when there is no electricity and store employees do not know you (anymore). Unless you can spend $100 in one place, carry smaller denominations of bills.

5. *Have water.*   Rotate bottled water in your home (so it stays relatively fresh), and keep enough to last a minimum of at least four days per person. You can store water in a bathtub, but that would be best used for washing and for flushing toilets. Have the ability to disinfect water that might be contaminated, in case you run out of fresh water.

6. *Have food.*   Canned goods are the best. If electricity goes and you have a refrigerator full of perishables, eat them right away. Toss out food that is no longer safe.

7. *Have transportation.*   If you do not have personal transportation of any kind, then know where you might be able to get it. If you have time, get out of the way of the pending event. If this is not possible, however (many catastrophic events hit without warning), have a backup plan for evacuation.

8. *Have a rendezvous point.*   If you have family members in the area, plan to meet at a certain location at some point. Keep in mind that your meeting place may also be affected, so choose both a nearby and a distant location.

9. *Keep hope.*   This is the single most important factor if you are immersed in a horrible event. It will sustain you and can save your life.

Index